what people are saying about McKenzie Wark's previous books...

D1744291

Virtual Republic

"Wark manages to couch an eclectic array of topics in a language that is personal, modest, audacious and playful." **Kate Macdonell** *Overland* "Ken Wark makes postmodernism useful." **David Carter** *UTS Review* "You are unlikely to agree... but it will challenge your beliefs and stretch your mind." **Lieutenant Colonel Ian Wing** *Australian Defence Force Journal* "This challenging, original work pushes thinking on the way public debate occurs." **Anne Coombs** *Australian's Review of Books* "Wark is 'the country's leading postmodern critic'. Which goes a long way to explaining why he has a weird name." *Townsville Bulletin* "Wark wrestles the beast of postmodernism and achieves an accessible and entertaining book." **Peter Mews** *Australian Financial Review* "A burr under the saddle of modern society, an iconoclast who juggles cultural imagery with adroitness." **Robin Osborne** *Southern Cross* "Wark, who sees himself as a kind of sage of pop has a suppler grasp of some of the... pieties." **Peter Craven** *Sunday Age* "Something of an anomaly in Australian intellectual life... he looks more the archetypal bohemian radical than an academic." **Andrew Stafford** *Studio For Men* "The book is easy to read and there is enough controversy... to draw any reader into a good debate with the author." **Ray Duplain** *Geelong Advertiser* "Relatively free of the foot-in-mouth obscurantism of much recent critical writing." **Andrew Riemer** *Sydney Morning Herald* "The Ned Kelly of Australian cultural criticism... a distinctive mix of high-technology savvy, historical focus and political insight." **Tim Watts** *The Big Issue* "It must be good for you because it's not pleasing to read." **Stephen Fenely** *Good Weekend* "Wark's defense of... Demidenko is genuinely out of step with orthodoxy and even in a sense brave." **Hal**

Colebatch *Adelaide Review* "Wark is one of the better known of that po-mo crew... being positioned as our next generation of critical theorists." **Gary Dunne** *Sydney Star Observer* "I always knew I had more to fear from Wark..." **Peter Craven** *Australian* "A head trip with heart." **Michael Adams** *City Weekly* "A full blown, postmodern romp through Australian cultural life in the 90s." **Anthony Elliott** *Weekend Australian* "This elevation of unknowns, opportunists, and the cabalistically academic over track record luminaries should send the Australian reading public... into gales of laughter. **Gerard Windsor** *Australian Book Review* "It felt as though the book were inviting me into conversation with it." **Lisa Gye** *Media Information Australia*

Virtual Geography

"A Mad Max, vector guerrilla always on call... a quite entertaining text." **John Docker** *Australian* "A Mad Max of the information superhighway... cuts in and out of events and texts with the speed of an edit." **Ian McLean** *Thesis 11* "An interesting and original grand narrative... a vivid and engaging portrait." **Simon During** *Journal of International Communication* "Lucid and compelling... a genuinely audacious thinker." **Darren Tofts** *Metro Magazine* "Original and provocative... wide ranging, quirky and dextrous." **Sally Singer** *Times Literary Supplement* "The author's... ability to provide insights into a world where unbounded information is circling the earth at the speed of light is startling." **Ron Cathcart** *Choice* "An important book... helps establish a new vector for cultural studies." **David Marshall** *Media Information Australia* "Wark must be credited for the breadth of his research, and for attempting to generate discussion on what remains a vast, underexamined territory." **Ben Goldsmith** *Overland* "An unusual work, even for a field as wild and diverse as cultural studies." **Mark Gibson** *Cultural Studies* "The vector inspector of the lit world... offers a smart map through the experience of everyday life." **George Alexander** *Photofile* "His accounts of events in this book are in fact quite masterful: virtuoso investigations which write media vectors into a variety of narratives." **Alan McKee** *Continuum* "A cross between Jean Baudrillard and John Pilger... a stimulating, even moving book, dense with ideas." **Mark Singer** *New Statesman* "Well on the way to becoming... the Ned Kelly of pop cultural critical theory." **Ade Peace** *Australian Book Review* "An immensely exciting and stimulating book. It is also, I think a courageous one." **Elizabeth Jacka** *UTS Review* "Wark's prolific, fluent voice in antipodean cultural and media studies is noted for its originality." **John Conomos** *Cinema Papers*

Dear Imo,

I got an extra copy
of this which I thought
you might like.

Love Sara
xxx

Jan
2002

celebrities,
culture and
cyberspace

the light on the hill
in a postmodern world

McKenzie Wark

Pluto Press Australia 1999

First published in January 1999 by
Pluto Press Australia Limited
Locked Bag 199, Annandale, NSW 2038

Copyright © McKenzie Wark 1998

Cover design by Wendy Farley

Index by Neale Towart

Typeset by Chapter 8 Pty Ltd

Printed and bound by Alken Press
128 Long Street, Smithfield, NSW 2164

Australian Cataloguing in Publication Data

Celebrities, culture and cyberspace

Bibliography.
Includes index.
ISBN 1 86403 045 3

1. Australian Labor Party - History. 2. Celebrities - Australia. 3. Political
culture - Australia. 4. Social evolution - Australia. 5. Australia - Civilization -
20th century. 6. Australia - intellectual life - 20th century.
I. Title

324.29407

radical writing

celebrities, culture
and cyberspace

contents

c y b e r s p a c e

chapter 1

30 years, 15 minutes

The service of philosophy, of speculative culture, towards the human spirit, is to rouse, to startle it to a life of constant and eager observation.

Walter Pater

The real trouble with intellectuals is that they are cowards in the face of the good.

Martin Boyd

It's Time

As a dedicated watcher of news on television, I'm used to bad news. The paradox of news is how constant an index it is of human folly. So there was a special joy for me in the late 90s in watching television news reports of the electoral success of social democratic parties in France, Germany and Britain. The endlessly deferred demise of the conservative ethos of Helmut Kohl and Margaret Thatcher gave me a feeling of modest optimism.

It could be that I wait for these rare moments of hope amid the constant drone of bad news because I was trained at an early age to expect them. I was eleven years old when Gough Whitlam won the 1972 Australian Federal election, and became Prime Minister. I had to wait another eleven years for another moment like it. Bob Hawke won the 1983 election for Labor when I was 22.

There may be little anyone can do about human folly, but the incremental overcoming of human misery seems to me, even in postmodern times of attenuated scepticism, to be something for which one can still hope. The incremental overcoming of human misery is the "light on the hill" of which another labour movement hero used to speak. As the historian Jill Roe points out, Australian Labor leader Ben Chifley probably borrowed that phrase from Matthew 5:14. "Ye are the light of the world. A city which is set on a hill cannot be hid."[1]

The light on the hill is a figure of fable in Australian labour movement culture, but given its origins, I don't think it's stretching things too much to think of any and every social democratic government that achieves some small step to overcoming avoidable human misery and suffering as an instance of the light on the hill. It is hardly fashionable to think of Bob Hawke's Labor government as a shining instance of the light on the hill. Maybe in the postmodern ethos of the 80s, it was just the hill. There was a fair share of human folly in Hawke's government. Perhaps that was inevitable, in that it confronted a rapidly changing international strategic, economic and communication environment.

The rise of an optimistic rhetoric about a "third way" between market capitalism and state socialism among European and American commentators comes as no surprise to me. One of the few prophecies I ever made as a writer that came true was that the collapse of communism would be a crisis for the right, not the left. As I wrote when the Berlin wall fell: "Hard conservatism always worked in a paranoid way, by drawing a line through reality, and putting everyone to the left of Churchill on the *other* side. That other side was a fearful thing, threatening, subversive, manipulative, indefatigable, a horrible thing which must be resisted at all costs. Now that this paranoid fear has revealed itself as a mirage, conservatism of this kind must enter into deep crisis. So much the worse for them!"[2] Without the cold war to hold it together, the liberal and conservative compromise that so often kept social democracy out of power unravelled. Old cold warriors looked for new scare-mongering campaigns to keep themselves gainfully employed.

One of the least discussed aspects of the third way is as a third way to follow the first two vectors along which social democracy communicated and organised itself as a culture. The light on the hill is about being an example to the world, an instance of hope for the overcoming of misery for all to see. Conservatism may flourish, as it did during the cold war, on fear and ignorance. Social democracy can only flourish as a culture on the basis of the communication by example of what can be done to overcome misery. The first way social democracy found to communicate itself was tied to the printed word and the uses that could be made of it.[3] The second way was via the electronic media. The third way is about taking social democracy into the emerging postbroadcast world. Fittingly, I've found a particularly succinct discussion of the third way, not in dead tree format, but on a web site, called *Nexus.*[4]

I'm not entirely convinced that social democracy fully understands the way that it has been changed by the broadcast era, let alone how it can change in the postbroadcast era of multi-channel broadcasting and the internet. That is why in this book I want to look at the culture of the broadcast era, and see what a study of the media, within which postwar social democracy had to publicise itself, can tell us about the ongoing struggle to provide some light on the hill in a postmodern world.

When Gough Whitlam won office in 1972, it felt a bit like Australia was finally catching up with the world, and that the radical optimism of the 60s had finally reached the colonies. But it is not always the case that the periphery lags behind the centre. The Australian Labor Party formed the first minority government led by the labour movement, and governed in its own right while most of European social democracy was still struggling for power. Early in the century, Australia was seen as a social laboratory for the world.

This is not because Australian Labor has displayed any more wisdom than other labour movement parties, and it has certainly had more than its fair share of human folly. Rather, Australian Labor's precocious achievements are more likely just a symptom of the uneven costs that the globalisation of the capitalist economy has extracted over the last century of its accelerated development. 'Globalisation' is not a new idea in the former colonies and peripheries. Economic existence there has always been predicated on a sober grasp of the centralisation of economic power — elsewhere.

The depressions caused by setbacks in global economic development in the 1880s and 1930s were especially savage in Australia. What made it worse was the realisation of the power that international capital held over a peripheral economy. This experience of being always and already subject to global flows of capital and information was a strong part of labour movement culture.

Reading the summary on the *Nexus* web site of discussions among English academics about the third way, I can't help thinking that, like earlier in the century, Australian Labor has been there and done that. The project that emerged for Australian Labor at the end of the 90s was how to have a second go at the third way. At the 1996 election, the electorate punished Labor for inflicting its brand of the third way on it during the previous thirteen years. Australia swung right just as much of Europe and America swung more or less left. When Australia elected a Labor government in 1972, it felt like lagging behind the social trend in the rest of the 'over-developed' world. When Australia elected a conservative government in 1996, it felt more like what may come if the third way is not managed without as much attention to the cultural fallout from economic change as to the reform of the economy.

Perhaps another meaning of the third way is that besides paying attention to economic and political matters, social democracy also has to understand culture, for it is through culture that the stress of economic reform is likely to be expressed. Culture in a postmodern world means media culture. The culture of everyday life has its ruses and guises for resisting or ignoring the media's bad news, but for social democratic parties in the postmodern world, access to everyday culture is mostly mediated by broadcast, and increasingly by postbroadcast, vectors. These days, social democratic parties often have quite tenuous links to the culture of everyday life, and find themselves reliant on their media profile to keep alight the light on the hill.

In this book, I want to look in some detail at how a particular national space of mediated, postmodern culture, actually works. Rather than trade in the seemingly transnational jargon of social theory or cultural studies, this book deals with the particulars of both media culture and everyday experience. One little-discussed aspect of globalisation is the rise of professional and scholarly jargons that appear to abstract from particular national-cultural spaces. Scholars develop concepts that can be applied anywhere, as a social rationalist companion to the economic rationalist thought that provides the legitimating rhetoric for economic globalisation. These placeless jargons may suit the multinational publishing industry, but that does not mean they can articulate the peculiarities of actual cultural spaces.[5] Broadcasting, in particular, still creates powerful national zones which are unlikely to be dissipated by transnational media for some time yet.

While applicable, in theory, anywhere, abstract and placeless intellectual work really seems to find the countries of the old imperial heartland more congenial. These are the spaces from which the credentialling of scholarship, the publishing of internationally distributed work and the legitimising of rationalising ways of thought all emanate. While transnational social theory and cultural studies often pay lip service to the unequal differences that float across the surfaces of a postmodern world, in practice, these ways of thinking and speaking still subsume them under concepts convivial to an imperial practice of thinking from the centre outwards.

But the 90s are a time when globalisation has come home to roost. The populations of the old imperial centres are as subject to colonisation by flows of information, and almost as vulnerable to the withdrawal of flows of capital, as the populations of the periphery have always been. Even social democratic governments can no longer rely on imperial privilege, and protect their populations from global forces. In this they catch up with what the periphery has experienced and had to manage for some time.

This weakening of the capacity of social democracy in the 'postimperial' world to exploit for national populations the benefits of being host to centres of capital and information is of course only partial. The European Community still functions effectively to skew power in world trade to the advantage of European populations. All the same, the weakening of this privilege may in the long run be as significant as the end of the cold war to the future of social democracy.

The 60s seem to me to have been a time in which the light

on the hill communicated itself around the world via the images of social change. The 80s seem to me to have been a time when many feared the candle snuffed and the times unfavourable for the incremental overcoming of suffering. In this book, I want to write about the 80s and the 90s as I experienced them in Australia, as a time in which the economic impact of globalisation and the reform of social democracy itself produced a distinctive experiment in the third way.

The Wonder Years

A lot can happen in thirty years. It's just over thirty years, as I write, since Prime Minster Harold Holt drowned. It's thirty years since Paris rebelled and rioted. It's thirty years, in short, since the high tides and green grass of 'the late 60s'.

One's first decade is like one's first love. You live it intuitively, at once excited and serene. I was a little kid during the 60s, playing handball in the playground of Lambton Primary School, in suburban Newcastle. The Vietnam Moratorium was to me a really fab red and blue badge, the first of what would become a collection. I lived the 60s unconsciously, having not then yet grown much self-awareness. Now I have to teach classes on those times to people for whom it is even more remote. As I write this, people born in the 80s are entering university.

Celebrities, Culture and Cyberspace is titled in homage to a book Craig McGregor published thirty years ago, *People, Politics and Pop*.[6] That was a book I found useful when I wanted to reflect on the decade I had lived intuitively. I would say of my book what McGregor said of his, that it is "a purely personal, impressionistic book, a sort of collage of the contemporary". *Celebrities, Culture and Cyberspace* is dedicated to my niece Katie and my nephews Scott and Tim. I hope some day it will explain something to them about this decade, the 90s, now nearly passed — their first in the world.

McGregor is one of the few writers of the 60s who I find I can admire today without invoking a sense of irony. Unlike some of his contemporaries, he didn't get stuck in a groove back then. His later writings are alive to the changes as well as the continuities of the 70s, 80s and 90s. Writing in the late

90s, McGregor declares that "modernism is no longer contemporary. It was the name given to a particular cultural epoch…. like the others, it had a beginning, a middle and an end. In its place, as a dominant cultural paradigm, blazons postmodernity. It is characterised, among other things, by conflict, dissonance, plurality, discontinuity, asymmetry, contradiction, decentring, fragmentation, subjectivity, ambivalence, populism, and a cacophony of simultaneous discourses".[7] I don't necessarily agree with all of McGregor's diagnoses here, but the point is his engagement. There is no shortage of gently greying pundits who reject the attempt to think the present in its own terms. The lesson this book seeks to learn from the 60s is about the need to start over, to try for a mental leap clear across the present, rather than to burrow snug into the worn warren of the past.

In the late 90s there was a link between the complacency and reaction displayed by many contemporary opinion makers and the rise of an even more reactionary and punitive mood in Australian politics and culture. This is why I think it is important to acknowledge and celebrate Australian thinkers who did not lose their nerve when confronted by changing realities. Craig McGregor is one such thinker; Donald Horne is another.

From the 60s to the 90s

What people think of as 'the 60s' includes a bit of the early 70s as well. It was a decade with so much energy to burn that, like an overly enthusiastic sporting event, it spilled over into extra time. In Australia, I think it convenient to date the end of the 60s to the election of Gough Whitlam's Labor government in 1972. That was when the enthusiasm for change achieved electoral success and mainstream expression in the person of Whitlam. By contrast, the 90s were a bit of a wash out. It's only 1998 as I write, but already the 90s seem to be over. I date the end of the 90s from the election of One Nation candidates in the Queensland election of 1998. That was when the populist reactionary culture of the 90s found mainstream expression in the person of Pauline Hanson.

Whatever happens from this point on, in some ways it's a

whole new ball game. Hanson's support declined in the 1998 Federal election, but she still had an impact. What Chandran Kukathas and William Malley, academics from the Australian Defence Force Academy, call 'soft Hansonism' became mainstream policy: denying refugees their human rights, restricting welfare access for migrants, fudging Aboriginal reconciliation.[8] John Howard's conservative Liberal and National Party coalition government, which came to power in the 1996 Federal election, did so by appearing to embody the reactionary mood rising on the right. While Howard made conciliatory noises on reconciliation after winning in 1998, it looked like another term with the TV cartoon *South Park's* Mr Garrison running the country.

I write at a different time in *Celebrities, Culture and Cyberspace*, to that in which McGregor wrote *People, Politics and Pop*. The late 90s, like the late 60s, were a time when the legitimacy of mainstream politics and culture came under attack. In other ways, the late 90s were different. In the 60s, the attack was from the radical left. In the 90s, it was from the populist right. My interests are also a bit different to McGregor's. He sought significance in the suburban, whereas it is the urbanity of Australian culture that I find fascinating. It was still news in the late 60s that the suburbanite was a more resonant image of Australian self-identity than the swaggie. It was still news in the 90s that with the move to apartment living, close to the city, urban self-identity was forming, in part as a reaction against suburbia.

Conflict moved from the clash between bush and suburban values to one between urban and bush values, with the suburbs poised as the swinging vote in between. This showed clearly in the 1996 federal election, where Labor held its vote in what journalist Terry McCrann calls the triangle, the urban and urbane space of Sydney/Melbourne/Canberra, but lost ground in the outer suburbs and the country.[9] The 1998 Queensland election demonstrated the strength of the resistance and resentment in the hinterlands to urban culture and its values.

The 1998 Federal election, where One Nation won only one Senate seat but polled around 8% across the country, showed that the vernacular culture and hinterland politics of Hansonism had national appeal. Labor also made a comeback in 1998. As columnist Gerard Henderson noted, "Labor won back part of urban, provincial and rural Australia outside the Sydney/Melbourne/Canberra axis …. However, Labor's failure to win sufficient seats in Sydney and Melbourne provides an ill omen for the future."[10] It may not be possible to put together the urban block who voted for Paul Keating and the parts of the suburban fringe who voted for his successor as Labor leader, Kim Beazley. This is why I revisit the cultural construct of 'suburbia' in this book, the study of which McGregor was an early advocate.

In place of the people McGregor used as his touchstones of cultural flux, I write about celebrity. Since the 60s, it is clear that any public life is one that the media both shapes and shadows. Andy Warhol's prophecy, back in the 60s, that "in the future, everyone will be famous for fifteen minutes", came to pass by the 90s.[11] Hopefully, the fame of populist celebrity Pauline Hanson will last only fifteen minutes, but whether that comes to pass depends in part on imagining a positive and popular alternative to the populist reaction that would drag us back thirty years and more. Hansonism is the herpes of the body politic. It is an itch that returns in times of stress.

A foretaste of the political significance of celebrity was rock star Peter Garrett's strong showing in the 1984 federal election, in which he came close to winning a Senate seat for the Nuclear Disarmament Party. While Garrett made the transition from entertainment celebrity to political celebrity, Prime Minster Bob Hawke reversed the process in 1986 when he appeared on the popular TV drama *A Country Practice* — giving a speech in the imaginary country town of Wandon Valley about nuclear disarmament.[12] By the 90s, celebrity was permanently intertwined with politics. The Greens capitalised on Garrett's initiative by running high profile Tasmanian activist and celebrity Bob Brown. The careers of Australian Democrat Senators Natasha Stott Despoja and Cheryl Kernot showed just how effective it could be having a base in the media rather than in the old style party machine of the Liberal and Labor parties.

Kernot's defection to the Labor Party in 1998 then proved an interesting test of the ability of a more traditional party to exploit the relationship between celebrity, politics and the media. A test the Labor Party failed, with Kernot going down to the wire against Liberal candidate Rod Henshaw, a popular radio broadcaster, in their contest for the seat of Dickson on the suburban north western edge of Brisbane. Independent candidate Peter Andren, a rural television journalist, won Calare, a diverse electorate including NSW country towns of Bathurst, Lithgow and Orange. John Schumann, former singer with the radical folk rock group Redgum, ran on the Australian Democrat ticket. He gave Liberal front bencher Alexander Downer a run for his money in Mayo, a seat that includes a brace of suburbs at the foot of the Adelaide Hills in South Australia.

If there was a lesson in those results, it was that celebrity candidates can do well in diverse electorates if voters feel they are still a local candidate who cares about them, but celebrity itself does not give a candidate a winning edge. So while celebrity provides a shared, public image for people to think about voting for, or in my case, write about, the way the public responds to celebrities is complex. The culture of everyday life contains a remarkable depth of skill in 'reading' media images, whether in politics or entertainment, and perhaps particularly when the two overlap.

Rather than write about politics, the second term of McGregor's title, I write mostly about culture. As cultural studies scholar Meaghan Morris once suggested, in the 60s everything seemed arrestingly political, but then everything seemed to turn obscurely cultural.[13] Sometimes religion is the battle ground for competing views of the world, such as in the mid 50s, when the Catholic-inspired Democratic Labor Party split from the Labor mainstream. Sometimes it is political ideology, such as the challenge posed by the new left and liberationist social movements of the 60s. In the 80s, culture became the arena.

In each instance the conflict over the definition of the good life seems to me to be what is at stake. The possibilities for leading the good life are expressed at different times in religious, political, or cultural institutions and terms. In Australian culture, the expression "fair go, mate" is often cited as the classic vernacular articulation of the good life, although practically everyone who makes the demand for a fair go has a different view of what might constitute a fair go.

As Donald Horne wrote in the 60s, fair go is "what happened in Australia to the ideals of Liberty, Equality and Fraternity. As might be expected, in the transmutation these ideals have been knocked about. But the whole thing cost no lives and it is ingrained into the texture of Australian life."[14]

In the 90s, Horne wrote a book that imagined a theme park called *The Avenue of the Fair Go*. In this tour of Australian political culture, Horne had a representative sample of Australian 'types' offer their differing views on what kind of good life the fair go posits. When a young woman with badges critiques it as a term "too White and too Male", Horne has his Aboriginal character reply that his Grandmother, who was brought up in the bush, would say, "well a fair go would do for a start."[15] Horne's particular insight in his writings of the 90s is that the fair go is a cultural matter before it is a political one, and that it is something that exists only in the different ways people construe it and argue about it, rather than being some identifiable essence common to all Australians.

The rise of Pauline Hanson showed how political operators could mobilise a populist movement with the help of a leader with an instinctive grasp of celebrity power and a distinctive articulation of a view of the fair go. Hanson's quavering voice and outer suburban style connected the lunar right to a widespread questioning of the legitimacy of political culture. The mainstream pundits pointed out with increasing exasperation that her policies were racist and discriminatory and made no economic sense. All of which was true, but missed the point. Populism is never about policies and politics, it's about culture and celebrity. Hanson's talent was in using the media to create an image that articulated the feelings of people who no longer believed the policies of the Labor, Liberal, or National parties.

From Television to Cyberspace

Where McGregor wrote of pop, I write of cyberspace. Pop was his word for the jetsam that drifted through the experience of everyday life, as the dominant media of the postwar world cranked up to top speed. But the vectors along which images and sounds come to us underwent subtle changes between the 60s and the 90s. Pop was a product of a mass media age, where industrial scale distribution channels churned out bright, sharp, high contrast images, aimed at the most general qualities of its audience. Cyberspace is an emergent culture born of a postbroadcast age, where the digital quality of all information breaks down the mass media image into many multiple and shifting coalescences of sense.

When McGregor wrote about pop, it was a topic that incited conflicting passions. The critique of mass media offered by many modern intellectuals was of its complete and irredeemable banality. McGregor was more subtle. He did not go all the way with Canadian literary critic Marshall McLuhan, who became a celebrity by embracing it. McLuhan imagined print media as a sort of fall from grace, and broadcast media as transcending the limits of print culture and launching us into the collective consciousness of the "global village."[16] In the 90s, the promise of cyberspace also incited a range of responses. McLuhan's prophecies about the coming of the global village enjoyed a revival, largely sponsored by the Californian cyberculture magazine *Wired*. New York critic Mark Dery's caustic term for this McLuhanite revivalism is "theology of the ejector seat."[17] While there is much that is illuminating in McLuhan's insta-matic aphorisms, I find McGregor's inquiring scepticism more consistently edifying.

Australian writers were rarely evangelical in their embrace of cyberspace. A more practical and sceptical handling of it prevailed among writers such as Dale Spender, Jon Casimir, Daniel Petrie and David Harrington.[18] As if to (over) com-pensate, John Nieuwenhuizen ranted against cyberspace as "cultural AIDS".[19] Both Nieuwenhuizen and his opponents in this debate tended to over-estimate the novelty of this partic-ular 'information revolution', as if there had not been a whole series of information revolutions in the past century, each of which brought a unique set of changes in its wake.

It is simply not the case that cyberspace boots-up out of nowhere with the internet. Nor is the internet a unique or radical break in vectoral history. Even before the federation of the colonies, Australia was caught up in a whole series of technological changes that generated new vectors for storing or distributing information. Communications historian K.T.

Livingston lists telegraphy (1840s), rotary printing (1840s), the typewriter (1860s), transatlantic cable (1866), telephone (1876), motion pictures (1894), wireless telegraphy (1899), magnetic tape recording (1890s), radio (1906) and television (1923) as significant inventions that created new communication possibilities.[20] Cyberspace is an emergent property that arises out of the cumulative growth of ever more supple, subtle, pervasive and invasive vectors of communication.

Rather than see things in a technological determinist fashion, where these new vectors drive changes in everything else, I think it makes more sense to adopt a 'technological possibilist' view. Livingstone has an interesting take on the extent to which the possibility of telegraphy made it possible for the competing colonies on the Australian continent to think about cooperation. He points out that telegraphy was a significant topic of debate among political leaders in inter-colonial forums in the long, slow process of federating the colonies. New technologies make possible new vectors, along which information can travel more quickly, more reliably, more accurately or in greater quantity. These vectors create a matrix which makes it possible to generate new forms of political or cultural action. These forms of political and cultural action can in turn shape the way the next generation of vectors is implemented.

The relationship between telegraphy and federation is an interesting late 19th century instance of such a connection between a vector and the kinds of action it enables, and which in turn furthers the development of the vector. Telegraphy brought business and political elites into an emerging national space, while many ordinary people lived in a more local matrix of vectors. In the 20th century, television and the telephone extended the national space into ordinary people's lives, while business and political elites connected into a growing global network of communication.

Television makes it possible to generate vast publics, attuned simultaneously to the same message; the telephone makes it possible to coordinate personal connections, exchanging particular and self generated messages.[21] Through the television and the telephone, quite different kinds of culture coalesce: one based on normative and majoritarian messages; the other at least potentially enabling the formation of marginal and minority cultures.

Through the television and telephone, quite different forms of political action can be generated. The election campaigns of the major parties use television to spray messages as widely as possible, trying to catch the transient attention of uncommitted voters. The telephone, on the other hand, is the weapon of choice of the machine politician, lobbying and persuading one on one. Or as the conservative parties learned, it can be used for aggressive 'push polling', where party operatives call voters and ask leading questions that are carefully targeted to particular local issues. Push polling does not try to gather information on voter intentions, but to change those intentions.[22]

Communications historians Graeme Osborne and Glen Lewis argue that there have been three persistent themes in Australian debates about communication. The first is a technocratic concern with building infrastructure for national development. For a long time debate centred on which kinds of government institution ought to implement which kinds of technology, but the rise of an argument in favour of market-led development in the 80s was not unprecedented. A second theme is the view of communication as an agent of social control. The critical literature which decries the controlling influence of media that rose to prominence since the 60s really just reverses the value of long-held assumptions about the power of communication. Wartime propaganda managers of the 40s saw control as a good thing, while journalists of the 90s who had to work in the shadow of corporate media interests took the contrary view. The third theme is the concern over the role of communication in community and culture. Some saw commercial media as having a particularly poisonous effect on community; others, such as McGregor, adopted a more subtle view of the relationship between communication and culture.

Each of these three themes takes on a new inflection as pop gives way to cyberspace. For Osborne and Lewis, the technological development of the vector, from the telegraph to the internet, "does not appear to have overcome the sense of social isolation or the existence of an inarticulate citizenship." It is not enough, they argue, to improve the technology. There is also "a fundamental sense in which the question of values needs to be addressed by students of communication if its role in community creation is to be better understood."[23] In *Celebrities, Culture and Cyberspace*, my aim is limited to looking into the development of values within the communications matrix emerging at the end of the century.

I agree with writers such as K.T. Livingston, Graeme Osborne and Glen Lewis that the historical dimension to communication has been unjustly ignored, but I would add that it is also necessary to develop concepts out of that history. I'm looking for concepts that not only grasp the past, but can articulate possible futures; concepts that not only grasp the technical and social aspects of communication, but the subjective and experiential side as well; concepts that might help articulate a debate about the fair go on the cusp between the broadcast era of radio and television, and the postbroadcast era of cyberspace.

Conceptualising Cyberspace

"I belong to the first generation in Australia born into a world in which television already existed", writes Deakin University academic Scott McQuire.[24] I think he also belongs to the first generation of Australian media theorists using this lifetime of experience as a background for thinking about how media technologies transform both our conscious and unconscious lives in an ongoing way. For those of us raised by television, the so-called Generation X, it is clear that our perceptions are different to those who preceded us, who were weaned on cinema and radio. We are no better, no worse, just different. What is emerging in Australian media studies is a desire to confront the changes to media form since television on the basis of this experience of a prior transformation of which we are the product.

"Cyberspace is the defining figure for a sensibility produced by mediated cultures", writes Darren Tofts from Swinburne University, another of the TV generation of media theorists.[25] In his experience, "cyberspace... invokes a tantalising abstraction, the state of incorporeality, of disembodied immersion in a 'space' that has no co-ordinates in actual space". While it may appear to some that technologies like the internet, multimedia, hypertext and so on created this space *ex nihil*, Tofts insists that "cyberspace has its own sedimentary record, and accordingly requires an archaeology". These are just the latest gadgets in a long process of technologising the perceptions through which our bodies negotiate the world.

McQuire and Tofts go looking in different places for the conceptual prehistory of cyberspace. Tofts is interested in technologies of writing, from the clay tablet to the typewriter to the internet. McQuire traces the effects of photography: "The ability to witness things outside all previous limits of time and space highlights the fact that the camera doesn't only give us a new means to represent experience: it changes the nature of experience". While he is shy of using the term, he sees in photography a cause for the "anxious fascination with cyberspace".

In my first book, *Virtual Geography*, I tried to tackle a different aspect of the evolution of cyberspace.[26] Ever since the telegraph, technologies have developed that permit the transmission of information that can move more quickly than people or things.[27] The telegraph, telephone, television are steps in the development of telesthesia, or perception at a distance. Being able to perceive events elsewhere makes it possible to think and act on a scale far beyond the local but with the speed of the immediate. The internet extends and refines these capacities.

While I take a different aspect of the past evolution of media form as the basis for thinking about the emergence and potential of cyberspace to Tofts and McQuire, I share a similar experience to these other two children of television. It is since television brought sound and pictures right into the living room that the degree to which media pervade and transform social space has really started to sink in, but it is only on the basis of being immersed in television that it is possible to think about the further potential for the transformation of culture by the development of these vectors.

There is a charming enthusiasm in Craig McGregor's experience of pop that I think is a bit lost on me. Pop was already going stale in my time, and like Tofts and McQuire I'm too old to experience the cyberhype about the internet without some irony. For McGregor, pop was a potentially liberating force; for some people cyberspace was also meant to liberate us — from the tyranny of pop culture and its mass media vectors. The art of writing media theory in the 90s, having experienced more than one wave of media change fire up the imagination, is to steer between the extremes of cyber-hype and technofear. But this 'third way' is not just a matter of muddling through to a middle of the road position. Those who stand in the middle of the road get run over. It is a question of examining what the real potentials are that lurk as yet undiscovered in the media's transformations of culture. The writers who gathered around the Melbourne-based *21C* magazine, including Darren Tofts, Mark Dery and myself, tried to articulate a historically and culturally sensitive reading of cyberculture that could be critical but not too negative, creative but not too naive.[28]

Thirty years ago there was something of an unholy alliance of the new left and the old right 'intellectuals' against new forms of media-driven culture. This raised its head again in the 90s. The conservative pundit and veteran cold warrior Robert Manne commanded support on both left and right by revamping the bogey of "permissiveness" and arguing in favour of a return to censorship. He thought the screen versions of Jane Austen's novels that were popular in the 90s were good models of family love. He seemed not to notice that they portrayed an era when women were barred from real jobs, from public life and could not even own and transmit property.[29]

Meanwhile, Senator Richard Alston, as Minister for Communications and the Arts, exerted influence to restrict our liberty to choose what we want to see on television, film and video. He relied on rather cruder and more theological scaremongering than Manne. There would be no more "electronic Sodom and Gomorrah", like the popular commercial TV sex and relationship show *Sex/Life*, if Alston had his way. As columnist Brian Toohey remarked, "Sadly, a wrathful God has yet to turn *Sex/Life* viewers into pillars of salt."[30]

Robert Manne's kind of nostalgia for a nonexistent past is no less absurd than the McLuhanite cyberhype for an impossibly utopian future. But alongside these tired themes of control and development, the third theme Osborne and Lewis identify, the theme of community and identity, has opened up into a much more productive debate. What I would call the virtual dimension of change, the creative potential to make things otherwise, has opened up within the space created by changing media vectors. Cyberspace contains within it many possible forms of community and culture that have yet to be actualised. What I call urbanity is the art, culture and politics of trying to realise the virtuality that celebrities embody, that culture expresses, that cyberspace enables.

Intellectuals and Talking Heads

In the late 90s many on what was once the left either acquiesced to the moral authoritarian views of Alston and Manne, or actively supported them. The idea of liberty seemed to have run out of juice between the 60s and the 90s. On the road to building a fair and just and free society, many seemed to decide somewhere that there was not enough petrol to get us there. Seeing the gauge waver around the half way mark, 'intellectuals' on both the left and the right declared the tank half empty, and advocated turning back. Few on the left or the right realised that the tank could also be seen as half full — with enough to press on. Between the 60s and the 90s, criticism became a pervasive form in which 'intellectuals' asserted themselves.

I'm not happy with the term 'intellectual'. As broadcaster Robert Dessaix discovered when he conducted interviews for a book and radio program on the topic, Australian intellectuals are wary of being called intellectuals. Unlike their French counterparts, "Any Australian whose name was included in a *Dictionary of Australian Intellectuals* would very likely sue for libel."[31] Dessaix dared to extend the term to a number of interviewees, including myself, who offered some meek protest, but no writs. No-one seemed too proud to prohibit Dessaix from bestowing such a title over the pretence of objections, but perhaps Australian intellectuals protest too little.

We can all observe that heads and shoulders frequently appear, on television and behind lecterns at writer's festivals and other literary pop festivals. These heads may or may not be attached to bodies. These heads are given time in which the top half of the head may hinge up and down relative to the bottom half, allowing sounds, emitted from the mouth, to form what talking heads qualified to speak about these matters call speech. This speech may or may not be attached to an intelligence, but that too is a matter for conjecture. Hence the term intellectual calls for an unwarranted assumption. On the evidence Robert Dessaix provides, intelligence is not consistently demonstrated by the utterances of talking heads — including my own. Empirically speaking, the term talking heads seems more accurate than the term intellectuals.

From the 60s to the 90s, the value of what talking heads say came to depend on their ability to say what was lacking in what they saw around them. Negative evaluation became the norm; the talking head became a nay-saying celebrity. What fell by the wayside was a creative and positive assessment of the potential that the actual state of things might contain for improvements in justice, liberty and fairness, or even for new and unprecedented values.

The 60s saw the rise of a radical attack on the conservative mainstream of the Menzies era; the 90s saw a conservative counter attack against the institutionalised forms of urbane libertarianism that existed during the Hawke years. The 60s was when economic luck seemed still to be holding; the 90s was when everyone realised the luck had run out. In the 60s, radicals confronted their society with optimism and marshalled a will for change; in the 90s, conservatives shouted down any talk of making life better, and preached compulsory morality as the only way to stop things getting worse.

I suspect that writing in the wake of the 90s might be harder than writing after the 60s. These are both periods when a writer of the left could not assume that her or his position in Australian society carried any legitimacy. The difference is that in the 60s there was a legitimacy to be won. As the *bon vivant* and gay adventurer Peter Blazey wrote of Melbourne in the 60s: "as the Vietnam war gathered pace, Carlton's social lepers became morally superior to South Yarra's silvertails who had manifestly backed the wrong horse".[32]

In the 90s, it was left-leaning talking heads, the writers and thinkers, Blazey's 'Carlton', who were tagged with the blame for the social ills of the times. The Canberra economists that sociologist Michael Pusey labelled "economic rationalists" had to carry the can for the economic inequalities and uncertainties of the 90s.[33] The social rationalism that accompanied it was sheeted home to the urbane instincts of the left. The popularity of the reactionary writing of Paul Sheehan is symptomatic of this.[34] Between the untimely death of the free thinking and free wheeling Blazey and the rise of the accusatory and scapegoating Sheehan, the times were a-changing — back.

Or so the new reactionary celebrites, from Hanson to Sheehan, imagined. But in some respects the dynamism of technical change in media vectors, from the 60s to the 90s, irreversibly altered the cultural landscape of Australia. The era of massified pop media began giving way to an era of diversified cyberspace. Where there's a vector along which people might imagine new ways of life, then there is hope. Technologies do not create utopias all by themselves. Rather, they offer the potential for proposing new images and ideas of the good life with which people might choose to think and act of their own accord.

The opening up of such possibilities does not mean that only good possibilities eventuate. The flourishing of the populist right owes as much to the ongoing media revolution as does Green politics and other radical social movements. Cheap and fast media vectors, from desktop publishing to the internet, enabled a much more diverse fringe of cultures to coordinate and organise themselves. The web site for Pauline Hanson's One Nation Party Ltd, established in April 1997, had 500,000 hits over the following 14 months.[35]

The dispersed media vectors of cyberspace were one factor that enabled populist movements to reach the point in the 90s where they could challenge the legitimacy of mainstream political culture from both right and left. The Greens brought down the Queensland Goss Labor government, and One Nation brought down the Borbidge National government that succeeded it. The major parties are no longer in a monopoly position in capturing grass roots electoral support on the ground and combining it with media clout.

In this book, I'm particularly concerned with the effects of this transformation on the fortunes of the Australian

Labor Party, and how it might respond to them. I think
Labor still offers the best chance for reconciling justice
with liberty, government with market, and adapting the fair
go to a changing world. In this book I side with the agenda
for radical economic reform and with the forces for radical
cultural change, but I temper this with a prudent affirmation of the value of traditional social institutions, such as
parliamentary democracy, and the institution of the Labor
Party which seeks power by composing electoral majorities
across urban, suburban and rural electorates. Labor has
always been the practical means of advancing change, but if
Labor is to remain the party of the people, it has to understand the culture of the people. The light on the hill, the
traditional image of Labor inspiration and aspiration, may
emanate from the cathode ray tube rather than the
kerosene lamp.

In the 90s, Labor faced challenges, not just from the other
institutionalised parties, but from new populist forces on
both the left and the right. What made it possible to organise
effectively outside of big media and big politics was, broadly
speaking, cyberspace. This is another factor that made the
90s a hard time to write about. I think the shape and speed
of media in this postbroadcast age make it a different kind of
culture, but because these media break down mass communication into smaller channels, it's very hard to generalise as
to what that culture might look like.

What made the possibility of challenging mainstream politics and culture a reality in the late 90s was the self-inflicted
loss of legitimacy of the mainstream. The public started
choosing their own talking heads from outside the mass
media tank, and the mass media had no choice, in the end,
but to accept Bob Brown and Pauline Hanson. Both are
curious examples of very different kinds of activist celebrity,
coming into the media from the provinces rather than from
the urban centre.

Green politics and One Nation populism articulate very
different visions of the rural good life. One came equipped
with trouty streams, the other with semi-automatic rifles.
Both were a challenge to the Sydney/Melbourne/Canberra
triangle and the uneasy *modus vivendi* between economic and
social rationalism sponsored by the country's urban talking

heads. In the 90s, the bush and the city joined battle for the hearts and minds of the suburbs.

Culture and Cyberspace

How is it possible that Australia exists? The geography of Australia is real enough. The state that controls the space of that geography is real enough too. So too the economy that produces and distributes its wealth. But neither geography, politics nor economics make Australia real to us as something present in our subjective experience. What makes 'Australia' seem real to 'Australians', as an abstract object of thought and abstract subject that is supposed to be thinking about it, is that there are celebrities, cultures and cyberspace.

In subjective experience, this thing called 'Australia' appears as a 'virtual republic'. It is a republic in the sense of being a *res publica*, a public thing, with the additional meaning of a public reality that everybody shares in making, if not equally so. What makes it a virtual public thing is the paradox that while it is shared by all who make it real by imagining it and articulating it, everyone imagines and articulates it as something different. Its existence is not predicated on any agreement as to its essential features, as the Hansonites would have it. Rather, its existence, like the existence of the 'fair go', is predicated only on the possibility of disagreement about its qualities. Australia is that which Australians disagree about; Australians are the people who disagree about the possible pasts, presents and futures of Australia. Or at least so I argued in my second book, *The Virtual Republic.*[36]

What makes it possible to become this people who disagree about this public thing is the existence of a matrix of vectors that thread images and stories together, and thread them also into people's lives. Images and stories, weaving in and out of everyday life, connect people to each other. From the telegraph to the telephone, to telecommunications, these vectors change, and in the process they change the way subjective experience of reality gets made. The subtle shift from a modern world experienced via people, politics and pop, to a postmodern world experienced via celebrity, culture and cyberspace is an effect of changes in the means of communication, but also in the accumulated techniques available in everyday life for reading what is communicated. Moving from pop to cyberspace, Australians start to see their collective and individual identities differently.

Australians have many different ways of thinking and feeling, but nevertheless share a cyberspace within which cultural differences are not only negotiated and adjudicated, but creatively combined. The most visible signs of this process are celebrities. They embody not just the particular cultures from which they come, they embody also something beyond. We may not like the same celebrities, we may not like any of them at all, but it is the existence of a population of celebrities, about whom to disagree, that makes it possible to constitute a sense of belonging. Through celebrating (or deriding) celebrities it is possible to belong to something beyond the particular culture with which each of us might identify. Cyberspace provides the vehicle, celebrities provide the fuel, and culture is the journey.

Cyberspace mixes images and stories from the cultures of different places. What celebrities do is articulate the possible points of difference and combination that arise between those cultures. Both the recognition of differences, and the possibility of reconciling them, are things that come about because of cyberspace. The emerging vectors of cyberspace are what made it possible in the 90s for there to be 'public things' in a world that long ago outgrew the space of the town hall or market square. The development of cyberspace is what made it possible to partially bypass the limitations of television as a substitute space for the public square.

Celebrity, culture and cyberspace are the concepts through which I want to explain how 'Australia' comes into existence as something people know in their bones, but about which there is a constant friction of difference, since no two people ever experience it as the same thing. Out of this chaotic dance of information passing between public life and private worlds, how is it possible to create a majority that has a positive sense of the possibilities for an open, dynamic, urbane Australia? That is the problem for the Labor Party at the end of the 90s. It has to find a third way between unpopular reform agendas and populist hostility to change.

Donald Horne, Intellectual Celebrity

The 60s teemed with new concepts. In the 90s, there were plenty of opinions, stories and rhetorics at work in Australian public life, but it seemed to me that fewer concepts were created. Like Sydney University's Elspeth Probyn, I want to "engage less in the negative critiques", but rather "take up an idea and push it along and see where it gets you", so as to "bring together a sense of the empirical with different theories that are abstractions of the observable".[37] Concepts are made by looking into all of the different experiences we have and asking ourselves what makes these differences possible. A concept attempts to express the process by which differences get made. It's a way of abstracting something from all of the particulars of experience.

Concepts are tools for thinking not only about how reality gets made, but about how else it could possibly be made. This is why there can be no radical thought without concepts, for without concepts it is not possible to think constructively about how things might be otherwise. Without concepts all we have is nostalgia for how things once were, or impossible, unobtainable ideals. Conservatives and utopians can get by without concepts, but not radicals. Radicals, as the name implies, want to get to the root of how things work in order to think rationally and creatively about how things might work better.

Between the 60s and the 90s, making concepts for and with an Australian public became a bit difficult. The liberation movements of the 60s proposed concepts, but they were marked by a tendency to read local experience through concepts from elsewhere. While some liberationists such as Anne Summers and Dennis Altman tried in varying degrees to adapt liberationist thinking to Australian experience, these were still thought of as local variants of international movements.[38]

The fate of conceptual work in Australia is that it is often perceived as too intellectual by the media and too popular by the academy. The media are unthinking but readable; the academy is thoughtful but unreadable. The media prefers talking heads who tell stories or evoke feelings that are immediately recognisable. The humanities and social sciences academy prefers work that develops received ideas within the framework of internationally accepted languages and styles. Mainstream media ceased transmission of new concepts from the academy in the 90s, and attacked the academy for its postmodernism and political correctness. Some 60s thinkers with entrenched positions in the media were by the 90s no longer producing new concepts.

There is no shortage of Australian talking heads, but rarely do they encase thinking minds. A more stringent test is required to distinguish thinking capacity from mere talking capacity. For a talking head to become a thinking mind — an intellectual — requires a practice of making concepts that are shared, via the media, with a public, where the concepts attempt to articulate the experiences of that public, at that moment. Just as there can be talking without thinking, there can be thinking without talking, or at least without the kind of public speech acts that I think define an intellectual's habit of thinking out loud.

The talking head is a rare kind of celebrity; the intellectual is an even rarer kind of talking head. There are talking heads through which people feel and dream, who articulate the emotional or erotic desires of a public. There are talking heads through which people narrate and moralise, who satisfy an instinct for stories and rhetorics that provide the comfort of belonging. But there are also talking heads who articulate the conceptual desires of a public — intellectuals. They articulate the desires for critical questioning and creative rethinking of what might otherwise be taken for granted about everyday life. Intellectuals may bring with them into public life the authority of an institution, such as a university or a newspaper or a church, but what defines their celebrity is that they risk this legitimacy. They stake it on the communication of an idea to a public that proposes to that public a new way of thinking about its very existence.

The intellectual is a rare event in Australia, but one of the most enduring, and endearing, is Donald Horne. Which begs the question of what it is about Horne's style of thinking that made this possible. The answer, I think, is clearly legible on the surface of Horne's mid-60s book, the *Lucky Country*. In that classic book, Horne stressed "the need to build up a certain kind of cleverness".[39] In the 90s it was no longer quite the case, as Horne wrote in the 60s, that "almost all Australian writers — whatever their politics — are reactionaries whose attitude to the massive diversities of suburban life is to ignore it or condemn it rather than discover it". But the desire to research and conceptualise everyday life here and now still met derision and indifference from those for whom the term 'culture' was reserved for other times and places.

Horne's crucial observation is that "Australians 'learn' their culture", and this formally acquired sense of culture is remote from lived culture. The accumulation of wisdom in the practices of everyday life from below receives scant recognition among the authorities who teach or review culture from above. The seeds of the populist rejection of 'political correctness' in the 90s are already present in this divide, to the extent that resistance to it was a popular flouting of the terminology and conventions of legitimate talking heads.[40] What is of enduring significance about Horne is that he tried to develop concepts out of Australian experience, rather than importing concepts and sticking them on top of that experience. The thing to learn from European culture was that the reason European writers and thinkers mattered was that the concepts they created had organic connections to the culture of everyday life — even when in opposition to it.

Rather than oppose to everyday life here and now the concepts emanating from Rome or Moscow, London or Paris or New York, it's a question of seeing how the practices of everyday life already have distinctive ways of thinking imminent in them. The fair go, for instance, might not be just a crude rendering of Liberty, Equality and Fraternity. It might have acquired some different senses of its own. There is still a long way to go in refining the experiences thrown up by the Australian milieu into concepts and perceptions. There is still a long way to go in adding to the vernacular language a conceptual dimension. These are essential tasks if what the populist reaction dubs Australia's 'cultural elites' are to overcome Horne's melancholy diagnosis of the second-rate, and also overcome the resistance of a large part of the Australian people to the very idea of thinking.

Beyond Criticism

If there is a part of public life in most need of the challenge of intellectual rethinking it is the media, as the media are the very means of communication by which publics form in the first place. There are intellectuals who criticise the media in terms of what is wrong with it. To them there can be no advance towards the good life without first fixing the channels within which the public argues with itself about it. But what seems to me less common are intellectuals who can conceptualise what can be done within the actual media. Or in other words, there is more of a critical than a creative culture of thinking about Australian media. Shifting the balance more toward the creative side requires a bit of a rethink about what the point of studying the media might be in the first place.

Critical media studies flourished in the wake of the 60s. It was the means by which a radical minority explained to itself why the majority did not agree with it. The masses had been duped by the media. From this simplistic starting point, often quite enlightened and sophisticated knowledge about the media developed. The irony is that while the theories improved, critical media theory lost its political edge. In the 60s, criticism attacked the legitimacy of journalism either in the name of its stated ideals of objectivity and independence, or in the name of a radical alternative. By the 90s, criticism still attacked the legitimacy of journalism, but mostly this served to legitimise the authority of the academic critic rather than advance a reforming or radical agenda.

In the 90s, criticism of the media took two main forms. Some talking heads criticised what was lacking in the media in terms of the stated ideals of liberal democratic society. Others criticise what was lacking in liberal democratic society in terms of a more radical ideal. Julianne Schultz, from the Centre for Independent Journalism, argued that the actual practice of journalism compares badly to the standards of independence, rationality and seriousness embodied in the ideal of a journalistic "fourth estate".[41] Victoria University academic John Langer critiqued this kind of critique of the media in turn.[42] He saw it as a "lament" which was obsessed with policing the boundaries between high and low forms of journalism. The lament was popular with journalists and former journalists, from Schultz to former commercial current affairs celebrity Jana Wendt and the ABC's media critic Stuart Littlemore.[43] Langer's critique of it was more common among media studies academics.

Lamenting talking heads decried the incursion of 'soft news' into the world of 'hard news'. They were against anything commercial, trivial, emotional or exploitative. They were in favour of news that is in the public interest, is rational and dispassionate. But as Langer pointed out, the lament style of critique takes for granted that news really can grasp the world in a factual and impartial way. The lamentation chorus were the biggest suckers for the assumptions news makers and journalists have about themselves. They assumed an ideal world in which news is just about transmitting information to citizens. There is no evidence that the media have ever worked that way, and good reasons to doubt that it ever could. As Langer pointed out, ritual, symbol and myth play as much a part in news as any other part of the media.

One alternative to the lament was critical media studies. This had its roots in the 60s, which inspired its rejection of the claim that news could aspire to be impartial and objective. It saw news as a purveyor of the dominant ideology. From the 60s to the 90s, this view became less simplistic. It no longer saw news as just a transmission belt for the dominant ideology of the ruling class. It saw news as a means by which the ruling class seeks consent for its policies by accommodating some of the aspirations of subordinate groups.[44]

Like the popular ABC comedy *Frontline*, radical media critics like Langer went beyond the lamentation, and asked what the trashy world of low journalism is all about. Langer argued that "other news", such as celebrity gossip, human interest features and disaster coverage are an integral part of the cultural universe of news and current affairs. Langer extended a subtle view of the way ideology works to secure widespread consent for the ruling order to the other news. Journalism's processes of selection, classification and representation produce the meaning of events in such a way as to naturalise the dominant way of looking at the world. But Langer thought the views of subordinate groups are more likely to be dealt with in the other news. It's the "crucial region where some of the contradictory tendencies in television get played out".

I think Langer was right to draw attention to phenomena like celebrity, but the trouble with his critique is that it seems to assume that nobody understands the selection and presentations techniques of the media except the media studies scholars who critique it. Both Schultz and Langer discount the creative uses people make of media in everyday life. Their views are self-legitimating, in that in their critique, the public are assumed to be unable to read the media without the intervention of talking heads like Langer and Schultz with the special ability to see what the media lacks. Langer also ignores the influence media studies itself has had on viewer tastes. I think it unlikely that a show like *Frontline*, or the English newsroom comedy *Drop the Dead Donkey*, could become so popular if the critical ideas of media studies had not themselves become a part of everyday culture. *Frontline* poked fun at what everyone already knows is wrong with current affairs journalism.

What a lot of talking heads who claimed authority to speak about the media still assumed in the 90s was that the way people read the media and make use of it is just some sort of natural given. Schultz assumed you just have to bring the production of media in line with its own ideal of itself and the public will be better informed. Langer assumed you can just study the texts of the media and from them you could anticipate the meanings people make of it. Others, such as Ien Ang and Virginia Nightingale from the University of Western Sydney, paid more attention to what people do with the media, showing that the public can be active readers who can resist and negotiate as well as consent to what the media says.[45]

While this was a big advance, there is still room for a fourth way of writing and speaking about the media. Rather than assume that texts generate meaning all by themselves, or that publics make the media mean whatever they like, why not see media studies as the business of enhancing the capacity people already have for reading, not just critically, but also creatively? As well as showing how the media does not live up to its own ideals, let alone the ideal of a radical alternative vision, why not equip a public with the interpretive tools to make other kinds of sense out of the media that confronts them in everyday life?

It's a question of applying to the popular reading of journalism and news the kind of concept many intellectuals now accept as a fair rendering of the workings of popular readings of entertainment culture. McGregor always saw the popular arts as containing people's "unexpressed potential", and he was particularly drawn to "Dionysian rituals of celebration", from the jitterbug to disco.[46] In his enduring interest in jazz music, there is a certain ethical view of popular creativity at work. Jazz is a great example of a spontaneous, popular creativity, one that takes the elements of the mass media form of popular music, deconstructs it into its constituent elements, and creates out of it a new lexicon of expression.

From the 60s to the 90s, this bebop art of releasing the virtual world of creativity from the actual material of a mass media culture spread from music to all kinds of media culture. *Celebrities, Culture and Cyberspace* is meant as a contribution to this art of making other kinds of sense, not just out of pop tunes but also out of celebrity images and news stories. It is also a book that wants to make a modest contribution to the problem of growing concepts out of the everyday experience of this jigsaw jazz of popular creativity.

An Itinerary

Over the next nine chapters, I want to look in more detail at how the media constitute a common world, within which cultures negotiate via images and stories that bear the imprint of famous faces. Those faces are a mix of political and cultural celebrities. I'm interested in both the politics of culture and the culture of politics. One effect of the proliferation of media vectors is that these things are no longer quite so separate.

In chapter two, I look at the general contours of the phenomena of celebrity. By looking at particular instances of celebrity, I want to show how subtle the machinery at work in this phenomena can be. Celebrity is a key with which to understand not only how popular culture works, but how the self-perceptions and self-interests of the people who participate in popular culture form.

In chapter three, I look in detail at two contrasting stories about celebrities — Kylie Minogue and Nick Cave. They are celebrities from the world of music who embody quite different concepts of what it is that people desire, and what kinds of popular images and stories can embody an idea of the 'fair go'.

In chapter four, I look at how a celebrity acquires legitimacy with a public, and how this can be used to cross the invisible border between the politics of culture and the culture of politics. Like Kylie and Nick Cave, Peter Garrett started out as a popular entertainer. He transferred the idea of the fair go embodied in his music and his persona into populist environmental politics. I examine how he made this transition.

Moving on from celebrity to culture, I look in chapter five at the way culture is experienced as stratified. I propose a way of thinking about class difference that is based not on property or wealth but on access to information. I look at the tensions in Australian culture between the cosmopolitan and the suburban as a latent class distinction between people with the capacity to benefit from access to information and people denied that capacity, and hence that benefit.

In chapter six, I argue that tensions about the costs and benefits of access to new information in an increasingly media saturated, globalised world has been a consistent theme in Australian movies and television in the 90s. Movies like *The Castle, Muriel's Wedding* and *Idiot Box* are read in terms of what they have to say about negotiating the changes that come in a culture more and more immersed in flows of information.

If there is a culture that ought to be able to articulate, from the bottom up, a vision of the fair go that embraces the information poor, it is the culture of the Australian Labor Party. But Labor lost its hold on the popular imagination in the 80s, despite its record electoral successes. In chapter seven I examine three of the most substantial media portrayals of the history of Labor culture, *True Believers, The Dismissal* and *Labor in Power.* Here I find that politics, no less than culture, struggles to maintain its confidence and its bearings as globalisation and cyberspace become more and more concrete determinants of the shape of everyday life.

In chapter eight, I approach the problem of thinking about cyberspace through the prism of 'generationalism'. I try to show how the synchronising effects of broadcast media produce generationalism as an effect. But rather than stick with the rather clumsy distinction between Baby Boomers and Generation X, I show how television provides a more subtle determinant of who might share a given repertoire of stories and images.

The academic disciplines in which I work, media studies and cultural studies, like to think they have an ethical and even political orientation. The problem is that I think this political orientation has ossified and become as estranged from new information as most other kinds of suburban Australian culture. So in the last two chapters, I try and open up some space for new debate about the kind of connection that can be imagined between the politics of culture and the culture of politics.

Chapter nine looks at the passing of the torch from Barry Jones, Labor's original thinker of the 90s, to a new generation of Labor talking heads — and one hopes, intellectuals. An examination of the ideas of Lindsay Tanner and Mark Latham, from the left and the right of the Labor Party respectively, takes up most of chapters nine and ten. In part, I'm looking for a third way, not just between right and left within social democratic culture, but a third way that might come after the old left of the labour movement and the new left of the social movements.

What I hope the reader might get out of these essays is a sense that radical and progressive change is still possible. What I hope to show is that re-energising the movement for change might be a matter of exploring what is to be done with the means actually at people's disposal for thinking about culture and the common world — celebrities, culture and cyberspace. What I hope for the future is that people born about now, who are not yet part of this common world, will look back on what we did and said and will not complain that we spent all our time complaining.

celebrities

chapter **2**

The murmur of the waves

The barbarians are no longer at the gate, they are inside the castle, redecorating.

Catharine Lumby

A Strange Kettle of Fish

My brother likes to photograph fish. He's an accomplished underwater photographer, and more than once has managed to make images that convey something of the serene ubiquity of the sea, across which some fish swims into view, sublimely oblivious of being made into an image by the camera.

My brother also takes pictures on dry land. It's a standard family joke that while he has the most up-to-date camera gear, it still seems to take him forever to snap the shot. Not that I can complain too much, as he has produced a beautiful record of my family's progress through time.

There is something vaguely embarrassing about having a camera pointed at you. I'm one of those people who squirm while waiting for the flash to pop. That my brother takes so long about it gives me plenty of time to dwell on this acute kind of uncomfortable self-awareness. I try to imagine I'm as blissfully unaware of the intruding lens as a fish.

As you can imagine, I was even more embarrassed to find myself before the camera in a fashion photographer's studio, standing before him in my best suit, becoming one of the endless series of images of people that clutter up the pages of magazines. In this case, a photo of the huge crow's foot around my left eye and my stubbly chin ended up in a stylish fashion magazine called *Studio for Men*.[1] I felt less like a fish in the ocean, more like a salamander in a bowl, existing solely to be seen by someone else.

My experience as something beneath even what broadcaster Helen Razer calls a "media celebutante of only minor notoriety" was mercifully brief.[2] Just the sort of thing you do these days at the behest of a publisher's publicist. But it made me think about how Labor parliamentarian Cheryl Kernot must have felt, becoming the cover girl for the April 1998 edition of *Australian Women's Weekly*. While Kernot is probably well accustomed to swimming in the aquarium, this was a little different. Kernot is a celebrity because of her prominent role in politics, but what the *Women's Weekly* cover made just that little bit more obvious is that she is also prominent in politics because she is a celebrity.

Robert Hughes once wrote of Andy Warhol that "he went after publicity with the single-minded voracity of a feeding bluefish".[3] A great line, but one that begs the question: what kind of fish that would make Hughes? As Catharine Lumby points out, the art critic has an altogether different relation to publicity and celebrity than the artist, but a relation to it all the same.[4] Perhaps Hughes and Warhol are species of fish that need each other — celebrity artist of pop and celebrity art critic of quality; bottom feeding bluefish and predatory critical shark.

There are probably as many different kinds of celebrity as there are of fish. There are celebrities who are like your standard goldfish — stock images of what is good to look at. There are celebrities who have some substance to them, ranging from the flaky salmon types to the strong meat of swordfish. There are celebrities that become celebrities by predatory behaviour among their own kind, like sharks. There are bottom feeders, thriving on muck, like flounder; there are rare exotics, like the tropical fish; there are celebrities with a capacity to shock, like stingrays; there are celebrities so well armoured you know very little about what makes them tick, like yabbies. Some prefer big tanks, some small; some like their water warm, some aerated. Some perform tricks, like seals; some appeal to us as much for their intelligence as their looks, like dolphins.

The media's world is like Seaworld, only it is celebrities, rather than marine life, that it turns into something that exists only so that we might see that it exists, and might experience our selves, our desires, our possibilities, and our interests via their fishy existence. Any desire, from comfort to passion and beyond, can be experienced via the act of celebration, by putting oneself in some relation to the image of celebrity. Even the desire for an idea or two about celebrity itself. In this chapter, I want first to celebrate images of celebrity that might produce ideas about celebrity, and then I want to look at celebrities who are themselves producers of ideas.

The Pleasure Machine

For all of the differences the celebrity kettle of fish displays, all these bright species can be graded along a continuum. At one end are the talking heads, at the other, the moving bodies. There are celebrities whose images appear because of what they say, and celebrities who are asked to say things as an adjunct to their appearance. This is why there is a continuum from talking head to moving body, rather than a divide. The appearances of talking heads matter, and what moving bodies say matters.

Take, for instance, a celebutante of 1998, Gabrielle Richens. She became an object of attention when the Rugby League football star Solomon Haumono broke his contract and bolted from Sydney to be with her in London. Richens was a model who appeared as a gyrating pole-dancer in a television ad for Virgin Atlantic airline, in which the aircraft was referred to as the "pleasure machine". In the coverage of the story, Richens quickly became "the model known as the pleasure machine", suggesting in none too subtle terms that she was so hot and sexy Haumono couldn't resist her. She was, in short, about as far up the moving body end of the celebrity spectrum as you can get.

Yet Richens was still required to speak, to the popular women's magazine *Cleo* and its male counterpart *Ralph*, both of whom put her picture on the cover with **THE PLEASURE MACHINE** blazoned underneath. The only significant difference between the two was that *Cleo* was more interested in her sexual style and *Ralph* was more interested in Solomon's.[5] All celebrities, whether they are moving bodies like Gabrielle Richens and Solomon Haumono, or talking heads like Cheryl Kernot, must produce both appearances and speech, although attention may not focus equally on them. Richens became a celebrity as soon as she was obliged to speak. She was a model who became a spokesmodel. The spokesmodel is a celebrity who has to speak because it appears; a talking head is a celebrity who has to appear because it speaks.

Celebrity, as the word implies, involves the celebration of someone, via the circulation before many eyes of their image. It might appear at first that what celebrity celebrates is weirdness. Celebrities form a freakshow of extraordinary appearances and outrageous soundbites. Popular culture is never without its wiles, and what is also being celebrated via celebrity is not just the exotic and strange qualities of an image elite but also the everyday and ordinary qualities of the people who choose to participate in the celebration. Celebrities become celebrities only partly because of their extraordinary appearances or statements; they become celebrities also because, no matter how otherworldly they may appear, they cannot but participate in the ordinary as well. This is why people were interested less in the policies Cheryl Kernot might talk up and more in observing how she reacted when a truck plowed into her house. Likewise, people were interested in the ordinary, everyday romantic folly of Solomon Haumono — the banal heart of the pleasure machine story.

Celebrities affirm both individual ambition and collective belonging. A celebrity is at one and the same time someone who broke from her or his community but who also affirms the capacity and identity of that community. "I don't know where people get the idea from that I'm trouble", Gabrielle Richens says to *Cleo* magazine's Paula McFadden, "I'm just a kid from Kent." This is true not only of a celebutante like Richens, but even of Elle Macpherson, a model who became not just a spokesmodel, but a supermodel, a talking head, and even an ironic version of an intellectual, with her famous quip that "I only read books I've written myself."

Elle Macpherson was an image of ambition fulfilled, and

yet she was still *our* supermodel. She belonged to the Australian people. She stood, within its limits, for the capacity to extend limits. She embodied a certain kind of desire for the good life. Celebrity may be all about appearances, but it always invokes something beyond appearances. Celebrities are the almost tangible evidence that one of ours can become something that might redefine what we think we can become. Celebrities embody the virtual in everyday life.

The apparatus that produces the appearance of celebrity, from the publicist to the stylist, from the copywriter to the photographer, is the pleasure machine. What the celebutante Garielle Richens was supposed to embody was actually a quality of celebrity in general. The pleasure of celebrity embraces the reciprocal link between the everyday and the fantastic, the banal and the magical. Imagine an ordinary suburban lounge room. The celebrity on the cover of the magazine on the coffee table, like the goldfish swimming in the bowl on the mantle, flashes a glint from another world, some strange aqua life. Celebrity is not just a trace of the extraordinary in the ordinary. What makes it tangible is that it is also a trace of the ordinary in the extraordinary. The goldfish may fascinate, but it still needs a regular feed. The celebrity may fascinate, but the trace of the ordinary habits of life, from domestic friction to eating disorders, connects even the most worldly celebrity to the mundane.

Never Tear Us Apart

When rock singer Michael Hutchence was found dead, there were many stories. Kings Cross parties buzzed with instant fables. And juicy gossip it was too, for it combined death under curious circumstances with a very high profile celebrity. In 1987, Hutchence's band INXS sold 9 million copies of their album *Kick* worldwide. In 1997, for a moment, at least, Hutchence left the ranks of golden haired Rock Gods, and joined the exalted company of the multiplatinum immortals. The irony of celebrity is that it offers the closest thing to instant global immortality, but only on a temporary basis.

Most celebrities, we are constantly reminded, are mortal. They age and they die, just like us. They have faults and foibles, just like us. And yet they are living proof that one can aspire to something beyond. Some celebrities become immortal. For a time. Michael Hutchence lives on. He lives, just as many household gods and saints around the world live, so long as there are people to idolise and worship him, who play his records, who keep his picture blu-tacked to the wall. This is the paradox of immortality: it can last forever, but only so long as there are humans to perpetuate the memory.

Celebrities are vampires that suck their existence out of us. Only it is not blood they demand as a sacrifice, but grey matter, a corner of memory. But celebrities do not colonise our memories merely on behalf of their own appeal. They are the embodiment of actions, statements, stories, about how someone with some mix of ordinary and extraordinary qualities responded to events that happened around them, and made something happen out of those circumstances. The lives of celebrities are fables, in which they appear as worthy of the events that happen to them. "Such is life", the bushranger Ned Kelly says, when he knows his end is near. He is worthy even of the event of his own death.

So, perversely, is another larrikin — Michael Hutchence, found dead in a room at Sydney's Ritz Carlton Hotel. He made the front page of the *Daily Telegraph*. "Hutchence's body was found naked, hanging by a leather belt from the self-closing mechanism on the door of room 524... He choked himself by kneeling down and taking the strain on the belt."[6] It might have been suicide, as the coroner decided; or as *Who Weekly* speculated, it might have been an accident that happened "when autoerotic sex went wrong".[7] For *Juice* magazine's Toby Creswell, it was like a plot point in a trashy airport novel: "So what would make Michael Hutchence, a man who had everything, take his own life — a mistake in a sexual game or a moment of depression, a suicidal impulse brought on by a raft of emotional, neurological and emotional causes?"[8]

The ambiguity about motive goes to the heart of the ambiguity of Hutchence's celebrity. The autoerotic asphyxiation story fits with his Rock God past, but the suicide story fits with the saga of his attempt to become a family man. In that version, Michael wanted to be with Paula Yates and her children, but their father, Bob Geldof, was winning the legal battle to wrest custody from the wayward Yates. All of which are private matters, ultimately unfathomable, but which became public property the instant Hutchence carked it. "Almost as soon as Michael's body was discovered," writes biographer Ed St John, "a Ritz Carlton staffer bounded onto the footpath outside the hotel and blurted the news to a handful of reporters and photographers. Before a single member of the INXS entourage knew anything about the singer's death, the news — initially reported as a rumour — was spreading like wildfire through the electronic media."[9]

On talkback radio, I heard many arguments about Hutchence, Yates, Geldof, child custody, responsibility, privacy, a whole host of ethical questions. Celebrities populate our ethical life. They are not necessarily more moral than ordinary people, often they appear much less so. The world celebrities invoke is closer to a pagan world than a Christian one.[10] A lot of criticism of celebrity stems from a Christian revulsion towards this celebration of figures whose punishments and rewards are all very much sought in this world rather than the next. Like the ancient Greek heroes, celebrities combine strong passions and abilities with mundane failings. They may be remembered as much for how these qualities led to their undoing as for how they made it. But whether tragic or heroic, a memorable celebrity is someone celebrated for being worthy of what happened to them.

It's hard to specify the common characteristics of celebrity. By definition one of the things a celebrity achieves is some kind of novelty, some new quality. But there are some characteristics that define a sort of range of family resemblances among celebrities. Like members of a family in a snap shot, each has some characteristic in common with another, but not always the same characteristic. I might have the same chin as my brother but a different nose, and the same eyes as my sister but different hair, and so on.

Celebrities, like goldfish or humans, are a species. Like each species, each new individual member of the species embodies a new combination out of the gene pool, which is the virtual sum of all possible new members of the species. A species of tropical fish in their specially heated tanks and celebrities in their specially lit media environment might fascinate us for much the same reasons. An exotic fish in vivid colours is a striking example of just how many and varied are the things that fish might become. An exotic celebrity is even more fascinating, for it is rumoured that celebrities as a species bear some genetic relation to humans. Humans and celebrities belong to the same genus; *homo sapiens* and *homo celebratus*. Celebrities are a virtual world of exotic things toward which humans might 'evolve'. The bodies of athlete Cathy Freeman or footballer Ian Roberts, the minds of scientist Paul Davies or poet Judith Wright — these are images of what, one way or another, we could become.

Celebrities embody the ordinary characteristics of some kind of community. Ned Kelly is an Irish Australian of the 1880s; Kylie Minogue is a suburban Melbournian of the 1980s. Celebrities produce images of the interaction of the qualities of someone from a particular community with other kinds of people. Kylie Minogue is the suburban girl like us who gets to rub shoulders with the rich and famous who are not like us. Michael Hutchence is the Sydney larrikin who takes that city's easygoing cosmopolitan style onto the world stage.

Celebrities have an ability in a particular field, but they end up circulating among images of people who have abilities in widely differing fields. Elle Macpherson's skill was as a model, but now we see her image alongside actors, businesspeople, politicians. Hutchence's skill was as a singer, but we see him arm in arm with a supermodel. Whatever their many and varied attributes, celebrities share the quality of appearing in the public world of celebrity. In a world where everyone leads increasingly specialised lives, celebrities specialise in appearing to live lives of general appeal to almost everybody.

Celebrities come into the world endowed with 'true stories' about their exploits that reveal something of their character and significance, but before long other stories attach to them which, whether true or not, define them — rumours. "Nellie Melba", said Manning Clark, "had a gardener — or that was his official designation, although his purpose was markedly different. He would wait backstage at the theatre and Madam Melba would suck him off immediately before she went on stage and sang because it relaxed her tubes, you see, improved her modulation".[11]

Celebrities require intermediaries who relay to us stories of their great and ordinary doings. Sometimes there are whole chains of intermediaries. The story about Nellie Melba comes from screen writer Bob Ellis, who is quoting historian Manning Clark who in turn relies on intermediaries who, when pressed, he cannot even name. Through intermediaries, celebrities spread their image across time and space, achieving not only temporary immortality but temporary ubiquity. These intermediaries cannot be trusted. Many rumours circulated about Hutchence's death, all supposedly originating with a friend of a friend who worked at the Ritz Carlton Hotel.

The irony is that it is not the image of any particular celebrity which achieves this ubiquity and immortality, but the pleasure machine of celebrity. When Michael Hutchence sang 'Never Tear Us Apart', it sounded like a romantic ballad, but it might just as well be a song about the strange love of publics and celebrities for each other. This is another side to the pleasure machine, quite different to its celebration of the link between celebrity and banality. Celebrity also lures a public with the promise of the inexplicable, ineffable side of living. Celebrities become immortal through displaying publicly that they are worthy of the event of mortality itself, of life itself. They live in public the surprise of life that the rest of us confront on the quiet.

Natalie Imbruglia's Haircut

When former *Neighbours* soapie star Natalie Imbruglia had a hit with her record *Left of the Middle*, her face appeared everywhere; on TV and in magazines, framed with a distinctive and fetching shag haircut.[12] As the stylists played around with her image, the face began to appear without the haircut. But the haircut also started appearing without the face. The distinctive Natalie Imbruglia haircut appeared on two magazine covers, but attached to the generic faces of models, rather than to the distinctive face of Natalie Imbruglia.

Celebrities, like humans, have bodies, and like humans they have faces too. Unlike humans, the faces of celebrities can be detached from their bodies, and attached to all kinds of inhuman things. Natalie Imbruglia's face was detached from her body and attached to magazines, CDs, posters stuck up in record stores. One night she became the face of my television. I had the eerie feeling that her head was floating in my television, like a goldfish in its bowl. But then I realised that this is what is at once so strange and so familiar about the postmodern world. All kinds of weird technologies insert themselves into our lives, but they seem so normal and friendly because they have recognisable faces on them. I have very little idea how a CD or a TV works, but the faces that mask their strange workings make them seem like familiar if somewhat demented friends.

This 'faciality' is a strange business.[13] It is a sort of mask for desire, but not just sexual desire. Sure, the face of Natalie Imbruglia or Michael Hutchence might appeal because we want to fuck them. They also appeal because we might want to be them, or be like them, or want them to like us. We might want to fuck the body behind the mask, or we might want this attractive mask for our own body, or we might want this mask to want our body. Or possibly even a bit of everything at once — the desires celebrities embody and that their faces mask are nothing if not polymorphously perverse.

The mask of the celebrity, the face we want, seduces us away from sexual desire. To seduce is to lead astray or turn aside, and celebrity certainly turns desire away from any straightforward satisfaction. This is what celebrities share with models. Their faces divert us, usually towards other images, or to products — or services. A fashion magazine, a sports magazine and a porno magazine might be about very different kinds of interests, addressed to different kinds of people — but on the cover of all three is a woman's face. Her face on the cover might channel the buyer's desires to pictures of her body, inside. But it might equally channel the reader's desire to pictures of men playing football in the case of the sports magazine, or women in frocks, if the genre is fashion.

A model's face is supposed to seduce, but when the inquest into the disappearance of model Revelle Balmain revealed a darker side of desire, it became a widely reported tabloid story. "Ms Balmain, who was 22 when she disappeared, has often been described as a model and, indeed, two weeks after she went missing, a gorgeous portrait of her appeared on the cover of the urban style magazine, *Oyster.*" *Sunday Age* journalist Caroline Overington reports that "Revelle might have done some modelling, but she was a prostitute for two agencies, VIP Hostesses and Select Companions. Statements from her clients, tendered to the court, described her variously as an escort and call girl, and as a 'nasty little gold-digger with a bad coke habit', who was paid to attend sex parties for businessmen at the Ritz Carlton hotel."[14] The story goes on to speculate that Balmain may have been murdered by a client, or perhaps someone she owed money.

The pictures that went with the Revelle Balmain story showed a generic models' face, a mask of make up, interchangeable with a host of others. Trained as a dancer, Balmain had not succeeded in parlaying that face into celebrity, other than as a posthumous celebutante, an image for a moral on the dark side of desire. Her face was the generic face of White Girl, the standard from which every other media face is a deviation. Gabrielle Richens, for instance, deviates from it in being Eurasian.

Far from being excluded from the ever expanding empire of cyberspace, minority faces are increasingly included, but they still appear as deviations from the standard, and the standard is still the face of White Girl. Even the faces of male models appear as deviations from White Girl. In Australian culture in the 90s, White Girl was the abstract image not only of what is desirable, but of desire itself — although she was inevitably shadowed by her ironic double, the Drag Queen.

Where White Girl is the generic appearance of seduction, the Rock God purveys the *sound* of seduction. His is a more active magnet for stray desires than White Girl. He too has his ironic double, the Bad Girl, who produces the aggressive sound of an active desire, but with a female rather than a male body. Bad Girls turned celebrities include Madonna and Courtney Love, who stage themselves as elaborate drag parodies of the Rock God persona. In short, both male and female images and sounds appear in the media as attractors for desire, but the way they work is not quite the same.

It would be wrong to think that those generic, interchangeable faces of White Girl are all there is to the empire of desire. Besides almost silent, almost anonymous

White Girl (it's striking how many models have only first names), and the wailing three chord wonders, the Rock Gods, there are celebrities. The faces of celebrities mask much more particular, much less abstract kinds of seduction. Browsing through my clippings files, I find these Australian faces gracing the covers of popular publications: Ernie Dingo, Donald Horne, Pauline Hanson, Kerri-Anne Kennerly, Kerry Packer, Nicole Kidman, Tim Costello, Cathy Freeman, David Williamson, Ian Roberts, Indira Naidoo, Judith Wright, Georgie Parker, Natalie Imbruglia — and two appearances of the Natalie Imbruglia haircut, framing the faces of anonymous White Girl models.

In this school of odd fish, only Nicole could be said to embody the impossible proportions of White Girl. Nicole was once a model, not surprisingly, but what makes her a celebrity rather than a model is that she not only appears, she speaks, she became a spokesmodel, an actor, a celebrity. The paradox of celebrity is that while it depends like much of the media on the face as the mask of seduction, celebrity faces can connect desire to a wide range of possibilities, both in terms of what kinds of community people are from and what kinds of people one might become. In the world of appearances, White Girl reigns, and every other image is a deviation from her ideal. But in the world of celebrity, difference has, I think, made more progress.

White Girl is a mask that hides that to which it seduces. Take off the mask — turn the cover of the magazine — and what confronts us next is another mask, another image. Her eyes often look back at us. Those eyes are not the window to the soul, they are a shop front window, in which we see our desire reflected in the form of commodities. You cannot buy her — unless you frequent prostitutes — but you can buy the things for which she is the mask.

And you can buy Natalie Imbruglia's haircut. From Imbruglia's head to the head of a model White Girl to the head of anyone who walks into a salon with the picture and asks to have it copied, a sign of what is desirable changes hands, or rather, money changes hands — and the haircut changes heads. Not just a sign of what is desirable, but a sign of desire itself. As a celebrity, Imbruglia embodies a host of signs, the combination of which constitutes Natalie

Imbruglia. But not only can this be the mask for many different pathways of seduction, leading to the purchase of a magazine or a CD, the mask itself can be what seduces, by becoming a sign of the very process of attraction.

I think Imbruglia would rather the public bought her CD than copied her haircut. This is the problem with the way desire works through media images — it goes off on any and every tangent. The mask of the face is an image that appears in sharp relief, a desert bleached by the light of the camera flash, magnet for our desires. But the voice of the celebrity can speak of its own desires. Put a pop CD like Natalie Imbruglia's ARIA award winning *Left of the Middle* on the Walkman, enclose your ears with the headphones; put a sea shell to your ear, listen to the murmur of the waves.

Dave Graney's Mysterious Kink

I put on another CD and listen, listening for clues as to the strange art of seduction that passes between celebrities and publics. For my money the classic Australian text on the pleasure machine of fame, and the seduction of celebrity, is Dave Graney's song 'Rock'n'Roll is Where I Hide'.[15] It narrates the fable of the invisible Rock God. He reveals the story of his "mysterious kink", his strange power over us, his public. It all started back in the day when he really believed he was invisible. The invisible Rock God would materialise every now and then, just for an instant, and launch into song, just to surprise us, just for a laugh.

And then we start to notice. We start talking about this invisible rock singer. The problem is, he finds himself materialising unintentionally. More and more we come to see the invisible rock singer, but we make fun of him, taunting him. He thinks he is invisible, we say to each other, expecting him to overhear us. It's not working any more. He remains visible. He has lost the knack.

But then he starts thinking, maybe it's not such a bad thing, to appear to his public as a singer who thinks he can't be seen, even though he knows in his own mind that he can. It's a special talent. Even better than being known for being invisible is becoming known as a singer who will do anything so long as nobody is watching. We want to watch, because we think that he thinks we can't see him. And we keep watching, because we also think he can't see us as we watch. We think he's blind; we think he's invisible.

We're all looking now, because we think he thinks nobody is looking. Now he can't *not* be seen. He's not looking at us now that he knows we are there, looking. Even if he were visible, we can't see him. We are not watching him, we are waiting to watch him dematerialise, right before our eyes. The invisible rock singer and his invisible public, each mis-recognising the other, each seeing what is not there and not seeing what is there. Each celebrating the presence of the other's absence in the absence of their presence.

Where better to disappear?, Graney concludes. The fabled singer, addicted to an unknown, long lost desire, remembered only as that which appears when the person becomes the celebrity. For when the person disappears into celebrity, what remains is the fable of disappearance. Graney lists some of the fabled attributes left behind by famous singers, from Mel Tormé, who became the Velvet Fog, to Johnny Cash, who became the Man in Black, to Iggy Pop who is remembered as the World's Forgotten Boy. He adds the signature of his own disappearance: Dave Graney, who disappeared and became the Best Dressed Chicken In Town.

Appropriately enough, when he appeared on stage to accept his ARIA award from the music industry for the record on which this fable appears, he was in a crushed pink velvet double breasted suit and a black 70s style afro fright wig. He was a fabulous, almost camp, parody of a Rock God. The joke was on him. Graney knew too much about celebrity to become one. Commercial radio avoided his all too knowing recognition of the double game of misrecognition played out between celebrity and celebrants.

In Graney's fable, it is not the public who are duped by celebrity, it is the celebrity who dupes him or her self with a celebration of a quality that is beyond mortal limits. What the public comes to celebrate is not the qualities of the celebrity, but the quality of the celebrity's belief in his or her qualities. Celebrity is the celebration of what is inhuman in the human. Celebrity is the celebration of the virtuality of humanity. Celebrity starts with the recognition of the self-transformation of the human into something outside itself.

It is a misrecognition, because this self transformation is merely an act of faith, and one doubled by the act of celebrating it. The trick is that there is no trick to this most strange and most commonplace kind of seduction.

Not-Mimi Macpherson

As cyberspace deepens and thickens, spreading over the social world, it brings images of celebrity into any and every corner of our private lives. The vector carries them everywhere: Dave Graney's face on the TV; Natalie Imbruglia's song on the radio. From station to station, via satellite and fibre optic, on any and every frequency — the electronic murmur of the waves.

The vector also works in reverse. As if in revenge for the intrusion in our private worlds, media vectors creep ever more intimately into the lives of celebrities. Lightweight cameras and sensitive microphones offer up to the public the occasional sacrificial image of the private life of the public image. This affects not only entertainment celebrities. As Stephen Loosely, once a powerful backroom figure in the NSW Labor Party once remarked: "The directional microphone is the enemy of machine politics."[16]

Where technology fails, there is still rumour and gossip, which fill in those parts of the fable where the public fable fails. Gossip is the pornography of the soul.

For instance: the story to the effect that Mimi Macpherson, sister of Elle, allegedly appeared buck naked in a tacky home made sex video with an alleged cocaine dealer.[17] The copies that circulated around Sydney were too degraded to tell, and she vigorously denied it. The woman in this tape isn't Mimi Macpherson. But the point is that regardless of the fact that it isn't Mimi Macpherson, celebrity encompasses images of public and private behaviour, relayed by intermediaries, in which elements of fact and fable mix. The denial cannot countermand the will to suspend disbelief.

The tape in question is a strange artefact. Its interest is doubly displaced. Mimi stated that the woman in the tape isn't her. There is no reason to doubt her denial. This Not-Mimi who appears in the video is thus twice removed from celebrity. She is not supermodel celebrity Elle Macpherson. She is not

Elle's celebutante sister Mimi. She is just a Not-Mimi, Non-pherson. All there is to it is that she has eyes remarkably like both Macpherson sisters. It's a shock when she looks straight into the camera and we recognise who it isn't.

Viewing the tape can be a repulsive experience. The woman who is Not-Mimi seems pretty drug-fucked. She lies languidly on the bed while a man sets up the video camera. It's hard not to take an instant dislike to him. He asks Not-Mimi repeatedly what her name is, and she refuses to speak her name. She decides it's a game and that she is supposed to make up a porn star name. Perhaps this is that party game where you take the name of your first pet, and the name of street where you lived as a child, put them together, and it makes your porn star name. (Which would make mine Rastus High). Not-Mimi doesn't want to play.

The zoom lens lunges groggily into Not-Mimi's crotch, which she covers with her hands and the sheet. "Finished now", she chimes. "What's finished?", he asks. "The movie", she says. Only this is not a game and the movie isn't finished. He takes ages getting the camera set up on the tripod, while Not-Mimi masturbates nonchalantly. He takes even longer peeling her out of the sheets and propping himself on top of her, so the camera will witness his cock bobbing up and down as he fucks her. A hairy bum moons the camera for a while, and he's done. He wanders around out of view. "Want another line?" a voice asks from somewhere out of frame. Not-Mimi is left to jerk herself off, slowly but surely. When she comes, he doesn't even notice.

Who gets off on what here? As pornography the tape is dull and amateur. It has value only in its false link to a famous name. The most genuinely intimate and the most spectacu-larly public never quite come together. The desire for the most open celebration of what is most closed never comes to pass. The impossibility of its realisation only fuels this desire.

What does this man who does the taping want? To profit by proximity, one can't help suspecting. But it might just be the desire to record an intimacy, to not let it pass. The trouble is that the recording gets in the way of the pleasure. He fiddles with the camera more than with Not-Mimi. The desire for the document makes the document fail to record the desire.

Why does Not-Mimi consent to the camera? Perhaps she is

too stoned to know what's going on. Perhaps she just likes the attention. The irony is that her desires and his do not really meet. She gets off on the game of *refusing* to perform for the camera. Then she gets herself off with her index finger. Neither has anything much to do with what he wants. Her refusal to perform frustrates his desire to film. Her indifference to him fucking her makes no difference to him. He comes all by himself, masturbating himself in her body. She comes by herself and for herself. She comes for the camera, but not by the camera. It sits idly by, recording its own impotence.

Celebrity is just like bad sex. Dave Graney's song puts the best light on the bad sex of celebrity, making the mismatch of desires between the celebrity and the public into an act of magic. But the Not-Mimi show is truly *bad* bad sex. Graney sings of the ability of the celebrity-effect to invoke something beyond the world of human appearances. Celebrity calls into existence the virtual aspect of our nature, its ability to become something different, something beyond what we expect of our species. Not-Mimi performs the side of this alchemy it is best not to see — for in the Not-Mimi show we see the intercourse of celebrity and public itself. It draws attention to the one thing that breaks the spell: the complete incompatibility of the public's desire with that of the celebrity. The sordid fact that both jerk off on the other, but can never come together.

Authorising Celebrity

"It seems Melbourne just can't get enough of Sam Newman — on or off the television screen. He is, as far as this city's obsessions go, bigger than the weather" says sportswriter Wendy Tuohy.[18] After canvassing several explanations for Newman's public rise and fall, she decides to ask an expert: "For David Marshall, the author of a new book, *Celebrity and Power: Fame in Contemporary Culture*, Newman typifies Australians' love of accessible heroes." And she goes on to quote Marshall: "We love to see them fly, but get a big kick when they fall… That makes them just like us." Hence the desire to believe, contrary to the facts, that Not-Mimi is Mimi — to set her up and see her fall.

Tuohy goes on to quote Marshall at illuminating length:

"Because they have been given this kind of celebrity status, unlike other things related to a merit system, we begin to look for ways to see how they might fall, which pulls them back to our status... There's a bit of a death-wish in Australian icons; we want to see something vainglorious — and that often produces blood. It's a bit like the attraction to motor sports." Marshall's explanations seem plausible enough to me, but what I find more interesting is that a journalist would call up this University of Queensland academic and ask him in the first place. The humanities and social sciences have been a source of authoritative talking heads for journalists seeking all kinds of expert-sounding opinion on all kinds of social and cultural topics, but not usually on the topic of the content of the mass media vector itself.

Another newspaper article quotes Marshall as an authority on the relationship between celebrities and media, which he describes as "a frantic, desperate dance." The journalist, Chris Cobb, then adds, on Marshall's authority: "When celebrities allow media inside their private lives, as they often do, the line between the public and personal is blurred, or disappears altogether".[19] What I find interesting is that the journalist Cobb and the academic Marshall seem to be speaking the same language, and about a topic of interest they both share with Cobb's readership — the workings of celebrity in the media. The difference between media and academia is blurred, but does not disappear altogether. Rather, like the relation between the public and the private lives of celebrities, they form a more intimate relation. Or at least they could. Marshall is an interesting instance of what the humanities usually resists — proximity to the media.

"Diana recognised that celebrity power was much more potent than the former symbolic power of the monarchy," Cobb quotes Marshall as saying, apropos the late Princess of Wales. "Celebrity power is liquid, changing and connected closely to the power of the people. Royalty relies on symbolic power and distance to maintain their renown." There was a time when the same could be said about journalism and the humanities academy. The former sought organic connections to popular culture, the latter distanced itself from it and insisted on its superiority. What is striking about Marshall's book is that it bridges this gap, bringing conceptual judgement about celebrity back in contact with journalism, which perpetuates celebrity.

It wasn't always the case that educated opinion sought to distance itself from the pleasure machine of celebrity. In 1750, Samuel Johnson thought that celebrity had its uses. "Fame may be used to smooth the paths of life, to terrify opposition, and fortify tranquillity." His conclusion was that "upon an attentive and impartial review of the argument, it will appear that the love of fame is to be regulated, rather than extinguished; and that men should be taught not to be wholly careless about their memory, but to endeavour that they may be remembered chiefly for their virtues."[20] Which is as good a rationale as any for teaching cultural studies.

William Hazlitt, no fan of Johnson, was rather more critical of popularity: "The multitude will agree with us, if we agree with them", he wrote in 1817. His pessimistic view was that "man is a toad-eating animal. The admiration of power in others is as common to man as the love of it in himself: the one makes him a tyrant, the other a slave."[21] Nevertheless, Hazlitt was an active participant in the public discussion of celebrity, seeking to judge and compare contemporary celebrity by the yardstick of the classical Greek heroes. Over time, as literary authority passed from the professional writers such as Johnson and Hazlitt to the academy, less of their active and critical participation in the world of celebrity survived. What matters about David Marshall is that he is one of those within the humanities academy almost brave enough to work for a return to such an engagement.

Central to the broadcast era was the relationship between the celebrity and the demographic. Celebrity was a kind of hyper-individual, someone who appeared unique, but who paradoxically had to appear unique to very many different people for many reasons. The demographic, on the other hand, was the way the instrumental knowledge attached to the culture industries understood the people who read and listen to the media. In his book *Celebrity and Power*, Marshall calls this development of celebrity and demographic a double rationalisation.[22] The demographic is rationalisation from above, part of the way the people who run the culture industries try to get a handle on their customers as an object of knowledge. But counter to this trend is rationalisation from below — the process by which people feel their way through what is happening in the world in terms of the plea-sure machine of celebrities appearing in the media. Marshall, who was like Tofts and McQuire, born into a world where television already existed, wants to open up ways of thinking about, and thinking through, the 'mass' in mass media. He wants to open the relationship of the audience to the celebrity and explore its complexities.

The very word celebrity has a curious history. Its roots refer us to both what is solemn and what is notorious. The word encompasses in its own history the ambiguity of celebrity itself. It covers the solemnity of Michael Hutchence's funeral at St Andrews in Sydney; but it also covers the notoriety of Revelle Balmain's alleged prostitution at the Ritz Carlton Hotel. The practices of the pleasure machine, Marshall reminds us, have a history, and quite a long one. When people complain that in the 90s politicians have to acquire the television skills of celebrities, they forget that politicians have always had to have the ability to appear effectively in the media of the day. Ronald Reagan might have been a master of the intimate television chat, but George Washington was no slouch when it came to parading down main street on a horse.[23] Both are skills in managing appearances. What changes is that the public space has became a part of broad-cast space, which is now becoming part of cyberspace.

Marshall's main theme is celebrity and power, and he pro-vides an illuminating history of the way generations of talking heads have spoken about the nature of popular culture and politics to the powerful. In the late 19th century, theorists of the crowd, particularly Gustav Le Bon, identified the crowd with the feminine and the irrational.[24] The crowd operates, he argued, by sentiment and instinct. The charismatic leader could maintain power by appealing to the crowd for legiti-macy, by appearing as the symbol of unity and aspiration — all the while steering the crowd towards the leader's own ends. At a time of optimism and rational progress, Le Bon introduced a pessimistic note, seeing in the crowd an uncon-scious force that had to be harnessed and controlled.

Marshall argues that the 19th century anxiety about the behaviour of the crowd contributed to the 20th century anxiety about the culture of mass society. Where the former feared the activity of the crowd, the latter decried the passivity of the masses. Where the former identified the bad influence as the populist leader, the latter attributed passivity to the effect of the mass media. Notable anti-media talking heads in the English speaking world included the poet and critic T. S. Eliot and literary critic F. R. Leavis.[25] The German philosopher-critics Theodore Adorno and Max Horkheimer contributed a more rigorous conceptual framework for critiquing the culture industries.[26] In both cases, the legitimacy of a critical and literate culture came to rest on its ability to assert its distance from popular taste. An inevitable consequence was a growing ignorance among those trained in literary culture as to how the culture of everyday life actually works.

In the 90s, it was often those who appeared in pop culture as its token bit of snob value, the literary journalists, who seemed most proud of their ignorance of the very medium that provided their livelihood. Put Andrew Reimer and Peter Craven, who reviewed books for *Sydney Morning Herald* and the *Age* respectively, together in a room and you might get some erudite chat about T. S. Eliot, but not much enlightenment about the media from which they made their livelihood. David Marshall points out the debilitating effects this disdain for the content of mass media had on thinking; Darren Tofts points out that it held back an appreciation of the form of the media vector as well. Media studies scholars such as Tofts and McQuire had to distance themselves from literary criticism in order to conceptualise media vectors. Cultural studies scholars such as Marshall had to distance themselves from it in order to think about how a mass media saturated culture actually works.

Marshall points out that alongside the modernist distaste for mass media's effects on culture arose a more empirical approach. With the backing of political and business interests, social psychologists started researching the actual processes by which media and culture work. Harold Lasswell started what is now a whole industry on the effects of mass media with his studies on the effectiveness of propaganda.[27] Paul Lazarsfeld was more sceptical about the direct effects of mass media, and thought the impact of its messages were mediated by what he called "opinion leaders" in the community.[28] Elaborate studies of the "uses and gratifications" the public gets from the media have proliferated ever since.

The taste for scientific-sounding results among such researchers made them assume that they were studying some immutable and innate human need that the media satisfied. They paid very little attention to the historically variable side of culture. All the same, the ideal of communication as a 'hypodermic' injection of a message into a public body that Lasswell initiated is still popular with those who would prefer an instrumental view of how media work, including many journalists. It also appears in negative as a paranoid vision of media power, in which media magnates inject their venomous and self-serving messages into a hapless public. This kind of fear has legitimised an enormous body of largely useless research that tries to identify the hypodermic action of the media, particularly on children.[29] Social psychology has a lot to answer for in propagating the view that communication is a sort of natural or chemical process. It has consumed vast amounts of public money that could be better spent actually educating people, particularly children, in how to read the media critically and creatively.

A more sensible approach emerged in the 60s. As the inadequacies of the literary disdain for the mass media became more and more apparent, humanities scholars went looking for conceptual tools for thinking about how culture and media work that are a bit more sensitive to particular historical circumstances than the social psychology tradition. Cultural studies grew in part out of the loss of legitimacy of literary culture, which seemed increasingly irrelevant and marginalised, but also out of the loss of legitimacy of the social science approach, which seemed subservient to the business and government interests that funded it. Cultural studies contained a radical impulse to critique mass media, but with a better knowledge of how it worked than literary criticism had to offer. But it also contained a democratic impulse to get to know how culture worked for different kinds of people in their everyday life.

Marshall is closer to this second view. He does not necessarily endorse any and every aspect of mass media culture. Rather, Marshall wants to understand how media and culture interact through the celebrity pleasure machine. This is what makes it potentially a genuinely democratic approach to the nexus between culture and politics. It is also what makes Marshall a genuinely credible talking head, a celebutante of celebrity itself.

Implied in the idea of mass culture is the idea that the images that circulate in the mass media are pretty much alike, and that the way they effect people is pretty much the same too. Cultural studies pioneers such as Stuart Hall preferred to speak of popular culture, a name that implies that the stuff is popular because people actually engage with it.[30] That people might negotiate or resist the images and stories of popular culture was one of the enduring contributions of the early cultural studies thinkers. The people produce culture, but not with media of their own making.

Marshall writes that "celebrity is a way in which meaning can be housed and categorised into something that provides a source and origin for meaning." Whatever thoughts, feelings, intuitions people may have, particularly about what may constitute the fair go, can be arranged under appropriate celebrity 'headings', each labelled with a celebrity face. "In politics, a leader must somehow embody the sentiments of the party, the people, and the state. In the realm of entertainment, a celebrity must somehow embody the sentiments of an audience." I would go further and suggest that both politicians and entertainers embody at least an element of something beyond, a certain hint of virtuality.

Both politicians and entertainers are "headings" under which people can identify components of what Marshall calls the "popular will". It's important to bear in mind that the popular will is not one thing, it is characterised by the differences in that to which people aspire. The differences in what people desire find a fluctuating equivalent in the differences between celebrities. When the pleasure machine fails to offer adequate scope for differences in the popular will, new celebrities appear to express it. The rise of Pauline Hanson is a striking instance.

One of the things that connects the cultural to the political is celebrity. Marshall contends that "the leader, although institutionally an element of the political sphere, must work to embody what is perceived as universal interest or common experience, which is defined primarily in the real of cultural life." I don't think it's quite the case that political leaders can only achieve political majority by embodying majority cultural taste. Rather, I think political leaders have to embody majority taste of a very particular kind. They must embody taste in leadership itself. When Paul Keating ran for re-election in 1996 under the slogan of **LEADERSHIP**, the problem was that he was too urbane an image of a leader. His razor sharp suits, enthusiasms for antiques, architecture, and classical music, combined oddly with his westie indulgence in verbal aggro. This was not an image of leadership that conformed to the suburban norm.

Marshall thinks that the rise of celebrity represents a collapsing of politics and culture together into a realm of consumption, but I don't think this is quite right. Celebrities occupy the subsidised, public broadcasting channels as easily as the private commercial ones. It is the distinction between public and private, rather than that between politics and the market, that is changing. The classic suburban house, ideal image of the private world, has not only walls and a security mesh door but a boundary fence around the perimeter of the property. What crosses these boundaries with impunity are the vectors of telesthesia — the telephone and television, not to mention the vectors of the internet.

Television, in particular, connects the private world into the public world in the most intimate manner. In the days of Prime Ministers like John Curtin and Ben Chifley, radio was starting to reach into this private world, but people who wanted to see them would have to put on their hat and coat and go to a public hall, or at least to a newsreel cinema. In the 60s, the distinction between public and private spaces in the world had almost entirely given way to the distinction between public and private time — on television. The evening news and current affairs shows counted as public time, while entertainment programming counted as private time.

In the 90s, the lament for the decline of the public role of news and current affairs pointed out, quite rightly, that private images were intruding into it — not least stories about the private lives of entertainment celebrities. But what this lament failed to notice is that public issues increasingly occurred in the private time of entertainment television. It's hard to think of a current affairs issue, from race and immigration to media censorship to the corruption of public office that has not featured in an episode of *The Simpsons*.

While Marshall's book still carries some baggage from the negative and critical approach to media studies, what is refreshing is his attempt to produce concepts that might account for the complexity of the celebrity pleasure machine. He does not slag off the fans of celebrity images as so many cultural dopes, duped by capitalism, or patronise their taste for 'kitsch'. Nor does he try to produce a pseudo-scientific calculus. He provides a useful history of the way business, government and cultural power has conceptualised its 'other': the crowd, the mob, the mass, and the leaders and celebrities who link one to the other.

Catharine Lumby's Appearances

Here are some more strange clues as to how the media-made public sphere might actually work these days: A woman appears on ABC Radio National's *Late Night Live* with Phillip Adams, voicing her ideas, but she also decorates Mikey Robins' panel on the ABC TV comedy game show *Good News Week*. The *Australian* critiques her at great length, then she pops up in black bra and panties in the music magazine *Juice*. Exquisitely photographed in *Vogue*, she wisecracks her way through the Foxtel comedy panel show *Mouthing Off*. She garners an endorsement from distinguished feminist philosopher Moira Gatens, and features as a talking head on the commercial TV show *Sex/Life*. Who is she? Macquarie University lecturer and *Sydney Morning Herald* columnist Catharine Lumby, promoting her book *Bad Girls: The Media, Sex and Feminism*.[31] Is she fighting the good fight, bringing feminism's thinking about the media kicking and screaming into the 1990s? Or is she selling feminism out to the bad guys who run the media?

These are strange things for a feminist, a journalist or a media studies scholar to do, and Lumby is all of these things. Inspired by the example of Meaghan Morris, Lumby explores the possibilities of appearing as a relay between points within various discourses and what they take to be 'outside' their domain.[32] Her thesis was that the contours of

contemporary feminism are both cause and effect of a transformation of the virtual republic. She not only produces a
theory of the postmodern breakdown between zones of discourse, she performs it.

Lumby argues that feminism challenges all of those ways of
speaking, from journalism to scholarship. Feminism alters
the parameters of what the public recognise as a public
thing, and also the parameters of who is recognised as entitled to address the public. Lumby's philosophy of the media
fits with her evolving practice within it. Both the theory and
its practice reflect a certain contemporary experience of the
way the media create points and moments within which one
can create a certain kind of effect for a certain kind public.

From the 60s to the 90s, more and more women entered
the work force, acquired their own incomes, and started to
spend them. The market and the media adapted to this
rising field of wants and needs. This is where Lumby directs
public attention — to popular media that burbling talking
heads often ignore and despise. If you want to talk about
what women ought to be, one has to know something about
what women actually read and watch and buy. A political
feminism that thinks in terms of solidarity and opposition
doesn't necessarily have a handle on these cultural forms
through which women forge identities and act as
autonomous subjects.

Lumby connects the emergence of women in the work
force to a change in the structure of the virtual republic. The
old alignment of women with the private sphere and men
with the public sphere broke down. Likewise the division
between daytime and prime time television that was built on
this social segregation. What was once considered 'women's
business' — the chatty, gossipy, touchy-feely, celebrity-ridden
stuff of daytime talk shows — had by the 90s worked its way
into the serious men's business of evening current affairs.

This 'tabloid' trend was widely derided, but as Lumby
points out, the prejudice against tabloid style news and
current affairs repeated term for term some old prejudices
Marshall identifies about the irrational and feminine nature
of the popular. Take, for instance, the way the body appears
in daytime talk shows as opposed to prime time current
affairs. The paternalistic style of the latter treats the body as

a statistical norm to be presided over by experts. An example might be an edition of ABC TV's *Lateline* in which four middle aged white men in suits talk about heroin addiction and treatment, while the only addict who appears is in the filmed introduction — and the program announces that she is already dead.

The daytime talk show style is quite different, and focuses not on expert opinion but on everyday experience. It deals with the body not as a statistical norm but as grouped examples of excess and personal struggle. For instance, whole shows might be devoted to the experience of anorexia, or to the sexuality of the 'big woman', or interracial dating, or breast implants. In daytime TV, the body is made to testify for itself, and the expert opinion is marginal.

Lumby argues that daytime television was originally designed to appeal to women at home, but as more women entered the work force, elements of these media rhetorics found their way into other media formats, thus producing the panic about the corruption of 'serious' media by tabloid 'trivia'. Lumby asks just exactly who is speaking in these denunciations of issues to do with women's health, safety and self-esteem as 'trivial'.

Lumby's book *Bad Girls* concentrates on interesting and positive examples of print and electronic tabloid culture, but I don't think Lumby would want to defend all of it. Part of the problem with the reception of this book had to do with the fact that it reached out to a suburban readership in a cosmopolitan manner.[33] Lumby found positive values and changes in the low and the pop, and confronted complex class and gender prejudices. In the 90s, refined suburban taste still justified itself in terms of a notional mass of undifferentiated pop trash beneath it. The whole idea of applying an aesthetics of distinction to pop challenged the divide upon which a suburban taste grounded its identity.

Lumby's conceptual challenge to suburban taste was not entirely new. It recapitulated the work of, among others, John Hartley in exploring the machinations of the popular.[34] What was new was that Lumby took these arguments out of the restricted circles of the cultural studies academy and rephrases them for circulation back along the vectors of popular media. Lumby crosses the boundaries between media and academia, whereas Marshall is content to position his scholarship in close proximity to the media. Lumby introduced an urbane critique of the assumed and unthought hierarchies that prevail in public life.

That people who consume pop media are not 'cultural dopes' was by the 90s a standard idea in cultural studies. Lumby's adversary was an image of a feminism that hates the media and celebrity and calls for more censorship. For instance: the supposedly left wing Labor Senator Margaret Reynolds, who worked hand in glove with the reactionary and anti-feminist Senator from Tasmania, Brian Harradine on the Senate Inquiry into Community Standards. What they had in common was that they would rather work away quietly at administrative control of culture than work within culture against administrative control of women's lives. Feminism can be about producing speaking positions for women, or it can be about suppressing speech. If politics, unlike culture, is ultimately a matter of choosing sides, Lumby sides with the libertarian party, which gives culture the most free reign.

This libertarianism is of a democratic variety. It puts a lot of trust in the ability of ordinary women to make of images what they will. Media studies scholars like Ien Ang discovered the diversity of the way people use the media through the qualitative study of media audiences.[35] John Hartley subjected popular media texts to scrutiny, and found that far from being an endless stream of covert ideology, media texts are actually designed to be open to quite diverse readings. I've argued that you also have to look at the increasing diversity of vectors along which texts shuttle between media producers and audiences.[36] But while close contact with media audiences, texts and vectors led to more subtle and supple concepts of the receiver end of the communication process, media studies in the 90s was still prone to somewhat paranoid views of how the media gets produced.

Lumby describes the media as a virus. She claims that feminists failed to grasp its elusive qualities. The meaning of an image doesn't reside in it, but in the way it circulates. She criticises influential models of the media process that try to locate within it an essential structure. She cites art critic John Berger and film theorist Laura Mulvey, who both posited an active male spectator for the passive female spectacle of White Girl.[37] Lumby does not pursue these theories into every last baroque twist that academic screen theory took since the 1970s. She charges these theories with being wrong at the root. They fail to address the complexities of the way images circulate and mutate as they meet an endless variety of different kinds of reader.

"Why teach women to read images in a way that makes them feel bad about themselves?" A good question. Rather than a feminism which negates what it sees with a critical reading, Lumby is interested in what I would call a 'virtual' practice of media feminism. "We're all media producers", she says. Not equally so, of course. And yet, why not start with whatever space of free interpretation is open for the creation of a free subjectivity? By becoming a self-produced media actor, Lumby embodies this idea in a 'controversial' form. For her, feminism is a way of 'controverting' the established practices of a paternal order. A virtual feminism moves beyond the bounds of critique and opposition, towards being a generator of new ways of becoming a feminist, always differentiating itself from itself.[38]

Feminist philosopher Moira Gatens reminds us of Hegel's remark that women are the "everlasting irony" of the public sphere.[39] What he meant was that women are immersed in private affairs, family ties and local concerns. They never achieve the abstract and universal quality of being public actors — and being men. For Lumby, this rational public sphere is neither possible nor desirable for women. It excludes women, or it forces them to exclude part of themselves in order to belong to it. But what's happened is that as women gain some access to autonomy, they pass beyond gaining entry to public life on the existing terms to gaining the leverage to change the terms of 'publicness' itself.

Women bring with them into this emergent virtual republic residues of another culture, one tied to the particulars of private life, to the body, sex and reproduction. Women also bring with them elements of an aesthetic learned from long years of performing as an object for others, elements of irony, artifice, masquerade — and celebrity. In Lumby's world, feminism is not about opposing nature to men's culture, but playing with an aesthetic subjectivity that can escape from masculine objectivity. It's not some special essence of 'woman' that women bring to public life, but particular capacities to speak about what arises from their everyday lives.

Lumby notes in passing that if you look at the popular men's magazines of the 90s like *Ralph*, it is masculinity that appears to be having trouble adapting to the current cultural climate, not femininity. Men are in trouble in the 'tabloidised' postmodern media — unable to articulate sense to sensibility. Another part of the 'man problem' may be the self-consciousness that arises from the existence of women independent and confident enough to objectify men and pursue their own ways of being sexual subjects. In the 90s, sometimes the boot was ever so lightly on the other foot, particularly in popular culture marketed to women. Which is not to suggest everyone became equal in the 90s, but that the old patterns of inequity became quite seriously destabilised, particularly at the level of appearances — in images and stories in the media.

Perhaps it is as much a journalist's instinct as a libertarian's, but Lumby resists the idea of a feminist politics in which 'bad' images of women will be constrained by administrative means and replaced by 'good' ones. Partly, she resists the claim to authority implied in the assumption that there are enlightened feminists who can decide on which images of women ought to be suppressed. Partly, she resists the idea that images have one intrinsic meaning independent of the context in which they are read. Partly, she thinks the media have evolved way beyond the image of it formed in feminist media criticism of the 60s, as recycled by 90's authors like Naomi Woolf.[40]

More fundamentally, Lumby opposes the idea that feminism can reject an image on the grounds that it is a false representation of 'Woman'. That would presume a feminism in possession of the truth of 'Woman'. Whenever 'positive' images of this essence are actually produced, they turn out to be based on preconceived norms about what 'Woman' ought to be and how they ought to be represented. The dream of a place outside communication where a pure self resides is a fantasy. Feminist talking heads have no more access to the truth of 'Woman' than Marxists had to the truth of the

'Working Class' — or for that matter, priests to the 'Soul of Man'. 'Woman' is as much a matter of images and stories as White Girl, and indeed sometime she seems to be White Girl with *attitude*.

Even the most tawdry image, of Revelle Balmain or Not-Mimi, for instance, is a public thing about which publics can argue — and can be encouraged to argue. Lumby's kind of feminism works through images, whether of White Girl or of Kylie Minogue, rather than attempting to reject images in the name of a higher moral order. Even more than some of the other members of that first generation in Australia born into a world in which television already existed, Lumby came to an understanding of how the vector shapes experience by experiencing it herself. Compared to the modest excursions into celebutante status of a David Marshall or a McKenzie Wark, Lumby grasped the production of celebrity from the inside. As a former model, she was not blind to the structural inequality of the media, in which White Girl stands as the gold standard of desire, from which every other image deviates. What she affirms is that cultural politics has to work within culture, both in trying to produce new images, and in encouraging a public to read for itself, critically and creatively.

A consequence of this line of thought is that there can be no feminism without a margin of liberty within the media for it to differentiate itself from itself. Administrative feminism can become an anti-feminism, for it shuts down some of the space in which women can produce images that differ. There can be no feminism entirely outside of the media. There can be no concept of feminism as a productive movement without a concept of the media as the matrix of vectors out of which it composes relations between women.

From the 60s to the 90s, advertising and popular media responded to complex demands inflected by the rise of feminism, and learned to live with it. But in the late 90s, the state started flexing its old repressive muscles again. The Christian right learned to appropriate feminist images and ideas. Senator Harradine's most often stated objection to pornography was that it "degrades women" — just as he thought access to work and safe contraception "degrades women". Old fashioned paternalism has learned how to speak in the language of a new 'maternalism'. But for Lumby, both these views are based on "coercive ideas of what it means to be normal." Both ought to be rejected accordingly.

Just as she wants to move away from a feminism that defines itself negatively, against patriarchal power, so too she wanted to move away from a politics that defines itself negatively, as resistance to the market. In *Bad Girls*, Lumby does not spell it out, but I think the underlying concept of the fair go is of a plural world of different kinds of institution — state and market, culture and media — and of a feminism that could produce different tactics in each.

Which perhaps accounts for why Lumby produces herself differently in different media contexts. She makes of herself a proliferating series of anecdotes, quips, cracks, images — and ideas. As always with celebrity, this school of virtual Lumbys succeeds just as much when people react against them as when people embrace them. The irony is that even hostile reactions are still part of Lumby's project: to create differences — productive, interesting, unexpected differences — within feminism, via the media, and within the media, via feminism. The scale on which she achieves this celebrity is of course quite small. All the same, its a unique experiment for media studies in the aesthetic laboratory that is the postmodern, media saturated public sphere. She refines the Bad Girl into a concept, and becomes a Bad Girl intellectual, an ironic rethinking of the mostly masculine practice of appearing as a 'serious' talking head.

If talking heads spent a bit less time denigrating celebrity and a bit more time thinking about it, there might be a more informed discussion of what constitutes popular sensibility about what constitutes the fair go. It might then be possible to conceptualise celebrity, rather than merely dismiss it. If talking heads could admit that they are celebrities, or at least celebutantes, they might circulate with more ease across a broader range of media vectors, informing more parts of the public search for what matters. That way the process of conceptualising the experiences that arise in everyday life might be more widely spread. As I've tried to show, everyday experiences of media, from dead Rock Gods and White Girls to quite lively pop songs and porn videos, all provide instances of public things from which concepts can be drawn.

Writers such as David Marshall and Catharine Lumby, who

are not afraid to approach, or even cross, the boundary that separates serious and 'masculine' parts of the media from what were once trivial and 'feminine' parts, end up becoming interesting examples of the intellectual as celebutante. They break out of suburban preoccupations with keeping things, unthinkingly, in their 'rightful' place, and pose challenging questions about the changing boundaries within the virtual republic between high and low, serious and not serious, politics and culture.

chapter **3**

The ass and the angel

*We pursue contact with wealth, talent, beauty, privilege
and influence as though they were viruses from which
we might seek contagion and self improvement.*

Helen Razer

Ned Kelly, Man and Myth

There aren't many Australian celebrities who have achieved
immortality. Ned Kelly is the only one I know who has firmly
made the transition. Of the Kelly gang's last shoot-out, the
showdown at Glenrowan, Colin Cave writes that it was a "the-
atrical masterpiece of which Tyrone Guthrie, Peter Brook or
even Cecil B. De Mille himself might well be envious. It
opens like a John Ford Western, with the bold ride into town,
the Gang brash and unafraid." Cave argues that this is no
accident — at least five photographers were present, "not to
mention the gentlemen of the press. The imagination warms
to the men who set it up."[1]

In his fabulous evocation of the Kelly gang, novelist Robert
Drewe has Kelly himself muse on this process of becoming a
celebrity: "In their overheated way it was the papers that
defined us, presented us as sure things, as blocks of type. And
when they declare you to be so-and-so, then you become it.
Strange the way they make you famous or notorious before
you are — and then you are in spades."[2] In Kelly's case,
forever. The "gentlemen of the press" may have created his

celebrity by producing a version of him in story and image, but his immortality requires the ongoing agency of another pleasure machine, one devoted not to producing, but reproducing traces of his image: in Sidney Nolan's paintings of 1947, Tony Richardson's film *Ned Kelly* of 1970, Robert Drewe's book of 1991. As I write this, another great novelist, Peter Carey, is reportedly working on his version. These well known artists present Kelly as very different things, and in each case he becomes it. This is the irony of modern immortality: each generation requires fresh images of what is immortal, which might then, retroactively, become the accepted image of all time.

There are plenty of celebrities in Australian cultural history with the potential to become immortal, but who's images are fading, or have not yet crystallised. Nellie Melba is in danger of slipping back into the past rather than being continually present among us. Her star seemed to decline after Lewis Milestone's undistinguished biopic *Melba* of 1953. The problem is a lack of resources for the reproduction of enduring celebrity. Don Bradman was, in songwriter Paul Kelly's words, "more than just a batsman, he was half the bloody team."[3] 'The Don' is still with us as I write, so it would be unseemly to speculate on his immortality. Mary MacKillop, on the other hand, has achieved sainthood, her own museum, and perhaps a lasting posthumous celebrity in the secular world.[4] But none of these have yet proven as durable as Kelly.

Ned Kelly became a celebrity in the first place because of the existence of vectors of communication and recording. These distributed and conserved images and stories that purported to be about him. But really, this pleasure machine produced him. Or at least, produced the Ned Kelly that people came to know as a celebrity. The telegraph tapped out tales of his movements, popular songs engraved in memory his supposed deeds, popular newspapers reproduced his image. But over the years, the memory trade has not always been there to recharge his celebrity and confirm his immortality within Australia. The Nolan paintings became famous in London. Richardson's film starred the Anglo-Irish Mick Jagger. Drewe's book was published by a local branch plant of a multinational publisher.

I think it matters that a culture both produce new images of celebrity for itself and sustain old ones to the point of immortality. It is through celebrity that we come to know both our ordinary qualities and extraordinary potentials. Indeed it is through celebrity that we acquire this habit of saying 'we' that makes it possible to think within the horizon of a culture in the first place. We who think we are Australians know few of the others who also think they are Australians. But most of us know at least some of the celebrities who define a common repertoire of people, a virtual world of possible Australians, past and present.

The Impossible Princess, Kylie Minogue

"All day, every day, I'm possessed by various characters. I have loads of them", says Kylie Minogue, enunciating a necessary though not sufficient quality for professional celebrity. She is Minnie to her friends, the Singing Budgie to those less kind. Celebrities are avatars, through which people experience their feelings and perceptions as belonging to a common world. But it is only through the difference between one feeling and another, one perception and another, that their qualities can become apparent to us. And so, year by year, fresh talking heads and moving bodies appear that make it possible to define such differences. A celebrity may appear to define a feeling, but soon enough another sensation will be defined by the difference between that celebrity and another, and soon enough, another in the series appears, making the first redundant. That's the way the pleasure machine functions.

Professional celebrity requires a constant reinvention. David Bowie and Madonna raised this to a fine art by becoming ever new versions of themselves, inviting a public to coalesce its feelings around differences, not between different celebrities, but between different characters generated by the same celebrity: Ziggy Stardust and the Thin White Duke; Madonna Sex Goddess, Madonna with Child. Kylie has had some success at this game, selling over 13 million albums and 20 million singles. "You have to have a lot of talent to be commercial", she says, and it's true, although it may be less a talent for singing or dancing than a talent for being a celebrity. A one hit wonder is an accident, but a professional celebrity is her own creation.

From what are little girls made? Sugar and spice and all things nice. From what are little celebutantes made? Snips and sales and soap opera tales. "*Grease* inspired me like nothing else", Kylie says. It is easy to imagine preteen Kylie in a suburban bedroom full of posters cut out of magazines, singing along to ABBA and Olivia, holding her hairbrush like a mike. As Dino Scatena says in his elegantly trashy celebrity bio *Kylie*, the Minogues "could have been one of the central families on *Neighbours*. Even their street looked like Ramsey street".[5]

It helps to have a relative in the business — in 1979 auntie Suzette took 12-year-old Kylie and little sister Dannii to their first audition. But it also helps that there is a media industry in which to accumulate a knowledge of how professional celebrity works, some skills in one of the branches of media production such as acting, and a relationship with an audience. What made Kylie possible was the fact that there was an Australian television industry with a strong base in Melbourne through which Kylie's relationship with a public might, in time, emerge.

It was sister Dannii who badly wanted the part at that first audition, but it was Kylie who got the job, a bit part as a Dutch orphan on the popular show *The Sullivans*. As a consolation, Dannii wound up on *Young Talent Time*. More substantial work came Kylie's way in 1984, in the *Henderson Kids*, alongside Nadine Garner and Ben Mendelsohn. Then in 1985, a part in *Fame and Misfortune*. According to Scatena, Kylie and friends would sneak off to watch *Countdown* being taped in a nearby studio.

The Countdown Generation

Countdown, that legendary weekly pop show, defined a whole style of Australian pop celebrity, of which Kylie is perhaps the most striking and successful product: innocently camp, intuitively urbane. Appropriately, she hosted the show's final edition. *Countdown* created a virtual space, across the nation, within which young people could express their own sensations, watched over by no more threatening an authority than everybody's favourite funny uncle Ian 'Molly' Meldrum.[6] What *Countdown* didn't do was create a virtual space within which young people could express their feelings in relation to older people.

Neighbours filled that gap. In 1986, Kylie appeared as Charlene Mitchell. Of the characters in *Neighbours*, Scatena writes that "there was a virtual UN of cross generational, socio-political belief reflected within the handful of households on this magical street". (Although as Germaine Greer once pointed out, no Blacks). Set in Ramsey street, in the mythical suburb of Erinsborough, it was a virtual matrix for the differ-ences with which mainstream white Australian suburbia were comfortable. And it worked: by 1988 the show had two million fans in Australia and another 13 million in the UK.

A lot of thought went into creating this Erinsborough, where millions of people would live, at least for half an hour in the afternoon. *Neighbours* was produced by Melbourne based commercial TV company Grundy's, originally for Channel 7, who dropped it after an initial poor showing, then for Channel 10. Reg Watson created it, drawing on his experience on such popular shows as *Prisoner*, the *Restless Years* and *Crossroads*. Like all of those successful shows, it con-jured up an imaginary world. In *Neighbours'* case, the show proposed an ideal suburban world.

TV SHOCK — TEEN SEX ON TV TONIGHT is great pub-licity for what was little more than a screen kiss, but that is how the Sydney *Daily Mirror* promoted it. It's one of the key things about celebrity: the producers, the audience and the media all have a common interest in its success. Celebrity is an index of media productivity. Celebrity only exists as a cur-rency exchanged, not only between its producers and con-sumers, but by some additional proportion of other intermediaries, and as something passed among people beyond its mere consumption. Celebrity is the human face of the media vector. Celebrity is who everyone is talking about.

For many aspiring actors, becoming a celebrity in a soap opera like *Neighbours* is the worst thing that could happen. It's an embarrassment to an artist who wants to be known only for 'serious' work. Kylie Minogue and her *Neighbours* co-star Jason Donnovan thought otherwise. To them, this *was* serious work. They had a naive and precious urbanity. They are what we might call organic celebrities, in that they grew out of the prevailing matrix of media vectors of their time.

Their idea of becoming a celebrity was defined by the popular media genres through which their own sense of self was formed. They became what they beheld.

Organic celebrity might be contrasted with traditional celebrity, which is the desire to resist the prevailing media vectors that shape one's experience and develop a presence in some older and more established zone that has, over time, acquired more legitimacy. For example, the soap star who would rather be acting in 'legitimate' theatre, or perhaps a part in a film under a famous director. Traditional celebrity respects what I would call 'suburban' conventions of reading forms of renown through high and low categories of taste. Organic celebrity grows directly out of proximity to the production end of media and invents its own categories of taste.

Far from being embarrassed by becoming soap stars, Kylie and Jason grew organically with the experience. Which was just as well, as the Channel 10 pleasure machine developed an aggressive promotional campaign, with radio interviews and personal appearances in shopping malls. These are now standard promotional devices, but at the time this was not the case. What really made it work was the organic quality of Kylie's celebrity, which developed with apparent natural ease from watching Olivia Newton-John on the screen and wanting to be her, to appearing on screen in her own right and experiencing other young girls wanting to be like her. It appeared so natural because for Kylie, television was not a thing apart, it was always a vector that traversed her world and her sense of self. "Okay, so it isn't *Gone With the Wind*," she said, "but it's popular…". There's something quite touching about the 'quality' image she chooses here for the comparison.

Charlene and Scott's wedding was the highest rating episode of a soap on Australian TV. Once Kylie won her Gold Logie award, where could she go from there? Here is where Kylie makes the leap from being a soapie celebutante to a professional celebrity, by developing another part of her pop experience, in quite a different medium. In 1987, Mushroom records released her version of 'Loco-motion'.[7] Once again, it helps to have an industry at hand if one is to become a celebrity. Mushroom were one of the few Australian music businesses of any size, and while they specialised in generic Rock God bands from the pub circuit,

Countdown had created a national space within which pop music for teenagers reigned. While Mushroom boss Michael Gudinski dreamed of taking oz Rock Gods to the world, it was Kylie-pop that would really open doors for him abroad.

I Should Be So Lucky

'Loco-motion' was the biggest selling Australian single of the 80s. So what next? There is a point in the development of celebrity where it outgrows the resources of a place like Melbourne. Or so the theory goes. *Neighbours* would introduce Kylie to the British, and the suburban Australian flavour of it seemed to be part of its appeal.[8] Erinsborough's image of suburbia was warm and sunny. Even the manual workers in Ramsey street lived in mansions. It was like America without Black People. The Australian qualities of *Neighbours* might appeal on television, but Mushroom wanted the guarantee of a London sound for Kylie's music, and so Stock, Aitken and Waterman (SAW) became the producers for her follow up to 'Loco-motion', called 'I Should Be So Lucky'. A hit in Australia and Britain, it also went to number 28 in the American *Billboard* magazine charts.

Kylie's London makeover fashioned her into SAW's 'millionaire next door' look. They produced happy sounding records with young, clean, well groomed and styled singers who appeared to be enjoying themselves and unlike the typical Rock God, did not whine in interviews about tedious drug problems. The irony is that this banality perfected appears to some people as far from innocuous, but as somehow deeply threatening. **I HATE KYLIE** t-shirts appeared on the streets, and legendary British avant garde DJ John Peel interviewed a cardboard cut out of Kylie, claiming that it had more personality. (The joke was on him. The cardboard cutout did have more personality — than Peel.) Craig McGregor saw a class dimension in the adoration of Kylie, summed up in the graffiti **KYLIE VS THE SNOBS**.[9] She had an urbane style that those exiled to the outer suburbs could use against the narrow tastes on the more privileged inner suburban world.

The SAW version of Kylie was an image that appeared to hide nothing, a bright sign with nothing dark inscribed on the reverse. A sign that resists interpretation, as there is nothing on the surface to point to some hidden residue of meaning. This indifference to interpretability was quite an achievement: The 80s-model Kylie was a discrete image with no distinguishing feature other than its own style. This is anathema to traditional ways of distinguishing celebrities on the basis of their qualities, by interpreting their hidden residues.

Both John Peel and the most ardent Kylie fan were defining themselves through the differences between kinds of celebrity, created in turn by particular repertoires of sound and image. For Kylie's teen fans, she produced just the kind of image and sound through which to produce an expression of joy that can be shared via Kylie. People more attracted to expressing themselves via a more traditional kind of celebrity defined themselves via different celebrity figures, but also defined themselves negatively via a distaste for Kylie. John Peel's fans might express themselves through, for example, Nick Cave, but also, as Peel's mock interview suggests, negatively via Kylie. This is a crucial thing about celebrity. You can dislike a particular celebrity, but it's almost impossible to avoid the pleasure machine of celebrity in general.

Kylie's success in Britain came at a price. Everything ended up being produced in London. Not only her songs but her wardrobe and the artwork for her records would all be express airlifted from London. Mushroom achieved a short term goal at the expense of a long term one. It was Kylie alone, not the whole team of people who had a hand in fashioning her image in Melbourne, who established a reputation in London. Not surprisingly, London is where Kylie herself ended up as well.

Perhaps there were dreams of Hollywood. The vehicle was to be the film version of *The Delinquents*, based on a novel by Criena Rohan, published in 1962. Two aspiring film producers owned the rights to this moving tale of teen rebellion, and Village Roadshow, a subsidiary of Hollywood conglomerate Warner Bros, agreed to finance it if Kylie starred. The producers were also thinking of Nicole Kidman for the lead role of Lola, but Warner nixed that idea. Warner also insisted that Lola's love interest Brownie be played by an American, and so the producers dumped Australian actor Ben Mendelsohn in favour of American Charlie Schlatter.

This 'Americanizing' of Australian stories is itself an old story, well rehearsed in Australian film criticism, but as Murdoch University film scholar Tom O'Regan points out, there are some benefits in the occasional big-budget Hollywood production for the local national film industry.[10] What I find so depressing about the film is not that Schlatter is an American, but that Ben Mendelsohn is both a better actor and a more robust celebrity. In any case it made no difference: when released in 1989, *Delinquents* was a box office hit in Britain, successful in Australia and a flop in the US.

Michael Hutchence was to the Sydney rock scene what Kylie was to Melbourne pop, its reigning presence. When they got together in Sydney in 1989, Kylie's style would change irreversibly. To paraphrase Greg Perano, Michael introduced Kylie to nightlife and Kylie introduced Michael to daylight. Hutchence wrote a song for her, 'Suicide Blonde', after Kylie's name for the hair colour she wore in *Delinquents*.

It's part of the fable now that Michael transformed Kylie. Some versions of the fable cast this in terms of an awakening of Kylie's sexual self-awareness; some versions as a matter of awakening her self-awareness as a star. In a way these are probably the same thing. What is sexuality if not an awareness of the possibilities between bodies? What is celebrity if not, in part at least, much the same thing? Or rather, it is in both cases a matter of seduction. Seduction, which, as the French essayist Jean Baudrillard insists, is not as goal directed as sexuality.[11] Seduction has no goal other than to perpetuate itself, to keep open the possibilities between bodies by means of the creation of alluring appearances. When Michael Hutchence died in 1997, a grief stricken Kylie would be photographed among the mourners.

Better the Devil You Know

As the 80s became the 90s, Kylie the pop creation became Kylie the pop creator. She took control — as much as that is possible in a pleasure machine that is forever assembling very large networks of diverse skills and technologies in order to produce and distribute images. At the start of the Australian video release of *Delinquents* there is a special "environmental message" from Kylie. The world she invokes when she appears expands a little. No longer just a happy-happy joy-joy world, but also a world in which bad people club baby seal pups to death. Celebrity has its uses.

'Better the Devil You Know' was a different kind of Kylie pop video, too. The pure sign of Kylie was acquiring some meaning. Shot in Melbourne, it shows a raunchy Kylie out of sync with the SAW formula, and developing her own aesthetic. She spent part of 1990 in America, working with other producers, refining her style. A pop record is always a collaboration, but a celebrity ought to be able to choose her collaborators. The 1991 tour extended the sex-bomb theme, but somehow it didn't quite seem right. As one critic said, "it's difficult to adequately describe the kind of numbness that begins to overcome you as you enter the seventeenth successive number". In the process of becoming something different, Kylie was in danger of losing the fans who wanted more of the same. *Smash Hits* magazine deserted her, but *Melody Maker* described her as a "genius of pop". Which is all very well, but *Melody Maker* sells a lot less copies than *Smash Hits*. Kylie fell foul of suburban anxiety about the mixing of high and low culture.

The metamorphosis Kylie was struggling to complete was perfected by the boutique record label deConstruction, who in 1993 performed a reconstruction on Kylie, transforming her into a "radical dance diva". Until now, Kylie was what one might call a general celebrity. It's true, she appealed mainly to teenage girls, but the mode of address of her appeal was universal. She addressed a potential audience by presenting an image of universal desire, seducing you into a world in which anyone could belong. From 1993 onwards she became instead a particular celebrity, signalling an address to a specific community, and implying a world of desire especially for them. In short, she became a Gay Icon. Her appeal to anyone else would be bound up with the appeal of gayness itself as a halcyon image of the fair go.

Confide In Me

The most sublime realisation of this new specific celebrity was her 1994 hit 'Confide In Me', which went to number two in Britain and number one in Australia.[12] It's a self-consciously camp performance, its seductive qualities built on the tensions between gayness and straightness. For a gay audience, it can be read as classically camp: as something from the straight world that can be read as if it belonged to a gay world.[13] It is actually doubly camp. It is also something from the gay world that can be read as if it were straight. It's not a symmetrical relationship. Kylie's celebrity is historically very straight, which is why she makes such a delicious Gay Icon. In becoming a specific celebrity of the gay world, Kylie hints at the homosexual dimension of all celebrity. After all, in the heyday of her straight celebrity, when Charlene married Scott, it's her image as much as his that was the focal point of desire for girls.

There is always a homosexual component to celebrity. But there is another way to see this: there is a kind of desire beyond sexualised gender. The desire to be led astray by images, to be escorted to another possible world. This is the virtual side of desire. It's what was really going on when Kylie made her famous 1994 appearance at the Sydney Gay and Lesbian Mardi Gras, dressed in a pink tutu, with matching Drag Queens. But were the Drag Queens imitating Kylie, or is Kylie imitating Drag Queens? To whom do the signs of seduction belong? In an urbane world, there are no easy ways to categorise things, to make distinctions of kind or grade. As the vector wends its way into every cranny of the everyday, images mix, combine, juxtapose, forming any and every organic relation with each other. Everyday life becomes potentially more and more urbane. In spite of the garish lights and the shout of colours, celebrity becomes something subtle.

Like all great celebrity performances, Kylie singing 'Confide In Me' is a double act in another sense as well. The listener can imagine a character who asks us to confide in them, as a way of seducing us to them. It's a line one might hear in everyday life. Yet it is not just anyone who is asking us to confide in them. It is Kylie. She is asking, also, for the listener's loyalty to her celebrity. She is asking us to use her as the medium through which to express a desire.

If 'Confide In Me' is a lesson in how to produce celebrity, Kylie's appearance in the movie *Street Fighter* is a lesson in how not to. Filmed on the Gold Coast, this video game action movie was a commercial success in the US, but it was not a success for Kylie. As she said, "it's very frustrating because you don't get to perform unless you're the star". A celebrity can only appear in someone else's tank if they can keep the airlock open to their own world at the same time. The *Delinquents* succeeds because, whatever Charlie Schlatter's limitations, the movie connects to Kylie's discovery of an urbane life out of the restrictions of suburbia. *Street Fighter*, on the other hand, contains nothing recognisable from either the world of Kylie's origins or her destination.

A more successful collaboration was her duet with Nick Cave. On the face of it, nothing could be more unlikely. The alternative rock swamp from which sprang Cave and Kylie's pop sensibility are not only poles apart, they define themselves by their differences from each other. Cave comes from a world where urban aesthetics meets badlands amorality in its purest form. Kylie comes from a suburban world that is careful — most of the time — to avoid both extremes. Which is probably why Cave wanted to do a duet with Kylie. He saw her as pop without cynicism, a true believer. He persuaded her not to disavow her earlier incarnations completely, grasping how her more calculatedly urbane later appearance added qualities to her earlier, more naively urbane pure pop style.

Cave is a strikingly original aesthete when it comes to pop, particularly attuned to unlikely combinations of qualities in performers. He sees the humour in Leonard Cohen and the angst in Karen Carpenter. A duet with Kylie made a certain kind of Cavian sense. 'Where the Wild Roses Grow' was recorded in 1995.[14] Kylie and Cave performed it on the British *Top of the Pops*. In the suburban cultural world they are incompatible opposites, but in an urbane sensibility, they work.

Cave once remarked to Kylie about performing with her that "I've had people try to hit me over the head with iron bars and urinate on me, but nothing has made me as uncomfortable as singing to that pocket of Kylie Minogue purists at the front who were shaking their fingers whenever I touched you or held your hands, defiling your sacredness." And indeed there is something sacred about a certain kind of organic celebrity. The gay photographic artists Pierre et

Gilles saw it too when, in their portrait of Kylie, they mock-canonised her as Mary MacKillop. For those of us living in a secular world, it's not likely that we will ever witness someone touched by God's grace. But in celebrity, we see everyday a pagan and profane alternative.

Nick Cave's Prison of Sound

It's not hard to imagine Nick Cave swaggering around at school, affecting a bit of David Bowie glam. Cave grew up in Wangaratta, not far from Glenrowan, in Ned Kelly country. Not only was Nick Cave a fan of the bushranger in his youth, but Nick's father, who ran adult education programs, organised a celebrated conference on Kelly. The Kelly image may have more to do with the origins of Nick Cave than any specifically musical influence, although young Nick did sing a bit in the choir. Not well, apparently, although he was fond of the bible studies that went with it.

Out of the endless flow of images and stories to which the media vector exposed young Nick, who knows what might stick? Ned Kelly, the Ramones, Carravagio, Merle Haggard, Iggy Pop, Brett Whiteley... Born in 1957, Cave, like a lot of people, was connected from birth to a wide range of media flows. It was a question of making something out of them. What defined Cave as an urbane artist was his skill in mixing things from incompatible categories.

Ditching art school for punk music was a common move in the late 70s. That seemed to be where the energy was. Not that the rock music industry paid much attention. There was pop and their was rock; there was *Countdown* and there was Mushroom records. Cave's band, the Boys Next Door, didn't fit into either. But it did one of the things art has to do — create a new world, show something else to be possible.

Eventually, Mushroom tried to milk the punk market, with a tacky new record label called Suicide. The sampler album that launched it — and sank it — was a bit sad, but at least it led to the first recordings of the Boys Next Door, and of Nick Cave singing fellow band member Roland S. Howard's classic punk torch song 'Shivers'. As the sound engineer Tony Cohen said of working with them, it was "a bit more fun than your average, stock standard, eighteen tom-toms, bloody whatnot". The Boys Next Door were not the kind of people who would be welcome in Ramsey street. They were trouble: private school yobbos who refused to grow up, but whose career would be a matter of shaping this juvenile refusal into a sophisticated refusal. They transformed yob punk into urbane art.

Melbourne hosted at least two punk scenes in the late 70s — one in Carlton that would be the training ground for dance music technician Ollie Olsen; one in St Kilda where Nick Cave would learn how to be a performer. Not just a performer on the stage, however, but the kind of total performer whose art and life become one process. Cave joined his body to a greater body of work of the European avant garde that runs from the romantics to the symbolists to dada and beyond. As Greil Marcus argues, this underground tradition was what the punk years grafted onto the basic blues roots of rock and roll.[15]

In Australia, rock was one of the last refuges of the Ned Kelly larrikin style, but the independent music scene was where it also displayed its vulnerabilities and staged its own collapse. After a few years of havoc and stupidity, it was time to leave town. Cave rechristened the band The Birthday Party, from a scene in Dostoyevsky's *Crime and Punishment* where Katarina Ivanova throws a dinner in honour of her late husband. The scene isn't actually a birthday party, but (to paraphrase Catharine Lumby) what is art if not the practice of getting things wrong, flawlessly?

In 1980, The Birthday Party arrived in London and found it in the deep fug of economic recession and cultural depression. It was not a good time. The live rock scene was declining and being replaced by nightclubs and dance floors. The music scene favoured synthesiser bands with leftist credentials. Anti-Australian sentiment was an acceptable form of racism in the English media. Cave lived in a dismal squat, reading Samuel Beckett. Gigs were few, but the band was not entirely without friends. They acquired some intermediaries: Ivo Watts-Russell ran a record label; Chris Carr was a freelance publicist; Bleddyn Butcher, a photographer — the rudiments of their own pleasure machine for perpetuating their image and story.

Apollo and Dionysus

There was something strikingly fearless about Cave's performances with The Birthday Party in those days. They were closer to what Friedrich Nietzsche would call the art of Dionysus, not the art of Apollo. In the way Nietzsche thinks of the ancient Greek culture, Apollo is the presiding concept in its sculpture. The dreamlike clarity and purity of form, the hard and sharp outline of the singular figure, these are the attributes of Apollonian experience, and of the art made from it. Dionysus is the god lurking in music. The drunken sway and the pounding rhythms, the forgetting of the self and its merging with pulse, these are the qualities of Dionysian experience. Apollonian art can be appreciated with detached and disinterested observation, but Dionysian art can only be experienced by giving oneself over to it.

Where Kylie Minogue appeared as a pure image, a perfectly proportioned miniature; The Birthday Party was an ugly brute, of value for the energy it evoked, not for the beauty of how it appeared. Where Kylie emitted a pure, angelic light of self-awareness; The Birthday Party were the guttural murmur of unknown beasts, wallowing comatose beneath the ripples of a swamp of their own making. Where Kylie becomes a celebrity by separating herself from generic White Girl, so Cave becomes a celebrity by separating himself from the generic Rock God.

What punk discovered was that by stripping away the surface artiness of rock music and taking it back to its roots in rhythm and blues, it becomes a simple and effective medium for exploring some of the neglected Dionysian territories of western aesthetics. Not an art of disinterested contemplation, but not mere entertainment either. Something both more sublime and more ridiculous. Punk took simple musical forms and ground them down until they liquefied, often dissolving into chaos. And they took their audience with them. The punk aesthetic had a Nietzschian impulse to show a public that "their entire existence, with all its beauty and moderation, was based on a veiled substratum of suffering and knowledge, revealed to them once again by the Dionysiac."[16]

The Birthday Party did not take itself too seriously. The crowd pleaser 'Release the Bats' was meant as a self-parodying joke.[17] But it was one that backfired, as it was one of the catalysts for the whole subcultural style of Goth, which aped the mannerisms of the black-clad band. This is perhaps the most cruel aspect of celebrity — being turned into a series of easily replicated clichés. Cave would later write of himself as the "black crow king", diminished by ubiquity in a world where all the crows are sporting black.[18] Urbane taste values its singularity. Cave was out of place in England, where rock music is part of the creation of 'subcultures', little pockets of suburban conformity that were much fetishised by the rock press and by cultural studies academics alike.[19] Cave's whole aesthetic was opposed to the idea of style, of simply mucking about with the Goth signs that would become so popular in the 80s. Rather, his was an art of experiences. His songs were not 'representations' of violence, death, eros and chaos, they were expressions of a kind of inchoate experience at the threshold of subjectivity. They were not meant to be performed for an audience, but *with* one.

Theatre of Cruelty

I only saw the band perform a few times, and often they left me with little but tinnitus and a headache. (But then as novelist Bernard Cohen says, "tinnitus is the spirit of the age."[20]) Sometimes they could catalyse a crowd into releasing itself into a collective experience of the possibilities of life outside of the self. An experience both exhilarating and terrifying. "We will try to centre our show around famous personalities, horrible crimes and superhuman self sacrifices, demonstrating that it can draw out the powers struggling within them, without resorting to the dead imagery of ancient myths." This is what Antonin Artaud proposed in his famous manifesto of the 1930s for a "theatre of cruelty", and it is, I think, an apt description of a good Birthday Party gig.

The Birthday Party's theatre of cruelty was a theatre of drastic action pushed to the limit. One that would break through the veil of words and return to its source — the vital signs of the body itself, that would awaken "the Gods that sleep in the museums", in a language of "those tortured at the stake, signalling through the flames".[21] Or like the "raps taps and gaps" Cave imagines, in his novel *When the Ass Saw the Angel*, with which twins-to-be communicate while still in the womb.[22] Cave searched for the same thing Artaud was looking for — a language "somewhere between gesture and thought".

With the music and lights pounding as fast as the body can stand, a good Birthday Party gig was a sublime instance of what Artaud thought culture ought to be — the double of life itself, raised to its highest intensity. It was theatre returned to its ancient roots. Theatre, Nietzsche claims, began in ancient Greece when a solitary actor stepped out of the murmuring chorus to speak. The intensity of Greek art for him lay in the mutually affirming energies of the rhythm of the chorus and the vision of the solitary performer.

In modern times, these distinct kinds of art, the orgiastic Dionysian revel and the Apollonian purity of form, separate out into different kinds of cultural experience. The grunge of rock divides from the bright sheen of pop. A dream girl like Kylie appears completely removed from the drunken slur of The Birthday Party. (Although sometimes they come crashing back together, as when Pauline Hanson, pure Apollonian image, addressed an admiring audience inside in a hall, while an angry, thrashing, swirling mob oozed anti-Hanson anger, right outside.)

Nick Cave is a paradoxical celebrity, because the art of Dionysus from which he stems is a great dissolver of self, a great liberator of energy from the prison house of identity. Whenever he appears as a celebrity, it is with the sense of immanent possibility that he may plunge into dissolution, and the residual memory that he has taken audiences along on that ride before. His celebrity is a constant reminder of celebrity's complete inverse — the senseless, selfless, mass. When The Birthday Party subsumed themselves in their waves of noise, and when Cave crowd surfed the audience, the actor returned to the chorus, and the chorus merged with the crowd. He was a reminder of the close relation between grace and danger.

"A general experiment in every direction" is how Tony Cohen described the recording of *Junkyard*. Even the title is a kind of debased monument to the poet Arthur Rimbaud's idea of the point of art being "to arrive at the unknown, by the deliberate disordering of all the senses".[23] I'm still quite fond of The Birthday Party's 'Hamlet Pow Pow Pow', in which the ghost of the Prince of Denmark returns as contemporary psychokiller. That Shakespeare's fable should end as it begins, with the return of the ghost to haunt the descendants, always struck me as an original insight. Shakespeare's play ends, even if not happily ever after. The nightmare logic of Cave's Hamlet-machine is the endless, deathless, repetition of the walking ghost, generation after generation, "Pow Pow Pow Pow Pow."

Celebrity Pessimism

The trouble with celebrity is that it catches up with you. An artist who becomes a celebrity can no longer be just an artist, but really has no choice but to be an artist *of* celebrity. Unless of course there is a line along which to escape. The Birthday Party fled Melbourne for London, then London for Berlin, took off for tours of America and other parts where they were not known. But it couldn't last. An art based on a refusal of being turned into a representation of something, a refusal of immersion in the fishbowl, cannot survive its own success unmodified.

"All the great works of art, it seems to me, are the ones that have a total disregard for everything else", Cave explained to the Melbourne writer Richard Guilliatt. Which might be a good way to think about Cave's career since The Birthday Party. The recordings would veer from good to bad, rarely passing though indifferent. But as the late 80s went by, Cave seemed more and more trapped in celebrity. His designated species in the fishbowl was that of pale-gilled, smack-addled misogynist Gothic monster.

But somehow I don't think this ever did him justice. Cave's writing is misanthropic — the men hardly fair better than the women. The world he invokes is an *Old Testament* landscape, but one without the light of redemption, where God has absented himself, where characters move and collide who have not internalised any sense of self-restraint or self-affirmation. This is a world without God, but also a world without the God brought down to earth and internalised that is humanism. There is a glimpse here of the world Artaud and Beckett approached from different angles and with different faculties, a world without the habits of conventional selfhood, a world of both wonder and fear.

This could be an exhilarating ride, as in 'Deanna', or a terrifying descent, as in 'Mercy Seat', where a condemned prisoner *demands* the electric chair.[24] In the philosopher Arthur Schopenhauer's dread utopia, "where everything grows of its own accord and turkeys fly around ready-roasted, where lovers find one another without delay… in such a place some men would die of boredom or hang themselves."[25] Cave would be one of those, had he not the capacity to create his own artificial suffering, and to create an artifice of suffering for those a little less susceptible to the banality of boredom.

The pessimist as celebrity expresses what the rest of a culture conspires to deny. Does anyone really believe that Hamlet's father's ghost is the last ghost in the line? Are we not always condemned to live? The celebrity as psychokiller and the psychokiller as celebrity both express what is elsewhere denied. The attempt to censor both only confirms what Nietzsche said, that we are not strong enough for the truth about this life: "happiness and virtue are no arguments".[26]

Cave's reconciliation with celebrity came with the recording of *The Good Son*, a record which abandoned the last traces of aural abrasion and evoked instead a subtle aura of loss.[27] For once a world of possibility comes into being, not as the music approaches, but as it recedes. It was a wonderfully untimely record, detached from fashion, and detached also from some of the smack-Gothic clichés of Cave's celebrity. The self-parody of himself in the film *Johnny Suede* as the white-clad Rock God named Freak Storm also assisted Cave's recovery of his own celebrity.[28] In that movie, Cave sings a few bars of a wonderful parody of one of his own train-long-suffering songs, before conning money out of a gullible wannabe — Brad Pitt.

And the Ass Saw The Angel

Cave's novel *And the Ass Saw the Angel* takes its name from Numbers 22:23. It is the dumb ass that sees the angel, not its human owner. Cave is one of very few celebrities from the world of music with a body of work that has theological significance. His work with The Birthday Party seems simply to assume a godless world. His later solo work is frequently pre-occupied with god's absence. "He curses his virtue like an unclean thing", Cave sings in 'The Good Son'. Cave is fascinated by characters who repeat the fall, who stage extremities of sin, but who, like the ass, perceive the absence of grace in the world through the violence they do to themselves and to others. Just as the lowly ass speaks of the presence of the angel, so Cave's lowly, bestial men speak of an absence of grace that others less lowly do not perceive. If he cannot have angels, Cave at least warms to more human signs of grace, and it is grace that I think he wants to recognise in Kylie's celebrity. Her image is the closest thing he can approach in a world where monotheism is dead and where Hollywood has replaced Mount Olympus as the home of the pagan deities.

The duet with Kylie Minogue was an inspired idea. A meeting of two Australian expatriates whose roads out of Melbourne to the stars took such divergent paths. That Cave's character kills Kylie's in this murder ballad seems apt too. If Kylie expresses a celebrity of the image, of the perfection of the image of the fair go, then Cave recognises this perfection at the moment his murderous character desecrates it. Cave and Kylie are the ass and the angel, Dionysus and Apollo, contagion and self-improvement. She is the sun pouring out its pure energetic light and he is the swampland that traps it and deploys it to decompose anything and everything into base matter.

The initial rise to celebrity of Cave and Kylie was only possible because the component parts of a pleasure machine for producing it was present in Melbourne in the 1980s. Both reached the limits of what the local productive capacity could support and the limits of what the local audience could absorb. These fish got too big for the tank. Both were obliged to reinvent themselves — and this is one characteristic of the species *homo celebratus* that humans do not possess — the ability to change form at will. Both Cave and Kylie kept discovering new audiences by becoming something other. In this way they avoided — most of the time — becoming parodies of themselves, by refusing to play to an audience's demand that they live up to their past images.

What makes them, despite their differences, such emblematic Australian celebrities of the 80s is that both embody a confidence about taking on the outside world. Cave had initially discouraging expatriate experiences in London, while it was where Kylie found hits and a home. It took Kylie a long time to be taken seriously in England, whereas Cave steadily acquired a high prestige if low volume celebrity. But both embody a confidence about the relationship of Australian culture to an outside, an urbane ability to mix the local with the international. They are to the world of pop celebrity what Paul Keating is to the world of political celebrity: embodiments of the 80s sense of possibility.

In the 80s, it became obvious that the aspirations of a generation, and also its sense of what the Jamaicans call dread, came not from church or community or family, but from the images and stories created by the pleasure machine of celebrity and distributed by the vectors of television and radio, recorded music and video tape. While Hawke and Keating opened the Australian economy to the global economy, Australian culture opened itself to the global cultural world. The fabled life-stories of Kylie Minogue and Nick Cave are expressions of that double process, as they became not only international celebrities, but also international commodities.

In the next chapter, I want to look more closely at another archetypal pop celebrity of the 80s, Peter Garrett. Like Kylie and Cave, he had a career that spanned the 80s and the 90s and, like them, he embodied some of the possibilities of cultural optimism of the Hawke and Keating years. By looking more closely at how Garrett's celebrity was produced, I hope we can get closer to an understanding of the relationship between celebrity and culture, and also — another archetypal 80s theme — the relationship between the market and politics.

chapter **4**

Homage to catatonia

Cultures are not manufactured, they grow of their own accord.

George Orwell

I Don't Want To Be The One

July 1987: It all begins with a slight but suggestive sartorial detail. A little thing, easy to miss amid the wash of Australian Bicentennial pseudo-events and bogus champagne. It was at the press conference to launch the first advisory report of the Constitutional Commission where, to my eyes, one little thing stood out from the usual run of the mill meet the press bun fight. There, wedged in between the bespectacled, grey suited dignitaries, with their tastefully conservative ties perched like floppy kippers between neatly pressed lapels; there sat Mr Peter Garrett in a faded black denim jacket and open necked shirt. As the report being launched told us, Garrett was "Lead singer for Midnight Oil; lawyer".[1] Evidently he was dressed in the style of the former of these two capacities.

Perhaps it was because I felt as out of place at this particular press conference as Garrett's jacket that I noticed. Surrounded by 'real' journalists in their low key work wear (tailored but not pressed), I stood at the back in a leather jacket and a t-shirt emitting stale cigarette smoke from the night before. I was not a journalist, I was a rock and roll writer. So naturally, the only way to get to a morning press conference was to not sleep the night before.

Looking at Garrett, fielding questions at the front of the room, it seemed to me that the "lawyer" appellation was less important under these circumstances than the "lead singer". This was what was most curious about the whole show. How was it that "Lead singer for Midnight Oil" could become the sort of qualification one lists at the front of advisory committee reports? Midnight Oil are a rock'n'roll band, after all. A popular act, admittedly. Yet if that were the main criteria, why wasn't the even more popular Michael Hutchence on the Constitutional Convention? And how was it that the most striking thing about Mr Garrett's *curriculum vitae* was the discreet non-mention of his most remarkable achievement: the fact that in 1984 this lead lawyer-singer came within a hair's breadth of winning a seat in the upper house of the Federal Parliament?

Clearly, something else was going on here. The perennial presence of Peter Garrett in the public eye through the 80s and 90s seemed to me symptomatic of the kinds of relationship that might have become possible between Australian popular culture, political culture and the culture industries as they emerged in those years. In this chapter I use Garrett as the pretext for essaying how these relationships might work.

The urbane critic has to be careful in territory such as this. Take the opening move of this chapter: the critic as the one who has an eye for the telling detail; the suspicious mind seizing on the metonymic part that explains the whole business. Both Garrett's celebrity and the ways I might write about it are caught up in the differences between formations of taste, such as those that define the urbane, suburban and vernacular as distinct cultures. So one has to be careful when writing about culture in general to pay attention to the frissons and frictions between different cultures that animate not only Garrett's appearances but also anything I might say about them.

Oils Ain't Oils

This is a case study of how celebrity built in one domain can be parlayed into another: from popular music to populist politics. Given the size of the music industry, perhaps this is not all that surprising. By the time Midnight Oil released their best selling *Earth, Sun and Moon* album in 1993, the Australian music industry was worth about $2 billion to the economy and employed some 80,000 people. Music exports brought in a net revenue of $90 million or more, and it was no small achievement that Australia became the third largest source of repertoire for the international charts. About 30% of contemporary music recordings sold in Australia were by local artists.[2]

The distinctiveness of the Oils was their ability to make a place in suburban taste for the idea that rock music could be both culturally legitimate and professionally respectable while at the same time drawing a sizeable crowd. As it does with the experience of any and every cultural artefact, suburban culture drew distinctions within popular music. On the one hand, there is *pop* music; on the other, *rock* music. The distinction arrived late in Australian taste, where the relatively small size of the market probably slowed the growth of distinctions within it. By the late 70s, however, it was well entrenched.

Countdown, the ABC's weekly pop music show, dominated popular music for most of its long life, from 1974 to 1987.[3] *Countdown*, had at its disposal a vector of national scope, and it synchronised the once rather parochial pop music markets. It was the defining tempo of pop across suburbia and beyond. But it also provided suburbia with a way to distinguish rock from pop. Rock was, by definition, what was too 'hard' for *Countdown*, which only played what is 'soft' — pop. Needless to say, the distinction within suburban taste between rock and pop is between the tastes of young males and females, but only partly so. It is also partly an age distinction: preteen and early teen pop fans are supposed to grow into late teen and early 20s rock fans.

Ironically, the pop music fan, too young to go to licensed premises to see rock music, may have imbibed a more subtle musical brew via *Countdown* than some suburban rock fans, for *Countdown* had a certain camp subtlety in the way it played with boundaries of gender and desire. *Countdown* had the added advantage of being available everywhere — television's vectors cut across the distinctions between urban and suburban life. The rock music business was more spatially segregated. In the inner city, punk and postpunk music spontaneously created its own subcultural world, rich in critical and creative strategies. But this was a ghettoised world, and in Sydney it was quite sharply divided from the suburban rock scene, where covers bands dominated. Midnight Oil were one of the few bands that grew out of an urban, punk scene to extend their territory out into the suburbs. They were assisted in this by ABC radio station 2JJ, which was at the time an AM band, Sydney-only government broadcaster, which supported the inner city music scene and extended its potential influence.

With the help of 2JJ, Midnight Oil were able to develop a following among both urban and suburban rock fans, combining the stress on independence and originality required by the former with the hard rocking entertainment sought by the latter. What both urban and suburban rock fans shared was the ethic according to which rock taste legitimised itself. In rock music, some relationship, some necessity linked the public to the music. Demand preceded supply, or at least appeared to. Those supplying the music, the musicians, had to work damned hard to prove to their public that they were indeed the genuine article, faithful and true, a suitor who will love, honour and obey.

Once firmly wedded to a rock music act, its public was usually tenaciously faithful to it — often for decades. This courtship occurred through the dense network of vectors which formed the media landscape of the time: clubs, pubs, parties, jukeboxes, record stores, fanzines. Like any other small business, a rock'n'roll band had to start small, investing a little capital, doing solid business, generating good will, word of mouth interest, building up a working stock of material, improving the product. Midnight Oil's drummer Rob Hirst said, "We had the option of going on *Countdown* and reaching three million people or doing 4000 out-of-town gigs and building up a following. We chose the latter."

The band accepted the financial risk themselves and tried to build their own following, bypassing the booking agents and front men and a lot of the petty thievery of the small time music racket. "We had a totally sympathetic bank manager," says Garrett. "If we had to borrow money from the bank, well, okay, that's just the way it was going to be — but we weren't going to let a bunch of thugs shut us down."[4] As educated young men from 'respectable' suburbs, Midnight Oil had access to more knowledge of business and better connections than many bands.

Like all rock bands, Midnight Oil reached the stage where it needed a major injection of liquidity, capital or access to a big distribution network if it was to break out of the small domestic market and get into big, international ones. As Garrett said, "the big business of North America that dominates the rock industry makes it prohibitively expensive for a young band to build a career without the support of a record company that takes on the role of a large bank. A starting price of half a million dollars for albums, videos and associated promotion is a normal figure in today's pop music world."[5] This is when a band 'sells out'.

With luck, a band might negotiate a deal with the big firms in the business without damaging the good will it had with its small family of loyal clients. In other words, a band would use the credibility it garnered as purveyors of rock music as a bargaining chip to play against 'the majors' — Polygram, EMI, Sony, Warner Music, BMG and Festival — so it could turn credibility into a base for financial success and exposure, and get a reasonable piece of the action as well. But it had to do so with a great deal of financial and contractual care. Rob Hirst: "It means recording albums cheaply and getting around having to sign contracts which tie you up and put so much pressure on you that, even if you had a mega-selling album, you still wouldn't recoup…. If you burn the record company for $200,000, then where do you go?"[6]

Midnight Oil kept their overheads low and built a following. The legion of Midnight Oil fans, from teenage tearaways and surfologists, to middle-aged suburban public servants, were a loyal, faithful public. Midnight Oil tried to keep the faith and at least the appearance of independence, even when they signed a distribution deal with CBS, then the most major of the major corporations in the music industry. 'The Oils', as they are affectionately known, worked long and hard to achieve this. (Just as Midnight Oil were bought out by CBS, so too CBS were eventually bought by the Japanese electronics corporation Sony. But that's another story.[7])

The ethics of keeping a discerning suburban rock public on side is at some remove from the way things work in pop music. Most pop music fails in the marketplace. Some pop music sells by the tonne, though not without the assistance of those parts of the pleasure machine that have the job of promoting the product, combing through it for the most bankable unit shifter, stamping it with the approval of the leading style authorities — and flogging it for all it's worth. As Garrett says, "Big record companies are constantly pushing out all this material, throwing it... into the funnels and hoping that sooner or later something is going to pop out the other end. And of course... something inevitably does. I mean, someone like Australian Crawl has popped out."[8]

This is how pop music appears to suburban taste where that taste has decided that rock represents something ethically higher than pop, but which still relies on pop in order to make the distinction. That rock is ethically higher than pop is a prejudice worth setting aside for a moment to consider the difference from another point of view, that of the strategy for creating a public and a market. In order to try and make pop music actually popular, a major record company that is promoting it has to invest heavily in packaging and promotion, and the band is obliged to sit still for this, to allow itself to be marketed, cling-wrapped, fondled and pawed by the magazine and TV people.

This is particularly so when the act lacks credibility. If it hasn't spent years scraping and saving and gigging and accumulating capital and goodwill out there in the minor and marginal vectors of rock culture. If it lacks this kind of base, then the act has little bargaining power with the major recording and publishing companies, and will more or less have to do as it's told, more like hired hands than a subcontractor. A case in point are Men at Work, who sold ten million copies of their first album and reaching number one in the British and American charts in 1982. Somehow they managed to sign themselves away to a ten record deal with CBS (now Sony). "They won't let us go" said manager Russell Deppler, "'til the day we die, we'll still be with CBS."[9] Like Australian Crawl, Men at Work no longer exist.

The distinction between rock and pop lies in the order in which the band tackles the various segments of the industry, who's money they use to do it, and who ends up controlling the process, owning the product and tapping the revenue streams that result. The central point, in terms of Midnight Oil and Peter Garrett's style of celebutante politics, is that the impetus in pop music comes from the company and in rock music from the band. In practice there is no neat distinction between the two, but a continuum. Suburban taste arbitrates, and decides which is which. What is at issue for the parties concerned is the extent to which the band is selling the audience it has acquired to the company and keeping some autonomy into the bargain, or selling themselves to the company in exchange for the company's investing in the purchase of the means to acquire a public.

From the point of view of urbane culture, the distinction between the rock and pop approach matters for somewhat different reasons. In the presentation to a prospective public of the relationship between the company and the act, urbane culture sees a reflection of its own bargainings in the workplace. The band who retains their autonomy *and* strikes the deal is a sign that this is possible for others too. A passing remark of Garrett's in one of his 1987 newspaper columns indicates what's at stake here: "Advertising: the last refuge in a sorry world for creative and ambitious people who don't mind manipulation in the guise of a profession and who profit greatly by the conundrum of our economic system. If we don't keep the big wheel turning and make sure that all that is produced is consumed, then as sure as night follows day, we'll all be ruined." Garrett could be talking here about anyone in any branch of the culture industry, from writing to music to art. He is speaking about the self-awareness, indeed the class awareness, of many urbane media workers who are trying to keep control and ownership of their creative work while negotiating access to distribution and investment.

After money, credibility is the second most precious commodity in circulation in public life. Once you can buy that, the rest is easy. This is why the majors are prepared to deal with acts like Midnight Oil and cede to it a certain amount of business and artistic autonomy. Credibility is inseparably wedded to the mythology of 'paying your dues' and is also a system of peer assessment, competition and support. Midnight Oil, touted in their early days as the hardest working band in the country, earned it — and enjoyed not a little commercial success along the way. Oils ain't oils; there is a complicated politics of credibility and success which traverses the whole of the 'culture industry' and blurs its boundaries.

The Power and the Passion

Within this framework, we can understand the double success of Midnight Oil and Peter Garrett. Midnight Oil are as well, if not better known for their extra-musical activities as their art. This is in no small measure due to the activities of Garrett, who has been 'frontman' in more ways than one, particularly since he achieved national media exposure as the Nuclear Disarmament Party candidate in the 1984 election.

Garrett's distinctive high domed pate and bush hat became familiar icons on television and in the press. The Garrett presence mounted the soapbox for everything from the Uluru/Ayers Rock hand-over ceremonies, to the anti-ID card campaign to 'Surfers Against Nuclear Destruction' (SAND) and a symbolic visit to Pine Gap, loud hailer in hand. Not to mention being hypothesised about on the TV show *Hypotheticals*. For an act which consistently refused to appear on *Countdown* both Garrett and the Oils achieved remarkably wide media exposure.[10] Indeed their refusal of *Countdown* is one of the fables for which they became famous. Perhaps Garrett's baldness has resulted from wearing too many hats.

Garrett succeeded in the 80s as a populist and progressive figure in the public domain precisely because Garrett and Midnight Oil achieved credible success in producing rock music. The Oils' authenticity is not really an issue. They conveyed the *sign* of authenticity according to the conventions of their fans, and that's what counted. There was an organic link between the Oils and their patrons which preceded the machinations of the major powers that be in the industry. Precisely for this reason, Garrett could appear in public, wear many hats, give voice to left-leaning populist causes, vent his spleen in op-eds for the tabloids,[11] stand for office, sit on sub-committees, all without appearing ridiculous to the fans of Oils music. This is the precious stuff of credibility, the magic elixir of rock'n'roll power and passion — and politics.

Rock Against Rock Critics

There is an approach to the analysis of taste that has an element of the urbane in it, that treats all kinds of taste as equally amenable to analysis. Likewise, there are approaches to culture that have an element of the suburban in them, manifested in an inability to avoid making pre-emptive distinctions. This has particularly dogged academic work on rock and pop music, which can't resist arranging these in a hierarchy, in which rock stands a bit above pop, but both are found wanting compared to criticism itself, which sets itself up as the authority that judges between them.

For instance, Marcus Breen has it that regardless of how 'sound' Midnight Oil's songs may be, when they "suffer a transformation and become an extension of the marketing nexus of the dominant cultural and social values, their meaning is changed."[12] Breen insists on the inevitable 'capture' by the corporate world, as if it were monolithic, and not in turn subject to the need to respond to popular desires and interests. In the case of Midnight Oil, what is of interest is precisely the way the band was able to work with the culture industry on terms that their *public* would accept.

Michael Birch rightly stresses the "ongoing relationship between the nature of cultural products and the technology of production and distribution."[13] He also gives an account of the influence of the kind of cultural studies David Marshall mentions on the study of popular culture, and the way that it looks at it as "a field of struggle, a battleground of ideology, a field in which dominated groups win space for themselves." So far so good. He also ticks off "scholarly work" which has "taken a phenomenon through which millions have found expression, and has spilled quantities of academic ink to find a definition of popular culture." This is even better, though one wonders why it's in the past tense. Birch is admitting to the futility of attempting to define pop culture other than nominally and relatively.

Just when things are going so well, Birch succumbs to a tedious nostalgia. He can't resist an invocation of the 'real'

60s, as he experienced it, and expresses a desire to rescue the critic's own times from younger critics who evidently don't understand them. This application of selective memory culminates in dark mutterings to the effect that "the 'political role' of rock music seems to have disappeared" and that for Australians "the implications of recent developments are even worse."

The bottom line with Breen and Birch is pessimism about culture industries, other than education, and cultural practices, other than criticism. In both cases, a rather general kind of 'social rationalist' theory is first deduced, and then applied to the specific case at hand. For example, the theory that successive cultural technologies tend to be more and more alienating, and estrange the performer more and more from her or his own work.

The example Birch gives is video: "the innocent days when a live band were just filmed making their music are gone forever." Innocent days? Notice that the alienating technology of today is compared with... the day before. As if the cultural technologies of the 70s were not alienating to those who first experienced them, relative to the 60s, and so on. The concept does not arise out of Birch's experience of Midnight Oil. It is derived from the literature and merely applied to Midnight Oil, and the critic's own experience escapes any serious attempt to perceive its effects on the process of conceptualising culture.

Birch, on the subject of Garrett and the Oils, claims: "The effect of a 'political' band... will always be negligible. The example of Peter Garrett's failure to enter the Senate, despite an enormous vote, is a perfect example of the treatment of performers in the world of rock music once they attempt to step outside it. Right wing bad actors can do it, but not people with bald heads. The business is now not just commercialised but industrialised." Firstly, Birch collapses politics into culture. Garrett putting the wind up the Sussex st Labor hacks and debating then Labor leader Bill Hayden live on national TV is not considered for what it is — symbolic action, ethical fable — but lamented for what it is not: an instrumental political act. The second and third sentences are the pessimism of insatiable criticism: the glass half empty. It would be just as easy to be overjoyed at how rattled the ALP were by Garrett's showing.

The last sentence takes off on a new tack, and sees the root of the problem in the evil industrial structure. Yet if we take this metaphor seriously, would we not have to argue that teachers and metal workers and soapie actors are all equally in hopeless political situations because they work in 'industries'? Perhaps that's why, like musicians, teachers and metal workers and actors, they sometimes form and join unions. The network economy of power, information and money is still there for all and sundry to struggle in, be they in 'industries' or not. Only when we measure such efforts by some fixed ideal standard do they pale, which is a good reason not to conduct criticism on such a basis, lest we all get miserable and depressed. What politics is, criticism should be — the art of the *possible*.

Rather than criticising a work of art for what it lacks, there is another way of thinking about it. One can try and identify the potential it contains within itself for exceeding the conventions and limitations of the day. Art expresses the potential for things to be otherwise. This is a conception of art I learned from Craig McGregor, and that he learned from the University of Sydney philosopher John Anderson.[14] The virtual lurks in the actual: in even the most mundane and debased kinds of culture, in pop songs and celebrity images, what hides in the light is the possibility of imagining better worlds. Better worlds that are not a hereafter or a happily ever after, but might actually be made out of the resources right here in this world. Criticism is fond of pointing out what this culture lacks, but what criticism itself lacks is a way of identifying the possibilities present within everyday culture. Criticism is too suburban; it lacks an urbane ability to see anything and everything as a possible resource for making the fair go. The point of this digression has been to identify this common flaw in academic writing about popular culture, one that it shares with many other suburban commentaries, and set it aside.

Best of Both Worlds

The credibility The Oils established with their audience provided the springboard for Garrett to establish quite another kind of legitimacy. Garrett expresses the possibility of becoming, not just a rock star, but on the basis of rock, a talking head. One that might grow organically out of the relation the vectors of rock establish between the artist and the audience. This is not quite the same thing as the 'organic intellectual' proposed by the Italian radical cultural theorist Antonio Gramsci. The traditional intellectuals, to whom Gramsci contrasted the organic intellectuals, were principally the clergy.[15] The organic intellectuals were for Gramsci the self-educating and self-organising elements of the labour movement. It is no longer the case that Gramsci's organic intellectuals are leading forces for social change resisted by traditional intellectuals. In any case, Australia at the end of the 20th century is a different place to Italy at the start of it. But Gramsci's way of thinking still works, if at a somewhat more abstract level. It is possible to identify different kinds of cultural legitimacy, with different kinds of bases and tendencies to lean toward or against creative cultural futures.

In an era in which publics form, of necessity, around media vectors, perhaps the organic intellectual can only come into existence as a talking head. A talking head is a celebrity who talks, one who appears on TV in close-up, opening her or his mouth to say something about something other than their own career or image. An organic talking head is one that grows a general ability and legitimacy of speaking about things out of the particular ability and legitimacy to talk about their own work and fame.

Organic talking heads are less likely to have an investment in the current fixed hierarchies of culture, since their credibility is less based in them than that of traditional celebrities. Traditional talking heads, such as those based on academic credibility, or the credibility of the established political parties, have a vested interest in the distinctions on which their credibility rests. But an organic talking head can express the possibility of a new kind of culture, one not based on, and limited to, the fixed orders of taste and prohibitions on cultural mixing and matching so dear to suburban life.

Garrett is an interesting case here, as his initial celebrity was based on the traditional distinction between rock and pop music. Garrett evinces a quite traditional distaste for pop. And yet by building on the base of rock taste, Garrett created the possibility of appearing as an organic talking head, parlaying the traditional authority of rock into an organic credibility in politics. David Rowe puts the up side of Garrett's aspirations in the 80s very nicely: "Rock and overt politics collide only intermittently, at particular moments when broad social movements meet performers with Brechtian aspirations. Garrett hopes to use his over-18 fans as a block vote and to link them to the heterogeneous clutch of organisations which is anti-nuclear. At the same time, he is playing Pied Piper to the nation's current and emergent youthful constituency. Garrett is… a spectral repudiation of Hawke's consensus, a metonym for the excluded and the dissident. It is encouraging to feel that… rock can still provoke dreams of a new synthesis in the slumber of fiscal austerity."[16]

Garrett used his position in a particular set of social relations which are to do with the business of manufacturing music, in order to give voice to his constituency. Garrett saw the constituency with and for whom he spoke as being more or less the same as the audience for whom he made music as part of the collective entity that is Midnight Oil. While Garrett took care to distinguish these roles in public life, the credibility of both were founded upon the same sort of rapport. After listing some of the issues that concerned him upon becoming Chair of the Australian Conservation Foundation, Garrett adds: "I want to communicate these things to young people, who I have had a relationship with over the years with Midnight Oil."[17]

The difficulty with this proposition is that because Garrett's base in music depends on the traditional distinction between rock and pop, his ability to articulate the interests of the whole of youth culture is limited. An environmental message from Kylie Minogue, and one from Peter Garrett, is necessarily addressed to quite different audiences. Just as the Kylie Minogue/Nick Cave duet expressed a combination of distinct cultural categories, so too a Kylie Minogue/Peter Garrett joint statement on the environment might express a combination of distinct cultural categories for a political end.

As independent outsiders with their own base of support, both Garrett and the Oils could deal with the business end and the press without being captive or captivated by either.

This relative autonomy, besides bestowing an aura of credibility, had certain other advantages. It gave Garrett access to the press and made him a relatively recognisable talking head. The Oils spent some ten years building up a name and a reputation, so they didn't totally need either CBS or the media to put them into circulation. Garrett was quite well known without all that, which not only gave him some leverage vis à vis the publicity machinery of the music business, it also gave him a tiny bit of leverage with the non-music media. Editors wanted Garrett because he was already known and hence good copy.

In their heyday, Midnight Oil and their management tried to use this to extract some degree of control over their image and message. They granted interviews selectively, and retained the power of veto over photo sessions. The Office, the management agency that ran Midnight Oil's affairs, applied the lessons learned in the music media to the media in general. There is certainly a lot to be learned from their example about messages that "suffer a transformation" (as Breen puts it) in the media process.

Garrett acquired two of the things political figures aspire to — a public constituency and media access — without a political party. His attempt to be part of one, the Nuclear Disarmament Party, was not in the end a success. Garrett's split with the NDP is a complicated affair.[18] Part of the problem may have been that Garrett's methods of work were so much at variance with those of a political party. Garrett worked out of a traditional relation to rock music culture, and transformed this into an organic relation to politics via the electronic media. He transformed himself from a cultural celebrity into a political talking head. Perhaps his style did not translate very well into the rorting and wrangling of a quite different kind of traditional organisation — the political machine. Celebrity was both the strength and weakness of Garrett's personal, populist style.

Take The Hardest Line

Garrett was ideally placed to act as a populist figure: not totally dependant on the culture industry, not answerable to a political machine either. For a rock populist, the best of both worlds is to work with both but be identified with neither. Garrett uses this double position to advance a vision of a stripe which is uniquely his own. It combines appeals to 'Australianness' with elements from the agendas of the social movements of the 60s. Populist political talking heads, like popular celebrities, embody quite particular expressions of possibility, drawn from quite particular social and cultural experiences.

Born in 1953, Garrett grew up in Menzies era suburban TV-land, where "Bob Dyer glued us to our seats."[19] As he recalls, "We danced in surf clubs and at the local hall, went to the sit-ins, checked out the new films, watched the street theatre and talked politics and drugs." His sense of possibility comes from "the ambitions of the Whitlam era — social and political reform, a more independent foreign policy, encouragement of the arts, provision of basic equitable treatment for groups that were less well-off in society…".

"Gough was tough til he hit the rough."[20] Garrett is one of those who maintained the rage when, as he puts it, "The brave new republic had foundered." Midnight Oil's strident anti-American rhetoric was congruent with the popular belief that there was CIA involvement in the fall of the Whitlam government. While the evidence, as gathered by radical journalist John Pilger for a TV documentary on the subject, appears purely circumstantial, Midnight Oil tapped the populist current that believed in the possibilities Whitlam signalled if only partly delivered. And they believed former CIA officer Victor Marchetti when he remarked that "The CIA's aim was to get rid of a government they did not like."[21]

Garrett articulated a sense of a fragile national sovereignty. "The twin tidal waves of Hollywood and Madison Avenue via the-world-according-to-the-Pentagon have left Australia gibbering and uncertain — an ineffective participant in the great drama that is the struggle of the people of the world to see peace and equity become a reality in their lives." He links vulnerability to outside influence to a lack of maturity. "The US bases in Australia — Pine Gap, Nurrungar and North West Cape — are three of the biggest pimples on the face of adolescent Australia." Vulnerability in terms of political sovereignty results in part from a lack of cultural self determination. "By embracing America without question we left a gap in our own cultural development.... Without an Australian vision to compensate for the failure of the American dream to realise itself we have developed a culture centred on retrospection and cliche."

The resources for developing a mature and sovereign nation are partly cultural, and for Garrett are associated with the vernacular figures of radical nationalism, like "the experience of the bush, characterised by a streak of reckless independence coupled with support for your fellow mate as its positive qualities." According to Garrett, these masculine virtues of the Australian legend need recovering and developing, as they stand in opposition to the traditions of colonial authority, be it British or now American. "Nowadays the form guide, instant lotteries and bucks nights have become a corral for those stuck between the perfect world of the advertisers and the strictures of family and state." In that corral are the energies of refusal that Garrett and Midnight Oil articulate.

As a way to maintain the rage, Garrett's populism broadened over the years from its rewriting of radical nationalist imagery. By 1990 a more ecumenical Garrett was talking on behalf of the ACF of "an abiding concern for the good of the earth", in the name of "we 'greenies', the counsellors of caution."[22] The path from articulating the needs and interests of the nation to articulating those of the land itself passed through Midnight Oil's serious engagement with the issue of Aboriginal sovereignty when they toured the outback, resulting in the remarkable *Diesel and Dust* album of 1987. As Garrett editorialised that year, "Faced with the possibility of extinction and armed only with a desire to see justice done by being able to return to the lands where their forefathers had lived for centuries, Aborigines embarked on a campaign for genuine home ownership. It's called land rights."

As if to offset charges of an excessively masculine interpretation of culture, interest and history, Garrett also wrote about the technology of *in vitro* fertilisation, and asked: "Who controls these reproduction technologies and to what ends?" While there is undoubtedly a pervasive if non-denominational spiritualism in many of Garrett's statements, this usually takes the form of a critique of the presumption of god-like powers over nature on the part of capital and western culture. Garrett's most interesting contribution to Australian political culture is in demonstrating ways in which older values can be aligned with more recent and seemingly different ones, and may be made more palatable to younger generations who may not even be aware of Australian radical traditions.

And it works. According to the journalist Paul Kelly, when Graham Richardson became Labor's environment minister in 1987, he sought out three Green leaders: Tasmanian Bob Brown, Philip Toyne (then ACF director) and Peter Garrett. Richardson wanted to campaign through the media to reach the grass roots of the environment push, by seeking cooperation with Green leaders the public respected and by publicising pro-environment positions on major environment issues. Richardson: "We had to win by getting back those preferences. I kept telling Hawke this, but I didn't have to persuade Bob. He knew that already. That's why he made such access available to Brown, Toyne and Garrett."

Garrett became ACF chairman in 1989, on Toyne's initiative. In that capacity he campaigned hard on the issue of the incorporation of the Coronation Hill area into the Kakadu national park. Writes Kelly: "a fortnight before the decision Hawke had a three hour meeting with Toyne and Garrett. He never had a similar consultation with BHP."[23] On Kakadu, the ACF prevailed on Richardson, Richo on the parliamentary Labor party, and the party, in the end, on the electorate, winning the subsequent Federal election on Green preferences. Garrett retired as ACF president in 1993, but was made ACF patron in 1995.

Midnight Oil emerged with a strongly traditional adherence to the distinction between rock and pop, but they approached the rock business in an organic way, developing new possibilities out of it. Garrett leveraged the celebrity he attained as Midnight Oil frontman to become an organic talking head on a range of political issues. He cut across traditional organisational forms and hierarchies in the process. The values for which Garrett stood drew upon a certain kind of suburban ideal, a domestication of radical nationalist images. He mixed these with more recent suburban concerns with observing proper distinctions, particularly the distinction between nature and the economy.

The paradox of populism is that it requires an urbane disregard for the traditional distinctions in political life, but it uses urbanity in order to propose to suburban culture an image of itself that it can enjoy in an organic relation with the populist celebrity, one that bypasses the traditional political apparatus. Midnight Oil learned how to bypass part of the music industry establishment and build an organic relationship with their fans, but one based on traditional notions of rock's distinctness from pop. So too Peter Garrett learned how to bypass part of the political apparatus in order to build an organic relationship with his constituency, but one based on traditional notions of suburban value.

The Hat

When I suggested Garrett wore many hats, that was a figure of speech. There is one hat that Garrett did actually wear, and it suited him on a surprisingly wide range of occasions when he chose to cover that bald head. The bald head was an inspired image. Together with his catatonic dancing and open, outstretched hand, the bald head was always an integral part of his stage presence. Off stage it came to mean more. To return, where we began, to matters of sartorial detail: if hair styles signified anything in the 80s, it was age itself. A haircut, particularly a 'public' one, is some sort of compromise between what befits one's age, what is fashionable, and how one wore it in one's youth. Garrett shaved the whole problem clean off. The shaved head became a popular gay style in the 80s, but for once a straight guy came up with this fashion statement ahead of the curve.

The gleaming skull bridged the gap between the old left and the new left; between surf culture and post punk marginalism; between suburban and urban sensibility. Certainly, all of the song writing members of Midnight Oil (principally Jim Moginie, Rob Hirst and Garrett) are of an age which puts them somewhere between the student radicalism of the late 60s and the punk rebellion of the late 70s; but the eclectic mix of attitude, iconography, ideology and musical styles which characterised the band's art tries to speak to like-minded souls from any and every period of cultural formation.[24] Hence the bold bald shine under the follow-spot at centre stage: a sign of open, honest, neutrality, catatonically animated.

Garrett's Aussie bush hat was another key icon here. While his bald pate gathered significance accidentally, his bush hat had a slightly more calculated air about it. As far as I'm aware its first public exposure was when Garrett launched the 1984 NDP campaign. It also appeared in 1986 in the context of a public event connected with the Constitutional Commission: the re-enactment of the proclamation of Australia as a nation.[25]

That Garrett was on to something when he donned that hat might be borne out by the subsequent attempts by others to appropriate it. In a daring display of image scavenging, Ian 'Molly' Meldrum took to wearing one as host of *Countdown* to cover his receding hairline. He made a big show of symbolically giving Bob Hawke one when the latter appeared one night in the guest compere's seat. Thus Garrett, the wearer of many hats, has put one particular hat in circulation which has since been worn on many formerly hatless heads.

At the very last *Countdown* annual awards show, Molly removed the hat to reveal a clean shaven pate, à la Garrett — no doubt meant as a show stopping joke to commemorate the antagonism there has always been between Meldrum and the Oils. The joke was on Meldrum. The *Countdown* public suspected that the avuncular Meldrum was going bald, and losing his grip on Australian teen consciousness, but perhaps not even Garrett himself knew if Garrett was bald. The spokesperson for the aspirations of youth reserved the right to grow old but not grey, gracefully.

The bush hat connotes the 1890s style masculinity that historical Russell Ward made famous as the 'Australian legend'. It's the headgear that connotes the rugged, self-reliant individuality of the fabled bush worker.[26] Garrett reclaimed it for suburbia, but a suburbia looking inwards, towards a reformulation of its relation to the bush. Garrett struck a pose as a new kind of pioneer, reimagining bush in terms of an environment that calls for a duty of care, and also in terms of the unsettled issue of Aboriginal justice. These are, at first sight, strange and unlikely things to put under that hat. Garrett's urbanity consisted in this willingness to try out new combinations of images, even if the images he was trying to combine and compose were of a new suburban settlement, a new spiritual order that reconciles black with white, environment with invader, sovereignty with spirituality.

"We're like the wall people are spewing up against, writing graffiti on and riding skateboards across. We're the canvas the country writes itself across", as Garrett said in an interview with Craig Mathieson, promoting the 1998 album *Redneck Wonderland.*[27] The title came from a bit of graffiti on a wall near the recording studio in Melbourne where the band were recording. Given the change in mood that signalled the premature end of the 90s at that time, it's not surprising that this ends up sprayed across the record. "Got you in my sights, spot lit by the fence. If you're small you're fair game, it's just common sense."[28] Midnight Oil found a reason to exist again, documenting the reactive populism of the 90s, trying to turn the same energies of refusal in a less reactive direction. Garrett even thought about running for the Senate again, on the Green ticket.

But the world beckoned, and in the Mathieson interview tensions surfaced: between Garrett's public political career and the band's export potential; between the 70s punk activism of the band's past and the electronic decoration added to the sound by a hip young producer, attempting to repackage the Oils for the moment. Garrett on *Recovery*, the 90s revamp of the *Countdown* TV music formula, looked a little out of place, trying to get a teenage audience to get up and dance. They seemed a bit mystified by the sincerity of this rock musical parent. Garrett, as always, seemed not at all put out by the clash of context. While firmly in the suburban rock aesthetic, in every other respect, cutting across differences and combining energies is what Midnight Oil were always all about.

culture

c h a p t e r **5**

Subdivision cultures

Taste classifies, and it classifies the classifier.

Pierre Bourdieu

Communication by means of art is an amusing misunderstanding.

Witold Gombrowitz

Paul Kelly, Songwriter

"I'm afraid for my country" intones the tall gaunt man, and 2 000 people fall silent and tune in to him, as if he knew their wavelength. Melbourne based singer-songwriter Paul Kelly has just commenced his set at Sydney's State theatre. In his unassuming way, this man spoke to much the same sore point in the national psyche as Pauline Hanson, but in a different style, and to very different result.

On this night at the State Theatre in 1996, I sensed why culture can matter more than politics. Politics is a parasite on culture. It takes the feeling of the majority and turns it into power. A popular artist works within culture, creating other ways that feelings might be put together. Here, tonight, Kelly takes the feeling of fear and worry that haunts this audience and separates it from the feeling of resentment. At the time, political leaders did it the other way around.

Through Kelly's agency, a public might connect worry to a quite different feeling. Insecurity can lead to altruism almost as easily as to a desire to cut off the dole to the young unemployed, Blacks, single mothers, recent migrants, whoever else is on the hit list of the resentment mongers. It was a question of acknowledging that fear plays a larger part than hope, and of moving from fear to a search for mutual reassurance rather than mutual paranoia. But that requires an artist's touch rather than a politician's, a singing head rather than a nodding one.

"This is the land of the little kings", Kelly sings.[1] It sums up a sentiment that crosses party lines. It speaks to the structure of feeling from which people's political judgement came. People were fed up with puffed up blokes who talked loudly and carried a little stick. That opened the door for Hanson, but it could open the door for other voices too. It is the role of the artist as celebrity to create alternative public expressions for everyday feelings.

"I've been careless", Kelly admits, and "I've done all the dumb things."[2] And yet he holds out hope for us average white blokes — and the women who love us. He doesn't neglect to mention the finer qualities to which we aspire — courage, generosity, purpose. He also expresses our willingness to listen and change. "We love you!" shout a couple of women in the front row. "Then I'm lucky," replies Kelly.

Here was another sensibility about how Australian culture can work. A man tells a few stories, admits a few limitations, exposes a raw nerve between the lines, invokes a past and a sense of belonging, names some things about which he cares, defines what matters from the past and should not be lost. And 2 000 people pick the points at which their own structure of feeling might connect.

This is one of the things a popular art is for, and why it matters. It proposes a simple template with which a cross section of people can shape their own particular fears, hopes and identities. The complexity lies in what people do with the template. Different people can use the same songs to shape different feelings, and yet feel like they all belong to something larger than themselves. Popular art is the heart and soul of any viable culture. It's a virtual republic out of reach of little kings.

Looking around the State Theatre foyer as the audience left the show, I noticed that Kelly's people were between 25

and 45 years old. They dressed neatly, and looked disproportionately Anglo-Celtic. Most were couples, and there were
as many men as women. This was the people of the white suburban heartland. This was a generation that grew up listening to the Rock Gods as they pounded out their 4/4
rhythm. This was the generation of the golden age of pub
rock, which in the late 70s broke out of its urban ghetto and
reached out into the suburbs. These people might have out-
grown pub rock, but not Paul Kelly, one of its enduring
products. They might have tired of the banality and repetition of the Rock Gods, but not of this Rock God who raised
himself out of the tedious beat and into the ranks of
celebrity.

"From little things, big things grow", as one of his songs
puts it. Politics grows out of culture and culture always grows
from the ground up. Even when culture uses the most mass-
produced images and stories, it requires local, particular,
contingent acts of affirmation, little gestures made in the
pores and folds of everyday life, for those images and stories
to acquire any significance. From the smallest connections of
personal feeling come the largest of public moods. Which is
why, with his ability to connect the pervasive anxiety of the
late 1990s to hope, dialogue and care rather than to resentment, preaching and cruelty, Paul Kelly made a difference.
Where there is art there is hope.

Paul Kelly, Journalist

There was another Paul Kelly besides the singer-songwriter,
who also became a celebrity in the 90s. There was the Paul
Kelly who was a respected journalist, editor of *The Australian*,
and the author of *The End of Certainty*, a key book about the
80s. In it, this other Paul Kelly argued that protectionist,
inward-looking Australia, with its dependence on state
benevolence, was no longer a viable economic basis for
Australian prosperity. This Paul Kelly added his considerable
journalistic weight to Treasurer Paul Keating's economic
reform agenda.

Kelly claimed that the Australian settlement "was founded
on: faith in government authority; belief in egalitarianism; a
method of judicial determination in centralised wage fixa-

tion; protection of its industry and its jobs; dependence upon a great power (first Britain, then America), for its security and its finance; and above all, hostility to its geographical location, exhibited in fear of external domination and internal contamination from the peoples of the Asia Pacific. Its bedrock ideology was protection; its solution, a Fortress Australia, guaranteed as part of an impregnable Empire spanning the globe. This framework — introspective, defensive, dependent — is undergoing an irresistible demolition."[3] The lucky country could not get by, on this account, in the emerging global economic and strategic environment. So changes came.

Kelly was aware that structural economic change cannot take place without cultural change. But he seemed to think cultural change could be effected from above. He saw that the Labor Party had staked its claim to leadership under Hawke and Keating on the strength of its own internal cultural reform. "Labor, once the bedrock party of the old White Australia, had undergone a more complete transformation on the issues of race and non-discriminatory immigration than had its conservative opponents."[4]

What Paul Kelly the journalist did not perceive was that cultural change cannot proceed from the top down. What Paul Kelly the songwriter intuited when he sang of the land of the little kings, was that the cultural resources were not adequate for coping with the anxiety generated by the sudden abandonment of the last tenets of the Australian settlement. Kelly the journalist, who gathered information from the powers that be, knew Australia had to change. Kelly the songwriter, who gleaned a sense of the mood at large, felt that change was being resisted within the culture, that a public had not really formed that grasped the new information on which the dash for change was mandated.

In cultural matters, both Kellys had suburban instincts. The difference was that the songwriter's suburbia was a somewhat less precious batch of postcodes than the senior journalist's. Kelly the songwriter tuned in to the emotional tone of a culture stressed by change. Kelly the journalist's policy, while at the helm of *The Australian* newspaper, took a cosmopolitan view of the necessity of economic change, but supported suburban cultural resistance to it at the same time. *The Australian* sponsored repeated attacks on political correctness, feminism and multiculturalism, and added the conservative editor of *Quadrant*, Robert Manne, to its roster of columnists. Under Manne's editorship, *Quadrant* had been in the vanguard of resistance to cultural change.

The Australian created space for a public debate between what Kelly called sentimental traditionalists, talking heads such as Robert Manne, who wanted to retain aspects of both the cultural and economic side of the Australian settlement, and international rationalists, who favoured economic change. But its pages were much more closed to advocates of cultural change. Kelly noted in his book the unholy alliances that formed on the sentimental traditionalist side, where Labor leftists line up with their old cold war nemesis, the Melbourne conservatives around *Quadrant*. But nowhere did he acknowledge the possibility of combining an acceptance of reforming the economy with a radical platform on cultural change, social justice and pluralism. In the absence of an airing of such an alternative, economic reform had a narrow base, and the third way suffered as a result.

From 1996 onwards both John Howard and Pauline Hanson picked up on the kinds of attack on cultural change that Kelly and Manne had sponsored. As they were strongly opposed to the racist element in this populist appropriation, these two prominent cultural conservatives were then forced to tack left. Hanson's celebrity accelerated the expression of grassroots reaction from below. Prime Minister John Howard tacked rightward in response, his soft Hansonism from above being his response to hard Hansonism from below. One lesson that was not drawn was that Kelly's economic modernism combined with cultural conservatism was an incoherent doctrine. It offered no resources for coping with the costs felt in everyday life of economic reform. It led inevitably to reactive refusal of the "land of the little kings", as no progressive way forward was publicly aired. Sponsoring talk about the republic, as *The Australian* did, was no substitute for a searching debate on how culture is supposed to cope with rapid economic transformation.

Paul Kelly the journalist correctly identified the elements of the Australian settlement that could not be sustained under the impact of globalisation. Paul Keating the politician at least recognised the need to change it, even if he did not quite grasp the means. What came apart in the 80s was the fortress suburbia the Australian settlement supported within its fortress Australia — a suburban culture that was until the 80s relatively untroubled, not just by economic uncertainty, but by something more fundamental, something Donald Horne identified a long time ago.

"Australia does not have a mind", Horne wrote in the *Lucky Country*.[5] Despite a passing fondness on the part of Prime Minister Bob Hawke and some of his Ministers for talking up, in the place of the lucky country, the notion of becoming the clever country, the idea didn't really become a part of everyday culture. The reason for this failure lies in the nature of fortress Australia. The Australian settlement did not shield Australians from economic globalisation — on that score it did not do too well. As the prices Australia received for its wheat and coal exports declined relative to the prices it paid to import Toyota cars and Sony video players, the Australian settlement simply failed as a guarantee of prosperity. But what it continued to protect Australians from were the pervasive flows of *information* upon which economic globalisation depends.

White Australia kept out troubling flows of information coming from cultural negotiation with migrants. Industry protectionism obviated the need to track detailed information about global economic opportunities. Wage arbitration retarded the flow of information about negotiating at the workshop level. State paternalism exempted citizens from thinking actively *as* citizens and exercising and extending their liberties. Imperial benevolence damped interest in information about the possible roles and niches for a sovereign Australian nation in a changing world.

These information deficits prevailed long after their economic impact became apparent. The cultural residue of the Australian settlement that persists is the culture of suburbia and its instinctive resistance to any challenge to its restricted and stable diets of information. What was resisted strongly in the Keating agenda, perhaps even more strongly than economic reform, was the idea that Australians would have to learn to think for themselves, process information, deal with intellectual as well as material uncertainty.

Suburban resistance to 'postmodernism', for instance, was about more than resistance to a particular intellectual fashion. It was about resistance to any challenge to the faith that this is a stable world with fixed coordinates and immutable truths, about which no more need be thought. It was suburbia's resistance to becoming more urbane in outlook. This was most telling in the public burblings of formerly progressive talking heads such as David Williamson or Beatrice Faust, who turned their backs on their former selves and appealed instead to the ideal of fixed truths, as if the mere invocation of the possibility of an end to intellectual uncertainty were the same thing as actually achieving it.[6]

When he became Prime Minister in 1991, Paul Keating made many mistakes in his efforts to promote economic and cultural change, but the task was not helped by the incontinent support of the talking heads of the 90s. Those who supported his economic agenda were often arrogant, politically illiterate and culturally philistine. Those who supported his cultural agenda simply refused to understand economic necessity and frequently pined for nostalgic solutions. Very few seemed to grasp the simple fact that globalisation changes the *information* environment within which a nation has to think through *both* its economic and cultural life and come up with appropriate political and social structures for producing stability and prosperity. The common wealth is made out of what information people can glean from the vectors that traverse its borders as much as from capital, labour and minerals.

Composing a new majority around the goals of economic and cultural change, a majority that accepts change as offering the potential for modest but feasible solutions to the age-old problems of achieving the fair go — justice and liberty, equality and community — that was a major problem confronting Australian public institutions, including the Labor Party, at the century's end. In the rest of this chapter I want to examine the cultural side of it. The culture of what I call suburbia appears as an immutable given in Australian life, one resistant to new information and to any changes to the Australian settlement. But progress might be made possible by reading it in terms of its anxieties, and proposing new solutions to assuage them.

Reading the Public

How is that we know with whom we belong? This is a question not just of belonging to a particular culture, but belonging to some sense of what Donald Horne called a "public culture" where those particular cultures intersect and overlap.[7] Interpreted broadly, the public culture is where a majority can comfortably negotiate who they are and who others are and how to get along. What I want to do here is try to construct an image of such a majority, and then move on to the question of how such a majority constructs itself. If there is to be an optimism about the future, then it might help to imagine a majority who might come to embrace a future not premised on denouncing minorities. Given that "cultural and intellectual elites" are among the minorities that populist reaction denounced, this might be of more than theoretical interest.

I'm going to use, as my source for thinking there is hope, an unlikely document: the *Silent Majority III* report released in August 1997 by Clemenger Advertising, who promoted themselves as Australia's largest Australian-owned advertising company.[8] *Silent Majority III* was the third time Clemenger commissioned a survey of Australian opinion, and there were interesting differences between them.

In 1977, people were most concerned about the lack of replacement dust bags for vacuum cleaners. In 1997, the survey found that "in contrast with a decade or two ago, the issues of greatest concern in the late 90s are 'big' topics embracing moral, ethical and economic issues." This, I think, is one reason to have hope. Far from being a "culture of forgetting", as Robert Manne claims, this is a culture that remembers a great deal of what it sees and hears, and has learned to use the media to think a bit conceptually.[9] In spite of suburbia's acculturated resistance to thinking itself part of a larger public culture, people think about the world the media exposes nightly in the living room.

If the survey is to be believed, then heading the issues of the day in the late 90s was the betrayal of trust by community leaders, particularly politicians. There was cynicism about the media, particularly news and current affairs. People resented the wealthy getting government handouts, and managers paying themselves more while giving their workers the sack. There was alarm about the integrity of the criminal justice system. Surprisingly, race and immigration issues were of less importance. After several generations of migration, it might be a more ethnically cosmopolitan world out there than some talking heads credit.[10]

The *Silent Majority* researchers used focus groups to generate a list of issues, and then tested those issues against a sample of a thousand people with a questionnaire. The methods used were hardly perfect, but the results are still useful, if decoded with some sensitivity. It's not hard to see in the survey what the political parties saw in their own polling before the 1996 election: a strong undercurrent of resentment. According to journalist Pamela Williams, the Howard camp capitalised on this kind of research, while Keating ignored it.[11] The resentment the public heard about during the election was resentment of dole bludgers and welfare cheats. The resentment the public didn't hear about, because Labor neglected to articulate it, was resentment of big business paying itself huge bonuses while downsizing the work force.

Added to this class resentment was a mistrust of professional authority. Teachers, media workers, police, judges, doctors, priests and politicians all copped it more than in the two previous reports. There was a striking rise in public scepticism about the media's roster of talking heads. Older people forced into redundancy and early retirement by the rationalisation of industry, particularly of the public sector, appear especially distrustful. Suburbia knew enough to be sceptical of authority, but this scepticism can work in different ways. It can open new ways of interpreting information; it can also block any further thought.

In the 1988 report, the main media related complaint was having to watch the same TV commercials more than once an hour. The 1997 version showed a much broader popular critique of the media. "Trial by media" and excessive coverage of some issues at the expense of others head the list. Crime was an issue in all three surveys, but the nature of the issues changed in interesting ways. In 1997, drugs were a less cited concern. Fear of violence against children had become weirdly sexualised, but the threat was seen as outside the home — teachers and priests. Domestic violence worked its way up the agenda, suggesting that, for all the talk about a backlash, many people were starting to see some aspects of everyday life through the perspectives feminism proposed. The link between the family and violence against women came out in the open. The link between the family and violence against children did not. There was a generational polarisation well in evidence. Older Australians were much more alarmed at social and cultural changes, at privatisation and 'Americanization'.

If the Clemenger survey is to be credited, the fair go was the big issue. A lot of people were distrustful of the procedures by which issues became public in the media, and by which institutions dealt with them. As Elaine Thompson from the University of New South Wales claims, the concept of the fair go is always a very contested one.[12] It is taken to be a distinctive feature of the Australian settlement, but its meaning gets read in wildly different ways. Pauline Hanson's idea of a fair go might be rather removed from Aboriginal activist Noel Pearson's. In the 90s, publicly available ideas about fairness were perhaps not subtle and supple enough to express the complex equations of fairness, based as they sometimes are on crudely bureaucratic concepts of minority and disadvantage.

What *Silent Majority III* suggested was that the popularity in 1996 of Howard and Hanson arose from genuine grievances, and ones that need not express themselves in terms of race. Opposition to Hanson might have been more effective earlier on if it articulated those grievances in other terms, rather than simply amplifying Hanson's racist articulations. I don't know that country people, older people, or suburban 'battlers' are necessarily more prejudiced than anyone else. But these were the groups who were less likely to have the resource of other ways of articulating their senses of injustice.

For instance, resentment of dole bludgers was more subtle than is sometimes portrayed. The people surveyed distinguished between genuine need and taking advantage. *Silent Majority III* found a lot of anger about the perception of new migrants going straight onto benefits without earning a right to them. On the other hand, there was not much opposition to foreign aid spending. Concern about Asian students taking university places away from Australians fell since the 1988 survey.

The problem these results pose is one of weighing up concepts of the fair go that do not have a common measure. In the social democratic consensus of Keating's government of 1991 to 1996, it appeared as if fairness was a matter of belonging to an identifiable category to which it could be administered. The problem was that very few people actually wanted to identify themselves with such categories. Suburbia saw it as a sign of 'falling back' that someone gets caught in the net of special assistance programs. As Paul Kelly's song 'Special Treatment' suggests, it's a loaded term.[13] On the other hand, a program that you don't have to be special to get, like Medicare, enjoyed broad public support.

While there was much talk about cultural difference in the Keating years, the concept of culture was never differentiated enough. Given a choice between thinking of oneself as part of one or other quite narrowly defined minority, or as part of a silent — and unspeakable — majority, many people chose the latter, and chose Howard. But the Coalition could do very little with this unspeakable majority, particularly as more and more people discovered that industrial relations 'reform' and cuts to education and welfare hurt them too.

People reacted against the linking of fairness to identity — as if you had to belong to a special category to get special help. So it was tempting, particularly for Labor, to abandon the whole rhetoric of the minority and join the jostling crowd of political populists angling for some alleged suburban battler mainstream. A more interesting challenge was finding new ways of proposing the fair go that could articulate differences into a public to which people could belong without putting themselves and their cultures into categories and hierarchies. This was a double challenge, both to Australian political culture and to cultural politics: to find new ideas and images; but also to grasp the way political ideas and images have to mesh with the way culture works, and with the way the media connects different kinds of culture together.

Reading As Public

"The only successful class distinction in Australian history," claimed the writer Geoffrey Dutton, was that drawn by urban talking heads to distinguish themselves from the silent majority of suburbia.[14] A distinction successful, ironically enough, because the people talking heads designated negatively as suburban came to embrace the term. They are the "silent majority" that Clemenger constructed via their survey.

Craig McGregor's book *People, Politics and Pop* was a polemic addressed to this distinction that urban talking heads made in the 60s between themselves and suburban nongs and drongos. Huddled in urban slumland was the 'real' working class, bumping shoulders with the 'real' cultural elite, the bohemians and writers. Meanwhile out in the suburbs, Alf and Daph mowed the lawn and on weekends had friends over for a barbie — ignored by both the old warhorses of the labour movement and the urban cliques.

McGregor was one of those who in the 60s broke ranks with those leftist talking heads such as Allan Ashbolt, Ian Turner, and Humphrey McQueen, who clutched their Great Books and their Great Music and shunned the whole idea of suburbia — even as they drifted into it.[15] McGregor announced to anyone who would listen that the great suburban mass, out amid the TV jungles and radio jingles, was actually quite a lively, interesting, valid culture. He switched sides, and went in to bat for a pop democracy. It was a brave and necessary move for the times. And he wasn't the only one. In its brief existence from 1972 to 1975, the Whitlam Labor government combined traditional Labor with suburban issues and a radical tone. Reason and progress took a long march through the institutions. For every three steps forward, there were two steps backwards, but on the whole, the institutionalisation of the fair go made incremental progress.

Of course, this suburbia that many Australian writers abhorred and that McGregor embraced, never existed. It was, as University of Melbourne cultural historian Chris McAuliffe discerned, a concept formed from an observation: from the experience of the suburb comes the description of it as suburban and then the concept of suburbia.[16] It was, as cultural historian Tim Rowse once said, a "necessary fiction".[17] Rowse critiqued suburbia in the name of a supposedly more true image of class conflict, one more recognisable to left wing talking heads of the day.

But McGregor recognised that rather than translate suburbia into what urban talking heads might recognise as an image of society, it was more useful to translate left wing ideas into the language and image of surburbia. This was because this image, no matter how much a fiction it might have been, was starting to have a real existence as a public world in which people believed and came to call their own. As McAuliffe says, "it is difficult to separate the suburb (a physical site) from suburbia (the states of mind associated with living at that site)."

Suburbia became what I call a 'third nature'. The roads and buildings and shops around us become second nature to us after living in a place for a while. They become something taken for granted. Likewise, the images and stories through which we understand how those roads and shops and houses connect to a larger public world become a third nature, a taken for granted world no less real than the tarmac of the road and the red brick of the houses, even though it is made up of words and pictures, transmitted by radio waves, or thrown over the fence by a kid on a bike with a newspaper round.

Suburbia provided writers and readers with a third nature within which to collaborate on creating an image of the times. In the second nature of our built environment we tend not to notice anything much until it changes. The street is just the street until the council sends a gang out to curb and gutter it, and people pause to watch. Likewise, in the third nature of our information environment we tend not to notice the stock images and stories, but rather we notice the elements the writer or producer proposes as something new. In the movie *Sum of Us*, there is nothing at all exceptional in the actor Jack Thompson playing the part of a regular Aussie bloke. He has so established himself as an image of what a bloke is that it's taken for granted. That he has a gay son in the movie is the 'new' element, but it is only recognisable as new in the context of a third nature of shared images.

Suburbia is a third nature that provides images of the fair go, and corresponding images of its opposite. In his book *Popular Reality*, cultural studies scholar John Hartley writes, "the public of modernity is coterminous with the readership of media."[18] What creates a public in the first place is some vector that connects people together, such as a newspaper, television or radio. What creates a public *culture* is, in addition, some shared images and stories about which people can think and feel by reading them *differently*. Against the background of third nature are new concepts, sensations and emotions about the fair go and the short shrift. Out of thinking, feeling, arguing or ignoring such information, people become a public, and create the common world of a public culture.

The concept of 'reading' and 'readership' that Hartley advances are crucial for any genuinely democratic approach to thinking about this unspeakable majority who come together as a public. The talking heads of both the left and the right often have full rhetorical command of what is good for the unspeakable majority. Talking heads on the right might speak of 'the people' and those on the left used to speak of the 'working class', but usually what most folks actually read and watch, let alone think and say, is completely ignored.

The rhetorical strategy is to suppose that there is a (false) public that is brainwashed by celebrity trivia, in the absence of which they would come to their senses and agree with this or that edict of the babbling and burbling talking heads, and form a (real) public. What actually gets written for, and distributed by, the more popular media vectors, and what gets made of it in acts of readership, is discounted or ignored, as if it were unspeakable. Thus talking heads on both left and right are often united in an authoritarian and anti-democratic approach to culture. Both sides are more interested in criticising what's *not* in popular media and criticising what's lacking in popular taste, than attending to the potential of suburban culture.

What is refreshing about Hartley's approach is that it takes seriously the idea that it is not just the talking heads who know how to read, but that silent suburbans also know a thing or two about how to make meaning out of a text. Both 'reading' and 'text' might apply as much to television and pop songs and movies and journalism as to the novel. Acts of reading that take place with the telly on in the suburban living room, or while listening to the radio in the car on the commute, are what constitute the actual public culture of the nation. It might not be the ideal 'public sphere' imagined by political theorists, but unlike the latter, it actually exists.

Ironically, what Hartley is doing here is the opposite of the usual caricature of cultural studies. According to that put-down, cultural studies brings trashy pop culture into the refined world of the literary classroom. But what Hartley does is go looking for the reading practices of the literary classroom out in the common world. He goes looking for examples of the way people read, and by reading, become a public. The public are a "reading public", and they read voraciously — movies, books, magazines, TV shows. And out of what they read, the public decide who they are, what they believe, what the common world is like, what ideas of the fair go to pursue. The public even has its own criticisms of the media, as the *Silent Majority* report shows.

Like Craig McGregor, Hartley's instincts are popular and democratic rather than elitist and authoritarian. What he adds to McGregor's intellectual sympathy with the popular is a more sophisticated way of thinking about exactly how the act of reading the texts distributed by popular media vectors actually creates a common world. McGregor announced in *People, Politics and Pop* that "I am Alf!"[19] Hartley's point is that it's not just a question of McGregor the talking head identifying with suburbia by reading himself into the text of suburbia. This is what everybody does. We all participate in a third nature of shared images and stories. McGregor chose, rightly in my view, to participate in popular ones. What Hartley adds is a sympathetic and constructive reading of the way reading itself works in everyday life.

This is not to deny the power that media proprietors hold. Being an Alf or a Daph is to have considerably less power than a Rupert or a Kerry. Being Craig and Charlene (children of Alf and Daph) is to have less power than Lachlan and James (sons of Rupert Murdoch and Kerry Packer). But the power of a newspaper or a government can only be exercised with the consent of Alfs and Daphs, Charlenes and Craigs. Their consent is won by proposing images and stories of the fair go. As David Marshall stresses, media and political talking heads continuously poll and survey Craigs and Charlenes to try and rationalise what it is they want.[20] This is the great mystery of publics: the way they form themselves, from the bottom up, by giving consent to shared images and stories of the fair go.

The media proposes, publics form themselves by reading what is proposed, and images of what those readings decide are proposed back to the public via opinion polls and surveys. It might not be the ideal of a rational 'public sphere', but it works. One could criticise what's wrong with it. I could join those talking heads who attack the monopolisation of ownership of the media and the centralist and undemocratic workings of the major political parties. Or I could join those resentful talking heads who attack the public itself for its lack of interest in media regulation and the democratisation of public life. But after I felt myself move, and the whole audience move at Paul Kelly's State Theatre gig, I decided there had to be another way.

So I took my cue from the *Silent Majority III* report. What's interesting there is the way that, in the 90s, a public formed that had quite a different criticism of the media. Rather than support proposals for reform to politics and the media proposed by urbane and cultured talking heads, a public formed that was rather more critical of urbane talking heads themselves. A significant part of suburbia rejected urbane proposals, and saw in them self-interest rather than the public good. Part of the suburban public started looking to the hinterland for different kinds of proposals, including those of One Nation. As to why is an interesting story, and that's what I want to get to next.

Suburban Resistance

Central to the rightward turn of the late 90s was the partial rejection of urbane cultural values. The irony is that while suburbia shunned the latest talking head proposals, they did so in the name of previous proposals from previous generations of talking heads. These previous proposals had come to define the taken for granted values, the third nature, of the 'suburban'. What was refused was a certain kind of proposal for redefining the public culture. Such changes attracted the label 'politically correct'.

The suburbia that Craig McGregor embraced in the 60s as embodying both a progressive and a democratic force was, by the 90s, in danger of becoming a largely reactive force. The irony is that it might have become so precisely to the extent that the authoritarian strand in the disposition of talking heads refused, particularly in the Keating years, to hear what this unspeakable majority was saying. Third nature is a powerful presence, as real as bricks and bitumen, and sometimes even harder to demolish and rebuild.

Understanding this resistance to new proposals seems to me a necessary prerequisite. Right through the 90s, there were plenty of interesting proposals for change. Michael Pusey called for a return to a nation building social democracy of the old postwar reconstruction type. Eva Cox offered a vision of a truly civil society. Moira Rayner talked about the process of rooting democracy in everyday life. James Walter lamented the failure of Australian political imagination. Fred Argy located Australia at the crossroads between economic rationalism and a progressive liberal view. Gregory Melleuish critiqued the limits of the packages that reformers offer for reimagining Australia. Humphrey McQueen defended popular sovereignty against the rhetoric of globalisation. Frank Brennan sought a way to balance the public good with individual liberty. Bob Ellis mounted 202 'arguments' against economic rationalism.[21] Each of these distinguished talking heads offered a critique of the limits of the economic and political imagination. They prescribed large or small doses of institutional reform, some of a radical and some of a liberal nature. Some wanted to change things, and some wanted to change things back. There were good proposals among them, and a stimulating dialogue to be had discussing them.

But whose dialogue? It ends up being a conversation among talking heads. It goes with being a talking head to specialise in talking about what is good for the public culture in general, but most people construe themselves as belonging to a private world. Suburbia is a largely privatised culture where the fair go is felt and lived through image and stories of the particular — a record of which is kept in the family household photo album. The difficulty is getting from the general to the particular. What intellectual talking heads needed was not only concepts about the fair go in general but concepts about how the general can be expressed in the images and stories of the particular.

Many of these talking heads had a genuine claim to be intellectuals. I have doubts about that claim in some of these cases, but there is a more pressing issue than critiquing their conceptual integrity. These talking heads offered the public concepts about the fair go in general. If they were intellectuals, they offered not just concepts about the fair go in general, but *new* concepts. Most of them spoke from a culture that felt at home talking about concepts, but they could not speak to a culture that felt more at home with familiar images and stories. I don't think it possible to consider the kinds of information these authors wanted to put on the agenda without first considering the conflict over the role of new information in culture that is working its way through the images and stories that preoccupied suburbia in the 90s.

Which is why, urbane talking head that I am, I feel obliged to offer a concrete location to place my own thinking for the reader. I am as much a product of a certain kind of second nature and third nature as everyone else, and I construct my public place out of private readings just like anyone else. The distrust evident in the *Silent Majority III* report was based on reading these private and particular interests back into the abstract proposals talking heads offered as their way of seeing the common world. And talking heads always carry a class baggage as a type of celebrity. So it might be better to come clean at the outset. I think and speak and write from deep within the urban triangle, where every sink has not two but three taps — for hot water, cold water, and chardonnay.

Kings Cross Saturday Night

The taxi eases up William st to Kings Cross, its passage slowed by traffic. We make a right beneath the running fire of the giant Coca-Cola sign and we're just over the border into Darlinghurst. It's Saturday night and the Cross is a Mecca for suburban thrill seekers, as it has been for decades. A public space of release from suburban constraint. But I am not here for that. Here I am an insider. My friends and I are heading for a private party in a back street, out of sight of the neon. There is more than one Kings Cross, although their boundaries are indistinct and overlapping.

The poet and journalist Kenneth Slessor wrote about Kings Cross with a special affection. "Its plan of living represents a cut across the organic structure of the Sydney ant-heap. Hovels are wedged between palaces. Millionaires look out of their 'luxury apartments', their silver and velvet suites, at the slum-world looking at them from the tenement next door or across the street. Among the termites of the yelling flat-blocks, ladies of unimpeachable virtue lend aspirin to ladies who come home barefoot with hiccoughs."[22] In the 45 years between when Slessor wrote those lines and I wrote these, all that's changed is that cosmopolitans speak of women in different terms, and the luxury suites of the 50s have moved down market. Giant new towers look down on them from even more expensive heights.

Wading into the party, I hand three bottles of vodka to Richard behind the bar. The room is a sea of black-clad bodies, providing a readymade background for the one bright mango jacket, clearly visible through the darkness. Richard and Dr. Death are mixing industrial strength cocktails. Richard hosts a TV show, while Dr. Death is an academic specialising in Holocaust studies, hence the grim nickname. Despite their different occupations they have much the same approach to the cocktail. I pass potent potions to Libby and Milissa.

Libby tells me a story about signing a violinist to the record company she works for who ends up giving her violin lessons. This astonishes her colleagues, as the new signing is a famous classical musician not known for tutoring absolute beginners. I move on to Colin and we argue about conceptual art. I whisper something in CD's ear as she stands, long and lean beside me in her black Betsy Johnson dress. Then I talk to Khym about her cookbook, which I tell her I am using all the time. She is making web sites for Microsoft now. Milissa and Neil swap publishing gossip. I meet an architect from East Timor called Paolo who is designing a new nightclub. I tell him I want to renovate and ask for his email address. Kaye tells me she has the full text of the Clemenger survey that's been on the news and that she can fax it to me if I want it. It fell off the back of a truck and her research assistant was there to catch it. I return to the bar to recharge my cocktail, and plunge into the network of black-clad bodies again.

Caroline tells me she is reading scripts for Fox now. I ask her what the worst one she's read is about. Before she can tell me I'm diverted by some gossip about a famous TV star with a very suburban image who is no longer welcome at the Sebel Townhouse after his room was found splattered with blood. Dale introduces me to Peter, who is working on the next Labor election campaign. We talk about the sex appeal of Pauline Hanson. I try to get some information out of Dale about his employers at News Corporation, but as always he is too discreet.

I congratulate James, our host, on his short listing for a literary award, and I ask Mardi, our hostess, if her doctoral thesis has been marked. She tells me that after an episode of the soap she writes for that featured an ill-mannered doctor, several people called or wrote claiming to have had the same experience — with the same doctor. Cassandra explains Indonesian politics since the fall of Suharto to me. Tony, my publisher, nags me about when this book is going to be finished and tells me about his new baby daughter, followed by more talk about home renovation.

Some very drunk young woman talks about how much she likes the work of a novelist I once had an affair with, and asks me about the novelist's sexual tastes. The Polish violinist whose name I forget disputes the greatness of Frank Sinatra's phrasing. Tony the architect mentions that a mutual friend is pregnant, which is news to me. He describes the progress on the refurbishing of the Sydney Post Office and we lament the development of East Circular Quay. Empty vodka bottles line the hallway. It's time to leave while I can still walk.

I don my coat and head out into Victoria street hunting for taxis, for the short ride from Kings Cross to Ultimo, back to my actual home from my spiritual home. The Cross is the neighbourhood where I lived, on and off, for much of the 80s, before discovering that I get more work done sitting in cafes in Ultimo where nobody knows me than in cafes in the Cross where there is always a friendly face and where there seems to be a fellow writer living in every other apartment block.

The taxis are hiding from me as I lurk in the shadows near the fire station, ready to pounce on the first that beetles along. It's a little risky on the streets so I'm trying to stay alert, dodging stragglers from buck's nights and hen's parties, slouching toward Bexley. I'm sensitive, not just to the drunks and yobs wobbling by, but also to the ghosts. I imagine the ghost of the poet Christopher Brennan hiding under his broad hat, ambling towards Liverpool street where he once lived. The ghost of Brennan's daughter laughs as she leads a gentleman friend by the arm, and her shoes clack on the pavement. There's Ken Slessor himself, with a skinful, wending home to what is now Darlinghurst rd. Dulcie Deamer, queen of bohemia, chatters with some bright young things from another time as she clatters off to a party in Macleay street.[23]

If there is a landscape of urbanity in the geography of Australian feeling then Kings Cross is surely a part of it. That people keep coming to the Cross from the suburbs for a big night indicates that it has not yet lost its place in the imagination. That people still choose to live there and practice contemporary forms of urban living add new layers to its cultural sediment. While Kings Cross has been the image of urban Australia since the 20s, by the 90s it was no longer its prime location. There is urbanity not just in Kings Cross but in every city and sizeable town. You find traces of it wherever different kinds of people decide to live, not just by politely ignoring each other, but by working out amongst themselves a collective style of public interaction, sharing aspirin and beer.

It is possible to live an urbane life in the suburbs. As McGregor says, suburbia, "like Kings Cross, is a state of mind."[24] Telephone and television make it possible to connect with others and with a shared agenda by remote control. The internet and cable television deepened inner suburbia's immersion in the urbane oceans of cyberspace. But in the 80s and 90s, suburbia became in many ways less rather than more urbane because of what McGregor calls the "growth of a privatised lifestyle". In the postwar years, suburbia meant incremental improvements in the size of the house, the power of the car, and the amount of stuff crammed into both, although there was still some time and energy left over from the pursuit of private materialism for some genuflection to public ideals. Fortress suburbia sailed along like fortress Australia — until the economic crisis of the 80s made this culture harder and harder to sustain.

As McGregor says, suburbia "has become stretched, broken up, subdivided, the victim of falling incomes and falling expectations, worried about jobs, homes and kids, and many of its members don't hold out much hope for things getting better in the future." All may look well from the yard, but sometimes behind the security screen door, the proud house may stand empty, the appliances flogged off to keep up with the repayments. There's no time and not much hope left for anything but defending the fortress from the debt collectors and the tax office. There's definitely no time and no hope left for coping with too many new ideas.

The refusal to take at their word the political and cultural talking heads appearing in the media has a real basis. For decades, suburbia consumed not just more and more stuff, but the idea that the fair go consists in consuming more and more stuff. This was, as a popular TV game show named it, the *Great Temptation.* By the close of the 90s, consumer culture had become the last *Sale of the Century.* A commitment to consumerism is an investment in the expectation that fortress Australia would secure an ever expanding space for material growth. When this expectation appeared unfounded, the legitimacy of the talking heads who idealised, and even the celebrities that embodied, this suburban wonderland appear in a more cynical light.

This sense of crisis in the Great Australian Dream of suburban home ownership and ever expanding consumption stripped some of the legitimacy from media and political talking heads. Those who produced and distributed the flows of information on which such a culture depended were caught napping, asleep at the wheel. Those who anticipated the cultural dimension of such a crisis did not get word out through the gatekeepers of public communication. The producers of the pleasure machine of popular culture had become as suburban as its consumers, and suburban in the worst sense — inattentive to change, difference, possibility. What was required, at the arse end of the century, was a new kind of urbanity, new proposals for living in what Paul Kelly called the age of uncertainty, what the other Paul Kelly called the land of the little kings.

Notes for a New Fable

Talking heads can only propose new concepts, perceptions, feelings. It's up to culture at the everyday level to accept or reject the images and stories vectored into their domain.

What was lost in the 90s was a sense that both are equally valid parts of Australian culture. Talking heads appealed repeatedly to the 'heartland' of suburbia, as if the 'headland' of urban Australia was somehow not a legitimate part of the body politic. Many country people complain that rural Australia featured as some unmentionable nether region. While I acknowledge the seriousness of the cultural absence of rural culture from public life, it was at least strongly represented in political life through the National Party's presence in the Coalition. Urbanity, on the other hand, depended for its political efficacy on its cultural legitimacy, and the undermining of that was a problem that for me was closer to home.

Media attention in the late 90s focused on Hansonite resistance and resentment out in the suburbs to new information. This begged the question: from where comes the ability and the confidence to invoke new information? These are notes for a new fable that might affirm such a capacity, such a confidence. I can only write about what I know from experience. I'm sure there are other places, other stories about this virtual side to Australian life. I can only encourage others to tell them.

Sydney has more than its share of the culture of urbanity, although its cosmopolitanism can be a bit overstated. As the irreverent sub-tabloid magazine *Strewth!* puts it, Sydney is "a postmodern pastiche of Bangkok's traffic, LA's freeways, London's liquor laws, the wankers of Paris, the smugness of the Vatican, and the dividing wall of old Berlin."[25] Still, Sydney has been a key centre where urbanity gets transformed from a fluid way of life into stories and images proposed in mediated form. It is in Sydney that most of the media industries have for much of the country's history had their centre. The urbanity of the 1880s, of Louisa Lawson and her son Henry, fed off and fed into the *Dawn* and the *Bulletin* and many other journals both high and low. So too, the urbanity of Kenneth Slessor and the 1920s fed off and fed into *Smith's Weekly* and a host of other periodical prints. Journals like these were until very recently the main vector along which urbane formulations of the good life might propose themselves far and wide. In these pages the acceptable threshold of urbanity of the moment could be stabilised and distributed.

Critics such as Sylvia Lawson are right to point out that the urbanity of the *Bulletin*, that famous incubator of the Australian legend, was a limited affair.[26] Its pages were where key elements of the Australian settlement were formulated, most notoriously the White Australia policy. Urban life is never completely cosmopolitan, and the urbane image of the fair go it generates and transmits over the vector perhaps even less so. But urbanity has to be measured in relation to the vernacular standards of the time with which it was engaged, rather than retrospectively in terms of the cosmopolitanism of the present.

As cultural historian John Docker said of the 1890s, it was a time when Sydney "experienced a continuing expansion of urban communications networks... It was accompanied by an enlarged reading public and by the development of a lively, active, urban intelligentsia."[27] The latter were kept in work by the culture industries, and Sydney's urbane life has lived off the culture industries ever since. As literary historian Peter Kirkpatrick says of Sydney bohemia of the roaring 20s, "everyone wrote journalism".[28] In Sydney more than anywhere else in Australia, popular media have been an engine that supported an urban culture who lived by fuelling the pleasure machine with their ideas and wit. The urbane images of the good life proposed by this urban experience coalesced into a suburban culture, as its public accepted these images to live by, and live within.

Richard Neville writes of venturing into Kings Cross in the late 50s and finding jazz and the cappuccino. "It gave me goose pimples, the sense that somewhere out there in the night was a secret city waiting to be embraced."[29] Kings Cross was also where, one night in 1963, the artist Martin Sharp introduced Neville to Robert Hughes and Louise Ferrier, all of who would work in one capacity or other on *Oz* magazine, the irreverent successor to the early *Bulletin* and *Smith's*, that Neville, Richard Walsh and others started in 1963 as an outlet for what Anne Summers calls their "late adolescent oedipal revolt."[30] Neville worked on *Oz* while holding down a copywriter's job and a movie reviewing column at the *Sydney Morning Herald*. Here again is the pattern of combining paid hack work with aesthetic ambition typical of Sydney's urban culture industries.

In the mid 90s, novelist and Kings Cross identity Justine Ettler was writing book reviews for *Who Weekly*, movie reviews for Microsoft's online entertainment guide *Sidewalk* and cashing the occasional royalty cheque from her bestselling novel *The River Ophelia*. Ettler was herself as pure a product of urbane Sydney as you are likely to meet. "I grew up in the very thick of Sydney's post-WW2 cocktail culture…", she writes in *HQ Magazine*, part of the vast magazine empire Richard Walsh went on to manage for Kerry Packer. In the late 90s, *HQ Magazine* became a sort of beige refinement of the kind of magazines through which Sydney's urbane culture has proposed countless images of the fair go.[31] *Strewth!* is its shit-brown alter-ego.

Urban Sydney, particularly Kings Cross, is sometimes pictured as a world apart, removed and detached from the suburban 'heartland'. Both urban and suburban culture find it a convenient fiction to imagine a border crossing somewhere that keeps suburbia safe from the hazards of urbia, and the urban safe from the boredom of suburbia. While separate in geographical space, and separate in the spatial imagination, the vector traverses the border, linking them together, but in an unequal relationship. The machinery for producing information is in the city, and so too is a key cultural world of many of its producers. Images and stories cross the border from city to suburb, and the judgement of the suburbs heads back to the city in the sales figures and ratings. If there is to be a reaffirmation of the good life in Australia, a release from virtuality to actuality of new imaginings of who we can become, it will in part depend on this process by which the urban proposes and the suburban disposes.

Bohemians and Urbanites

The Kings Cross world of writing and drinking, partying and thinking that I described descends from a world Peter Kirkpatrick labelled "bohemian." Tony Moore picked up this theme in his ABC TV documentary *Bohemian Rhapsody*, which put images to this fable I am sketching of urban and urbane Sydney.[32] By describing it as an urbane rather than a bohemian world, I'm trying to enlarge the concept of what kind of culture might take place where many different ways of life intersect in urban space and many different tastes collide in the media produced out of that space.

Dreamtime Alice is a memoir by another Kings Cross identity, Mandy Sayer. In it she eloquently invokes the bohemian life of her father and "his musician mates and flamboyant theatre friends, who were always immersed in some hilarious tragedy."[33] Sydney once had a flourishing jazz push, about which John Clare has written.[34] There was even an intellectual bohemia of sorts. Anne Coombs documented the Sydney Libertarians of the 50s, followers of the freethinking philosopher John Anderson, who were bohemian in their refusal of a suburban work and leisure ethic, and pioneers of sexual practices such as cohabitation and serial monogamy that subsequently became suburban norms.[35] But bohemia is only the most visible part of urbane culture. The image of the writer or artist as bohemian is part of our third nature, but what's lacking from that image is the diversity of urbane life.

Bohemians have a romantic view of life as art and art as a life apart from work-a-day boredom. Urbanity seems to me to be a way of life in which refusing a working life or denigrating the allegedly poor tastes of suburbia are only some of the options. Confronting and offending it, as the *Oz* magazine crowd did is also an option. An ironic embrace of it, à la Craig McGregor is also an option. Appearing as taste maker and consumer guide for suburbia as *HQ Magazine* does is also an option. Urbanity embraces all of these ways of life. It's one of the things that makes it urbane. It's not just different kinds of people from different kinds of culture, it's the mixing of different criteria of taste that make urbanity distinctive.

What distinguishes urbanity is that it experiments with new practices of the fair go. A striking instance might be the way urban Sydney has been the space of an ongoing struggle to extend tolerance to homosexuality, which culminated — eventually — in law reform. Its public cultural expression was that unique institution, the Sydney Gay and Lesbian Mardi Gras.[36] The urbane is the propositional engine of modernity — and when modernity's routine production of the new gets boring, of postmodernity. Urbane culture grows in close proximity to flows of information. The economy that supports urbanity is one of inventing and managing flows of information, be it in the form of images or stories, news or ideas. The conversations I reported from the cocktail party are a sort of cross-section of the ant heap of such an economy.

I can't help but see things from the point of view of an urbane life — it's just second nature to me to live and work in such an environment. It's a preference for living close to the roaring traffic of information. But if I want to understand what suburban life is like, or what bush life is like, I cannot do so from the inside. I have to either become a tourist, or rely on information I can gather from one media vector or another. I could gather statistics, for example, but that won't tell me how it *feels* to live another kind of life. What might be more useful is to do what everybody else does when they want to know about other people's lives: look at the images and stories about them that constitute its common world.

Australians watch on average three hours and thirteen minutes of TV every day. About 83% of Australian households own a VCR.[37] Most Australian homes, at least in the suburbs and the towns, are close to a video rental store. If it's a matter of enjoining a conversation about the fate of fortress Australia after the fall of the Australian settlement, video and TV are the vectors that most readily traverse different cultures of place, informing them with a cyberspace. TV and video provide a common third nature of information, despite differences in the experience of the second nature of the built environment.

The screen, particularly the small screen, can be as narrow an aperture through which to communicate new information as a magazine or journal. The TV comedian Paul McDermott sums it up in a vivid anecdote: "It's amazing the amount of blusher, rouge and foundation they paint on to make you look lifelike for the cameras. That's the thing about television and performance, it's an illusion. If you didn't wear make up it'd be pretty scary, like those mornings when you drop acid and your pupils are enlarged because you're accepting so much information that you see a landscape completely different from what you normally see. Very tricky for everyone at home."[38] But as many people who have been tripping in front of the television know, there's still plenty of information coming down that vector to overload the sensorium. It's just a question of subverting the habit of filtering it out.

What I want to do in the next chapter is use some television and film images from the 90s as the pretext for proposing an understanding of what it is about this land of the little kings that the unspeakable majority of suburbia resist and resent and refuse. While I won't be getting so much information out of this landscape that it will look like an acid trip, I hope a notion or two about how to think more creatively and productively about the future might flicker across the screen.

chapter **6**

Screening suburbia

Australia is a huge rest home, where no unwelcome news is ever wafted onto the pages of the worst newspapers in the world.

Germaine Greer

Instead of despising the suburbs we should work to improve them.

Hugh Stretton

Suburban Television

Once, when I was a kid, I was walking down a suburban street at night, when I noticed a rhythmic flickering of light from inside the houses. Though screened from view by the drawn curtains, the lights from a row of separate houses were all pulsing in time. And then I heard the music and I knew: everyone was watching the same show — *Number 96*. At night suburbia locked its doors, turned its back on the street, and watched the common world go by on TV.

This was a third nature in which existed the rural life of *Bellbird*, and the suburban dramas of *Certain Women*. But it was the slightly urbane and certainly risque world of *Number 96* that people turned on — and that turned people on. Chris McAuliffe is a perceptive cultural historian who, like Tofts and McQuire, Lumby and Marshall, is of that generation raised on television. He notes that while in the 70s "television persisted in contrasting city to country in programs like *Matlock* and *Bellbird*, it also began, with series such as *Number 96* and *Certain Women* to represent urban life as a heterogeneous mix of age, gender, ethnicity and sexuality."[1]

What I remember as distinctive about *Number 96* is that it was an apartment block rather like the one in which I lived as a teenager in Newcastle. I had a suburban childhood, but an urban adolescence, which is perhaps why I'm sensitive to the difference between them. But in TV drama it was rare to see much acknowledgment that the urban even existed — except on *Number 96*. Some of the voices and characters on the show were suburban enough. But then there was Don, the gay character, played by Joe Hasham. There weren't any gay people in my building, as far as I could tell, but there were some elsewhere in the neighbourhood. They kept themselves to themselves, but *Number 96* gave them an existence in public culture, and made that existence seem to me like third nature.

Australian television of the 90s also created a public culture divided into urban, suburban and rural zones. It included Les Hiddins, the *Bush Tucker Man*. He was a rare image of the self-reliant, khaki individualist with whom the *Bulletin* of the 1890s populated the outback. A rather more urbane image was Paul McDermott, doing his monologue at the start of the ABC comedy show *Good News Week*, dressed in a Valentino pin-stripe suit.[2] McDermott played host to this game format show which, in true urbane style, had no glittering prizes. His opening monologue, scripted by some of the country's top joke writers, satirised the week's news stories, adding an ironic layer to the temporary information of the moment. McDermott excelled at this kind of urbane display of verbal skill, and according to *HQ Magazine* journalist Amrutha Slee was approached by one of the major parties to run for parliament.[3]

Where Hiddins was laconic, direct and spoke broad Australian; McDermott was witty, ironic and spoke the cultivated tongue. McDermott's celebrity was as urban as Hiddins' was outback. McDermott displayed the ultimate urbane quality, which is a mastery of information about information itself. Hiddins appeared as having information only about things in the world, although he would pause for a story, should one be required to immortalise the meaning of a place to permanent memory.

In between the figures of Hiddins in his bush hat and McDermott with his delicate hairdo, was the man in the smart denim pants and woolly jumper. There's something slightly odd about people clumped around their televisions in the living room at night watching a show about a man who stands around in people's back yards during the day. What I found curious about *Burke's Backyard* was the way a gardening show could express so much about the suburban ideal of the good life.

The broadcaster Allan Ashbolt wrote about Sydney's upper North shore garden suburbs, at a time when the Vietnam war obliged suburbia to come to grips with some new information about the world. The suburban, wrote Ashbolt, "…tries to establish a symbiotic relationship with nature. Through the process of cyclical change and transformation, of organic decay and growth, he seeks an emotional equilibrium denied him in the devitalised, mechanistic routines of financial, mercantile and cultural power centres. The garden represents his one important opportunity to understand the mainsprings of creative energy and, further, to project his moral imagination, his essential humanity, into objective forms." The trouble for Ashbolt's suburban was that "the garden shows him the way to serenity, but only the city can buy him the leisure to choose it."[4] In *Burke's Backyard*, all such qualms are banished.

Don Burke appeared as a bearded, middle-aged man with a relaxed stance. He usually popped up in a yard, talking from somebody's private world of plants and pots, talking the common language of the garden as an expression of the fair go. Burke praised gardens that showed originality and creativity, but the stress was on creating a private world behind the fence. Creative flair aside, the fair go is about stability and consistency, having a yard that, over the course of years, becomes a world set apart from the common world. If there is skill and ability in this suburbia it is deployed for the benefit of the shrubs.

If there were people from a common world here they appeared as 'celebrity gardeners' — Poppy King or Pauline Hanson seen outside their public role in business or politics. What was curious was the way *Burke's Backyard* offered an image of a public life composed of private places and passions. Burke appeared as the public figure as gardener, as someone who shares a suburban dream of tending one's own plot, controlling and managing a stable world behind the fence. It took some art to compose such an image. Estranged Hanson adviser John Pasquarelli alleged that the pot plants Pauline appeared with were not her own but had been bought on a $600 government grant for the purposes of decorating her electoral office.[5]

Les Hiddins went out into the natural world, where he does not just gather roots and berries, he gathers information about how to live off the land. Paul McDermott didn't go anywhere much beyond the cab ride from his home to the ABC studio, but his skill was in appearing to be abreast of the latest information sheeting along the vectors. Don Burke, by contrast, did not go out into the larger world, he created miniature ones within the fortress of the backyard. This is the distinguishing mark of suburban culture: its desire to maintain a separate world, into which new information can be allowed only selectively. Whether it is what plants will be permitted to grow along the back property line, or what shows the kids will be allowed to watch on TV, what distinguishes suburbia as a culture is less its physical form or location, as its *territorial* approach to information.

Suburbia can read and accept new information — as even the *Silent Majority* report showed. But it does so slowly. Suburban culture is a museum of past modes of urbanity, filtered of anything too frivolous or harebrained, but denuded too of a certain complexity and innovative spirit. The difficulty is that the Australian settlement got caught in the flux of volatile global economic and information flows, to which it adapted too slowly. There is a significant lag built into the backyard culture of everyday life.

National Broadcasting

On television, the urban and suburban have imaginary homelands. There is a bias in television towards the suburban — not surprising given that suburbia is the locus from which most television shows are read. What might be a bit of a worry though is that television seems to me increasingly made by suburbans for suburbans, without the creative tension of an urbane contribution at the production end.

By the 90s, suburbia captured even the ABC, which you would think would have some sense of duty towards trying to get new information past the high pass filter of suburban culture. The days are long gone when an anti-suburban provocateur like Allan Ashbolt could get to feed the vector. In the 90s, the ABC had nothing half as brilliant as *The Simpsons*, which is truly a classic work of television art. Its urbanity came through in the ambivalent way it imagined the American small town world of Springfield as caught in a complex web of internal and external forces. If there is new information reaching us through television in the 90s, it was more likely through *The Simpsons* on Channel 10 than *Hettie Wainthrop Investigates* on the ABC.

In the imaginary homelands of the ABC, Kings Cross appeared as an image of the urban in the TV series *Wildside*, which pictured it as a grim and colourful underworld.[6] It was a suburban image of the urban: the urban as the place of danger and crime. Cops and social workers patrol this sink for all that suburbia would like to imagine drains away toward the city. In one striking episode, two convicted paedophiles become the suspects in a child abduction. When the little girl turns up dead, her father corners the two with a shotgun on the roof of an inner city building. One, it turns out, is innocent — but he jumps to his death, tired of a life as a permanent suspect. The other, we discover, is guilty.

While it may be a good thing that information about sexual abuse is out in the open, a topic for television drama, what was striking is the way the paedophile appeared as an urban predator, detached from home and family. Suburbia is still not ready, it seems, to process information about more intimate forms of sexual abuse, inside the family, the home, the neighbourhood. In ABC TV's subdivisions, crime comes to the suburb from without. Suburbia is a neutral, innocent, self-contained, self-absorbed world that can accept information about the world at large, provided television observes the convention of seeing evil as something external to its world. Evil is something banished inwards, in *Wildside* to the city, or outwards, to the periphery, as in movies like *Idiot Box*, *The Boys*, and Geoffrey Wright's *Metal Skin*.[7]

This suburban picture of the urban was not necessarily any more accurate than urban images of the suburban. 'Representation' is not really the point. If we want to critique media images for their lack of reality, this is pretty easy sport, for no image is ever equal to that which it represents. What's more interesting is to think about how people use these images to map the relationship between different kinds of place that stand as emblems of ways of life. How, for example, would a 1998 ABC viewer think about her or his place in the world in relation to *Wildside*, on Wednesday night, and *Sea Change*, on Saturdays?

Sea Change pictured a small coastal town as a rural version of communitarian paradise.[8] A world peopled with quirky characters who have their petty hatreds of each other but still form a community. We see it mostly from the point of view of Laura (Sigrid Thornton), a former big city lawyer who becomes the town magistrate. It's a show very much centred around Laura's public and private judgements. It is hardly an accurate representation of small town life, or anything else. Rather, it is an expression of that strong desire, in a suburban world perceived to be under siege from new information, to retreat to the country.

Where *Wildside* was a suburban view of the urban, *Sea Change* was an urban view of the rural. Or rather, of a renewal of a relaxed and comfortable relation to information that suburbia might acquire from this fantasy of the rural. But perhaps there was some truth in Samuel Johnson's judgement on those who leave town for the country: "The utmost they can hope to gain is the change of ridiculousness to obscurity, and the privilege of having fewer witnesses to a life of folly."[9]

If there was a positive image of the urban as a place and the urbane as a culture in ABC drama of in the 90s it was on *Heartbreak High*.[10] With its weeknight six o'clock timeslot, few working adults were probably even aware of its existence. At least here the ABC managed to produce an image of the urban subdivision of imaginary space that wasn't about grit and grime, crime and chaos. The show followed its diverse range of young characters from the schoolyard to a range of encounters on the fringes of an urban world. A predictable strain of moralising aside, the emphasis was on encounters that require new ways of adapting to new information. While a suburbanised ABC could express the adaptability of the young, it exempted suburban adults.

Castles in the Stream

In the Australian spatial imagination, suburbia runs in bands around an urban core. Like the rings of Saturn, they are finely graded orbits of particles, surrounding an urban ball of hot air. Out beyond that lies empty space. The larger and richer and denser particles cluster close in the inner rings, and by finely graded degrees they become less rich and more sparse on the way out to nothingness.

The movie that epitomised the suburbia of the outer rings in the 90s was *The Castle*. It tells the story of the Kerrigan family, who live at number 3 Highview Crescent, Coolaroo.[11] Dale Kerrigan (Stephen Curry) narrates a family fable about an encounter with the unknown world of big business and big government. Dale introduces us to the Kerrigans, and to their home at Highview Crescent. Throughout the movie, conspicuous signs proliferate of the outer suburban culture to which the Kerrigans belong. But while the visual repertoire of the film encourages the audience to read the Kerrigans as very culturally specific, as located in an outer band of the suburban rings of Saturn, the story cuts through this ring to reveal it works in a very different way. If the visual world of the film makes the Kerrigans into almost everyone's idea of outer suburban taste, the narrative world makes of them a heroic expression of a nobility that crosses the distinctions between the bands of suburban culture.

The Kerrigans live near the airport, right under the flight path. One day a property valuer appears, and Darryl Kerrigan (Michael Caton) proudly shows him around his pride and joy, the house his family has made a home, and to which he continually adds extensions that seem never quite to get finished. The property is a nightmare of what the architecture critic Robin Boyd called "featurism", which "…may be defined as the subordination of the essential whole and the accentuation of selected separate features."[12] It displays everything Boyd would have loathed about outer suburban taste. Darryl points to the fake chimney with particular pride, as it adds, in his estimation, "charm." The incredulous look of the valuer permits the audience to take this ironically and side with the valuer against the excesses of outer suburban taste, placing themselves in an inner suburban locus of superior taste and knowledge.

The valuation, it soon turns out, is for the compulsory acquisition of the property by a giant consortium called Airlink, who want to build a freight handling facility on the land. Airlink have the authority to buy up the whole street, and the Kerrigans find that the elderly retired man, the divorcee and the Arab family they share the street with are also to lose their homes. Darryl resolves to fight this, and takes his case to the local council. In a telling remark, he responds to the sympathetic noises of the council officer by asking, in an impatient tone, "will you please stop pretending to be on my side." However we might read the doubtful taste and closed world of the Kerrigans, it's hard to feel sympathy for the complete disregard authority shows them.

Darryl enlists the help of local solicitor Dennis Denuto (Tiriel Mora) to take his case to court. We see Dennis in his suburban solicitor's office, swearing at the photocopier, which he never quite manages to get working. Dennis has his heart in the right place, but he lacks the skill with information to get the Kerrigan's case across. "In summing up", he addresses the judge, "it's the constitution, it's Mabo, it's justice, it's law, it's the vibe. No, that's it, it's the vibe." The judge, played straight by the distinguished actor Robyn Nevin, is unimpressed.

While waiting for the judgement, Darryl strikes up a conversation with another man waiting around the courtroom, Laurence Hammil, or Laurie, as Darryl immediately starts calling him. Laurie (played by veteran actor Charles 'Bud' Tingwell) is at the courthouse to watch his son's first appearance as a barrister. Darryl, who addresses Laurie with the openness and equality that befits a mate, shares his own sense of pride in the achievement of his daughter Tracey, who graduated from the hairdressing course at the technical college, the first Kerrigan with a tertiary qualification. The conversation ends about there, as Darryl is summoned back to hear the bad news, that he has lost the case and the Kerrigans will be thrown out of their house in two weeks.

Just when all appears lost, and the Kerrigans are packing up their appallingly tacky collection of stuff, Laurie appears. He is, it turns out, a constitutional lawyer. He thinks the Kerrigans have a case. Laurie puts it to the High Court that under Section 51 of the Constitution, the government can only acquire someone's property "on just terms". Airlink's offer to compensate the Kerrigans for the loss of their house is not just, because that house is also a home, and the price of a home cannot be assessed by a property valuer. "Competing rights cannot be weighed, one against the other", he argues. Social justice is a bit more complicated than putting a price on things. Valuing goods is not the same as valuing the fair go. "That's what this is all about, being just."

The Castle proposes that no less a force than the Constitution guarantees the right of suburbia to resist change from without. If there is to be change, it must be "on just terms". It cannot simply dispossess people who have done no harm other than in remaining somewhat insulated, within their suburban castle, from the forces at work in a wider world. Regardless of the degree of irony with which we might be invited to read the Kerrigan's taste, there is little doubt that the emotional pull of *The Castle* is toward extending our sympathy to the Kerrigans. If there is to be change, it should respect the rights even of outer suburbia. Airlink can build their freight handling facility on the site of the old quarry, which might cost more financially but will cost less in human terms. Change has to be negotiated rather than imposed.

Sympathy is, in *The Castle*, what accumulates as the fable unfolds. When his daughter Tracey marries Con, we see Darryl's speech at the reception, in which he makes tasteless jokes about the Greeks, who, he says, "have a bit of a reputation." But through the private connection between his own family he comes to accept Con and the Petropolis family by extending the sympathy he feels for his family. When it turns out the whole of Highview Crescent suffer the same fate as the Kerrigans, he contacts them all, organises the court action on their joint behalf, and puts up poor old Jack's share of the costs. Sympathy need not stop at outer suburbia. "I'm really starting to understand how the Aborigines feel",

Darryl exclaims at his lowest ebb, recognising that they were dispossessed of their land on unjust terms too. And it is the sympathy Laurie feels for Darryl, who is a nice bloke and means well, but cannot comprehend what is happening to him. His sympathy is for someone who lacks a kind of information that has suddenly become vital.

Information is a recurring theme of the movie. "What do you know about lead?" Darryl asks the property valuer. Apparently there is toxic waste under the site somewhere, but Darryl knows nothing about it. After the Kerrigan case makes him famous, Dennis will represent the people affected by the lead too. When Con and Tracey, (played by Eric Bana and Sophie Lee) return from a trip to Thailand, the Kerrigans can't wait to get information out of them, for nobody in the family has travelled in a plane before. "The place is full of culture", Con tells them. "Chockas", confirms Trace. When Tracey tells her mum (Anne Tenney) that she is "not having kids until she is at least 23", Sal remarks, "times have changed."

Things may not have changed as much here in outer suburbia as among people who might feel they are a ring or two closer in than the Kerrigans, but the Kerrigans are neither stupid nor completely ill informed. They live under the flight path but until Tracey and Con's honeymoon, have not travelled anywhere — except for son Wayne who went to jail. They live on the edge of the vector, but lack the means to participate in the movement bustling about it. Darryl drives a tow truck, so his whole life is about the accidents generated by movement. *The Castle* expresses the predicament of suburbia, about to be Airlinked into the world by globalisation; it expresses a sympathy that can cut across the stratification of suburbia when confronted with change, and it expresses the terms on which change is acceptable — "on just terms."

Suburban Cinema

Australian cinema throughout the 90s also proposed more troubled and troubling images of suburbia than *The Castle*. P. J. Hogan's movie *Muriel's Wedding* is about leaving a provincial, suburban world and coming to the city.[13] Muriel (Toni Collette) wants to get out of Porpoise Spit, where her father

Bill 'The Battler' Heslop (played by Bill Hunter) reigns as the local political boss. Muriel hasn't had a job in two years. She finds both her peers and her family oppressive. "I know I'm not normal but I'm trying to change."

Muriel has her own style, but there is no place for it in Porpoise Spit. She takes off for Sydney, where she achieves her ambition of becoming someone. "Now my life is as good as an ABBA song!" She gets her face on the cover of *Woman's Day*. But after a few diversions, she finds that the good life means being with her friend Rhonda (Rachel Griffiths). She finds a way of life for herself in an urbane world. The film embodies some key urbane values: friendship extended to strangers; the right of self-invention; the cultivation of life as style; a subtle and contingent process of inventing new versions of the fair go out of the virtual lexicon of culture.

A very different kind of 90s movie about a very different kind of friendship is David Ceasar's *Idiot Box*. Mick (Jeremy Sims) and Kev (Ben Mendelsohn) are two fringe suburban likely lads, unemployed and bored.[14] Mick has urbane tendencies. He makes up poems that everyone tells him aren't poems, because they don't rhyme. Everyone's a critic. "I reckon if you say something is a poem, then it is", says Mick, spontaneously inventing conceptual art for himself.

Kev has other ideas. Watching a news story about a bank robber on TV, he hatches a plan to rob a bank. They are armed with Mick's concept, distilled from years of TV cop shows, about the five ways robbers get caught. This story runs in parallel to that of the successful bank robber who, unknown to Kev and Mick, lives nearby. His problem is that his junkie wife puts so much of the take up her arm that he has to keep robbing banks to keep her going.

As Labor parliamentarian Mark Latham points out, there were markedly increasing spatial inequalities across suburbia in the 90s.[15] This is particularly noticeable in Sydney, with its class divide between the more affluent coastal pockets in the east, north and south, and a vast western periphery in which there are serious pockets of poverty. *Idiot Box* is a black parody of the differences within suburban culture, with its parallel stories of successful and unsuccessful outer suburban life. The successful, skilled, professional bank robber cooks a roast dinner for his junkie wife. Meanwhile, unskilled, unemployed characters plot an amateurish attempt at breaking in to the same industry, but fail through their lack of skill. Kev's mum says of him what Muriel's dad says of her — "useless." Muriel succeeds in inventing, at least for herself, a use. Kev fails. Both have much the same resources to go on: whatever the media tosses up on their front lawns and chucks into the living room.

These two movies are examples of the sort of things the media proposes to a public — in this case, propositions about the ways out of suburbia. Interestingly, both are also about ways of using the media itself as a resource from which to draw proposals. As the neighbourhood drug dealer says about his own 'idiot box', "you can sit home and see everything in the world and see how it works. Whole worlds in a box in your room." If bank robbing was not such a good proposal for Kev to take up, Mick at least learned how to go down on his girlfriend thanks to videos. What keeps Muriel going while her father tells her she is useless is her ABBA tape, which proposes to her another kind of fair go, and which enables her to seek out a life "as good as 'Dancing Queen'."

Both *Idiot Box* and *Muriel's Wedding* play with a third nature of suburban images that previous movies and TV shows and magazine articles proposed and which have become part of a public world. They rely on suburbia as their enabling fable. Suburbia is a complex of images and stories as much as, perhaps more than, any actual place. 'Suburbia' made the experience of a suburb tangible and arguable; and by feeling and arguing through such fables, people made them real. In participating in the process, a people became a public. As John Hartley says, suburbia is "an image-saturated place which is both intensely personal (inside people's homes and heads) and extensively abstract", it is "a place where people make themselves".[16]

But unlike Hartley, I am not so sure that Australians can continue to live within the enabling fable of suburbia. It has not been a flexible enough space for self-invention. Uncertainties and insecurities generated by the economic rationalisation of the 80s and 90s produced new images and stories that made the old suburban dream seem unstable and unsustainable. A movie like *The Boys* points to a quite different kind of proposition about suburbia, as something threatened and threatening.[17] Even more than *Idiot Box*, this is a counter-fable of suburbia with no way out.

As University of Western Sydney academic Diane Powell argues, in the 80s and 90s 'the west' and 'the westie', the place and the people of Sydney's western suburbs, became images of suburbia gone wrong. They were "the areas constructed as *problems* and their people as *victims*."[18] While not unprecedented, such a concern seems to me to point to a struggle to redefine an enabling fable for Australian culture through new propositions about what the fair go might be — and might not be.

Beyond Suburbia

Two suburban movies that place stress on absorbing new information were *Sum of Us*, directed by Kevin Dowling and Geoff Burton, and Baz Luhrmann's *Strictly Ballroom*. "You should read a few books. There's more to life than what you see on television", or so Harry (Jack Thompson) counsels his son Geoff (Russell Crowe) in *Sum of Us*. Harry is a widower. He pilots a ferry around Sydney Harbour, lives in the traditional working class suburb of Rozelle, and drinks at the William Wallace. He's a character not far from the straight up Aussie blokes that are the backbone of Jack Thompson's celebrity. What is different about Harry is that his son is gay, and that Harry accepts and loves his son regardless — if in his own fashion.

That Harry has an open mind is the element that diverges from the 'ocker' character that is part of Thompson's range. Harry has not only had to think through and learn about his gay son, but has also had to rethink his memories of his grandmother, and the lesbian relationship she had late in her life. In order to understand his gay son, Harry does his research. He goes out with Geoff to gay bars one night, so that he knows something about the life. He buys gay porn magazines to find out what is and isn't safe sex. These mags are his undoing, as he leaves them lying around the house when Joyce, (Deborah Kennedy), the new love in this old widower's life, comes around.

These scenes of the open mind seeking out ways of incorporating new information are juxtaposed against the less understanding Joyce and the family of Geoff's love interest Greg (John Polson). Greg's parents find out Greg is gay when they see his image on the ABC telecast of the Mardi Gras parade. You can't learn everything from television, but they learn the one thing their son hides from them and that his father in particular can't accept. Suburbia appears as a zone of partial urbanity and partial conformity, and appropriately enough the film takes place mostly in Sydney's inner west, close to the city, but not in it or quite of it.

"You're all so scared you wouldn't know what you thought": the issue is not homophobia, but fear of new dance steps. And that might be as good an image as any for the problem of how suburbia is to incorporate new information into itself. Scott (Paul Mercurio) wants to dance his own "crowd pleasing" steps in the big ballroom dancing contest. The powers that be see this as a threat to their authority. The last thing suburban authority wants is too much new information.

Authority here is Barry Fife, played by that great Australian actor, Bill Hunter. As Barry Fife he is cast in a role not unlike his town counsellor in *Muriel's Wedding*. He is the suburban Aussie bloke gone a bit off. In *The Dismissal*, where he plays Whitlam government Minister Rex Conner, he's gone right off. In *The Adventures of Priscilla, Queen of the Desert* he shows a more open minded attitude, more like Jack Thompson in *Sum of Us*. But over the years, from *The Dismissal* and *Newsfront* to *Muriel's Wedding* and *Strictly Ballroom*, Bill Hunter's ability to convey stubbornness seems more and more to cast him as a fortress of outdated authority rather than of moral resilience.

Strictly Ballroom is, among other things, a movie about where new information comes from. Scott finds a partner for his crazy new steps in Fran (Tara Morice), who helps him learn by leading him back to the source. Scott wants to dance Latin, and, as it happens, Fran's father is a fabulous flamenco dancer. Like Scott, Fran comes from a dancing family, and a dancing culture, and like Scott, she wants to find a way to make the old steps new again, combining different flows, movements, rhythms, styles.

Cultural studies scholar Professor Graeme Turner noted in the early 90s that films like *Strictly Ballroom* imagine a "multi-

plicity of Australian identities". What *Strictly Ballroom* proposed to its public was "not the submerging of difference
within a consensual model... but the more difficult task of
maintaining differences even as they are blended to form
something new — a hybrid dance form."[19] What I think
became clearer in the late 90s was the spatial dimension of
the struggle for this hybridity. The proposal of hybridity is an
urbane one, but the site of the conflict is the imaginary place
of suburbia. *Strictly Ballroom* is interesting because what it
proposes is that the materials for an urbane, hybrid culture
are already present in suburbia. Fran lives nearby to Scott.
But their worlds have remained separate, until Scott's spontaneous urbanity leads him to seek new steps. The urbanity
of the film consists in proposing to suburbia its own virtuality, proposing to it that the potential already exists within it
for difference, hybridity, multiplicity.

The threat to suburban stability and order posed by the
recognition of the homosexual or the migrant is, among
other things, the threat of new information. She or he
requires that suburbia invent new moves, new ways of combining different forces, so new variations on the fair go
might emerge that accommodate what is new. Finding ways
to cope with new information keeps the fair go alive, by pre-
venting a fall into fear of change and strangeness. The experience of coping with new information can give rise to a
conceptual understanding of the link between the particulars of a life and the good life in general. This is because new
information breaks through the experience of everyday life
as second nature, as something that is just obvious that
doesn't require a second thought.

When the images and stories on the screen are a work of
art as well as entertainment, they break through the experience of cinema and television as third nature, as something
that is just obvious that doesn't require a second thought. Art
expresses a virtual world that cannot be taken for granted.
This, incidentally, is why the artist figures as a threat to suburban second nature as much as the migrant or the homosexual, even though artists can in every other sense be
'normal' — white, heterosexual, and male.

This is also why the artist, and the art, that is also a stranger
in terms of sexuality or ethnicity is doubly threatening. The

threat then is not only of exposure to new information in the form of stories and images, but also the possibility of a new concept about how images are supposed to be read, for these works of art cannot be accommodated within the existing practice of the good life, but must either be refused, or accepted as incitements to think the good life otherwise. *Sum of Us* and *Strictly Ballroom* reveal differences that are already present in the space of suburbia, but just not acknowledged by it.

An encouraging sign is the existence in the 90s of a small group of films that express a dawning suspicion that the blockage of flows of information through suburban culture might be a problem. These films deal with the question of whose interests are served by such a blockage, and also with the question of how to cope with such information when it does circumvent the blockages to its flow. In Kathryn Millard's film *Parkland*, Cate Blanchett uncovers bad information about the suburban Adelaide of her childhood, where her policeman father turns out to have been corrupt.[20] In John Ruane's *Dead Letter Office*, Miranda Otto decides that the whole bureaucratic system of readdressing lost mail has gone astray.[21] Both these films advance an even more challenging idea: that the whole practice of filtering and blocking information that is at the heart of suburban culture needs to be questioned. Interestingly, in both cases it is young women who have made some kind of break from suburban space that do the questioning.

The power to restrict information seems to be the province of an unseen "upstairs". In both *Dead Letter Office* and *The Interview*, this upstairs remains unseen — not the least of their powers is the restriction of information about their own actions and interests.[22] *The Interview* depicts a particularly paranoid world in which cops interrogate suspects, while the cops are themselves suspects, interrogated by internal affairs. As in *Parkland* and *Wildside*, Tony Martin plays the hard boiled copper, a flawed bloke caught between knowing too much about the bad life and knowing too little about the powers that be. He is the empiricist as hero, who has lost faith, who doubts everything, who is flawed and knows it, but who keeps working on making it come out, if not right, then at least not too badly. He has no concept of the fair go yet, but he keeps looking for clues, regardless. In *True Love and Chaos* as well as in *Dead Letter Office*, Miranda Otto similarly embodies a certain kind of curiosity, although of a more private and less compromised kind. She detects what suburbia would willingly forget about the imperfect workings of its idealised family.

A life without access to information is the bleak scenario of *The Boys*. Of the three boys, Brett (David Wenham) knows just enough to manipulate the other two, taunting Glen (John Polson again) with the information that his lousy job is paying less than the basic wage, and reminding Stevie (Anthony Hayes) that nobody is going to pop out of the television and tell them they've won the lottery. The three boys have so little information to go on that when they go out to settle an old score at the bottle shop, they find it is closed, and nobody can remember the location of the all night convenience store, so they can't rob that as an alternative.

In *Strictly Ballroom*, Barry Otto plays the antithesis of the Bill Hunter style of Australian masculinity. Where Hunter's celebrity contains a kernel of paternalist authority, Otto's presence often invokes weakness and acquiescence. As in *Strictly Ballroom*, so too in *Dead Letter Office* and even *Kiss or Kill*, Otto is the Australian man too completely suburbanised, in the sense of giving in to the allegedly 'feminising' aspect of suburban culture. As Chris McAuliffe notes, suburbia has a gendered polarity: "the suburb as private, domestic, passive, consumerist, conformist — as feminine; the city (or bush) as public, active, self-sufficient and individualist — as masculine." Barry Otto is the suburban male pacified by the rituals of suburban everyday life, "an acceptance of regimentation that was the antithesis of both the larrikinism of the bush and bohemianism of the city."[23] But he almost always carries with him a secret.

Bill Hunter is the suburban male whose reached a compromise with the feminising effect of suburbia, although hardly a happy one. The toupée eventually slips off his head in *Strictly Ballroom*. In *Muriel's Wedding*, his fate is both more tragic and more ambiguous. The suicide of his wife thrusts him into the domestic management of his household, but he still has enough political pull to get Bob Hawke to send a telegram to her funeral. Only in *Priscilla* is he rewarded with a happy ending, for abandoning his Filipina wife and going bush with a brace of Drag Queens.

In this context, *The Boys* is the dark side of that bush larrikinism, exiled from the bush to the outer suburbs. The boys' individualist and active urges take the form of violence against women. The intellectual and emotional trauma of *The Boys* lies in its bleak assessment of the intractable nature of an Australian masculinity at many removes from any suburban convention. These are boys not even a mother, in the end, can love. It's a film about what the inner suburbs fear about the outer suburbs — and these are the imaginary coordinates of suburbia's spatial sensibility.

Welcome to Woop Woop

What makes Stephan Elliott's *Adventures of Priscilla, Queen of the Desert* interesting in this context is that it is about the confrontation of the urbane with the bush without too much suburbia in between.[24] Elliott's tactic is to recycle the culture of the ocker, but in a rather different context.

As the poet and columnist Max Harris put it, "the most fascinating event, coincident with the Whitlam era, was the resurgence of that ill-educated, dogmatic, incoherent, and arrogant psychological phenomenon — the Australian ocker."[25] The ocker was a creation of urbane culture of the 70s. As a way of popularising urbane artistic and intellectual dissent, artists and writers used the ocker as their vehicle for the transgression of suburban strictures, once the province of the larrikin. Those suburbia resisted because of their intellectual or creative excess felt a kinship, or rather a mateship, with those suburbia charged with physical excess. Hard thinkers linked arms with hard drinkers. What John Docker identified as the "carnivalesque" seized upon suburban landscapes whenever the ocker arrived to turn the place upside down.[26] The ocker's progress: belching, farting, puking, pissing, shouting, drinking, gorging, fucking and fighting across suburbia — it was a physical expression of an urbane fantasy of revenge against suburban conformity.

The ocker was not universally popular. It hardly need be pointed out now that he was a male fantasy, although surely a self-satirising one. Bruce Beresford's 1972 film *The*

Adventures of Barry McKenzie is hardly a fable of triumphant masculine power. His 1976 film of David Williamson's astute and knowing play *Don's Party*, is striking for its honesty about the ocker as "bullshit artist" and about his failure to understand the women with whom he shares his life. Things improved a bit by the time one of Paul Kelly's blokey characters could ask "what makes such a sweet guy turn so mean?"[27] All the same, the ocker rampaged across the screen and into the hearts of suburbia. He was an ambivalent, rather than a critical weapon, absorbed back into the fold.

Max Harris identified the crucial flaw with the ocker, and the urbanisation through the ocker of the fabled frontier ethos of mateship: "It is a social imperative which calls for blind aggressive loyalty to your tribal group, whether they be made up of criminals, thugs, or theologians." The trouble with the ocker was that he exacerbated the suburban tendency to resist new information. He was famously impervious to feminism.

This is what makes *Priscilla* such a striking fable. It uses the road film to stage encounters where characters confront the unknown and are thrown back on their wits, forced to improvise, to become new versions of themselves. As such, it is no different from other 90s Australian road movies like *True Love and Chaos, Doing Time for Patsy Cline, Kiss or Kill* and *Heaven's Burning*.[28] In the road movie, the encounter with the unknown happens somewhere else and to someone else, not in suburbia. In *Priscilla*, the innovation is in the recycling of the ocker mentality in the most unlikely form — the ocker drag queen. Ockers, like larrikins, could dress like dags, but they could also be as 'flash' as Ned Kelly. The ocker drag queen simply gets the love of well cut cloth and the company of other men out of the closet.

It's on the basis of excess — excess in drinking, fighting, dressing and wisecracking that *Priscilla* transports its three ocker drag queens, played by Terence Stamp, Hugo Weaving and Guy Pearce, across the gap between the urbane world of the Imperial Hotel in Newtown, Sydney, and the vernacular bush world they have to cross to reach Uluru. Their kinship with Bob, played by Bill Hunter, the honourable ocker, is cemented by a mutual understanding of the role of excess. Cultural differences are negotiated with a drinking contest or a song, cultural conflicts settled with a bit of biff, and in the end three mates in sequins take the ocker fantasy back to its imaginary homeland, the bush frontier. An old image from the cultural wardrobe has done some new work in introducing the idea of differences in sexual preference, and transmitting it over the media vector. *Silent Majority III* might complain of too much homosexuality in the media, but I suspect that *Priscilla* slipped under that radar and was welcomed, regardless.

The Stockman's Hall of Fame

Priscilla cut against the grain in the 90s, for it was a time when suburbia became not merely layered, for it was always layered into inner and outer bands, it became divided. Part of suburbia looked toward the city and its urbane aspirations, while part of it felt increasingly locked out of the fair go and turned resentful, making common cause with the rural hinterlands. Many people benefited from the opening up of the Australian economy during the Hawke and Keating years. But the benefits were very unevenly shared. Inner suburbia connected more with the global opportunities than outer suburbia. There was not much joy in it for Coolaroo.

In my book, *The Virtual Republic*, completed in 1997, I spoke of some different proposals for imagining Australia. The idea of Australia is itself, after all, a 'public thing'. It is an object that, despite being a fantasy, is one that different people apply themselves to thinking and dreaming about out loud. Two imaginary Australias I mentioned were the virtual republic and the vernacular republic. The virtual republic I was trying to imagine is, I now realise, an urbane one.[29] It is an image of an Australia that people compose out of the most useful and interesting conjunctions they can imagine of their many and various differences. It is an image of an Australia not limited by any preconceived idea about how things might fit together or how they might change over time. An image of an Australia that can become whatever Australians make of it, drawing on whatever resources are at hand, from any and everywhere — just as Muriel does or the boys of *Priscilla* do.

The vernacular republic, evoked by the poet Les Murray is essentially a rural one.[30] It is an Australia based in the language of the land which is easy going, tolerant and egalitarian up to a point, but which is hostile to urban culture and its outward looking cosmopolitanism. It is a mental image of Australia bound by its past to the perpetuation of values forged out of distinctly rural structures of feeling. It is an image of an Australia that ought to be bound by its past to reject innovations that might obscure this essentially rural nature of its being.

Graeme Turner was prescient in identifying the "revival of rural-nationalist mythologies" in the 80s, and identified the opening of the Stockman's Hall of Fame in Longreach, Queensland as an emblematic space for it. The building itself, Turner pointed out, borrowed elements of "urban postmodernism" and combined it with traditional materials, resulting in something like a "cross between the Sydney Opera House and a shearing shed." The Hall of Fame, as Turner foresaw, was a site that could readily become a media image. It's popularity indicated that the signs of what Murray calls the vernacular republic still had the "capacity to revive and resituate themselves within a changing Australian identity."[31]

Murray's was a genial and fair-minded vision, except when it came to urban culture's talking heads, which he termed the Whitlam Ascendancy and its successor, the Hawke Ascendancy — talking heads who supported Labor governments in exchange for access to state power. Murray sees urban and suburban talking heads as equally prone to foreign fashions and remote from the authentic cultural roots of Australia. But he tends to define 'roots' negatively, by criticising the vernacular republic's enemy.

In the right wing populism that rose out of the hinterlands in the late 90s, and captured time on all the media vectors, there is an element of Murray's refusal of the legitimacy of urban culture. The difference is that the populists combine it with resentment of Aborigines and Asians and perhaps even Jewish bankers and anyone else who might make a convenient scapegoat. At a time when the rationalisation of banking, public services and telephony led to a decline in the quality of life in the bush, combined with the ill effects of unfair competition from subsidised primary produce from Europe and America, not to mention the tightening of gun laws following the massacre at Port Arthur, rural Australia

had a gutful. At a time when the rationalisation of manufacturing led to the disappearance of blue collar jobs and the
rapid decline of former manufacturing centres, not to
mention that new jobs being created in the economy
demanded quite different skills and were often located in
quite different places, a lot of manual workers also felt that
the Hawke and Keating years handed them the rough end of
the pineapple.

Both groups increasingly refused even a passive consent to
the culture and values of the urban triangle of Sydney/
Melbourne/Canberra. At a time when urban culture finally
came into its own in Australian cultural life, as not just a
noisy resistance to suburban values but an active creator of
an alternative to it, the space within which Australian culture
negotiated its differences came under pressure from the hinterland. The virtual confronted the vernacular as rival
claimants for the imagination of a mostly suburban public.

This may be why Prime Minister John Howard chose the
Stockman's Hall of Fame at Longreach as the site at which to
make an appearance defending his 10 point plan on native
title. It was also where Pauline Hanson chose to announce
her Aboriginal affairs policy during the 1998 election campaign. Or rather, her non-policy: "Under One Nation policy,
the issue of Aboriginality would no longer exist as benefits by
virtue of race would no longer exist," she said, before the
event descended into a screaming match between Hanson
and the press.[32] That performance was a low point in the rash
of media coverage of hard Hansonism. Both hard
Hansonism and Howard's soft Hansonism appealed to a vernacular alternative to urbanity. On Hanson's part, an alternative to both the economic and cultural side of urbanity; on
Howard's part, more selectively to urban support for reconciliation on terms that would be fair to Aboriginal people.

I will return in the next chapter to the question of why the
Hawke and Keating experiments in economic and cultural
change ran aground in the mid-90s. Right now I want to
define further the urbanity that I think was a crucial element
in the cultural landscape of the 80s and 90s. Since I see the
world through its distinctive structures of feeling, it seems to
me important to localise my own point of view within the
milieu that shapes my sensibility and way of thinking.

Media vectors criss-cross space, offering images of different ways of life to people living in different kinds of environment. But there is one major asymmetry: the partially overlapping worlds of urbane culture and urban space still have greater access to producing images and stories due to their proximity to the culture industries. It is urbane culture that has had a disproportionate hand in shaping the 'three nations' that confronted each other in the 1990s: the urban triangle, suburbia and the hinterland. The irony of this story is that it is not about the power of 'elite' urban taste, as the populist critique from the hinterland would have it. Rather, it is about the way the suburban culture of the 90s came to be haunted by images proposed by urbane culture of previous generations.

As well as trying to read the surfaces of culture through the images the media celebrates, it helps to go in the other direction, and ask about the vectors along which images and stories travel. As Richard Neville says, "*Oz* going offset was like Dylan going electric." The cheap and quick offset printing process revolutionised the print media vector in the 60s, computerised desktop publishing revolutionised it again in the 80s. In the 90s, there was a tectonic shift going on from broadcast TV to pay TV, from the pop tempo to cyberspace. This upset quite a lot of the strategies put in place over the last thirty years to stabilise a suburban zone in which a majority of Australians could create images and stories about themselves. Cyberspace plus globalisation put an end to the cosy fortress of Australian culture making.

By the end of the 90s, there was no longer a consensual space to which talking heads could address their appeals for a new order. While this tempted some, from Robert Manne to John Howard to Pauline Hanson, to pine for a happier time, in truth, the coherence and conformity of Australian postwar suburbia was always more apparent than real, purchased at the expense of ignoring minority and suppressing dissent. The means were few by which minority sensibility could express and communicate itself. Even majorities lived in relative silence. In the 50s and 60s, let's not forget, few Australian films were made, and Australian television was dominated by American programming that was made according to strict censorship and production code rules.

The 50s was not a better time; it was a time that just lied to itself better. The Menzies age was a self-deluded age.

Ideas about what Australia ought to become, like any other media artefact, are subject to decisions based as much on judgements of taste as practical reason. So too are propositions about who should be prime minister, or whether to become a republic, or whether to don the glad rags and celebrate Australia Day or the Gay and Lesbian Mardi Gras, or indeed whether Aboriginal and white Australians can live together. All of these things are clusters of feelings, perceptions, stories that people perceive in a large part through the media, and judge according to criteria of taste. Since there are different kinds of taste, people arrive at different feelings about these things. These feelings are something that affect us long before we have even heard an argument or a policy, let alone formulate an adequate concept.

To be able to think about imagining Australia as a public space or a political space, questions of taste and the cultural distinctions that taste shape have to be addressed. There are many different and overlapping kinds of taste and they form many different kinds of culture, and many different kinds of culture in turn do their best to define and maintain their particular structures of taste. But one enduring structure through which distinctions are made is through the creation and maintenance of the suburban. Sometimes, the suburban is made out to be synonymous with what is Australian. By defining at least two other kinds of public culture that are not suburban, the urbane and the vernacular, I want to get to the heart of the conflicts over what it is possible to imagine for Australia.

Class Struggle in Sylvania Waters

There is a suburbia to which vernacular and virtual republicans might propose their respective images, there is a suburbia to which media magnates and political parties might pitch woo, but there is also a suburbia that everyone wants to disown as quickly as possible. *Sylvania Waters*, a documentary series about Laurie and Noeline Donaher and their family, who lived in that suburb, screened in 1992, created a frenzy of public debate, and was forgotten as quickly as possible.[33]

"Noelene Donaher seemed to confirm some people's worst fears" about suburbia, writes John Hartley. "She was the Australian dream incarnate, but was it a nightmare after all?"[34] She became an instant celebrity, but as Graeme Turner notes, the public celebration of Noeline was "actually compromised by the embarrassing proposal that she was 'typical'."[35] To film historian Tom O'Regan Noeline was from a "long line of Australian monsters."[36] Multiculturalist scholar Mary Kalantzis complained that the show presented yet more images of a white suburban stereotype, and that the program's producers should have explored some of suburbia's ethnic diversity.[37]

Sylvania Waters was something of a touchstone for an emergent Australian cultural studies.[38] Like the Not-Mimi porn tape, *Sylvania Waters* demonstrated the simultaneously fascinating and repulsive consequences of reversing the direction of the vector, channelling information out of, rather than into, the most intimate and private space. And like the Not-Mimi tape, it demonstrated the degree to which everyday life borrows its codes from the screen in the first place. Where Not-Mimi jokes around as if playing a porn actor, Noeline strikes rather more stagey poses from 80s TV soap operas like *Dallas* or *Dynasty*.

Sylvania Waters was a project instigated by the BBC. The stereotype of the suburban Australian sometimes plays a role in British culture as the acceptable face of the despised minority — its possible to say about Australians what the well mannered would no longer say about Blacks or Jews. Some of the offence felt by the Australian public about *Sylvania Waters* was I think quite genuine, and perceived this barely suppressed racism in the motives of the BBC. While as O'Regan says the motive may well have been a desire for the "unveiling the quotidian Australian 'reality' behind the public face presented by *Neighbours*", it appeared in the Australian context as an unwelcome flow of information, back into suburbia, about what suburbia would rather repress.

Within the Sydney context, the refusal to identify with the show was motivated by a more subtle form of prejudice. As Craig McGregor notes, "Australians have a very well developed awareness of the prestige of the various suburbs in which they live."[39] Sylvania Waters is an outer suburb, but one that lacks the 'heartland' credibility of the outer west. Labor holds or can win most of the outer suburbs, but Sylvania Waters is in the safe Liberal seat of Cook. In the spatial imagination, it is a suburb south of the soul, place of the acquisitive, consumerist dream come true, but somehow lacking the redeeming qualities of the other Liberal strongholds such as the urbanity of the inner east, or the conservative respectability of the inner north. What the other compass point colludes in attributing to it is an unexamined aspect of the whole of suburban culture — at the end of the rainbow lies only boredom and bickering, and the absolute, resolute lack of self-awareness of Noeline Donaher.

When *Sylvania Waters* was made, the differences between suburbs, in terms of income and opportunity, were starting to attenuate. Research by Bob Gregory and Boyd Hunter showed that between 1980 and 1990, the average taxable income in wealthy eastern suburb Double Bay grew twice as fast as in the outer western suburb of Cabramatta. In leafy north shore Lindfield, income grew one and a half times the rate of Fairfield out in the west. Not just income, but employment and educational opportunity are also increasingly divided.[40]

Both Craig McGregor and Mark Latham have drawn attention to the way this research indicates a spatial aspect to inequality.[41] While Sydney suburbs might look like a neatly graded continuum from poor suburbs like Green Valley out west to the more desirable Lindfield on the northern flak of the inner suburban ring, these gradations mask an increasingly marked class conflict. If the vernacular language, spoken eloquently by Les Murray, and in more crude and resentful tones by Pauline Hanson made inroads into the outer suburbs in the late 90s, it was as a way of voicing resistance to the increasingly unsustainable fiction that the suburban fair go was a matter of incremental improvements in income — and postcode — as we all grew relaxed and comfortable together.

In Sydney, a significant break with the suburban dream appeared in the 90s in the form of a reversal of the migration of the 50s and 60s from city out to suburbs. The children of many of that generation of suburbanites headed back into the city and new patterns of urban living.[42] This was most noticeable in Sydney, but was mirrored in other Australian cities. At a time of increasing class difference, the inner city started to look like a safer place to be than the outer suburbs. Movies like *Idiot Box* and *The Boys* expressed a less than cheery view of outer suburban prospects.

Interestingly, urban Sydney had only had one strong and regular broadcast media image, in spite of its disproportionate wealth and cultural resources. The televising of the Sydney Gay and Lesbian Mardi Gras, which began in 1994 was probably the strongest expression of both an urban and an urbane culture. The telecast survived harassment from Senator Richard Alston and organised protest letter campaigns and was the ABC's most popular telecast in 1994.[43]

One way of defining class is in relation to access to capital. Workers spend what they get, while the bosses get what they spend. There are many other ways of distinguishing classes on the basis of wealth, power or status. What I would like to conclude with is a sketch of an approach to class in terms of inequalities of information. First, there are the information rich. There are those who own and control the vectors along which information travels — the Murdochs and Packers, for instance. They may also own stocks of information — intellectual property can be as valuable as real estate. There is also a larger group of people who can command the information analysing and gathering power of others. All of these make up the information rich.

At the other end of the scale are the information poor. This may be not only a lack of access to information vectors, and the stocks and flows of information that they might make available, but also a lack of access to the training that equips someone to make use of information in the first place. In between these extremes are the knowledge workers, who have access to the training to use information, but generally do not own the major vectors along which it travels, or the stocks of it with which they work, and who may be at the command of someone else as to what information to work on and how.

As the Australian economy moves away from manufacturing towards more information-intensive industries, and as these are integrated into the global economy, the class differentiation across the suburbs may very well have moved from a differentiation driven by property and income to a differentiation based on access to information and the capacity to use it. Suburbia based its distinctions of status on owning things. It did not put too much store on owning information or the capacity to use it, other than in the purely formal sense of getting a good qualification to get a good job.

What is turning up more and more on the Australian screen is an anxiety about the instability of this suburban world, where learning was a one-off thing necessary to get your place in the suburban landscape, after which life could be about the accumulation of things. The growth of an urban culture might also be related to the growth of an information economy. Urban space has for a century supported an urbane culture that put more emphasis on a public life in which information was more valued and more frequently sought and exchanged.

At the moment this is just a working hypothesis, but it seems to me that if the concept of a move from a manufacturing to an information economy has any validity, then this will have significant cultural and political consequences. It may undermine the whole basis of suburban culture, to the extent that it put a premium on the private acquisition of things rather than a public culture of accumulating and trading knowledge and information.

Whatever tensions inner suburbia might feel in such an environment, they are likely to be magnified in outer suburbia, where access to information resources and training is very scarce. This may produce not just relative inequality, but a complete disenfranchising of an outer suburban fringe. A vernacular culture with ties to the bush and to the past might have much more appeal there than a virtual culture emanating from an urban and forward looking information class.

Such a possibility places special pressure on Labor, as the party that once represented the organised industrial working class, but which acquired a following across several saturnine rings of suburbia. The cultural terms of that kind of class alliance may no longer exist. If the culture of suburbia is in transition, and nobody really knows to what, then the culture of Labor has to change and adapt if it is to forge a new Australian settlement, one that embodies versions of some of the values of the fair go.

chapter **7**

True believers

*It may be that true believers in original sin can face life
only if they view it ironically.*

Edmund Campion

That Labor Feeling

It was the only time in my life that I felt the membership card
for the Australian Labor Party that I keep in my wallet
burning a hole in me, searing flesh. I was at the Sydney Hotel
Intercontinental on election night, 1993, where Liberal
leader John Hewson expected to make his victory announcement. Only it was soon clear that the Liberal Party had lost.
It was just a matter of waiting around for Hewson to make his
appearance, and concede defeat. Bored journalists milled
around. Young Liberals in pressed slacks tried to be cheerful.
Liberal women, with hairdos that could only have been set in
shape by long hours in a wind tunnel, carped about media
bias. The canapes turned soggy. The straggle of listless
bodies only highlighted the emptiness of the room.

I chatted to the writer Linda Jaivin, an old Kings Cross
mate, who with her shock of orange hair looked even more
out of place there than I did among those amazing Liberal
matrons. Those Liberal women are the backbone of the
party. Craig McGregor once described them as "ageing, well
groomed, polite, carefully enthusiastic women whom one
felt instinctively would… reserve their worst scorn for any-

thing vulgar."[1] Tonight they are not happy. "At least one Liberal woman is sniffing and there'll be more tear stains on Country Road khaki before the night is through", Jaivin will write of this night.[2] They seemed to feel as though something had been stolen from them.

Somebody turned up the sound on the TV at the back of the hall. As Paul Keating appeared on screen in Bankstown, a modest crowd gathered at the Intercontinental to listen as he claimed victory for Labor. The mood was a bitter mix of arsenic and bile. Paul and Annita Keating walked across stage in Bankstown and on screen at the Intercontinental. "This is the sweetest victory of all", he said, as the Liberal ladies hissed. "This is a victory for the true believers." That one got a laugh. I felt out of place among these eastern and northern suburbs people but wondered if I would feel any more at home out at Bankstown in western Sydney, a place I have never been.

But when Keating spoke of how, under his government, no one would be left behind, something else took hold of me. I was no longer here, amid the Liberals, and Keating seemed no longer there, in Bankstown. He spoke, and I listened, on some other, more sublime plane, a plane that might be made of the vector that connected us, and connected many thousands of others, a vector of radio waves and sound waves and video phosphorescence. A plane of light and sound made possible by the crackling static surface of television. But there was something more. What Keating articulated was the actual existence of a virtual world that connected people into something greater than themselves, something beyond the graded distinctions that layer suburbia from inner privilege to outer deprivation.

Whatever Paul Keating's qualities as a political leader, he was, in that moment, a fair dinkum celebrity. It did not matter that the Liberals around me muttered and grumbled. It is not always a celebrity's job to be liked. Rather, it is a celebrity's job to appear, for as many people as possible, to articulate the possibilities of the moment. And that he did, brilliantly. That it was possible to come from Bankstown and become Prime Minister of Australia. That it was possible, in this topsy-turvy world, to be from the Labor Party and still manage to parlay that cranky old institution into power. That it is possible to feel as if things are possible — for this, in the end, is the real gift of celebrity. It opens up a plane for the possibility of possibility. A public's sense that through the appearance of this celebrity, something appears that is virtually imaginable is a step toward its becoming actually so.

Fables of Labor and the Labours of Fables

Bob Hawke was a celebrity when Labor elected him leader of the party, and his celebrity contributed, though in an intangible and unmeasurable way, to Labor's 1983 election win. By the time Hawke won his fourth term, he was rarely able to stroke the public with quite the same heat. He became Prime Minister in small part because of his celebrity, but he held power mostly on his political skills. I agree with Craig McGregor's assessment that Hawke was "a post-McLuhan politician, one of the first to realise that it is in the electronic media that a great deal of the passion play of contemporary politics is enacted."[3] That is not to say that all of politics is about celebrity, but celebrity is often in part about politics.

In 1993, after Paul Keating's election victory, a fair chunk of the Labor government became temporary celebrities with the ABC's screening of the epic five hour film *Labor in Power*.[4] The classification warns of "medium coarse language", for the stories are mostly told in what the participants themselves describe as "colourful" terms. For besides being a chronicle of Australian political influence and celebrity, *Labor in Power* is also a fable about a certain kind of culture — the Australian Labor Party. A culture Keating so brilliantly evoked in his 'true believers' victory speech, tapping that structure of feeling that connects the Labor faithful to its leaders, despite the failures, the compromises, the vicissitudes of events.

Labor in Power is a fable in the same way that Norman Lindsay's *Magic Pudding* is a fable.[5] Bunyip Bluegum meets up with Bill Barnacle and Sam Sawnoff. Because Bluegum appears to be so nice, Bill and Sam decide to share with him their magic pudding. This decision turns out to be a good one, for while Bunyip Bluegum can't stop the pudding thieves from stealing the magic pudding with all their ruses and tricks, he always helps get it back with a few tricks of his own.

Fables, the literary theorist Tom Keenan says, are about failure. "What is at stake in the fable is, more than anything else, the interpretation and practice of responsibility — our exposure to calls, others, and the names with which we are questioned and which put us in question."[6] The pudding thieves play on the pudding owners' gullibility, tricking them with false claims. Like the time the Possum poses as a fire fighter, distracting the pudding owners with the fun of fighting a fire while his co-conspirator the Wombat steals the pudding. Things are not what they seem, the fable warns, things that seem true are often just made up — as indeed are fables.

Fables, if you've ever hung around the Labor Party, are one of the things that bind its culture together. In 1998 I was at a fundraiser for Tanya Plibersek, Labor candidate for the Federal seat of Sydney, where I heard Max Solling tells some great stories about the former inner city municipality of Glebe. It's part of Leichhardt Council now — subject of a more contemporary fable — that great documentary film *Rats in the Ranks*, about how Labor councillors and Labor apostates run their patch.[7] Once upon a time, Glebe was a municipality all of its own, and for a while, a Labor one.

I always wondered why Glebe's park is called Foley Park. Over entrees, Max told the story of Doc Foley, Labor machine man, who built his power on giving free medical help to the locals during the depression — in exchange for their loyalty in party business. Senator John Faulkner provided the main course for the evening — the tale of the cleaning up of the corrupt Glebe branches in the 80s — some of the last remnants of the old right wing machines of the Foley type. Most of the branches around Glebe belong to the left faction now, and the right wing ones are honest branches. But the park is still called Foley Park. There's a moral, or perhaps a lesson, in that somewhere.

At first glance it appears that the difference between left and right wing factions in the Labor Party is that on the left people think fables have a moral, while on the right people think they have a lesson. The left seeks the truth behind the shifting appearances. The right seek knowledge of how appearances work and can be made to work. What they have in common is being true believers — a paradoxical phrase —

in the fables that are the party's accumulating stock of the wisdom learned of failure.

I used to be a true believer, and a labour movement leftist, but these days I've lost faith in anything but the practicalities of forming electoral majorities out of a commitment to min-imising what Bob Ellis calls "avoidable suffering".[8] Minimising avoidable suffering — if there is a feeling that structures the whole of Labor culture, I think that's it. The rest is the folly and fantasy of master thinkers, who think pol-itics is a matter of imposing a grand plan on people, against their will, because the master deems it good for them. That is also a feeling that structures Labor culture. All that changed is that the grand plans used to come from the left with its fantasies of state control; then the follies came from the right with the conviction that the market is the one big answer.

The Virtual Party

The Labor Party still passes on fables as an oral tradition, but Labor owes its perpetuation to another means of telling stories as well — to the media. In the media, Labor appears because it has power, and it has power because it appears. Mostly, Labor appears as part of an adversarial practice. Journalism, in the English speaking world, owes a lot to the legal and parliamentary tradition of adversarial justice, where rival orators plead pro and con. Truth is served by a balance between sophistries, neither of which is ever to be too readily believed.

The rise of the swinging voter parallels the pervading of culture by the media in which the adversarial style of jour-nalism is the norm. Labor has had to refashion itself, in part, into a participant in this media created adversarial world. It's a long way from the backroom style of the old party bosses like Doc Foley. It has become a virtual party, creating its elec-toral bloc out of any and every possible private desire it can attach to the ancient signs and current talking heads that constitute its public existence.

Sometimes, the fables of Labor appear in the media as something closer to the story telling style of oral history. There are at least three epic fables of Labor broadcast on national television in living memory, one for each of Labor's three recent periods of government. Besides *Labor in Power*, there is the Kennedy Miller production, *The Dismissal*, and *True Believers*, written by Bob Ellis and Stephen Ramsey.[9] In this chapter, I want to write about these three Labor epics. The videos of them are not too hard to find. They may lack the detail of the many books published on the Labor Party, but they embody a good deal more of the structure of feeling, the memory of which is what Labor culture has to work with as it reinvents itself, for the umpteenth time, for its public.

It's not often that Australian television gets around to telling its epic stories, and with the decline in funding for the national broadcaster, the ABC, it has become less common. This is a worry, because the media, particularly the electronic media, account for a large proportion of what people know about a wider world, beyond the borders of their suburb. While education might be charged with a larger responsibility than the media for extending popular memory and awareness beyond the here and now, it's hard to educate people without popular screen productions. Through long years of training, Australians have acquired fine intuitive skills in reading screen texts, but are sometimes less interested in the written word. If education is to include the fables of past encounters with crisis and conflict on a national and international scale, then educators need the programs with which to teach.

Politicians often seem puzzled by the lack of interest the public feigns in the machinery of government. Like most obsessive hobbyists, politicians don't understand why others aren't as fascinated as they by fly fishing or fretwork — or federal governance. They have no-one but themselves to blame. Both sides of the house have so intimidated and neglected the ABC that the national broadcaster has neither the time nor the inclination to pay much attention to making governance a subject for anything but the passing show of current affairs trivia.

The Unrepresentable Hero

True Believers was an apt title for the ABC TV series Bob Ellis co-wrote on the fables of John Curtin, Ben Chifley and Doc

Evatt. Two of these Labor leaders lost their lives and one lost his mind in confrontation with the events of the 40s and 50s.

The first scene has poor old Jack Curtin, Prime Minister from 1941–1945, on his deathbed.[10] We see through his eyes the cluster of his successors who will have to prosecute the last part of the war effort. It's telling that while the series tries its guts out to maintain for the viewer an intimate yet distant regard for such legendary figures as Chifley and Menzies, no actor appears trying to carry off Curtin's mantle. That would be too great a task. John Curtin: modest, austere, reserved, always troubled by melancholy and self-doubt, was an unlikely soul to be chosen, as he put it, as "fate's weapon." And yet through the anxieties of war he kept the country together. Even more remarkably, he kept the Labor party together.

Contemporaries claim Curtin was a great orator. This is difficult to understand in an age when cyberspace extends its embrace to almost everyone and everything. Even on radio, Curtin sounds like a man used to speaking to large groups of unruly men in cavernous halls. In the newsreels, he stands well back from the microphone, swaying rhythmically, the words expressed from the movements of his body as much as his mind. Hand in a waistcoat pocket, guarding his belly, he unleashes his mind. The words swoop and squall in elaborate arabesques.

Sometimes he even quotes poetry. He responds to the Japanese attack on Pearl Harbour with lines from Swinburne. He writes of the need to seek American aid for the war in the Pacific with lines from Bernard O'Dowd. "Without any inhibitions of any kind, I make it quite clear that Australia looks to America, free of any pangs as to our traditional links of kinship with the United Kingdom." In the same remarkable 1941 essay for the Melbourne *Herald*, he admits that in his attempts to mobilise Australians for war, he engaged in an "experiment in psychology" aimed at "the somewhat lackadaisical Australian mind." While Australians have always been patriotic, he claims that "response to leadership and direction has never been requested of the people, and desirable talents and untapped resources lay dormant."[11] He was the first Australian leader to experience power as the ability to direct the energies of the nation toward the production of a new version of its collective self. The experience troubled him greatly. That he was troubled by power is a key quality in what endures of his celebrity.

Curtin's talent for fashioning himself into the very image of leadership in action, and the wartime conditions restricting dissemination of dissenting information, made Curtin into a quite unique kind of celebrity in Australian history. The fantasy he stood for still had distant echoes half a century later. "This government's policy of full development of resources, full employment of man-power and full provision for social security is a basis not only for Australian reconstruction, but also for a stable and peaceful commonwealth of nations."[12]

Fifty years after Curtin's death, this dream of a state-directed mobilisation of resources still haunted the imagination, not only of the Labor left but also of Pauline Hanson's One Nation Party Ltd. Whether Hanson's policy of reintroducing conscription was suggested to her by her mother or by her minder John Pasquarelli, both would surely remember the now fading echoes of the wartime media mobilisation of which John Curtin was once a celebrated and revered symbol.[13] Curtin was a credible figure for the drive to send conscripts into the Pacific war not least because he came from the anti-conscription wing of the labour movement, and appeared to suffer a crisis of conscience about sending Australian conscripts into battles that were not fought for the immediate defense of Australia. Some of the ethos generated by the mobilisation of propaganda that accompanied conscription clearly sticks in the minds of some older Australians.

What is remarkable about *True Believers* is that while it narrates the trials of federal Labor from Curtin's death to Doc Evatt's 1954 electoral defeat and the decline of Labor's postwar fortunes, the image of Curtin himself does not appear. I wonder: how many Australians my age or younger are more familiar with the faces of Churchill or Roosevelt? How many students at Curtin University know who the place is named after? Perhaps Curtin is not only unrepresented in Australian media culture, but unrepresentable.

Curtin's successor was Ben Chifley, Prime Minister from 1945 to 1949.[14] In *True Believers* the actor Ed Devereaux manages to convey the towering pillar of ordinariness that was Chif. Simon Chilvers makes an excellent Doc Evatt, and conveys the volatile mix of bludgeoning intelligence and tender self regard. But Curtin himself is absent. Perhaps the film makers did not dare pull him down from his pedestal, and make of him a fable's more equivocal character, bent by and against the twist of a story's events.

Things Worth Fighting For

The moral of *True Believers* might be that when confronted with the vertigo of circumstance, Labor has to stick true to its identity, to its principles. Events reveal the true inner essence of the party, which its leaders either uphold or betray. But the lesson might be that events reveal the ambiguities of the party's identity. At trying times, all the different currents are exposed for what they are, and in order to survive the party has to remake itself in a new image out of the flux and chance inheritance that it always contains. When I first saw the series, I thought the former; now more than a decade later I think the latter. That ambivalence is at the heart of Labor culture.

True Believers pictures a pipe-sucking Chifley talking to the great nation building bureaucrat Nugget Coombs, as both lean on a scale model of the Snowy Mountains dam and irrigation scheme. Chif dreams of orchards and farms, but as he and Coombs know, the Federal government will not have the powers in peace time that it enjoyed during the war to mobilise the resources of the nation. One strand of the drama involves the clash between Chifley's vision of a benevolent state with control over the banking system, and resistance by the banks and business interests.

Chifley's pursuit of state controlled national reconstruction is one of the issues that lead to the defeat of Labor in the 1949 election. Was this an historic defeat of a labour movement that for once had the nerve to stick to one of its principles? Or was Chifley naive in his view that the government could be trusted not to abuse such extensive powers? A powerful scene shows Chifley and Robert Menzies (John Bonney) toasting each other's health on the eve of the 1949 election. The heart and soul of the Australian people is at stake, says Menzies. The heart and soul are always there, Chif replies, the politician's job is just to seek it out.

As it turned out, Menzies was right. The electorate did not want the continuation in peace of wartime state authority. A rising white collar segment of the electorate could not be persuaded to see the nation as one giant social factory. "I try to think of the labour movement not as putting an extra sixpence into somebody's pocket, or making somebody Prime Minister," a defeated Chifley said, "…but as a movement bringing something better to the people: better standards of living, greater happiness to the mass of the people. We have a great objective — the light on the hill — which we aim to reach by working for the betterment of mankind…. If it were not for that, the labour movement would not be worth fighting for."[15] Only someone always seems to be stealing this radiant possibility, right out from under the Party's nose. That sense of loss is as much a part of the structure of feeling of Labor culture as the ever-absent light on the hill itself.

If seeking equality and community means a loss of liberty, the creation of what the freethinking opponent of Labor's master thinkers, the philosopher John Anderson, called a "servile state", then the ends do not justify the means. "For the measure of freedom in any community is the extent of opposition to the ruling order, of criticism of the ruling ideas; and belief in established freedom, or in state-guaranteed 'benefits', is a mark of the abandonment of liberty. The servile state is the unopposed state."[16] Yet many in the labour movement insist on seeing the means of state control not only as justified by such a goal, but as an end in itself.

The Evatt Enigma

Chifley and Evatt could not be more different kinds of Labor celebrity. Chif's simplicity was legendary, and his is a simple legend — the self-educated engine driver who stoked the boilers of government business as efficiently as a railway steamer. That plain speaking, gravel voice, with its simple rhythms and rising intonation; "our Ben" talking to the nation as if addressing a gathering of family and friends in his native Bathurst. Bob Ellis once described it as a "voice like burnt vegemite toast."[17] He ruled federal Labor caucus with

his ferocious affection. A moving scene in *True Believers*
shows Chifley pop off home rather than attend the party for
the jubilee anniversary of the opening of parliament.
Menzies, radiant in white tie, beaming like a night club pro-
prietor with a full house, receives a message. He silences the
band and makes the announcement, Ben Chifley is dead.
"We have lost a very great Australian."

The Doc is different. Dr Herbert Vere Evatt, who succeeds
Chifley, is a different kind of Labor leader.[18] Educated by the
university and the profession of law rather than on the shop
floor, night school and the trade union movement, Evatt
speaks a different language. Between Curtin and Evatt, Labor
oratory acclimatises itself somewhat to speaking for the radio,
addressing people in their private homes rather than in a
public hall, but as Judith Brett argues, it was his opponent
Menzies who was the master of the radio vector, using it in
particular to address women, in the home, in a language and
with a mode of speech suitable for the private domain.[19]
Evatt's speech sounds a more masculine style, and in film
footage, he always seems to wield his right arm as if it were an
intellectual club. It was Menzies who crafted a public style for
the privatised world of an emerging fortress suburbia.

In *True Believers*, Evatt appears as a well meaning lunatic —
a quite different portrait to the hagiographic treatment of
Chifley. And yet there is for me at least something truly
moving about this brilliant, flawed, self-destructive man, so
engagingly portrayed by Simon Chilvers. He took on
Menzies, the courts, the media and the electorate to twice
defeat Menzies' attempts to ban the Communist party. The
powers Menzies sought, first through legislation and then
through referendum, were an even clearer breach of liberty
than Labor's desire to centralise control of banking and
investment. Menzies would use, not the threat of depression
and fascism at home, but the threat of Stalinism abroad as
the excuse for a servile state at home.

The enigma of Evatt is the force with which he could act
upon seemingly contradictory ideas. As the wartime
Attorney-General, he could be even more enthusiastic than
Curtin or Chifley for aggrandising state power. "In the fires
of war we have fashioned a new machinery of government
diverse yet unified, with its roots in the people and yet with

effective central direction; we have, too, fashioned a system of economic regulation by which we have built and maintained a gigantic war machine and at the same time protected our people from want and misery. We profoundly believe that this machinery of government and this system of control and organisation are necessary and well adapted to handle the equally difficult and urgent problems of the post war period." Or even more bluntly: "Total war calls for the organisation of the whole community. Australia has moved and is moving towards total organisation."[20]

Evatt's finest hour, in *True Believers*, is his single-minded campaign against Menzies' attempts to acquire extraordinary police powers for the anti-communist witch hunt. Communism would split the party. John Derum plays the part of B. A. Santamaria, the lay Catholic activist who organised anti-communist cells within the trade union movement to combat the reds. Derum captures Santamaria's trademark combination of gentle voice, self-sanctified airs and ruthless energy. The series ends with the party besieged from the left by the Communist Party, from the right by Santamaria. Evatt's judgement sours and his mind unravels, his lucidity probably sapped by arterio-sclerosis. Mercifully, *True Believers* spares us his year of public decline. But not before it has conveyed a lesson about the dangers of staying too loyal to a leader, for too long.

A Certain Hauteur

November 11th of 1975 is one of those days when many people can recall their whereabouts when they heard the news. I was on a bus on the way home from school. Daydreaming, looking out the window at the passing shop fronts of Hunter street, Newcastle, a newspaper poster brought me back to myself with a shock: **KERR SACKS WHITLAM** it said, in funereal black capitals.

The Dismissal covers the last 12 months of the Whitlam government, from December 1974 to December 1975.[21] These days, despite all of the nostalgia for Gough Whitlam, Labor Prime Minister from 1972 to 1975, despite all the social reforms his government pushed through, I find it hard not to agree with Paul Keating that it was "amateur hour." Or perhaps it was what Labor Sentator John Button more generously describes as "magnificent chaos".[22] Or as Hawke says in *Labor In Power*, the Whitlam government would be remembered for whether it got the economy right or not — and it did not.

In a frightening scene in *The Dismissal*, Rex Connor, Whitlam's resources minister, unrolls a map of Australia. He sweeps his hand across the map, along the line of the pipeline he wants to build, right across the continent. He jabs his finger at the north, where he wants uranium enrichment plants. The whole continent is just mineralised wealth to this master thinker. Bill Hunter plays Connor as a gruff Aussie bloke on a mission from the people. He needs *billions* of dollars for his grandiose schemes, and he doesn't care how he gets them. He's Bill Heslop, mover, shaker and fixer of Porpoise Spit Council — on a frighteningly grand scale.

Among Labor's most enduring fables is that of the Money Power, the hydra-headed beast of international capital that plots and conspires to steal the magic pudding from dinky di Australians.[23] Chifley wanted to nationalise the banks in order to put an end to their imperial dominance; Connor wants to borrow 'Petrodollars' from newly rich Arab states, and so circumvent their strangle-hold on capital. He wants mineral wealth exploited by Australian owned industry, even if, by borrowing to the hilt, the Australian government and thereby the Australian people, take all the risk. The fair go for Connor, even more than for Chifley, flows from the developmental state.

Jim Cairns, the Treasurer, also wants money. Cairns was once a radical celebrity, made famous by the Vietnam Moratorium movement, but as a Minister he appears out of his depth. John Hargreaves plays him as thoughtful, introspective, a long way from Connor's unreflective ambition. But it's the same vision of the light on the hill, as something only a master thinker with a plan and a pot of cash can deliver.

The main drama of *The Dismissal* is the constitutional crisis, the sordid circumstances under which the Liberal opposition gained control of the Senate, blocked the government's budget bills, forcing the Governor-General to act. The portrayal John Mellion invents for Governor-General Sir John Kerr, imagines him as pompous and permanently pissed.

Whether he was right or not to withdraw Gough Whitlam's commission as Prime Minister and hand it over to Malcolm Fraser is the great unknown that this fable commits to memory. To me this pales in comparison to the efforts of Connor and Cairns to raise money abroad to fund their schemes.

Had they procured these loans, Australia might really have become a banana republic, saddled with a mountain of public debt and a plethora of environmentally destructive quarries, turning minerals into exports at ever-declining prices. It might be a heretical thought even for a lapsed true believer, but it may be that not only Australia but the Australian Labor Party are lucky such plans never came to pass.

Labor in Power: The Movie

As with *True Believers*, and *The Dismissal* so too with *Labor in Power*. It's a fable about Labor's encounters with what is other to its nature — power. Depending on how you look at it, the moral of *Labor in Power* might be that Labor deceived the people to win power, but in deceiving the people deceived itself, and while it still thought it was a Labor government, in truth it had betrayed its identity. Or, the lesson of *Labor in Power* might be that you never can say much about things based on appearances, and you never can tell when your own appearances might deceive you as to who you are supposed to be, but that it is possible, in spite of it all, to keep going, to be in power, to have that disenchanted pudding — and to share it with your mates.

"He was a real Australian", says ALP pollster Rod Cameron. "He's the embodiment of the Oscar Wildeism that the flatterer is seldom interrupted," says former New South Wales Premier Neville Wran. They are speaking of Bob Hawke, long time leader of the Australian Council of Trade Unions, while black and white images go by of a Hawke who conveys a sense of elan even through the veil of old film footage. Pictures of Hawke drinking, laughing, and, in the language of the day, posing with a bird on each arm. It was "not a pretty sight when he was really on a bender", says Wran, but it didn't stop him garnering a Father of the Year award in

1971. "The one who should really have the title is my wife. She has to be father as well as mother most of the time," quips Hawke. Max Harris identified Hawke's tactic early on: "Mr Robert Hawke is highly educated, but he affects a rasping, aggressive style... The rasp, the ready aggression, the appearance of being on the look-out for an intellectual punch-up, is an atavistic survival of the old-style Australian ockerdom."[24] Hawke played to the same structure of feeling as Barry McKenzie.

Hawke was a Labor leader who appeared every inch a man of the people, just like Ben Chifley, only he was a different man and his were a different people. Ben was stolid, Bob was flash. Ben was self-effacing, Bob was nothing but face. While it took an actor of Ed Devereaux's skill to play Ben Chifley, it took an actor of Bob Hawke's skill to play Bob Hawke. When the comedian Max Gillies appeared with Hawke on TV, doing his famous impersonation of Hawke, what seemed to make Hawke uncomfortable was that Gillies impersonated Hawke better than he could impersonate himself. Hawke's Hawke fiddling with an earlobe and patting his hair looked like a bad copy of Gillies' Hawke. It's fitting, now that politics with a basis in social space has been replaced by politics with a place in media schedules, that *Labor In Power* has the principle actors re-enact themselves.

We don't see much of Paul Keating's rise to prominence in *Labor In Power*. Rising through the ranks of the right wing of the New South Wales branch of the Labor Party, Keating swam against the tide. While many of his contemporaries turned left during the Vietnam era, Keating stayed loyal to the Catholic social thought in which he was schooled. While Hawke was a Rhodes scholar, Keating is perhaps the last in a long line of leaders whose school was the Party itself.

That he listened to NSW Labor renegade Jack Lang's stories is not hard to believe, given the lack of respect he later showed for the memory of Curtin. That he was once a protegé of Rex Connor appears at first harder to believe, given his preference for market led rather than state directed growth. But like Connor he still believed that the light on the hill shone to illuminate a master plan for making the economy perform better than it would without Labor's efforts.

Bill Hayden led the Federal Labor Party from its nadir of 1977, but he would not reap the benefits of Labor's changing fortunes in the 80s. The conservative Fraser government was in trouble in the early 80s. The "resources boom" Fraser promised in the 1980 election failed to materialise, but the unions grabbed their share in advance in the form of increased wages, which achieved little besides bumping up inflation. Dogged by scandals involving 'bottom of the harbour' tax avoidance schemes, Fraser's coalition government was on the nose. As a consequence, so too was Bill Hayden's leadership of Labor. Sniffing an opportunity to win government, the Party movers, shakers and fixers wanted a leader who might hold the public's attention — a celebrity.

Hawke and Keating met at the Boulevard Hotel in Sydney in 1980. Hawke declared that he was going to challenge Hayden for the leadership, but that his ambition to be Prime Minister didn't extend beyond a couple of terms in office. Or so Keating claims. Hawke says he simply suggested that the reform program he had in mind would take that long in government. But Keating formed the impression that if he backed Hawke, "there would be something in it for me." As in many a memorable fable, a great political partnership is about to begin on the basis of mutual misunderstanding.

Early in 1983 Labor's shadow cabinet met in Brisbane to spill the leadership. "These things were discussed in an atmosphere of high drama and emotion", Hawke recalls. He took the leadership from Hayden just as Malcolm Fraser calls a snap election. "I believe that a drover's dog could lead the Labor party to victory," a despondent Hayden declared. But the drover's dog was Hayden, who brought the flock safely across the wilderness, but who the party judged a bit too mangy for the home stretch.

The Messiah

"Reconciliation, recovery and reconstruction" are Hawke's watch words. He wants "to bring Australians together in a united effort until victory is won." It's a campaign well suited to Hawke's particular attributes as a celebrity. His openness to people, the sense that he can participate in your joy and pain, his genuine belief that there is always a way to avoid confrontation, to combine the strengths and energies of different people together. There are no bad guys in this campaign other than the Liberal government. Through Hawke's body, a small smudge across the screen, pass the possibilities of the moment. His presence is an invitation to join the possible world he embodies, and to acknowledge, through so doing, both the potentials and limitations of this world in which we live.

Richard Farmer, a Hawke adviser, speaks of Hawke on election night. Relaxed and composed as he celebrates his father's birthday, "he knew it was his destiny, to be Prime Minister." Farmer bears witness to a private moment that, made public, adds lustre to celebrity. "I found it a bit eerie, how calm he was." A celebrity at ease in the twist and snap of events — at least according to Farmer's testimony for the cameras.

Hawke says he is "determined to try and make this a long term government." The key is abandoning what both Hawke in his memoirs and cabinet member Peter Walsh in his confessions both call the "magic pudding" myth.[25] "Cut and come again", the magic pudding said. But for Hawke, government is not just a pudding to cut and cut and throw to the party's supporters until thrown out of office. The bad example of Whitlam's government is the fable that guides him here.

There is something paradoxical about fables, and magic puddings. One becomes responsible by heeding the bad example. Government is not a magic pudding that you can cut and come again. But it is another magic pudding, the Whitlamite fable of how not to govern, that governs Hawke's sense of responsibility. Not doing things the way Whitlam did them becomes Hawke's own personal magic pudding, a fable he will cut again and again without ever exhausting its fabulous authority.

Things are never quite what they appear, particularly deficits. Hawke discovers that the Treasury department's estimate of the deficit is 9.6 billion dollars, some three billion more than publicly anticipated. Hawke and his new Treasurer Paul Keating use this new deficit as a stick with which to attack the departing Fraser government, and as a stick with which to beat off their own magic pudding promises made during the election campaign. This is the stick and stick approach to government, rather than the more usual stick and carrot. It is also a bit of political good fortune. Politics is the art of exploiting the potential of the moment, and as each moment differs from the next, it's not a profession for the dull witted. Hawke had the nous to exploit the bad news of the deficit to advance his agenda of economic modernisation.

For economist and Keating adviser John Langmore, this change of policy is "a shatteringly disillusioning experience". No longer would cutting employment be the goal, but cutting the deficit. This government is not what it seems. But to Paul Keating, Langmore was just a "true believer in the mixed up orthodoxy of the Labor party of the 50s and 60s." Labor abandons its Keynesian economic policy of expanding the deficit to assist the poor, create jobs and pump up the economy. There is no magic pudding that you can cut and come again. Government revenues are finite, dependent on tax revenues collected through an unfair system, in a small country connected to a very big world. Labor's responsibility is to fix this small economy, so that there might then be taxes to raise, and pudding to share around. This will be a government, not of social equity, but of economic reform. The fable Langmore tells in *Labor in Power* is not the magic pudding but an odd version of a biblical one: after the seven lean years of the Coalition government come the seven bountiful ones of Labor government. But government is no more a magic harvest than a magic pudding.

Some see the evil hand of the Treasury department in this. David Morgan, a senior Treasury official says: "Treasury got more of its agenda up under the decade of the Hawke-Keating government than under the rest of the postwar period." But it did so, he claims, by accommodating itself to the agenda of the government of the day. Did Hawke and Keating abandon the true principles of the Party? Or did they reinvent them? Certainly, they were a long way removed from the social reform and distributive justice of the Whitlam years, and were perhaps even further from the national development and bank nationalisation program of the Chifley years. But like Chifley, they thought you had to make the economic pud before you could, like Whitlam, share it about.

The Accord

The Hawke agenda became clearer at the National Economic Summit of April 1983. Bill Kelty, head of the Australian Council of Trade Unions, says, "what we wanted was a long term Labor government with a long term strategy." That strategy, which the Summit was called upon to witness, involved an Accord between the government and the unions, where the government promised tax cuts in return for wage restraint and a social wage, including Medicare. The tax cuts would make up for some of the lost wage claims, it would encourage business to employ more people, by not pricing workers out of a job, and it would help reduce inflation, by lowering the wage component in price rises.

There is more to it than that, but basically, it is an exchange of promises between government and unions. As Kelty says, the Accord "forced the unions to come to terms with the process of government very early." They had to see that they had a responsibility that stretched beyond the immediate demands of their members, since a short term action like a wage demand had long term consequences, for inflation, employment and investment.

Hawke believes the Accord can work. Keating doesn't, and neither does Treasury. But the Treasurer and Treasury disagree on another issue, the floating of the Australian dollar on the foreign exchange markets. Fearing a Labor win, money flowed out of the country. When it starts to look like this is not a magic pudding government, the money flows back in. As the money flows in and out, the Reserve Bank raises and lowers its value. These price changes don't just affect the relation between buyers and sellers of Australian dollars. They effect the buyers and sellers of everything that comes in or goes out of the country. With the dollar high, imports are cheaper, and the pressure on inflation from the cost of imports is low. With the dollar low, exports are competitive on world markets, but imports are expensive.

The idea that the Reserve Bank is really in control of the value of the money going in and out of the country will turn out to be an illusion. The amount of money was now so great that, as Hawke said, it would be "an exercise in futility" to try and stop it. The Reserve Bank could set a price and could buy and sell dollars, but trying to keep the Australian dollar at a rate that the market disagreed with could be a very expensive exercise. So why not just allow the market to decide its value? The Reserve Bank likes this idea, but Treasury does not. Hawke favours a float. Keating, not yet sure of himself as Treasurer, has to stand up to the advice of his own department, which has not quite given up on the idea of controlling the foreign exchange as a tool of national economic development. In *Labor in Power*, Keating looks calm and self-assured as he recalls this decision, but it is a striking instance of the risky side of political fortune. Even the best advice can be based on incomplete information, or even downright wrong, and yet sometimes a decision cannot wait until tomorrow.

The dollar floats, and the world does not end. Emboldened, Keating proposes deregulating the banks and issuing licences to foreign banks. As Barbara Ward, a key Keating staffer says, this was "a difficult one for the Labor Party." But at the National Conference in July 1984, Keating persuades the Party to make it policy. As Neville Wran says, this is "equivalent to stealing the holy water." As Bob Hawke says, "the job we had in government was to change the Party."

The man for the job is Keating. As Labor cabinet member Peter Cook says, "he was so certain about what he said." He is a true believer in a new kind of fable. Not the fable of the magic pudding, but the fable of the invisible hand. Keating will be so happy when *Euromoney* magazine names him Finance Minister of the year in 1984. He came to believe it himself. Like Doc Evatt before him, international acclaim would make him a true believer in the rationality of his own judgement.

Labor's popularity is so high that "it was just obvious we had to go" to an election, according to Senator Graham Richardson. Bob Hawke is a celebrity. He is beyond politics. But the use the party wants to put this toward is increasing its electoral majority. With the election in motion, Hawke's wife Hazel informs him of their daughter's heroin addiction. The news so unnerves Hawke that in a television interview viewers see him licking a tear that has dribbled all the way down to his lip.

People love Hawke precisely because he blurs the line between the public and the private. But in the election campaign, his private grief stains his public performance. No matter how much people love him, they will not necessarily vote for him, for Hawke's own ambivalence about his own ambitions has become transparent. And besides, the celebrity that extends his appeal outside of politics is being used for the most elementary political purpose, the extension of the mandate. As Rod Cameron says, in retrospect, the calling of an early election for 1984 was "probably Hawke's greatest political mistake". Hawke is no longer the messiah. Keating says this is when "he stopped nourishing us."

But for the Labor caucus, as opposed to the cabinet inner circle, Hawke's failure might be less on the policy front than his waning celebrity. His inability to turn his popularity into a second big Labor majority is significant because it contradicts the theory that politics is driven by celebrity and that in the postmodern age the electorate has lost the critical judgement it allegedly had in the good old days. In the contemporary media landscape, people judge celebrities, political or otherwise, according to rational, emotional, ethical, aesthetic *and* cultural criteria. The media vectors of television and radio make it possible to assess Hawke's celebrity along all these axes, and the public judgement is mixed.

Part of the difficulty is that different publics use different kinds of judgement. Long exposure to Hawke makes it harder for urbane, suburban and vernacular Australians to all see what they want to see in him. People look for different things in different kinds of celebrity, but one running for office has to find a majority in whom to inspire a feeling of trust, and Hawke struggled to pull that off a second time.

There are publics who are rightly disdainful of lengthy recitations of policy, for they know that politics is only partly about policy. Politics is also about the ability to manage complex and shifting situations — and in the more open economic times Hawke created, perhaps even more so. The irony of economic rationalism is that it opened up the country ever so slightly to global economic possibilities, but in the process it actually heightened, rather than lessened, the political nature of the times, and the political aspect of the experience of time. Politics experiences time in the present tense.

Pundits, columnists and commentators experienced time in the past tense. Economists will experience time in the future (imperfect) of forecasts and 'expectations'.

What makes *Labor in Power* such an interesting fable is that it is about how events test character. It is about politics as Machiavelli understood it — as fortune's test of virtue — rather than about politics as the policy wonk and wankers would have it. "Since... all human affairs are ever in a state of flux and cannot stand still, either there will be improvement or decline, and necessity will lead you to do many things which reason does not recommend."[26]

Consumption Tax

With Hawke's relative failure in the reelection bid, Paul Keating started acting as a more confident and independent public figure, and to acquire his own kind of celebrity. This would become very clear in the tax reform politics of 1985. Hawke was an organic celebrity. He grew out of organised Labor and created his own relationship with a public out of that experience. Keating would be a more traditional celebrity, but drawing his legitimacy from two very different kinds of traditional institution: the diction of the NSW Labor power broker would be made to articulate the idea of the Treasury experts. Behind these differing kinds of celebrity lies different ideas about how knowledge works in politics, as we shall see.

The magic pudding of government revenue comes from the very unmagical, although rather mysterious, taxation system. During the election, Hawke responds to a radio interviewer's questions about tax reform by agreeing that a tax summit might not be a bad idea. And so, after the election, Hawke announces a tax summit for July 1985. Keating disapproves of the tax summit, and this exposes fundamental differences between the way Hawke and Keating understand governance. Hawke wanted to consult widely, construct a consensus, and perform the semblance of consulting and constructing in public, so that the media might transmit the image of consulting and constructing far and wide. Keating thought such a complex and fundamental question as taxation policy ought to be nutted out behind closed doors by the experts first, and pitched to the public via the media afterwards.

Hawke puts Keating in charge of developing the tax policy that the Labor government will propose to the summit. Keating comes up with three options. Option A: fixing the loopholes in the current system. Option B: expanding sales tax. Option C: reducing income tax by introducing a whole new tax on consumption. Keating favours this last option. It will be, in David Morgan's words, "by far the biggest reform we had since federation." Treasury puts in "the most massive bureaucratic effort that I've ever seen" to come up with a consumption tax reform package that Keating takes to the tax summit. But Hawke is cautious.

The tax issue reveals a fundamental difference between Hawke and Keating. A difference not of policy or conviction, but a difference of epistemology. Epistemology, the theory of knowledge, is not a topic much discussed in politics, but here it becomes crucial. Hawke's approach to the problem of knowledge rests on the assumption that everyone with an informed opinion of a topic like tax reform is probably at least a little bit right. Keating's approach is that of everyone's view on the matter, one view must be substantially right and the others wrong. Hawke's approach is more empirical, building a view bit by bit from the bottom up, summarising and synthesising views. His ability to sum up even a lengthy and meandering cabinet discussion is legendary. Keating's approach is more rationalist. He hears competing arguments and judges one to be wrong and the other right.

After a marathon two and a half day cabinet meeting, Keating gets his Option C consumption tax up and running. It is a massive, top down rationalisation of the tax system with a comprehensive plan of reform, put together by some of the best minds in the economic ministries. Keating takes his "tax cart" on the road, in an election style campaign, working the media across the country. But he can't sell it. Opposition is so strong that, three days into the tax summit, Hawke dumps it. He opts for a pragmatic, incremental change based on Keating's less radical options rather than the revolutionary Option C.

Keating concedes at a press conference: "It's a bit like Ben Hur — we crossed the line with one wheel off". This may be a low point in Keating's political career, but as a celebrity it is a memorable, and hence successful, moment. Keating defines himself gracefully in relation to the failed policy, adding substance to the celebrity, even when announcing the failure of the policy. People judge celebrities by how they cope with events, and Keating pulled it off. After the summit, Keating gets a fringe benefits tax, reforms to business entertainment expense deductions and a capital gains tax through cabinet, as well as a cut in the top marginal rate. And he does it, he feels, without Hawke's support — a betrayal he will not forget. The lesson Keating draws is that consensus is an obstacle to change.

Banana Republic

Distracted by its tax agenda, the government misses a looming issue coming at it from without. The May 1986 trade statistics reveal a $1476 million deficit. As Keating recalls on *Labor in Power*, "we could no longer pay our way without substantial remedial change". At a function for a backbencher, staffers find a phone in the kitchen for Keating to talk with Sydney-based radio announcer John Laws. Audible in the background is a catering worker, resentful — so the fable goes — of Keating's presence, banging dishes in the sink. This will become the fabled interview in which Keating makes his warning about the dangers of becoming a "banana republic" economy. Hawke, on tour in China, is not amused.

Things get worse. The Expenditure Review Committee of Cabinet is where key economic ministers make many of the hard decision on government spending. Ministers from the spending departments pitch their programs for health, welfare, education or defence spending, and the committee reviews them — and prunes them. The committee meets in July 1986 for an even less pleasant task. In July, the floating Australian dollar — sank. Keating sits in the Committee room with a pocket screen in front of him showing Reuters quotes on the dollar's descent. The foreign exchange markets lost confidence in the value of the Australian dollar — and of the economy behind it. Finance minister Peter Walsh is close to despair. As we will recall in his confessions: "How the hell were we going to get out of it?" By cutting government spending.

The theory is that the current account deficit is so bad because Australians spend more than they save, and spend a lot on imports. The aggregate statistics bear this out. So if the government cuts its spending, this should have some effect, not just on the budget deficit, but on the current account deficit too. So with the presses printing the budget stopped at the eleventh hour, the committee meet to cut an additional 1.5 billion dollars from it as quickly as possible.

"The decision was radical, and also tough for the party", Hawke recalls. The revised budget lifted a ban on uranium sales to France, saving 70 million. When the ban was in force, the Government bought the stuff and stockpiled it, rather than selling it to France. This was in order to honour an existing contract with the mining company. Actually, the ban suited France, as the contract price was higher than the market price, and the ban freed the French to buy cheaper uranium than if it was obliged under its contract to pay for the Australian uranium. But it was the principle of the thing that angered the Labor left. When Keating presented the budget, three backbenchers walked out. Left winger Nick Bolkus thought it was "one of the silliest" decisions. Even right winger Graham Richardson conceded that it was "just really dumb". The moral of the story for the Labor left was that no principle was sacred to this government. Labor's support declined. As Rod Cameron said, "ordinary wage and salary earners were not benefiting out of a Labor government". Managing the big numbers, even when it produced reasonably good outcomes in terms of growth and new employment, did not make the electorate happy. There is more to politics than economic management.

It's a curious concept, 'economic rationalism'. It rests only in part on experience of how the economy actually works, and partly on a theory about how it works, but also in part on a theory of how it *ought* to work. Trying to change the economy in the light of economic rationalism brings with it certain problems. Change is driven by the normative idea about how much better the economy will work in the future if Labor changes it in the present. It envisages a change from political to economic time, where change that cannot be measured, the eventfulness of fortune, gives way to uncertainty that can be quantified, the calculus of risk. This pure, quantifiable time never arrives, but it acts as a permanent alternative dreamtime, the purity of which stands as a measure of the impurity of the sordid political time of the present.

As a critique of the irrationality of Australian economic institutions, economic rationalism performs very well. It's not hard to show why any given institutional arrangement fails to measure up to the ideal of a perfect allocation of resources by fully competitive markets acting on perfect information. It is a critical moral philosophy, but it is an imperfect guide to positive action. It suffers the same fate as other critical moral philosophies in the postmodern world. It falls victim to doubts sustained in the course of its application. It appears, after all, not to be the light on the hill. Yet it remains, like all moral philosophies, a useful critique. Critique of any kind is a poor stand-in for a practical, empirical approach to policy, and politics. Like all species of rationalism, it prizes its internal logical unity more than its compatibility with the multiplicity of experiences with which the world of economic events confronts us. It prizes its rationalism at the expense even of reason, which might counsel scepticism about the ability of the mind alone to comprehend, let alone take charge, of the world.

Richo the Greenie

"Graham has always been a zealous fellow", says the urbane Keating, with his sallow irony. The more calculating Richardson sums up his sudden enthusiasm for the Green movement a little differently: "It was a very happy mixture of good politics with what was right." Cue footage of Richo bobbling awkwardly through the bush. Leading environmentalists took him for a bush picnic. "He was deeply concerned his Reeboks were going to get dirty", says the Australian Conservation Foundation's Phillip Toyne. Together with Peter Garrett and Bob Brown, Toyne becomes a fulcrum figure in recomposing a Labor majority.

Two things pull Labor through the 1987 election: Keating finds a $540 million hole in opposition leader John Howard's tax package, denting the credibility of the Liberal's election campaign. Richardson gets leading figures of the environmental movement to endorse Labor, and Labor squeaks in with the help of Green preferences. Whether Richardson was responsible for this policy or not would be hotly disputed, but what mattered in the moment was his capacity to augment his own celebrity by claiming that it was his idea all along.

"By 1990, no Australian child will be living in poverty." It's a promise Hawke makes for the cameras at Sydney Opera House and will regret thereafter. "I just had to wear that cross", he says. What's interesting is how it happened. According to the *Hawke Memoirs*, it was a matter of whittling the campaign speech into finer and finer shape, and not noticing a subtle but crucial change. There is a difference between saying that under a Labor government no child's family need lack the funds to keep a child out of poverty and the claim that no child will live in poverty.

Or as Mark Latham points out, there's a difference between providing people with the welfare payment to get by and providing them with the social capacity to lead a life of self respect. A half century on, we're really a lot closer to Ben Chifley's light on the hill. The social safety net wartime Labor dreamed of is now substantially a reality. But by the light of that achievement, a new light appears, on a still more distant hill. This one lights the way to government that does not just throw money at need, making a need a private matter solved by the purchase of things, but a government that can also see in need not just a material lack, but a deficit in the organisation of public life itself. With its "targeted" benefits, the Hawke and Keating governments provide money for needs, but generate a public mood that resents the categories identified by the targets. As materially beneficial as targeted welfare spending may be, it is culturally detrimental — and in the end, electorally detrimental. That no child will live in poverty is not a promise any amount of money alone can deliver.

That media hiccup aside, the campaign goes well, with Labor's support falling in suburban heartland seats, but with gains in marginal seats that offset the losses. Hawke promotes Richardson into cabinet, and he becomes Minister for the Environment. He supported a campaign against logging in Tasmania. Peter Walsh calls this "decadence". John Button calls it "indulgent". But as Toyne says, Richo "was about knocking people down and dragging them out" and he prevails. Of the "post materialist" agenda, the Green stuff fairs better than land rights. Hawke's promises on that score are, according to Charles Perkins, "like snow on the desert sands".

Richardson was a complex character. He titled his memoirs *Whatever It Takes*, and styled himself as the ultimate machine politician. A less flattering portrait is journalist Marian Wilkinson's *The Fixer*.[27] Both books are a fascinating insight into the culture of NSW Labor's machine politics. It is one of the few organisational cultures that really fits with the classic style of muck raking journalism that Wilkinson brings to it. Petty crims and prostitutes rub shoulders in this book with business tycoons and international statemen. Where Richardson paints himself as a true believer in the traditional Labor creed of helping the little guy, Wilkinson sees him as helping himself and a handful of mates.

Yet in concluding her chapter on "Graham Green", she quotes Bob Brown: "Richardson made the difference when it came to the forests. Without his appearance on the scene in a whole host of environmental issues around this country, from the tropics of Queensland to the snow covered tall eucalypts of southern Tasmania, they would not be World Heritage, they would not be protected and they would not be, the heirlooms they are going to be for this country." The irony is that Richardson's private morality was in the end irrelevant to at least this part of his public action. If there is a virtue in the culture of machine politics, it is that it is a machine for meshing the desires of its operatives for power, prestige and pots of loot with that of the voting public for a fair go for the majority.

Crash Landing

"This is the one that brings home the bacon", is how Paul Keating explained the 1988 budget at a press conference in the new parliament house. What is not clear is whether it is everyone's bacon or Keating's own he is speaking about. Pure product of machine culture that he is, there is no necessary contradiction. Having got the economy on track, Keating thinks it's time — time for Hawke to step down. Hawke refuses.

In August, in an appearance on *Lateline*, Hawke indicates that if Keating leaves Treasury, he can be replaced. It is a remark Bob Collins recalls thinking was "unforgivable", but Keating, he says, "was being emotionally immature". Hawke and Keating strike the fabled Kirribilli House agreement, under which Hawke will step down after the 1990 election. It's the second time that, meeting to strike a deal, these two characters put off the inevitable conflict between them.

During the fracas between Hawke and Keating, somebody with a phone frequency scanner intercepts a phone call between Richardson and Keating, in which Richardson is speaking on a mobile phone. The call makes its way into the public domain. It is a remarkable event, this public airing of the private talk of public figures. It's as embarrassing as the Not-Mimi tape or the Donaher family. It's is political rather than domestic or sexual pornography. I wonder how we would think of John Curtin if we had access to his private calls too? Perhaps what made Labor leaders of the 80s and 90s seem smaller than life is that, compared to their predecessors, we saw too much of them up close. Their celebrity was intimate, mundane, rather than statuesque.

"This is a beautiful set of numbers for us", insists Keating. "I kept saying there were very depressing messages from out there", recalls John Button. Credit growth fuelled asset value inflation. Punters borrowed cheap money from banks who competed too aggressively against each other for market share in the new, deregulated environment. Investors parked a chunk of borrowed money in Sydney real estate. Throughout 1988 the economy raced away. Interest rates were too low, and the economy overheated.

Or so it appears in hindsight. The economic advisers at the time are more concerned about the 1987 stock market crash, which is one of the reasons for the low interest rate settings. They are thinking in terms of the precedent of the 20s, when tightening credit exacerbated the crash. But this is the 80s, and while the crash clips the wings of a few high flying business celebrities, speculative growth continues. The surging economy sucks in imports and inflation takes off. Keating meets with the Treasury and Reserve Bank officials and they jack the interest rates up and up and up.

Until, finally… "you could feel it. Something snapped", as

Keating adviser Don Russell recalls. Keating refused to insulate home loan rates from the credit squeeze. "We ran the risk of alienating everyone who owned a home in Australia" as Richardson says. Richardson, who begged for an exemption for home buyers, nevertheless recalls Keating's style admiringly: "It represents a commitment to authority, and the way it is exercised".

Trouble on another front. The Europeans subsidise agricultural exports. Deciding that if you can't beat them, join them, the Americans follow suit. This hurts Australian agriculture, and there are rumblings from the bush urging the government to threaten to pull out of the Western alliance. Hawke proposes APEC — an economic forum of Asian powers — as an alternative. Meanwhile, the country slips into recession.

In February 1990, Hawke calls an election. Labor wins it on the second preference strategy, an approach for which Richardson claims the credit. Rod Cameron calls it the "biggest single reason for the success of Labor's campaign". But after the election win, Hawke alienates Richardson, refusing to give him his choice of portfolio in the new government. "I thought that was a bit rich", deadpans Richardson.

The economy heads south. The forecasts from Treasury and the Reserve Bank, the Prime Minister's Office, the Statistician — they all turn out to be wrong. "We were acting on information that was just wrong", recalls Michael Duffy. Perhaps the lesson here is that there is something to be said for "being prepared to listen to anecdotal evidence" as Hawke puts it. But this was a government that ignored what politicians learn from talking to people and relied instead on the models and the numbers. It was a rationalist rather than an empiricist government. In March 1990 Keating is still saying it will be a soft landing. Which prompts Peter Walsh to speak of "the hazards of self delusion". Keating famously calls it "the recession Australia had to have". He claims in retrospect that this was Hawke's view also. Hawke's response in *Labor in Power* is direct: "any claim that I was consulted about that phrase beforehand is an absolute lie".

Bill Kelty pushes for industry assistance, but the government is obsessed with telecommunications competition policy. "I was a bit manic about it", Keating later concedes. He is manic about the rational view of the relationship between knowledge and government, and refuses to consider a more empirical, suck it and see approach. The financial journalists egg him on. Keating is relentless in his pursuit of his own agenda. "He can bruise not just the ego but the spirit, and that's when he goes too far", counsels Richardson. But Keating is like Achilles denied his prize. His pride is hurt. On Hawke's leadership: "It became a joke".

Placido Domingo

Keating's 'Placido Domingo' speech is a strange text He gave it to the National Press Club, in December 1990: "When I walk out on that stage, some performances will be better than others. But I'll always be trying to spring the economics and the politics together. Out there on the stage doing the Placido Domingo." And doing it better than his more prominent rival, Luciano Pavarotti. "Leadership is not about being popular. It's about being right, about being strong. And it's not whether you go through some shopping centre tripping over the TV crew's cords. It's about doing what you think the nation requires."[28]

In this famous speech, supposedly given off the record to the annual dinner of the National Press Club in December 1990, Paul Keating condenses everything about himself that people love to hate and hate themselves for loving. He flatters and he scolds. He praises the "participants" and bags the "voyeurs" in the struggle for change. He even has the nerve to dismiss John Curtin as a "trier" rather than a leader. Australia never had leaders, he says. "We're an accident... we never said this place is ours and we are going to run it for ourselves."

With the past thus dimmed, the future looms brighter on the horizon. "We have this chance", but it requires "national will and national leadership". Keating then defines the nature of this leadership as "having a conversation with the public", which, in a perverse sense, is what he was performing in this very speech. Performing, like Placido Domingo, in the shadow of one he thinks is a lesser performer, who gets bigger cheers from the crowd.

"There's an S&M glow about Keating," as Meaghan Morris observes in a profound essay on watching the Treasurer.[29] In the instance of his National Press Club speech the exquisite torture comes from it being so quotable. By tradition, speeches given at that occasion are deemed to be off the record, so journalists look for a way to bend the rules, and get Keating's best lines into print.

Like Doc Evatt, Paul Keating has all the hallmarks of a master thinker, of someone who thinks he can talk to the people on the basis of a higher knowledge of their interests and needs.[30] He is loved by yuppie swine and talking head types for the fearlessness with which he asserts the prerogatives of the strong will and sharp mind. "A Labor government is a rare breed of horse. You don't ride it by cracking the whip and jabbing your spurs into its flanks. You coax it, soothe it, talk to it, ease it along and point the way ahead."[31] Keating's lesson is that only a smart and wily drover can master such a dumb animal.

The showdown with Hawke has come. Even this private moment is watched, via closed circuit television, by the Prime Minister's staff in the next room. Hawke sits back relaxed; Keating animated, pacing. Hawke was annoyed by Keating's claim that Australia had no great leaders. "The mouth was the mouth of Paul Keating but the words were the words of Jack Lang." To Hawke it is an insult to the memory of Curtin. It is of course also an insult to Hawke, but I think Hawke was really offended by Keating's lack of respect for Labor saints. The Kirribilli deal is off. "Bob had an easy ride through public life", remarks the contemptuous Keating, who prided himself on doing it alone.

"We threw that year away", recalls Collins, of the time the government spent marking time while Keating challenged Hawke. The Gulf war delays Keating's run. The government lowers tariffs — "a bit quick" in John Button's view. "I just did not believe that they had got the economy right", adds Bill Kelty. Senior labour movement figures in daily contact with business decision makers think the economy is in a bad way, but the government still runs economic policy by the numbers and the models. Keating makes his challenge in June 1991, and loses. He retires to the backbench. He thinks about art and clocks and other things, or so it appears.

Coronation Hill

It takes five and a half hours of debate to decide, but finally Hawke supports Aboriginal opposition, on religious grounds, to mining at Coronation Hill. Even Kim Beazley, a loyal Hawke supporter, feels forced to confront his leader across the table and insist that he "make a decision". But it is not the decision Labor's hard-heads want. In *Labor in Power* Hawke is still indignant: "the hypocrisy of people who claim adherence to the Christian religion, who can easily accommodate the mystery of the holy trinity, pouring scorn on the beliefs of others because it doesn't make sense, just left me appalled beyond measure." Even with hindsight, it seems to mystify some of the cabinet members as to what this intangible thing was that Hawke felt called to answer to and protect.

John Kerin, Keating's replacement as Treasurer brings down the budget in August 1991. It fails to impress, and Hawke drops Kerin in December after a botched press conference where he confused economic terms. "There wasn't much future for the government under that leadership", is John Dawkins' assessment. Then comes the Liberal Party's *Fightback!* package. A vigorous and fresh John Hewson presents a policy to the public that would accelerate economic reform, particularly on the taxation front. "The government was struck dumb", says Keating, "*Fightback!* finished Bob off, not me."

By December 1991 there are six ministers asking Hawke to go. As Gareth Evans puts it to his leader: "Pull out digger, the dogs are pissing on your swag." Robert Ray's advice to Hawke is to get out while on top: "back of our minds, Labor Party needs some icons." Bob Collins, who spins Labor fables with bar room drama, recalls "the smell of death". Second time around, Keating polled 56 votes to Hawke's 51. Hawke's press conference after his defeat is emotional, personal. "If this was eleven years ago, I would be getting very thoroughly drunk."

Sweetest Victory of All

"Why won't you call an early election?" demands Hewson, in parliament, sitting at the dispatch box. Keating rounds on him from the other side of the chamber: "The answer is, mate, because I want to do you slowly." It's a rare occasion where the broadcast coverage of Parliament makes good television. Keating released his *One Nation* statement in February 1992. "We had to change our position", recalls Keating, "reordering the debate, saying there was a role for government." With Hewson presenting the Liberals as a potential government of accelerated economic reform, Keating tacks the other way, and with *One Nation* presents a package of employment and training measures. Keating lost faith in the advice of the Reserve Bank and the Treasury: "The judgements lacked guile". There are one million jobless.

Somehow, he pulls it off. In March 1993 Keating leads Labor to an unexpected win, his "sweetest victory of all" as he calls it on election night, out at Bankstown. This is where we came in. Bob Ellis was at Bankstown on that night, when I was at the Intercontinental. "Then suddenly, very quickly, I was at the side of the stage... and Keating, in half profile, was at the microphone, and the crowd was saying, 'We want Paul, we want Paul', and he was saying, 'You've got me.' And then there was silence, and he said, 'This is the sweetest victory of all'... and then like a tennis ball tossed back over his shoulder to me alone, 'This is a victory for the true believers', and I drank in the moment knowing few again would ever equal it...".[32]

There are those who feel that the moral Paul Keating's celebrity stands for is the possibility of the destruction of the traditions of the Labor Party. Dean Jaensch titled his book on the subject *The Hawke-Keating Hijack*. Peter Beilharz called his *Transforming Labor*. Graham Maddox juxtaposes *The Hawke Government and the Labor Tradition*.[33] These books chose to judge the Hawke government, and Keating as its economic prime-mover, by the standards and values of the Labor culture of the past, although the authors are not agreed on exactly which values in Labor's past are its true essence. While even less sympathetic to the Keating view on creating wealth in order to share it, is Carol Johnson's book *The Labor Legacy*.[34] At least Johnson recognises that if Labor has a tradition, it is one of virtuality, one of inventing pragmatic working relations with capitalism that secure something for Labor's constituences. Labor's tradition is a modern one, a tradition of fresh invention. The lesson of her study is not that Labor betrayed anything, but rather that it tried what it always tries, to create a working relationship among conflicting parties, an effort that eventually unravels.

I did not look upon Keating as a transformer or a hijacker of a legacy or tradition on that night. I think the lesson is rather that Labor in power always attempts the impossible. The problem is as knotty as this: The application of a belief in which many do not believe to appearances that are not what they appear, by people who's limitations can only be known in the middle of events that will expose limitations, guided by a knowledge of how politics and economics spring together that can only be verified to the extent that this knowledge fails. If that means we can expect less from Labor's leaders than faith might once have implied, then it is all the more reason to insist that Labor deliver what little it can deliver to minimise avoidable suffering.

The quality of a celebrity might be measured by the combination of love and hate she or he inspires. A Labor celebrity is measured only by the love of those who know in their hearts that their suffering, and that of those close to them would definitely have been greater had they not believed enough in this cause that it might cause at least this little. But there is no master plan, no magic pudding, and if there is a light on the hill, it is not that its glow has dimmed, but that it illuminates a spectrum of the mind that has not yet been brought to bear on rethinking the Labor fable.

cyberspace

chapter **8**

Generational ganglands

The true critic is he who bears within himself the dreams and ideas and feelings of myriad generations, and to whom no form of thought is alien, no emotional impulse obscure.

Oscar Wilde

The Itchy and Scratchy Movie is the defining moment for our generation. How would you like it if someone had said you couldn't watch the moon landing?

Lisa Simpson

Hugh Mackay's Generations

"Generation X didn't OD on the sofa," writes Camilla Nelson in *The Australian*. "We became angry."[1] I'll say! It's the subjective side of a very real problem: Australia at the end of the 90s was a mature economy with an ageing population. Those already in the money made deals amongst themselves to keep things that way, while a generation of Australians was warehoused in the education system.

Sooner or later they came out the other end. As cab drivers talking about discourse analysis, waitresses qualified in econometrics, shop assistants with interesting theories about child psychology. Diverse people with diverse talents, all with one thing in common: resentment for older and often less talented people who hogged the trough and will hog it for some time to come, what with health care, pensions and superannuation.

As the lucky country ran out of luck, issues of inter-generational equity appeared on the horizon. Inequalities occur across space, and can be detected by comparing the opportunities for the lives people can live when the population is broken down according to postcodes. Inequalities also occur across time, and can be detected by comparing the opportunities for the lives people can live when the population is broken down according to age cohorts. These two kinds of disenfranchisement can overlap. The rise in rhetorics of generational conflict in the 90s was largely cultural, expressing competing claims for attention among age cohorts with different cultural tastes. It also expressed something more serious. Pockets of very high youth unemployment, concentrated in particular localities, offered the bleak prospect of entrenching a permanent disenfranchisement. As Mark Latham says, "It is plainly intolerable for a nation to have one-tenth or more of its citizens and neighbourhoods disenfranchised from the new economy, with this level of disadvantage then being conveyed to the next generation through the tragedy of educational under-achievement and skill exclusion."[2]

The social psychologist Hugh Mackay devoted his book *Generations* to studying the way this perceived generation gap opened up in Australian culture.[3] He identifies a generation of Baby Boomers, born in the 50s, who grew up in an atmosphere of optimism and rising expectations, and who staged a 'revolution' against the values of their parents. Mackay calls this the Lucky Generation, who live secure within the comfort zone of suburban affluence.

The children of the Lucky Generation are the Baby Boomers. Like Helen Townsend, author of *Baby Boomers*, Mackay finds they were raised in an atmosphere of postwar material security, but against the background of the permanent emergency of the cold war.[4] They applied the cultural training of the cold war, with its permanent mobilisation, to the increasingly less materially secure years of the 80s and 90s. They became prone to stressing out about the present, and feeling nostalgic for a mythical 60s of peace, love and a good bonk.

The children of Baby Boomers, born in the '70s, are what Mackay wants to call the Options Generation. He did not succeed in shifting the media away from its consensus term, Generation X, so that is what I will call them. Canadian author Douglas Coupland borrowed the name from a '70s punk band, who in turn pinched it from the title of a '50s 'problem youth' book.[5] Generation X are the "most highly educated and media stimulated generation". They experience cyberspace, not as something new, but as something always already there. As the writer Beth Spencer says, being Generation X "means being part of the first generation to grow up on television."[6]

This might be why, in Mackay's terms, they are also the "bored generation", as media-generated novelty has, in their lifetime, become routine. As Ari, who could be a typical Generation X person from one of Mackay's research focus groups, puts it: "There must be thousands of movies I've seen on television." Mackay says that Generation X are used to the idea of insecurity where work and relationships are concerned, having grown up with rising unemployment and parents to whom an argument about squeezing the toothpaste tube in the middle is grounds for divorce. Generation X don't share the Boomer optimism about the future of Australia that Boomers inherited from their parents. But they tend to rate their own awareness of differences and difficulties pretty highly. They think they can handle things. They experience private hope and public despair. They keep their options open, making things up as they go along. Or as Ari says, "I may see no future but I got ethics."

For Mackay, people born in the '60s are Post Boomers, a sort of coffee break between generations, who "want to make an art form out of creating a lifestyle", but are otherwise of little interest. As I was born in 1961, reading Mackay's book makes me feel as though I share only some of the Boomer traits, but that I have already experienced some of the frustrations with them that Mackay reserves for his Options or X-ers. Catharine Lumby, also born in 1961, describes us in similarly relational terms as the "Squeeze Generation".[7] Perhaps it's this in-betweenness that makes me reflect on how debate comes to a consensus about the very existence of these kinds of Capitalised Cohorts as public things.

Mackay's method involves both group and individual interviews. A lot of the interviews appear to have been conducted at a time when generationalism was a live issue in the media. Mackay presumes that the main influence on generational identity is the relations within the family between generations. That may well be so, but there seems no clear way to distinguish the influence of the private world of the family from the influence of the public world, particularly the media. The rhetorical tools and images that Mackay's interviewees use seem to me to be drawn from the media. Which is not to say that the family counts for nothing. Rather, there exists a combination of influences, where the raw experience of being a mother or daughter, a grandfather or grandson, is assessed and interpreted in terms of images and stories made available via the vectors of radio, television, videos, magazines and the internet.

Heartbeat of the Literati

The synchronising of experience is a characteristic of modern life. The literary critic Georg Lukács writes in *The Historical Novel* about the way that, since the French revolution, mass mobilisation for war created a whole new kind of "mass experience." When a lot of people experience the same events at the same time, "this must enormously strengthen the feeling first that there is such a thing as history, that it is an uninterrupted process of changes and finally that it has a direct effect upon the life of every individual."[8]

The synchronising of media experience is a characteristic of postmodern life. Where warfare once mobilised a generation and moved it about in space; the media now mobilise a flow of images and move them about in space. Communication vectors, most of which developed as part of the modern war machine, tend to become ever more global and synchronised. Now they produce a synchronising of experience even in the absence of a mobilising conflict. This may be why common generational structures of feeling have been growing quietly stronger, unnoticed by a media and a public which imagines that generational difference was a one-off '60s thing'.

The whole idea of generationalism, the idea that there are

common experiences that define an age cohort, is a media artefact. It is a perception that has only come to exist in the first place as the media have synchronised the circulation of information. Starting with the first mass circulation newspapers, then the radio, cinema and eventually television, perhaps no more than four or five generations have lived in a media environment that made it *possible* to circulate images and stories about generations that people could use to think through their experience. And so we have had the Lost Generation, the Me Generation, and Generation X.

Mackay's book is very interesting and enlightening about what images and stories people have come to accept as categories they can use for defining their identity and the identity of others. But it is less useful as an explanation of how the whole process works. To do that, I think we have to ask about what kinds of media are available that can synchronise people's perceptions, what stories and images are available via which media vectors, and most importantly, who gets to make those images.

The mass broadcast vectors of radio and television produce the phenomena of people experiencing the same images simultaneously. Radio and television work their way into everyday life. The images and stories they carry propose templates for reading experiences in everyday life. The existence of a shared point of reference, in the form of this synchronisation of images, makes the subjective experience of generationalism possible. While the images may be common, the experiences in everyday life that they can be made to express are not. What a generation shares is not the same experiences, but rather different experiences read via the same images.

Generation X is not the first generation produced by the media, but it may be the first to reach widespread self-awareness about the constitutive role of the media in its self-definition. As Ari says: "Mum is part of the television generation as well". Which might explain why Ari treats the media more ironically than your average Boomer. He grew up not only on television, but observing his Boomer parents, who came to it later in life, relate to television as well.

In the 90s, the marketing and advertising industries began thinking seriously about how to target Generation X consumers. Advertising started internalising the kind of critical and ironic distance from advertising that marketing researchers identified as the hallmark of contemporary media reading practices. The Heartbeat market research group, for instance, labelled consumers in their 20s and 30s the Literati, on the assumption that what distinguished them was a distinctive level of literacy about media and marketing.[9]

Somewhat younger than Mackay, the Heartbeat team videotape their focus groups and make their research results available to their clients on CD-rom. Their construction of the generational object, in this case called Literati rather than Options Generation or Generation X, similarly reflects a more media-saturated view of everyday life. According to Heartbeat, the Literati "feel pulled in different directions by the multitude of choices and options open to them. The internet, the world media, the global village. Information is everywhere. They are trying to think holisitically in a global world." The lesson for media and marketing, is that the Literati "are looking for signposts they can rely on and brands which offer stability and a sense of direction for the future." They are literate and discriminating about media images.

According to Heartbeat, the Literati are no dopes. "They switch off from messages that, as Cherman from Ipswich told us, 'don't tell the truth, but don't lie'." They respond to both fantasy and reality but not attempts to pass one off as the other. They are "a generation of realists" and "they do not suffer phoneys". Yet they crave "symbols of their beliefs". And yet are sceptical of images and stories that offer too much. "The cult of celebrity has taken a very different turn…. The Literati reject icons that seem ideal." In place of the perfect glamour of the 'golden years of Hollywood', it's the mix of the mundane and the otherworldly that appeals.

The cultural studies scholar David Marshall writes in *Celebrity and Power* about how celebrity is part of a double rationalisation.[10] Business and political leaders try to rationalise the wants and desires of populations from above with various quantitative and qualitative research tools. Heartbeat's CD-rom, like Hugh Mackays' *Mackay Reports* are an attempt at constructing popular culture as an object of reasoning and calculation. While quantitative data is still useful, by the time Generation X arrive on the scene, reasoning about popular desires has started to get way too complicated for simple surveys. Both the way Generation X rationalises the world through media images, and the way media managers and marketeers try to gauge what kinds of images Generation X will embrace, has become an ironic double game. After all, Generation X is itself a rationalisation of the messy behaviours of different people's everyday lives.

One thing that is certain is that the Sony Corporation, for instance, has created a more powerful relation to the Generation X public than any political party. Politics as a whole becomes just a branch of the media and a species of celebrity, and as such has to compete on unfavourable terms with other kinds of media image and story. In the 90s, the major parties tried to insert traditional political images and personalities into the kind of media Generation X might read. In the 1998 election, Labor leader Kim Beazley appeared in the 'youth culture' magazine *Juice,* and appeared alongside popular band The Whitlams at suitable photo opportunities.[11] This was more a case of communicating the old politics to emerging publics than of trying to read and articulate a new politics that might emerge out of the Generation X or Literati culture — if such a thing can be said to exist.

Richard Neville on the Frontline

While marketeers might embrace younger people as consumers, and political parties might chase after their votes, the media industries have not been universally enthusiastic about the new sensibility that is spreading across popular culture. The constitution of generational identity via the media often takes place negatively, by defining a generation in terms of properties it does not share with another generation. This creates not only the perception of generational identity, but also of generational conflict.

Hence the popularity, in the media, for defining younger people in terms of what is *wrong* with them. Boomer talking heads are always looking for reasons not to give young people the car keys. There is no shortage of superannuated commentators who can think of nothing more creative than to blame all our problems on young people. Ageing pundits queue up to denounce any idea anyone ever had since they last read a book. Yesterday's heroes of left, right and off-the-map can't stop themselves from adding new bits to a self-serving fantasy that portrays the youth of today as deluded dopes. They just don't get it. But they won't shut up about it.

Take, as a representative Boomer talking head, Richard Neville. The former co-editor of *Oz* magazine has mellowed into a kind of new age sage of suburbia.[12] He says of Quentin Tarantino, who he thinks is a "skilful but ultimately shallow" film director, "everyone is so dazzled by technique and there is not really a lot of substance in what he says."[13] But let's consider another hypothesis: It's Neville who is skilful but ultimately shallow. The lack of substance in his complaints about Tarantino is the first piece of evidence against him. He is simply incapable of hearing what this film maker has to say. Where a younger Neville attacked suburbia for its resistance to new information, Neville in middle age has become the mouthpiece for just such a suburban narrowing of the channels.

Many of the talking heads and gatekeepers of the media are Boomers who acquired their positions during the expansion of the media, culture and arts industries that dates back to the Gorton and Whitlam governments of the 70s. That old curmudgeon Les Murray calls them, with a certain Celtic irony, the Whitlam Ascendancy.[14] I prefer to call them the Burblers. This is the sound they make in the media — burble burble. But it is also the place — suburbia — from which that sound comes. The Burblers have retired, one way or another, from public life, and make their pronouncements from private retreat in the suburbs. Cut off from the urbane give and take of a properly public life, they become cranky and preoccupied with grudges and nostalgia. Their perceptions no longer knit together into a consensual map that younger people can accept — not least because part of that consensus is a demonising of new ideas and fresh cultural movements.

At first sight, alienating younger readers and viewers might seem like a puzzling thing for market-driven media to do. In an episode of the comedy TV show *Frontline* called 'My Generation', the executive producer of the fictional TV current affair show *'Frontline'* explains why his show routinely portrays young people as uneducated, unemployable, drug-taking little aliens from Planet Nintendo: "Our audience likes feeling superior to the younger generation."[15] Since most of the advertising between which the fictional *'Frontline'* runs is for superannuation schemes, young people "are the one demographic we can afford to alienate." Given that most of the anti-youth stories that *Frontline* portrays as running on *'Frontline'* covers are stories that have actually run on 'real' current affairs shows, I think we can take it that the explanation is pretty accurate.

Looking at the formation of a generational rhetoric in the media from my supposedly Squeeze Generation location, it seems to me that a lot of us in our 30s who were scratching around trying to carve out a space in the media, the arts or the academy got caught in the middle. The easy way out, particularly in the first half of the 90s, was to create something that would please the Burblers: rehash the same images and stories, confirm their perceptions of the world, and in particular, be the token young(ish) person who could be trotted out to bash any new idea firmly on the head. The Young Fogeys who learned to burble got ahead, and are now entrenched in the culture industries. For them, the bar was lowered.

In the late 90s, the axis started to shift, if imperceptibly at first. Since the only voices the Burblers ever hear are each others', their collective drift into irrelevance went unnoticed amongst them, while those alleged young 'victims' of political correctness and poststructuralism and postmodernism and the slacker mentality got on with writing their novels, putting up their web sites, finishing their doctorates, polishing their stand-up comedy, rehearsing their music — and filling in their dole forms. What they have to say often has a harder edge. "There is a last, and very cherished, urban myth", says Ari, "that every new generation has it better than the one that came before it. Bullshit…. There's no jobs, no work, no factories, no wage packet, no half acre block. There is no more land. I am sliding towards the sewer, and I'm not even struggling against the flow. I can smell the pungent aroma of shit, but I'm still breathing."

Success is the best revenge. As material success is increasingly denied them in the 'real' world, Generation X spend their energies creating a virtual culture instead. The response is as creative as it is angry. The emergent culture of today is a secret picnic. If there is something positive in the media artefact of generationalism it is the possibility that Generation X could become the first truly virtual generation. Virtual in the sense of embracing the possibility of staying true to the main benefit of being young — the ability to thrive on new information, to absorb it creatively into one's being. Were Generation X to become the first virtual generation, it would become the last generation. It would refuse the limited set of possibilities that go with being defined as a generation.

The pressure to stay within the bounds of generational and suburban conformity appears in the media to come most strongly from Burbler Boomers who have embraced the impoverishment of suburbia and would foist it on the young as well, and so both generationalism and suburbia appear as something linked in a lot of the art that tries to escape from those norms. It is the remarkable skill for connecting new information to the continuity of experience that Burblers seem to most loudly resist and resent about their offspring.

Generationalism is to time what suburbanality is to space — a refusal of possibilities beyond an arbitrary norm. Overcoming generationalism is like overcoming suburbanality. People escaping the former intersect with the people escaping the latter, and the point of intersection is urbanity. In this chapter, I want to talk about the work of a few contemporaries of mine who seem to me to be on the frontline in defining and establishing an urbanity that arises out of living deep in the broadcast age, but which might also look forward to the emergence of the more distributed vectors of cyberspace.

Mark Davis in Gangland

"Once being young was a romantic adventure", writes Mark Davis. "Not one that ended in the popular stereotypes of the dole queue, the teen gang, the single mother, or the feminist daughter." Davis' book *Gangland* arrived in 1997 as a breath of fresh air.[16] It set out in clear and detailed form exactly how the Burbler world view in Australian culture contributed to this now national trend of demonising the young and the marginal for all the nation's problems. Finally, the Burblers were brought to book for their part in the decline of confidence and the rise of reaction.

The theme of *Gangland* is the "culture wars" of the mid 90s, in which young people "get to side with the popular, the postmodern, the untruthful and the self-deceived" — at least in the paranoid mindset of ageing Burblers who are losing their grip on reality, the agenda, and the public imagination. "Many of the protagonists are former cold warriors out of a job." Unlike the youth unemployed, they were able to invent their own make-work scheme, by transferring the cold war sense of permanent emergency from the reds under the bed to the young person lying flaked out — probably on drugs — on top of it.

Politics and religion are no longer the arenas where values and interests are thrashed out. Now it's culture. Only the Burblers try to maintain their authority by proclaiming a monopoly on the cultural high ground, at the expense of the young. This "gerrymander of the ideas market", as Davis calls it, is detrimental. "Our cultural landscape is currently peppered with examples of a desperate, backward looking stasis, a fearful hanging on, manifested as a long, slow, unproductive whinge."

Burblers link ethical and aesthetic decline to the idea of the young as failures, but if there is a cause of decline it is this constipation of the media sphere — unable to purge itself of the less nutritious parts of the Burbler gang. The Burblers like to monopolise the rhetoric of 'standards', but the fact is that sorting out what is durable and what it ephemeral in Burbler culture is a part of the ongoing debate about standards.

A leading symptom of the Burblers' decline is "legislated nostalgia" — a term Davis borrows from Douglas Coupland. Legislated nostalgia is that excruciating feeling one has while being made to endure the endless repetitions of a dewy-eyed fantasy about the 60s, as summed up in the title of Richard Neville's memoir, *Hippie Hippie Shake*.[17] The 60s was not a magical time. It was a time like any other, but now it is endlessly presented through the golden lens of nostalgia rather than a genuine, critical cultural history.[18]

The denial of a positive space in so-called high culture and literary life for young people fits with a more general repressive climate. Local and state governments increasingly deny basic rights to youth with special policing powers, sentencing laws and curfews. After the fatal stabbing of police officer Peter Forsyth, by what the *Sun-Herald* decided was a "gang of young drug dealers", in my own street in Ultimo, Sydney, I felt a brief pang of anti-youth hysteria myself. A feeling some of my neighbours already experienced: "residents have raised serious concerns about dance parties", the *Sun-Herald* reports.[19] But it alarmed me that when new police powers were suggested as the remedy for knife attacks, the suggestion was that it was only and always youth who were the people who needed to be searched for weapons.

These measures were advocated in spite of the fact that, as three community welfare experts declared, "there is often an inverse relationship between the depiction of 'the juvenile crime problem' and the actual nature and level of offending."[20] The media coverage of the Forsyth stabbing shows why Davis is right in thinking that generationalism is more than just a matter of a few Burblers needing to be pensioned off. Media-generated perceptions of generational attributes can contribute to public perceptions. As Ari says, "the rich don't fear the unionised worker, they don't fear the militant. They fear the crim, the murderer, the basher." And we might put a hard and fresh young face on him in our imagination without thinking.

Davis is particularly good on the hysteria around political correctness. He fits it into a cold war style of moral panic about race, women, young people, and the mentality that declares the end of western civilisation on the grounds that kids wear their baseball caps backwards. The remarkable thing is how much air time and how many column inches well-entrenched pundits wasted proclaiming that they were being 'censored' by political correctness — Paul Sheehan built a career on it.[21] Davis points to the self-evident absurdity of this. "If this is dissent, then it's a stage managed affair indeed — diversion designed to make tame orthodoxies look stale." It's a sure sign that a Burbler is clueless about contemporary reality and has run out of ideas when she or he spends time declaring that their old ideas are somehow under ferocious attack from often unspecified and unnamed young whippersnappers. But then, as Davis says, "they've been breathing each other's air for too long."

Davis faults the Burblers not only for detrimental effects on the politics of public culture, but also for the stagnation and boredom of literary high culture. Their "greatest single talent is elevating the middlebrow." So in book after book we get endless repetitions of the literary aspirations of suburban taste. Allegedly universal "values" are merely asserted, never justified or scrutinised. The Burblers have presided over a suburbanisation of Australian letters, cutting it off from anything that might challenge its pretensions.

Burblers make a habit of confusing storytellers with thinkers, talking heads with intellectuals. Time and again, storytellers shoot their mouths off about concepts they don't understand but nevertheless don't like, with few professional thinkers ever getting a word in edgewise. We need both stories and concepts in a public literary life, but reviewers, publishers and publicisers have, since the 60s, pushed one at the expense of the other. "Too often what passes for debate… is no more than an attempt to discredit motives and credentials."

Burblers have created an anti-intellectual culture. Davis offers as evidence a string of quotes from the Young Fogey style of high journalism of the broadsheets. For instance: "For many deconstructionists there is no such thing as truth and falsehood, good writing or bad; or indeed, no reality outside of texts." To which Davis responds dryly: "No theorist argues anything remotely so ridiculous." An increasingly educated population are coming to see this.

Davis effectively turns the tables on our leading Burblers. Where they see decline and fall everywhere but in their own backyard, Davis locates the problem squarely with Burblers and their lazy minded ways. It's not women, minorities or the young that are the problem. The problem is that an ageing Burbler ascendancy can't or won't make an effort to understand the contemporary range of experiences and points of view.

If there is hope, then for Davis it comes from a spontaneous, bottom-up urbanity that bypasses Burbler-dominated vectors. Out in community radio, zine publishing, web sites, listservers, self-organised campus reading groups, and at performance nights at the local pub — people are doing it for themselves. People are working through the cultural issues and experiences that the mainstream put in the too-hard basket.

As Davis says, young people know more about the media than their elders. They didn't come to the current media vectors late in life, they grew up with them and learned their ways and means early. When *A Current Affair* host Ray Martin decided to abandon the last shred of his 60s leftie cred and front for a sordid report by Mike Monroe that attacked the unemployed Paxton kids, not everyone took this sorry bit of hate-TV lying down. Some were busy hand-printing Paxton Fan Club t-shirts.

The publication of *Gangland* was significant not just because it identified the paralysis generationalism has caused, but because the reaction to the book by the Burbler crowd proved a good deal of its thesis. The principle targets of his attack commandeered as much media acreage as possible to denounce *Gangland*, thus proving its hypothesis about the ability of the Burblers to monopolise a good many vectors along which images and stories pass into the public realm. But the more encouraging side of the *Gangland* affair is that some of the media's gatekeepers demonstrated that their responsibility transcends generational rhetorics. A little bit more room opened up in the media.

The irony is precisely the exclusion of younger voices from serious consideration in the media that created the speaking position from which Davis could appear as the critic of such exclusion. As a result of his intervention, a few people in their 30s elbowed their (our) way into talking head status. The onus is on them (us) to create still more room for those still excluded. As part of that process, I want to write about what was distinctive about the experience of my contemporaries. This is not meant to legislate for a new nostalgia. Rather, trying to identify some differences and continuities from the 60s to the 70s and 80s might be a way of providing an enabling fable for others to mark their own experience, of the 90s and beyond, in terms of differences and continuities that may still be emerging.

Christos Tsiolkas Gets Loaded

In a now famous scene in Quentin Tarantino's film *Pulp Fiction*, Butch (played by Bruce Willis) gets free from a pair of psychos intent on torturing him in their dungeon, out back of a pawn shop. As he makes his escape, he pauses. Still trapped back there is a man who wants to kill him, a man Butch has cheated, but to whom he still feels a moral obligation. He decides to go back and rescue him. But first, Butch must choose a weapon. He picks up, and rejects, a baseball bat and a chain saw, before finally settling on a samurai sword as his weapon of choice.

Butch examines and rejects weapons that he, the other characters in the film, the film's makers, and a viewer like Ari who has seen a lot of movies on TV, will recognise as belonging to particular kinds of movie. Butch basically has to decide what kind of movie this is to become. Is it a slasher flick like the *Texas Chainsaw Massacre?* Is it in the gangster genre, like *Scarface?* No, it isn't, and the chainsaw and baseball bat are discarded. It's not Hammer Horror either. It's a samurai film. The theme is not blood lust or revenge, it's honour. This is a film about justice, about an ethics of living outside the law.

For perhaps the first time in the history of cinema, the film makers, the film characters and the film's audience share a moment of full recognition, free from irony or parody, that we all share a certain media culture. Not one that determines who we are and what we do, but one that offers a range of actions and conceptions form which we have to make choices. It is the self-conscious production and interpretation of shared images that constitute a virtual reservoir of possible action, possible worlds.

While there is a synchronising effect that goes with the globalisation of cyberspace, it isn't necessarily a homogenising effect. Global media vectors make different people experience the same images at the same time, but what people make of them differs from place to place. This is why a trans-national generationalism appears as a real effect of media globalisation, but not quite in the way some of the pundits think. It doesn't make people think or feel the same way, it just means that people tend to think and feel, at the same time, but in their different ways, via the same set of images.

When parallels to Coupland's *Generation X* started turning up in Australian writing, the Burbler response was to see it as just an effect of the global marketing of the Generation X aesthetic. But this missed something quite fundamental. Punk got going independently in several different places at once on the principle of "here are three chords, now form a band".[22] So too did the so-called Grunge Lit get going on the basis of: "here are 26 letters of the alphabet, go write your novel."[23] Both punk and grunge began as local and autonomous appropriations of a shared media moment.

Grunge writers were just a particular kind of young writer who used the repertoire of images that they had in common with others who pay attention to media aesthetics. That these books sold well is less a tribute to the marketing genius of publishers, and more to the simple fact that readers recognised in grunge writing a common world of media experience. Grunge fiction, like *Pulp Fiction*, played with a common world of film aesthetics. What readers recognised in the writings of Edward Berridge, Justine Ettler, Andrew McGahan, Luke Davies and Christos Tsiolkas were writers who articulated a widespread sensibility about what kind of milieu this is we live in, even if they made, and indeed we all make, rather different things out of the possibilities it generates.[24]

"I've just got up and I'm already bored", says Ari, as if anticipating what is expected of him with a wry smile. The joke is that a lot of readers found Ari himself rather interesting. He is the central character in Christos Tsiolkas' novel *Loaded*.[25] He also appears in the film based on the book, called *Head On*, played by Alex Dimitriadis. While it is an enjoyable film, it isn't half as interesting as the novel, and strangely, has less to say about cinema than the novel.[26]

Over the course of an energetic 150 pages, Ari traverses the four corners of Melbourne, the same city where Mark Davis terrorised the resident Burblers. But Tsiolkas takes his bearings less from the inter-generational tensions of Melbourne's suburban talking heads than from its migrant and working class suburbs. When it comes to the affluent and consumerist side of postwar Boomer life, as Ari says, "the wogs, being peasants, do it best… They have migrated to escape the chaos of history and they know, they know fundamentally, that property is war."

All the same I'd like to think that Davis might have cleared a space where we can hear the voice of Ari that Tsiolkas created. Tsiolkas' achievement is in creating a character through which we can read the limits, but also the possibilities of a certain historical moment. He gives us a richly detailed portrait of a young Greek male's suburban Melbourne. Mike and Carol Bradyland it ain't, but some of the qualities Tsiolkas sees through Ari's eyes define a wider milieu. "I keep thinking of some young girl in full chador, her veil covering her Walkman, walking down a street, ignored by all these Muslim men, and she's listening to 'Like a Virgin' or 'Justify My Love'. And going home, alone in her bedroom, touching her cunt, liking it. Bless the Madonna."

Interesting how the girl, the street, the Muslim men, no less than the song, could be in Melbourne, or Jakarta, or Islamabad. Media vectors create possibilities, but what people make of those possibilities is not determined entirely by media vectors. Media make it possible for Ari to fantasise the girl with the headphones. If she exists, may have a quite different fantasy space within which she hears Madonna. Like Ari, she may well partake in a fantasy space of global proportions, and in which Madonna is a shared image, but otherwise different.

"I can't recite a poem, any poem, but my mind is an automatic memory teller of pop music", says Ari. And what he withdraws from it is the "soundtrack to my happiness". For Ari, "favourite songs, like favourite films, like favourite people, change day by day, moment by moment." There is no one tune that sums up the times, just as there is no one personality type that defines a generation. Ari describes Joe as someone who "keeps his crew cut because he still wants to dip one foot into the pool of freedom." Aha! The Options Generation. But Ari, on the other hand, has opted out of all that. "There are two things in this world guaranteed to make you old and flabby. Work and marriage. It is inevitable."

The only thing that confronts everyone in the same way is the thing that confronts everyone as the same thing: money. "We all have to sell ourselves…. but you don't have to sell all of yourself. There is a small part of myself, deep inside me, which I let no one touch. If I let it out, let someone have a look at it, brush their hands across that part of my soul, then they would want to have it, buy it, steal it, own it. Joe's put that part of himself up for market… he's just waiting for the right bid."

Ari resists, and expresses that part of Christos Tsiolkas that resists. Or rather, unlike Ari, Tsiolkas takes to market a book that has hidden in its folds a little taste of that which cannot be traded, not even on the black market: the possibility of making something out of postmodern capitalism other than more of the same. Some of the resources for this lie in resisting the corrosive flow of marketable media, the resources of friendship, camaraderie, love.

Some of the resources are also out there in the ether, in the signs and flourishes the media vector spreads from Melbourne to Morocco. Urbane images and stories that are useful precisely because they are ones that Butch or Ari or the girl in the chador can all recognise and share with others as a mutual recognition. "The images have stayed in my head." In the end what is distinctive about the art that begins with Generation X is the recognition that the time has come to talk about, and even to enact, the fair go, via the very images that a commodified world would substitute for the fair go.

The Squeeze Generation explored the ironic possibilities of playing with those images, but Generation X created a new world out of them. An image is not defined by its origin. The limitation of suburban taste is to categorise images according to their origins. Urbanity begins when images are understood rather in terms of the shifting contexts in which they might be made to yield different meanings. The limit imposed on culture by Burbler aesthetics is to shut down the virtual play of meaning in the everyday that freeing images from origins creates.

Generation X is a term which has outlived its usefulness as an enabling fiction in every sense but one. It named a new kind of urbanity, one that could arise right in the heartland of suburban space. An urbanity tuned to the virtual hiding within the matrix of images that media vectors insinuate into the heart of the suburban. In the overcoming of genera-tional boundaries lies the possibility of releasing the virtual potential of cyberspace, the virtuality of time.

Essaying Urbanity

If it's true, as Mark Davis claims, that in the media environment of the late 90s, Generation X get to side with the "untruthful and the self-deceived", then the enthusiasm for young fiction writers might be part of the problem as much as part of the solution. Young people are expected to write "grunge fiction", but not other kinds of fiction — and certainly not nonfiction. This is why I want to concentrate on what is mostly nonfiction writing, in autobiographical essay form, by some of my contemporaries: Christos Tsiolkas, Beth Spencer and Chris Gregory.[27]

Its a remarkable experiment — two writers of different ages and backgrounds collaborated on the one autobiography, a document of the spaces between them. Christos Tsiolkas (born 1965) and Sasha Soldatow (born 1947) composed *Jump Cuts* as a medley of alternating voices, arguing and inventing, and popping out to buy CD's to test Sasha's theory that Beethoven invented jazz. Until finally there is a break in the text. Tsiolkas withdraws from the dialogue. As Soldatow records, "He accused me of treating him as Generation X, a term I don't use because it is just another journalistic beat up."

And so it is. Whether Soldatow likes it or not, generationalism structures at least some part of the exchange. Tsiolkas thinks through the 90s in part as a reaction to the way Soldatow thinks through the 60s. He reacts, particularly, to the baggage Soldatow carries from the 60s liberation movements. While these might have been anti-authoritarian movements, "your moralism is equally authoritarian", charges Tsiolkas. "I now have a knee-jerk reaction to the term *Third World*. It makes me want to leave the conversation, exit the room and watch more television." Tsiolkas sums up the lesson for Generation X of the 60s: "Self-righteousness does not equal idealism. Purity does not equal truth. Sex does not equal liberation."

Soldatow counters that "your generation doesn't understand the breadth of meaning we tried to slam into this word *political*." What he doesn't quite grasp is the breadth of meaning Tsiolkas finds, not in the word culture, but in the practice of it, in everyday life. A veteran of hardcore urban movements such as the Sydney libertarian push and the Melbourne liberationist Pram Factory, Soldatow seems to see in Tsiolkas an heir who cannot quite be trusted with an inheritance. "Something happens when the past, in this case mine, is resurrected. It comes to be redefined according to other people's needs."

One of the things Generation X means is this redefining of what is useful about the 60s. As a label for a group of people it is alarmingly arbitrary. As a way of designating a new kind of fable about the past, and a new bunch of talking heads who are proposing such fables, it's quite apt. As the writer Beth Spencer says, "X is that letter on typewriters used to obliterate errors and slips, to mark the lost and forgotten. It also implies a kind of generic, no-name status. As such the term was a reaction against the Boomer ethos that everything worth doing or experiencing or saying or writing about had happened in the sixties; the view that saw the seventies as just a sad, embarrassing mistake."[28] Whether it is rewriting the 60s, or filling in the *Blankety-Blanks* of the 70s, Generation X is a revisionist fable, one with consequences for living in the present, too.

Generation Moonwalk

In the Boomer mythology of the 60s, it was a time of activism in the streets. I can remember being taken to a Vietnam Moratorium march when I was about nine. There were cops on horses. I was scared, and held my big sister's hand. Most of my memories of the world of the 60s are not of marching in the streets, but of sitting cross-legged in front of the television. The big event of the 60s is not really Vietnam, but what Cate Rayson in her book *Glued to the Telly* calls "the ultimate television moment".[29]

When Neil Armstrong walked on the moon, I watched it on television from a bed out on the verandah of the children's ward at Royal Newcastle Hospital. I had both legs in plaster casts, and always thought my intense memory of that television event was peculiar to me, and generated by the callous irony of being immobilised while Armstrong cavorted among the moon dust. Recently, I've discovered three writers who, one way or another, also have memories of that event:

Beth Spencer (born 1958), Christos Tsiolkas (born 1965), Chris Gregory (born 1970). While there is a wide gap between their ages, I think they can be constructed as 'Generation Moonwalk' in that they can locate themselves and identify themselves in relation to this shared media event.

While I was in a hospital bed on that day in 1969, here is how Spencer remembers it: "When I was ten, Neil Armstrong and Buzz Kennedy landed on the moon and 'the world' watched with bated breath, fuzzy grainy pictures in which very little happened over what seemed like hours and hours cramped five in a double desk in the grade five and six class-rooms at Bayswater State School." (Actually it was Buzz Aldrin, but the conflation of the moon shot with JFK is interesting in itself) Meanwhile, elsewhere: "I was a small child when the North American astronauts landed on the moon. A crowd gathered in my parents lounge room to watch the historic landing", writes Tsiolkas.

Gregory remembers it, oddly enough, even though he was too young to even be alive at the time: "I was born about nine months after the first moon landing and you can figure that one out for yourself. My grandmother told me that my parents held a big party for the first moon landing. They bought their first television set for the occasion, and maybe I attach more importance to this correlation than I should."

Encouraged by the remarkable coincidence of finding the moonwalk in all three of these autobiographical writings, I decided to email all of the authors I found useful in writing this book, to see if Generation Moonwalk might be something to which others belong too. Scott McQuire (born 1962), emailed back: "I can remember getting off school to watch at a friend's house across the road. All the other kids were watching in the assembly hall. I got bored and went off to play after a while." Sure enough, the vector of television lodged varied memories of the moonwalk in some impressionable young minds. Rather than summarise, I want to present these varied memories, cut from the same media template, in the author's own words.

Darren Tofts (born 1960) recalls the moonwalk "vividly". He writes, "I was in grade three at Holy Name Primary School, in East Preston, then one of Melbourne's more notorious northern suburbs. I was taught by a Malaysian nun (itself exotic), and we had a portable TV set brought into the class especially... There was a very strong sense of occasion about it, that we were watching something very special... There was a sense that it was a television event, as much as a historical one."

Catharine Lumby (born 1961) also connects the moon-walk with school, and television: "I remember about one hundred of us sitting in the infants school hall squinting at this tiny black and white screen. It was incredibly exciting and afterwards I rushed home and begged my parents to buy me an orange plastic model of Apollo Eleven. It was big enough to sit in and practice your moon landings."

Mark Davis (born 1959) writes: "I can remember my dad getting me up in the early hours of the morning to watch either the launch or the landing. I don't quite recall exactly which.... My mother had gone to bed and my two younger brothers were considered 'too young'. At first I thought the house must have been burning down or something, but then he lead me, half asleep into the lounge to watch this thing, which, given that TV was always switched off in our house at 7-30, after the news... So it was a real bonding moment for me and dad. He sat there with a glass of beer and affected a suitable silent *gravitas* while the whole damn thing took place. I admit I was impressed too."

Interestingly, what Mackay thinks of as the primary means by which generations come to appreciate their relation to each other, through family contact, is here mediated by the place of television in everyday life. "I'm not sure if I had fallen asleep at the actual moment", writes David Marshall (born 1958). "We were staying up all night on a hot July night and my memory is everyone was sleeping or trying to stay awake around the set in various sprawled states. It was definitively a family event because it occurred in mid-summer in Canada."

The quality of the moonwalk as something produced by a television vector was not lost on the young Mark Davis, who like Lumby, experienced it as a template for a child's desires: "That it was happening live, right that very minute, it was real impressive. Over subsequent days and weeks my brothers and I collected every single piece of memorabilia/souvenir which was published in the papers (and in colour too — another, parallel, technological marvel), and made them up into a scrapbook each, which I still have."

Brady Bunching

The moonwalk is clearly a television event that children experienced as something presented to them by parents or teachers, or in my case, by the nurses at the hospital. A more distinctively generational experience was Brady Bunching. *The Brady Bunch* performed much the same role for people growing up in the 60s and 70s as *Neighbours* did for people growing up in the 80s and 90s. It provided a widely shared matrix of images and stories within which young people could place themselves independently of their parent's influence. In a rare break from the restricted range of suburban images of the time, it showed a blended family that comprised two parents (Mike and Carol), three girls (from oldest to youngest: Marsha, Jan, Cindy), three boys (Greg, Peter, Bobby) and a maid (Alice).

If television is a mass vector for distributing a crude set of images far and wide, email is a wonderfully subtle vector for generating much more precise cohorts. After getting interesting answers on the moonwalk, I tried asking whether people watched *The Brady Bunch.* "Oh sure", writes Darren Tofts, "Religiously, in fact... I wanted to fuck Marsha. I suppose I was Greg; being the eldest of 4 brothers, and pretty much the same age as Greg, I s'pose I identified with him re the teenage thang; he was cool, always bordering on being a grown up, while Peter and Bobby were definitely trapped in a neoteny time warp."

David Marshall: "I only watched *The Brady Bunch* at my next door neighbours [the Van Berkels]. I can't quite explain why this is the case other than they were regular viewers and we weren't — although I was over there a lot. (They may have had a better antenna for that particular station — maybe the same station that showed *Star Trek.*) So I associate it with the Van Berkels and I associate the identities of the Van Berkels with the Bradys. I never saw myself as one of them, although I related to the younger boy because he was the youngest in his family as I was in mine. But in terms of dress style — Greg. Sometimes I thought of Peter like my brother Alan."

Christos Tsiolkas: *"The Brady Bunch* was a little like reading Enid Blyton books; it was comfortable and safe, as was *Gilligan's Island* and even though every episode was different it was always the same (and comforting for that). I look back on it as succour during my transition from early childhood to youth, borne out by the fact I didn't mind the re-runs. My favourite Brady? Christ! Jan, I guess, for the obvious reasons. In particular what stands out is her envy of Marcia's beauty and the getting glasses episode. I'm nerd-identifying there… As for the one I was attracted to, all of them! I started serious wanking relatively young, around nine or ten, and I do remember an early scenario involving Mr Brady, Peter and Greg all going for it. At the time I think I was attracted to Greg…".

Catharine Lumby: "Always watched *The Brady Bunch* after school and — natch — I wanted to be Marcia but identified with Jan. Oddly enough I had a crush on Mr Brady who turned out to be gay in real life. But then I also had a crush on Joe Hasham who played Don in *Number 96* (more photos taken off the TV) — so maybe it was just a fag hag thing."

The Countdown Generation Revisited

While it's possible to construct quite an interesting cross-section of generational impressions by Brady Bunching, the distinctive text for Australians who were teenagers in the 70s has to be *Countdown.*[30] As Scott McQuire says, *"Countdown* in its early years was a fixture." For Darren Tofts, *"Countdown* was a defining phenomenon for me… *Countdown* was a vital and irrepressible part of life. When you weren't watching it you were talking about it; in the dark days before video you would just be hanging out for it… ".

Catharine Lumby: *"Countdown* was the big event of the weekend for most of the early to mid-70s as I remember it. I got hooked when I fell in love with Tony Mitchell, the bass guitarist in Sherbert. To my horror, I distinctly remember taking photographs of him off the television and pretending they were live snaps."

Darren Tofts: "It was a focus of what was going on in the

fashion, the sounds and the attitudes of the street life of the suburbs. It was a kind of reassuring measure and recognition of how people actually lived; the whole sharpie thing was huge in [Melbourne's] northern suburbs, and it was sharps who would be rubber-legging it in the studio while Hush played 'Boney Moroney'; then it would be down to the local church hall dressed in 'connie' cardigans and Batsanis shoes to rubber-leg to a cover band playing 'Boney Moroney'."

Beth Spencer: "I was into pop music very young, from about age seven… By the time *Countdown* came along, I watched it, but not so religiously, and I think in a rather disdainful way I'm afraid. It was probably far too popular-music and crass and teeny-bopper (and possibly too Australian) for my tastes by then. (Then I went to uni and had to eat my words as we all danced to AC-DC and Skyhooks.) But I do have to say that when *Rage* ran some old *Countdown* episodes a few years ago in the wee hours I found it utterly excruciatingly toe-curlingly evocative and familiar. (The hair-styles, the clothes, the very extra-ordinary Australian-suburban of it). I taped some of these and I'm still building up the courage to go and watch them again (for research for current book)…. So I guess I have mixed feelings about *Countdown*."

Christos Tsiolkas: "Yes, I watched *Countdown* as a kid. I was still in primary school when it began and one thing is very clear for me, within the schoolyard of North Richmond Primary and within the environs of Blackburn and Box Hill, the show had an effect in shaping a sense of popular music and culture. *Countdown* definitely affected my earliest exposure to non-Greek music. It did shape taste but not straightforwardly; maybe taste for many people was defined by their opposition to *Countdown*. I'm thinking in particular about the effects of punk, new wave and the rise of independent music. As an emerging queer, the exposure to androgyny and sexuality was not unimportant. Even though Molly's sexuality was never declared, there was much camp bantering, I remember. And also, I found much fantasy material from my viewing of *Countdown*. In particular I have a strong memory of Mum declaring Status Quo as *maliare* or 'longhairs', dismissing them, but me being completely entranced by the worn crotches on their jeans."

Mark Davis: "Against the grain I suppose, but I found the whole era regrettable. Only ironic distance saves it now! If it shaped his taste it was only as a kind of negative theology." Davis rates its wider influence as "absolutely mega-huge. It seemed to be all anyone ever spoke about at school the following Monday — which is why me and my downbeat friends took such pleasure in being anti-everything *Countdown*. It was definitely a show that broke new acts, made tastes and so on; and those bands that Meldrum didn't like were also assured a kind of notoriety if they evidenced the right sort of anti-*Countdown* 'code' in dress, sneer and so on. I remember when Meldrum called the Sacred Cowboys the worst band to ever be on TV. You couldn't move at their next gig."

Chris Gregory: "Yeah, I watched it religiously like all other kids my age, the repeat from the week before on Saturday and the new episode on Sunday, but I'm probably one of the last ones. People a couple of years younger than me may have watched *Countdown Revolution*, but it wasn't the same and didn't have as strong an appeal." Just as *Countdown Revolution* took the place of *Countdown*, so *Rage* and *Recovery* might some day form the basis of a shared memory, a sense of the contemporary, and a new pretext for creating a generation. *The Simpsons* may take the place of *The Brady Bunch*, and *South Park* of *The Simpsons*. As with *Countdown*, and *The Brady Bunch*, they might be the shared images out of which different senses of self emerge.

This is only likely if broadcast television remains a key vector that attracts a wide audience. Another possibility is that generational difference will be marked by the emergence of a postbroadcast sensibility. Rather than majorities tuned to mass images and a minority alienated from it, there might instead emerge a plurality of minorities, who all have to negotiate with each other. This might replace the situation that still prevailed at the end of the 90s, where minorities negotiate within the gaps created by broadcast media texts. For instance, Mark Davis and Beth Spencer quite self-consciously identified themselves as punk outsiders in relation to *Countdown*. Christos Tsiolkas and Catharine Lumby experienced moments of sexually ambiguous, or even 'queer' desire, in misreading the roles *The Brady Bunch* offered them.

Culture Generators

The moonwalk was a single, synchronising event. Perhaps not an event for 'the world', as Spencer points out, but certainly one that a lot of people in television-rich suburban Australia shared with others so endowed around the world. The TV series works less through its eventfulness and more as a chronic repetition of a fixed repertoire of characters and situations. Either way, what the media event or television series produces is an experience of the contemporary. Catch-all terms such as Generation X are usually based on a catch-all mix of supposedly key media experiences for a majority of contemporaries. What might be more interesting, I'm suggesting, is to break it down into specific cohorts that shared exposure to particular texts, and then look at what kinds of shared sense emerges in connecting disparate experiences of these media moments.

It's through a patchwork of shared media that the diverse experiences of growing up in the 60s and 70s can be narrated, and is starting to be narrated, in the books and essays published by Gregory, Spencer and Tsiolkas. Broadcast vectors are generators of shared images. More diverse vectors of distribution, from the printed book to the internet, generate more specific and different kinds of images and stories, but increasingly, these take as their raw material elements of the shared experience of media. In the writings of these contemporaries, I think there is a suggestion of how an emerging, postbroadcast culture might work. One still based on media experiences a majority share, but exploring the differences and specificities of that experience, rather than homogenising it under mass labels, of which generational labels are a conspicuous example.

As Spencer writes in an illuminating essay: "Being X means being bound together as adolescents by endless repeats of *Gilligan's Island* and *Get Smart,* as we immersed ourselves in the lives of *The Partridge Family, The Munsters,* and *The Brady Bunch* as our own families became increasingly cracked and dysfunctional." Of course not everyone watched the same shows. Not everyone even had a television. But still, TV shaped a kind of experience, and now shapes a kind of memory.

Spencer's experience of what she calls "outer outer sub-urbia" was an Anglo one, but Tsiolkas grew up in much the same kind of suburban Melbourne, among people who spoke mostly Greek. "The only English I knew was fragments and verses from pop music", he recalls. While it's a different experience, it had some of the same resources, thanks to the common world flowing into the privatised homes of suburbia from the vector of television. "My brother and I used to play television shows together. We'd play *Gilligan's Island* or the *Brady Bunch* and I often ended up being Ginger or Mary-Ann. We never thought it strange."

"When I was four years old I watched the *Aunty Jack* show every week", writes Chris Gregory. "I was afraid not to watch, because at the end of every episode Aunty Jack would say: 'if you don't watch my show next week I'll rip your bloody arms off.' If I missed an episode I would sleep in my toybox so Aunty Jack could not find me….". Spencer and Tsiolkas also report an invasion of the imaginative life by images to which they had been exposed by media vectors. Spencer dreams of a day out with Madonna: "we shopped around for hours and eventually Madonna chose a Sister Mary MacKillop showbag with crucifixes and beads and angels wings (that looked like cicada wings)…". Tsiolkas recalls that when he was young, "I masturbated over Jack Thompson…".

Not only did the desires of the body connect to this flow of images, so too did the consciousness of the mind. Recalls Tsiolkas: "I have one memory of the Vietnam war. I'm a kid, playing with Dad on the floor, and I hear my Mum start sniffing. There's footage on the black-and-white television screen of soldiers carrying dead men through a muddy swamp." It is also the young Christos' source of concepts with which to interpret his own experience. "It was from black Americans that I first learned of the world racism… The mini-series *Roots* changed my world." And it led him to read black music politically, and to seek out black writers, such as James Baldwin. On the other hand, "Nietzsche did not teach me that God was dead. I learned about it from an Elton John song, 'Levon'."

This flow of images and stories, sometimes even concepts, from without provides a sometimes discordant accompani-ment to suburban everyday life. Gregory recalls visiting relatives and listening to a cousin playing ABBA on a home organ "with a rhumba accompaniment" — shades of *Muriel's Wedding* here. His mother uses this as a pretext to impress on him the lesson of the suburban capacity to make distinctions: "my mother would tell me that the home organ was a tacky instrument, a degraded piano." She wants her son to be a cut above, so she enrols him in piano lessons. Only something goes awry. "We owned three televisions," writes Gregory, "but I was not supposed to have the television in the recreation room turned on while I was practicing the piano."

Spencer also experienced the kinds of distinction suburbia maintained. "Well the boys from Caulfield Grammar... might blithely flirt with a pretty girl from the outer outer suburbs, they might even form intense friendships (hours on the telephone, thrice-weekly letters) but they would never marry one." Caulfield, which was Nick Cave's school, might be located in the suburbs, but was not of it.

In the gap between the suburban space, where as Spencer says, "the television hums quietly in the background", and the worlds the television vector reveals, what opens up is a primary experience of irony, of displacement. Gregory starts to see something strange in his family's Franklin Mint limited edition collectables, there is something just a bit off about the idea of "instant heirlooms", kept in the "living room, where nobody went because there was no TV." A young Chris Gregory puts two and two together: "At an early age I realised that I was living in a world full of *bad design*. I had needed no leap of faith to conclude that I lived in a badly designed world."

Spencer recalls: "I used to work in one of the first shopping complexes when I was fifteen, making sandwiches and serving afternoon teas and meat pies on paper plates.... I had platform shoes and I was proud of knowing that the brown stuff on top of the cappuccino (instant) coffee was cocoa." What passes for knowingness, distinction, in a suburban context has been subtly undermined by paying just a bit too much attention to other worlds.

There are two other worlds that attract as suburbia loses its charms. More than their American counterparts, Australian Generation X fables involve a turning away from suburbia and a return to the city. Spencer recalls: "I loved coming to

the city when I was a teenager. So bloodless and artificial."
Which can be read as an ironic compliment. "I would go
shopping in the bargain basements and Indian Shops, buy
my lunch at Soul Foods and visit the Art Gallery and the
museum."

The break with suburbia is not a universal generational
experience. Many people chose to follow their parents'
example and seek a happy life there. As Spencer writes, "My
brothers and sisters invite me out to visit their homes to
admire the microwaves and the new cars and the games
rooms and the swimming pools. They feed me frozen
dinners and show me photos of their little girls dressed up
like child prostitutes for the callisthenics team." Suburbia
never quite looks the same to those who left it, and they are
the one who, in print form at least, get to tell its story.

The temporal gap between generations intersects with the
spatial gap between suburban and urban. The strange thing
is how a suburban environment, based on observing distinctions and restricting flows of information, could still provide
these three writers with the resources to critique it. Chris
Gregory declares: "I never talked to my parents about anything much. They did not read or listen to music. All they did
was work and come home late and fall asleep in front of the
television and then wake up for long enough to go to bed."
Beth Spencer writes: "I keep my life safe from my family and
I keep them safe from my life. Not so difficult because they
are fairly incurious about my world although they somehow
assume approval for theirs." The suburban gap, unlike the
generation gap, is not so much oppositional as a structure of
mutual indifference. As Tsiolkas says, "I moved away as fast as
I could because I identified the suburbs with vapid conformity. I'd heard of a more colourful world."

"I came to the punk scene late. Its music had infiltrated the
suburbs", Tsiolkas writes. "I stripped myself of a former
life…, the life of a plump suburban proud-little-Greek-boy."
Revisiting the suburbs in the 90s, having become something
like the urbane person he wanted to become, Tsiolkas finds
it a changed space. "Now the newsagent opposite my old suburban school stocks gay periodicals." Spencer is not so sure
— to her it is still the suburbs. Tsiolkas, while fleeing the
suburbs, "granted them three graces. The best jokes are

heard in the suburbs. You get the best drugs there. And the most gorgeous guys live out there."

Spencer remembers 1972 not just as the year Gough Whitlam won the federal election, but also as the year Helen Reddy won a Grammy Award for her song 'I Am Woman'. Sheryn George, former editor of *Australian Women's Forum*, a particularly urbane publication that infiltrated the suburbs in the 90s, says she used to know all the words to that song. In a perceptive essay on growing up female in the 60s and 70s in suburbia, George notes its particular tensions: "Basically, looking sexual wasn't on, yet everything was infused with sex when I was growing up. TV, parties, the beach, posters, music. The forbidden was alluded to everywhere. Although girls were supposed to be beautiful — even sexy — the nuns and shows like *Class of 74* suggested good girls hated actually having sex, even when they were married to their one and only true love."

Somehow, through some vector, information leeches into suburbia, from somewhere. "In sixth grade, three bolshie girlfriends and I sang a song at the end-of-year concert called 'Women Are Real People' (WARP)... I have no idea where we dug it up from. (I have a dim memory of Marcia being briefly empowered on that most sexist of programs, the *Brady Bunch*.) We must have looked pretty funny, four stubby eleven-year-olds holding up placards in defiance of our oppression, but the irony of our protest acronym spelling 'warp' was lost on us."[31]

This was the other line of escape open out of the suburbs besides the city: the media, or rather, cultivating an urbane way of appreciating media. This may mean actively seeking exposure to a broader repertoire than was available on TV. "The image... seduced me from an early age", Tsiolkas writes, and, "the image has been ubiquitous in my life." But there are images and images. "Unlike television, which was immediate, part of the house, the huge screen in the movie theatre was a space through which I disappeared into fantasy." Spencer: "I love matinees. I avoid Saturday nights, because it's always couples. I prefer daytime, midweek: playing solitaire with the old, the homely, the chip rustlers and furtive chocolate eaters, the hanky-bringers." Gregory: "What I saw on television and at the Monster Movie Matinee provided me with a substantial part of my imaginative life."

The results of such an exposure could be somewhat mixed. Tsiolkas reports that he learned about Students for a Democratic Society through Haskell Wexler's radical McLuhanite film of 1969, *Medium Cool*. Gregory recalls that: "All I wanted to be was the guy who wore the Godzilla suit and got to stomp all over a miniature Tokyo." Either way, what results is a kind of urbanity, what Spencer calls "a secret hidden left-handedness of the soul."

The Urbane and the Sceptic

The space of the city is by itself not enough to produce urbanity. It is quite possible to experience the city in a suburban way. Gregory thinks Liberal Premier Jeff Kennett's everyday experience of the city is entirely suburban. He sees it under glass, through a windscreen, shuttling between home and work, barely setting foot in it. "Perhaps Melbourne was one of the last places where someone could still see the city as something more than an obstacle to movement", Gregory laments. The tollways carve corridors for suburban drivers to get in and out of it in the privacy of their cars, without risking becoming a public.

Gregory writes about the great Hong Kong film star Jackie Chan making a movie in Melbourne, a city chosen as a cheaper stand-in for New York. Gregory wants to meet Jackie Chan, who makes much more interesting films, in Gregory's view, than usual Australian suburban melodramas. He thinks he and Jackie have something in common. "I wanted to tell him how much of my own work involved the imposition of incongruous scenes upon real physical locations." Gregory's writing crosses the flow of his body's movement across physical space with the flow of his mind's awareness of media space. Two kinds of vectors intersect: movement in space, on trams, in cars; movement of media, along phone lines and on video screens.

The urbane love the idea of their home city. The urbane think of the city as home. Gregory clearly loves his Melbourne. He gets fascinated by the way so many of its buildings are copies of more famous buildings in more famous cities. This antipodean city is itself in love with the idea of the city, only its idea of the city is Rome or London. And so why not New York? Gregory sees Jackie Chan's creation of a New York film in Melbourne as something akin to the creation of a 'Roman' cathedral there. "What Jackie Chan is doing makes sense, given that the history of Melbourne has been a constant process of imitation and reproduction anyway."

Aesthetics, or the concept of art, matters a great deal to Gregory, Spencer and Tsiolkas. Writing about aesthetics is a problem, because critical writing is itself an art, and the form of expression has to be right too. Gregory comes closest to a unique expression of a postsuburban aesthetics in his essay on the extinction of mock chicken, one of the culinary delights of what Gregory describes as his "white trash" suburban childhood. "I liked eating mock chicken. At the time I liked mock chicken more than I liked real chicken. The texture was more consistent, and the skewer was much more convenient and less disturbing than real chicken bones. Eating mock chicken was like eating a cartoon chicken."

What is aesthetic about this writing is the way Gregory is able to see even a degraded frozen meal experience as an expression of style. "Mock chicken was the product of more optimistic times, when people believed that human beings could improve on nature." Gregory gave up piano lessons. He gave up aspiring to a suburban idea of refinement. Rather than aspire to an ideal kind of artistic perfection in an unthinking way, he achieves a very thoughtful relation to the degraded and far from ideal materials he finds around him, from monster movies to mock chicken.

Gregory does not let the matter rest with an ironic, postmodern reversal of values, making mock chicken superior to chicken. Some secret hidden left-handedness of the soul obliges him to press the revaluation of values a bit further. Can we really assume that we know the value of chicken, the thing against which mock chicken is to be measured? Gregory questions the value represented by the word 'chicken' too, and thereby undoes the judgement he has just passed on its relation to mock chicken.

"The chicken is an elegant and highly sophisticated piece of modern technology", he writes, and then describes in alarming detail the industrial production of chicken. Mock chicken may be a failed improvement on nature, but a chicken is not an artefact of nature any more, but of technology. There is no old value to go back to, now Gregory wants to treat the modernising aspirations of the mock chicken eaters to gentle parody. The idea of a return, a rustication, is a suburban one, a way to grasp a stable value — 'nature' — now that improving on nature no longer seems possible. Gregory, by contrast, embraces a movement forward, but without the luxury of believing in it. "I feel the same way about chicken as I imagine more politically conscious people feel about the democratic system or universal suffrage."

There is something sceptical in these writers that I find congenial, as if it came from some shared experience. And yet it is a committed, active, ethical kind of scepticism. I find it utterly removed from the supposed "relativism" that Boomer critics identify, in their crude way, as the postmodern style. What I find in Spencer, Tsiolkas and Gregory is not relativism or the destruction of values, but the revaluing of values. What I find is not the destruction of the distinction between high and low art but a constant questioning of just where and how aesthetic quality can emerge, out of any and every media flow or everyday situation.

There is a scepticism about time, about cause and effect, about how actions in the present create conditions in the future. There is also a certain commitment, passion, will, which I think connects more to space than to time. The space of urbanity holds these disparate writers together. The urbane is a shared fantasy in which differences can be articulated, simulated, celebrated. It's common to think of 'suburbia' as a fantasy space which generates a certain kind of Australian culture, but why is there no 'urbia' to which suburbs might contribute? This urbia is already a cultural alternative to the suburban. Perhaps, if cyberspace really does break up the majoritarian quality of mediated culture, it might appear, retrospectively as the beginnings of a political critique of suburbia as well.

Pauline Pantsdown's Disco Nation

Secret hidden left-handedness of the soul doesn't quite go far enough to describe the achievement of Simon Hunt, better known to a wider public as Pauline Pantsdown. It's more of the order of Dave Graney's "mysterious kink". Pauline began life as a Drag Queen at one of Jamie and Vanessa's parties in inner city Sydney. While these parties had a strong gay flavour, they were popular with a wide range of young urbanites. Pauline performed 'I'm a Backdoor Man', a song put together out of bits of Pauline Hanson's speeches and media performances, cut up and rearranged on a computer, and with a dance track of Hunt's own composition added.

The ABC Radio 'youth network', Triple J, started broadcasting the song, and it quickly became popular with listeners on the request show. 'Backdoor Man' features the voice of Pauline Hanson speaking lines such as: "I'm a backdoor man. I'm a homosexual" and "I'm a backdoor man for the Ku Klux Klan, with very horrendous plans. I'm a very proud potato."[32] It didn't take long for the writs to arrive. Hanson's lawyers sought an injunction to prevent Triple J from broadcasting it, and sued for defamation. They pleaded that the song could be taken by ordinary people to mean that Hanson engaged in unnatural sex acts, and was the "receiver of anal sex."[33] Queensland judges took a dim view of Pauline Pantsdown's free speech rights, and found in favour of Pauline Hanson's right to protect her reputation. What made the decision offensive to common sense was that Hanson's lawyers succeeded in arguing that the public has the reading skills to understand that the expression "backdoor man" refers to anal sex, but not to understand that the recording is in the genre of satire.

Ironically, the expression 'backdoor man', has quite another history in popular music. In Chicago blues legend Howling Wolf's famous performance of the blues standard 'Back Door Man', he is bragging about his success as an adulterer, but more specifically, his success as a black man in fucking white women.[34] Somehow I don't quite see Pauline Hanson as a black man who fucks white women, although if we follow Hanson's lawyers down this track of attributing reading ability to the public, this is what that part of the public who are blues fans would supposedly be led to believe by the song. Of course if this public has any reading ability, they would most likely see Hunt's cut-up art as satire, and make no such assumptions about Pauline Hanson's racial or sexual preferences.

Pauline Pantsdown was not easily silenced. She released another song, 'I Don't Like It!'.[35] The CD shows Pantsdown in Hanson drag, draping herself in the Australian flag. "I don't like it, when you turn my voice about", runs the opening line. This time Hunt's digital deconstruction draws attention to itself and its relation to Hanson right from the get go. "My language has been murdered", Hanson — or is it Pantsdown? — says. The back half of this line would most likely remind the attentive reader of Hanson's famous death video, on which she says, "If you are seeing this, I have been murdered." It was a bizarre last will and testament left in case of her assassination. 'I Don't Like It' went to number 13 on the ARIA national music chart.

Simon Hunt changed his name by deed poll and ran as a Senate candidate in New South Wales. Journalist Caroline Overington reports of Pantsdown's campaign performance: "In truth, Pantsdown does not do Mrs Hanson's voice very well and, more importantly for a political satirist, she is not particularly funny, but perhaps that's the point."[36] Pantsdown's campaign appearances included Kingsteam Sauna, *The Today Show*, the Sydney Gay and Lesbian Mardi Gras Sleaze Ball, and a fish shop — Fish Records on Oxford st. A strikingly urbane mix.

Juice magazine described Pantsdown's election policies as being "as shallow (and full of piss) as a kiddies swimming pool."[37] Simon Hunt stressed that the point of the Drag Queen version of Hanson was to highlight the fact that both were "completely constructed". The same frocks and hairdo, on a man's body, draws attention to the colour and shape as artifice. If there is a difference between Hanson and Pantsdown, for that latter it is "that I make up the things I say myself." Neither got themselves elected in 1998. Pantsdown polled only 2295 votes. This other Pauline directed preferences to two other Senate candidates. One of whom, Aden Ridgeway, had a narrow win, and became only the second Aboriginal elected to federal parliament. It would be nice to think that Pantsdown made a difference.

To me, Pauline Pantsdown is a singular expression of an attribute I recognise as contemporary: the capacity to deconstruct messages received and become, in the process, the apparent author of a unique take on what the vector throws at us all, revealing the sense-making machinery at work that produced the apparently seamless, obvious "mock chicken" world of third nature. I can't speak for how Pauline Pantsdown arrived at such a capacity for finding the virtual in the banal. Maybe that lies in Simon Hunt's experience of suburban life as being somehow awry. "Or maybe it began that day," as Beth Spencer says "back just before I was born, when my father walked into the house carrying a brand new television."[38]

Spencer says that she makes her writing out of "everything from all the stories and anecdotes people have ever told me, to bits from *The Donahue Show*, the *Bible, In Bed With Madonna*, books on infertility and birth, lines from popular songs, gossip items from *New Idea*, fragments from philosophy texts, tourist information, characters from detective novels, excerpts from 1960s school text books, and so on." The material for her art is "The cast-offs or the mass-produced — all the things floating or left lying around out there. The space junk."

But like Pauline Pantsdown, this got her into trouble, and here is where the politics of culture meets the culture of politics for them both. With Pantsdown, the issue was defamation. With Spencer, the issue was intellectual property. What constitutes "fair use" of the material in which other people hold the copyright? Erring on the side of caution, Spencer sought permission to reproduce every last stolen soundbite in her book, even tracking down rock legend Lou Reed and pleading with him to intercede and have some ludicrously high charges dropped so she could use a few words from one of his songs.

Some of my most cherished and personal memories are copyright, and the copyright is owned by someone else. I do not actually own my fantasies about Marcia Brady — or Alice the maid. On the cusp between the broadcast era and cyberspace, the wealth of creativity blocked by Burbler gatekeepers of the mainstream and majoritarian media pours like sand through the cracks opening up in the edifice complex. What appears on the horizon, besides this virtual opening, are the limitations that will have to be addressed through a more subtle and diverse politics of information, media, communication and culture.

chapter **9**

Regenerating Labor

> *While it has been said that the meek shall inherit the earth, they are unlikely to do so while leading the Australian Labor Party.*
>
> Graham Richardson

The Future of Barry Jones

"Respected by all, feared by none", is how one journalist sums up the career of Barry Jones, who among many other things, was Minister for Science for seven years under the Hawke government.[1] If anyone had a vision of where Australia was headed, and how Labor culture was failing to anticipate the effect of the cascading changes of the 80s and 90s, it was Jones. This chapter revisits his legacy to map out the space Jones anticipated Australia would find itself in, and then turns to a younger writer from within the Labor Party, Lindsay Tanner, to look at what questions emerged at the end of the 90s, when Australian culture landed more or less where Jones predicted.

It is fitting that Australia's first postmodern politician became a celebrity through his television appearances. In the 60s, he appeared 208 times on Bob Dyer's quiz show *Pick A Box*. If Jones is the only Labor politician of his generation who could safely be described as lovable, it is in part because his celebrity originated in these televised displays of his broad erudition. He was the acceptable face of that suburban oddity, the man who knew too much. He was the perfect go-between for urbane knowledge to the suburban public, and vice versa. With his rumpled suits scrunched over his shoulders, his salted beard, and a gaze that seemed to search out something on a high diagonal in the sky, Jones embodied an idea of what it's like to be a politician with a brain.

"Am I interested in ideas? Yes. More than power? Yes." It's a fatal admission, and a sign of what kept Jones away from real authority within the Labor Party or in government. Jones was the political celebrity of the lost idea. While he did get some additional funding out of Hawke for the sciences, his main legacy may well be his perception of the problem building up for Labor culture as it confronts an ever more complex cyberspace, and tries to turn its cultural values into power through public debate and the political process.

If the survival of democracy is predicated on the *informed* citizen, then the information revolution is a political revolution too. Jones understood more clearly than most that government is as much about information as it is about power, and that information technology transforms relations of power. This is one of the most remarkable themes he took up in his provocative book, *Sleepers Wake!*. While other institutions have modified themselves, often beyond recognition, in order to make the transition to cyberspace, parliament has changed only incrementally.

In the century since federation, the number of members sitting in the House of Representatives went from 75 to 147, and the number of people they represented went from 3.7 million to 17.8 million. The number of people in the public service they had to oversee went from 11 thousand to 350 thousand, but the number of hours members deliberated went down from 866 to 603.[2] The amount of public expenditure per person may have increased spectacularly, but the amount of it actually brought before the House for review in the annual budget papers declined. In short, more people and more public service, producing more information that is subject to less and less scrutiny by elected representatives of the people.

For Jones, the consequence of this trend is disturbing: "The democratic system may become increasingly irrelevant as a means of determining and implementing social goals, or allocating funds on the basis of community needs, if elected persons do not understand how to evaluate and relate segments of information in which each expert works." Power has shifted from representative government to "strategically placed minority groups occupying the commanding heights in particular areas of society — technocrats, public servants, corporations, unions." A list to which the *Silent Majority III* report clearly adds the media. As cyberspace accelerates, more vectors carry more information, and more information leads to an increased division of labour, as people specialise more and more to capture a specific part of the information flow and bring it under their authority.

One unexpected consequence of this shift in the balance of power is that it fed into the rise of Hansonite populism. Former Hanson minder John Pasquarelli insists that she simply refused to absorb his briefings. "In response to my criticism of her slackness, Pauline, in a fit of pique, swept some of the briefing notes on the floor saying, 'I can't retain, I can't retain'."[3] If this is true, it worked in her favour out on the fringes of suburbia. Having witnessed popular politicians such as Bob Hawke succumb to the specialist apparatus of the public service and elite academic policy specialists, part of the appeal of Pauline was the notion of the idea-proof politician.

The Information Proletariat

Jones identified early on that "Australia is an information society in which more people are employed in collecting, storing, retrieving, amending, and disseminating data than are producing food, fibres and minerals, and manufacturing products." This is the primary sense in which Australia can be called a "postindustrial" nation. Changes to what the economy produces also changes its class structure. Jones identified the potential for the formation of an "intellectual proletariat" composed of people locked out of the benefits of the information economy. Education is the main ticket into the inner suburban and urbane knowledge class who have the specialised skills to process information. The educated protect their knowledge assets closely, and try hard to make themselves a hereditary caste, passing on the culture of knowledge to their children.

Exiled west of this strata of comfortable urban and inner suburban information burghers is the information proletariat. A 'checkout chick' passing groceries over the scanner is doing the manual labour of cyberspace, producing the raw information on which, eventually, the supermarket's managers will base their business decisions. An unemployed machinist who cashes his dole cheque and gambles it on the nags is also, strangely enough, part of the information proletariat, as his bets contribute to the statistical matrix that is the cyberspace of the gambling industry. A couch potato lying on the sofa with a bag of chips zapping the remote is part of the information proletariat. The ratings figures, on which advertising rates for the commercials being zapped are based, is a statistical projection of the number of couch potatoes. Information proletariat is what the Kerrigans would be if *The Castle* didn't end happily ever after.

The information proletariat gets little benefit from the information it generates, on which so much of the postindustrial economy depends. They are locked out of the education that might give them some leverage in this economy. They are assumed to be passive objects from which specialists of all kinds, in health, education, economics, welfare, marketing, extract information, and onto which they project plans and impose decisions. These info-proles increasingly resent the way information is used as a power over and against them, they resist it. The unspeakable majority refuses, more and more, to be spoken to or for.

The radical proletariat that Karl Marx imagined was denied the material benefits of capitalism. His proletariat sought knowledge in order to overthrow such an unjust order. What arose in the late 90s was a radical proletariat that had some minimal level of material benefits guaranteed by a Labor-sponsored welfare settlement, but was denied the virtual benefits of cyberspace. So the info-proles resisted knowledge and the unjust social order that went with it. The lesson, or the moral, is that unless the fruits of the production of information are shared, cyberspace capitalism will be resisted, just as industrial capitalism was resisted, until the labour movement won a share of the material benefits. The agenda for Labor beyond 2000 is clear: it has to spread the cultural and economic benefits of cyberspace.

This is Labor's problem: to make itself the power that might broker the interests of the information proletariat. Blue collar voters who in 1996 voted for the conservatives, who in 1998 voted for Pauline Hanson's One Nation Ltd, have to be persuaded that it was not really in their interests to resist the postindustrial order. This means Labor has to find benefits for those chunks of suburbia that have been shut off, or wanted to shut themselves off, from absorbing and applying new information. At the same time, it has to persuade the more urbane beneficiaries of cyberspace that it is also in their interests to defuse such resistance.

"The community is the collective victim of profoundly unequal access to information", Barry Jones wrote in 1995. By 1996, I think it fair to say that whatever outer suburbia did not know, it knew that it was the victim of this new kind of inequality. Resentment of this kind of inequality took the form of what I would call bad information. The info-proles were armed with the attack on "political correctness" and "postmodernism" sponsored by *Quadrant* and *The Australian* that were amplified and simplified by talkback radio's "emperors of air".[4] Resistance flourished as a deliberate flouting of the consensus values of cyberspace insiders.

Ironically, this might involve the use of the same vectors of cyberspace for the creation of just such a culture of resistance as are used for profitable and productive ends by others. The online newspaper the *New Australian*, with its front page links to both One Nation and the National Front is a good example. Writing before Pauline Hanson put Ipswich on the map by winning the Ipswitch-centred seat of Oxley in 1996, Barry Jones wrote that "in Ipswich, a town with higher than average unemployment, nearly 70% of the homes with children have computers." He uses Ipswich's local government sponsored internet access program as an example of the "capacity of computers to enhance the learning experience." Some adults may be learning how to resist the open information vectors of cyberspace by using those same vectors to create a cosy third nature that can repel new information, reading and writing for the *New Australian* and many other publications flourishing on the net.

As John Howard learned the hard way, playing with bad information is playing with fire. This populist resistance only looked thoroughly stupid. It was composed of people who, no matter how humble their formal education, had sophisticated and finely tuned bullshit detectors. These they fired up the instant they came across political celebrity, spreading itself about on television, radio, or the popular prints. Hard as it may be for the inner rings of suburbia to grasp, the outer rings who make up this populist revolt did not need their patronising attempts at enlightenment so much as a good reason to actually join the emerging public consensus on how to speak and act in postindustrial society. The infoproles, banished to the outer outer suburbs by declining demand for blue collar labour, saw no reason to attach their class interests to those of inner suburbia, where education provided some kind of bridge into the emerging global information economy.

Irrational resistance was a reasonable choice, and it worked. From the emergence of Hanson through to the 1998 Federal election, all the political parties, the urbane media and cultural talking heads, the burbling high moralists, everyone directed their attention to figuring out how to prevent the spread of populist culture and the bad information in which it revelled and on which it thrived. Much rhetoric was aimed at the resistance, but few good reasons were given for giving up resistance and joining the public consensus.

Part of the resistance was the National Party's problem. The junior party in John Howard's Coalition was clearly under pressure after it lost significant ground to One Nation at the Queensland election of 1998. It staved off the electoral challenge of One Nation in the 1998 Federal election. Even though One Nation actually polled more votes across the country, it won no lower house seats and only one Senate place. Part of the resistance was Labor's problem, as blue collar suburban culture was clearly a component of the resistance that Pauline Hanson's One Nation Ltd was able to co-opt. They are the symptom of a long term problem for Labor, and the title of Barry Jones's book *Sleepers Wake!* might just as well be directed at the culture of the Labor Party. As former Labor Senator John Button observed, "in Canberra Jones was surrounded by sleepers slow to wake."[5]

Bib and Bub

In the wake of the 1996 demise of the Keating Labor government, quite a few journalists set about attempting to identify new talking heads and new fables for Labor.[6] It was a time when, as Craig McGregor said, Labor found itself "with a dwindling working class base and a non-aligned middle." It would have to look beyond the blue and white collar workers for its majority.

At the end of the 90s, it seemed unlikely that survivors from the Hawke and Keating years could win back voters who associated Labor with high velocity economic reform that increased uncertainty and anxiety, even though many Australians benefited from the growth of a competitive and outward looking economy. Perceptions can often be slow to catch up with events. At the end of the 90s, there was still what John Button called "a hankering for the good old days when employers and union members shared the spoils of protection from imports in higher profits and wages, and consumers paid the price." Many pined for a return to an economy run on the 'not my department' theory: "The bosses blamed the unions and the unions blamed the bosses. There were scapegoats for all occasions."[7] Labor's senior talking heads seemed either to be tarred with the reform of the old system, or tarred with being its former functionaries.

Two Labor professionals stood out from the pack as potential new stars who escaped from the mindset of the old system and the culpability for reforming it. They both had something more than an image to burnish; they had ideas to brandish: Lindsay Tanner and Mark Latham. Latham published a significant book *Civilising Global Capital,* early in 1998. Tanner was working on one, tentatively titled *Open Australia,* due for publication after the 1998 Federal election.[8] The media often linked their fortunes, making them appear, in Latham's typically terse language, as the "Bib and Bub" of a potentially new kind of Labor culture.

In a world of ever more specialised information in ever more formalised formats, the book-length essay is still one way of creating an information vector that can address people as citizens. A good essay links together experiences, stories, concepts, arguments, and shapes a dialogue, within and beyond its pages, that connects people in a network of sense-making, rather than treating people as the object of specialised authority. Not many people might read either Latham's book or Tanner's, but word filters out, from those who have read them, via intermediaries that make up the pleasure machine of policy and political talk.

Of course people with a strong desire for policy and politics would like to think these are more worthy desires than other kinds, and that the machinery that propagates them is somehow more rational than that which propagates other kinds of desires, condensed around other kinds of images of celebrity. But let's be honest: pop stars, celebrity skin and fashion spreads get some people hard and wet, but a good policy document is what it takes to light some people's fire. A consideration of Latham and Tanner's future in Australian political culture has to take account of the strategies they pursue, which includes seeking credibility through writing in a curiously heightened way.

While hardly the first Labor politicians to write books, what was curious is the way the media responded to Tanner and Latham as, respectively, an intelligent politician and a political intellectual. They appeared as Labor talking heads who might qualify for leadership in the postindustrial, post-modern, information age. In the rest of this chapter and in the next, I want to look at the writings of these two young(ish) Labor celebutantes of the late 90s, and see what kind of future the fair go might have by their lights.

Craig McGregor once described Mark Latham as "the talented NSW right winger", and Lindsay Tanner he nominated "a key thinker on the Victorian left." Given that it was McGregor who spotted Paul Keating's potential when he was just a junior shadow minister, his interest in Tanner and Latham has some weight.[9] Both Tanner and Latham may have to wait their turn, as Labor's Federal front bench was still dominated at the end of the 90s by survivors from the Keating era: Kim Beazley, Simon Crean and the woman the media tagged "Labor's star recruit" Cheryl Kernot. Both Beazley and Kernot co-operated with hagiographers who wrote books about them, but this is not quite the same thing as attempting to make a mark on the public with one's own writing.[10]

Tony Wright, a journalist from *The Age*, recounts a telling anecdote from the 1998 Federal election campaign about the relationship between these older Labor politicians and the next generation: "What happened was that Beazley, in one of his numerous genial chats to journalists down the back of his VIP Boeing 707, told the truth. Asked on his last flight of the campaign about aspirants to leadership, Beazley mentioned, among others, Latham and… Tanner. Beazley agreed that the two, known as *The Young and the Restless*, were likely to be worthy contenders in the future, and used the throwaway line that they were a bit 'intellectually proud'."[11]

Tanner became Shadow Minister for Finance after the 1998 election, and was discreetly silent about Beazley's jibe. Latham, in the journalistic vernacular, "spat the dummy" and wound up on the back bench after airing complaints about the "palookas" on Beazley's staff and the lack of a real policy debate with the Labor Party. Whether Bub ever makes any more headway than Bib towards leading the party, one thing that these events make evident is the tensions within Labor culture about the relationship between concepts and policies.

Labor in Cyberspace

The changes Labor itself unleashed when in office created an economy, a polity and a culture that were considerably more dynamic than the quiet backwater in which people of my age, who I'll call Generation Gough, were probably the last to experince. The sense that there may be profound qualitative changes afoot in the 90s contributed to the resistant mood of the information proletariat and the reactionary instincts of Hansonite populism. No less worrying were the signs of soft Hansonism, even in the Labor Party, which took the form of a desire to make up policies that kept as much of the old suburban way of life alive regardless of its intrinsic quality or sustainability. Resistance to the need to invent new concepts for a new situation, to find new ways of grappling with complex information, seem to me to form a part of the disdain Beazley voiced for the "intellectual pride" of those Labor figures who saw the need to think again — and who claimed the capacity to think it through.

As Tanner wrote in 1991, a bad year for the Labor govern-ment, a division emerged in the Labor Party during the Hawke and Keating years. This was not the old division between left and right wing factions, but one that "straddles factional boundaries. The division is between those who may be described as 'rationalists' and others who may be seen as 'traditionalists' (or in each other's opinions, sellouts and troglodytes)."[12] Tanner identified the slogan of the troglodyte traditionalists, as "returning to our traditional base" and that of the sell-outs, or rationalists, as "adapting in a changing world." In the 1998 Federal election campaign, it was clear that Labor's traditionalists were exerting a strong influence. The party did well with its "traditional base", piling up useless swings in outer suburban seats it already holds.

The trouble was that Labor needed to appeal to both its traditional base and also to people who had benefited from the Hawke and Keating rationalisation of the economy. These appeared to be mutually exclusive goals. Labor needed to hang on to the loyalty of what had become the information proletariat, growing increasingly anxious and resistant in outer suburbia, and it needed to reposition itself as a forward looking party that understood the new agendas driven by urbane beneficiaries of an open and information intensive economy. It needed to be a party that could draw morals from its fabled past, but also that could draw lessons from the events of the present.

The moral of Labor's 1998 defeat was that the past Labor needed to return to was not any particular sacred relic of policy. Instead it needed to review the way those policies had arisen in the first place — as the expression of an alliance of popular interests and desires. Labor proposes, but the elec-torate disposes. Party apparatchiks might write the policy, but the public knows how to read. It can read the qualities of the party's talking heads and savour the texture of their speech as well as it can read any other kind of celebrity or commercial.

The lesson was that Labor did not need to substitute a new catechism of rationalism for it old dogmas, but to become a more empirical user of information and accumulator of knowledge. When Paul Keating said on *Labor in Power* that he stopped relying on Treasury advice because while he thought it was well informed and intelligent, it "lacked guile", this was a potentially important moment in the party's understanding of itself as an information gathering organisation. I think Keating realised late in the game that power in the postindustrial age means being able to draw intellectual confidence from scepticism rather than from dogma. He chose the word guile carefully, and what I think he meant by it was a certain kind of cunning that comes from knowing that knowledge is artifice.

If Labor is to survive in cyberspace it has to ask itself what its relation to information is, what kinds of knowledge it can claim to draw from the information it taps, and what kinds of skills it needs to communicate its knowledge. Anne Summers noted right at the start of the Hawke era that one kind of knowledge Labor was gathering with increasing effectiveness was survey polling data and focus group studies. "One hallmark of the reconstructed Labor party is its restrained and reassuring language... it would be possible to compile a glossary of key words... It would include such words as 'realistic', 'responsible', 'stable', 'moderate', 'careful', 'decent'. The words, and the themes they enunciate, come in a large part from the research on swinging voters and they thus reflect the values which significant sections of the Australian electorate respond to."[13]

Despite the populist rhetoric in the 90s to the effect that leaders were 'not listening' to suburbia, Summers marvelled at "the extent to which voters themselves are writing the speeches which the political leaders deliver. The notion that policies should be based on research rather than on ideology and long-held principles used to be anathema to Labor politicians." It was progress to be able to make policy that drew on information about the desires of the public and the language in which it was expressed. This makes more sense than the authoritarian practice of rationalising from belief, given that what counts as the catechism of true belief in the Labor Party was usually a matter of ideological control by functionaries rather than democratic information gathering. What Latham objected to in the party's attempt to formulate a soft Hansonite election policy platform in 1998 was that what the public wanted was not filtered through any serious attempt to conceptualise the sources of popular opinion, or how opinion could be moved to sound policy. A successful party cannot inform its policies solely by dogma or the polls.

On the other side of the process, all of the major parties acquired elaborate machines for grabbing space in the media vectors to communicate in as carefully managed a way as possible whatever policy was decided. As much as this too is an object of complaint within the electorate, the density of the vectors of cyberspace make it inevitable. As Summers wrote of the 1983 election campaign, "the parties were geared to monitor what politicians were saying and to blow any little phrase up into a political storm. The technique was totally dependent on the technology of the tape recorder, the transcribing machine and the vocadex." And of course such technologies have improved remarkably since 1983.

So on one side, any Labor politician and any Labor policy or slogan will be road-tested by the polling and focus group process — as long as the party apparatchiks have anything to do with it. And on the other side, any Labor politician and any Labor personality, policy or slogan will also have to get out to the people via a professional media apparatus. As John Button remarked, "in Chifley's day there were armies of passionate true believers... they turned out in their thousands for political meetings in public halls. Today's politics are filtered through television and radio. Elections are more like contests between rival management teams."[14]

All of this is bolted rather unhappily onto Labor's old industrial age machinery of decision making, and the historic culture of the branches. Some of those branches are strong. In Sydney's inner west, where I live, they have been an evolving part of the neighbourhood for a century. Party branches have not exactly spread outwards evenly as the city has layered ring after ring of suburbs around itself. There is a dedicated and intelligent membership of the party, but the resources Labor devotes to its education are minimal. The only consolation is that this ossification of the branch structure is not unique to Labor, but is shared by all of the major parties.

One thing that does mark out the Labor party as a unique culture is its longevity. It survived longer than any of the other major political cultures. It survived far worse times than the defeat of 1996 — I've only presented a few fables from the second half century of Labor's saga. That history should provide some confidence, and also some lessons and morals for a reinvented Labor's second century. Labor made the transition from an agrarian to an industrial labour movement party. The as yet unacknowledged challenge is to make it also the party of those who work with information, without forgetting those left behind in cyberspace, the information proletariat.

If Labor is a culture then it is flanked on one side by the problem of celebrity and on the other by the problem of cyberspace. By celebrity, I mean the need to create an image for the vectors of the media, through which the public reads proposals for what it could desire. By cyberspace, I mean the need to learn empirically from the great wealth of information available and create the peculiar kind of specialised knowledge that is the guile of the political generalist. For while Barry Jones is right in complaining of the capture of power by well-educated specialists dedicated to discrete kinds of information, Labor politics is also a kind of education in a kind of specialised knowledge — specialising in putting different kinds of speciality together.

One thing that Labor may have to integrate is a more forward-looking knowledge about the media, and not just the current affairs media that focuses on politics, but also the wider cultural significance of the media. If the basic idea of the previous chapter is even partly right, then it is increasingly from the media that people get the raw material out of which to shape their values and sensibilities. If the media is edging out the family as a locus of identity and self-awareness, then it must surely be overtaking less pervasive institutions such as the political party.

Generation Gough

It's one thing to say Labor could pay more attention to the politics of culture, but by the same token, academic work in fields like cultural studies could benefit by paying more attention to the culture of politics. In the 80s and 90s, when Labor was in power, cultural studies mostly positioned itself to the left of Labor, working the cultural margins that mainstream politics excluded.[15] This was partly a response to Labor's majoritarian politics, which did not really offer much to the most marginalised groups, particularly Aboriginal Australians.

Partly, it is also an unintended consequence of the influence in Australian cultural studies work of American readings of the formative English work in cultural studies. Lacking a mass social democratic party, the American reading of the English work emphasised the 60s radical side of cultural studies. Part of the motivation for this book is to try and draw the culture of politics and the politics of culture closer together again, in a specific context. It was no longer the case, at the end of the 90s, that cultural studies could comfortably position itself to the left of Labor, when Labor itself no longer attracted electoral majorities.

In thinking about the nexus between the culture of politics and the politics of culture, the moment that stands out is the period of the Whitlam Labor government, 1972 to 1975. While this is widely recognised as being a moment of both political and cultural transformation, I want to look also at the way the media operated to generate a synchronising template of those times. Besides being culture and politics, the Whitlam fable is also television. For some of my contemporaries, it was more television than anything else.

When I asked Darren Tofts about his experience of the Whitlam years, he emailed back: "Yes, I remember Whitlam being sacked; in fact my entire sense of it was derived from the television coverage; my recollection of how I felt about it at the time was of a sense of something that had gone drastically wrong; that this was just not on. Though I have to say that other things were equally pressing and momentous in my own life at the time; one was being a 15-year-old in a repressive secondary Catholic school, where corporal punishment was *de rigueur*, and sexual intimidation was a regular occurrence. The other thing was *Countdown*."[16]

An email reply from Mark Davis sets a vivid scene of the intersection of politics and culture in the Whitlam years, as a young person experienced them: "The election in 72 was another signal moment in Davis family history. To set the scene, we lived in a large housing commission estate on the edge of a country town — made of fibro, every third house the same floor plan, and so on — where we were 'billeted' because my father was a teacher. We were always 'broke', and accommodation was short. The estate was almost entirely populated by other teachers, Aborigines, what were then called 'new Australians', and the burnt out wrecks of cars. My parents, of course, were Labor. On my bedhead in those days was a forlorn 'Swing to Labor' sticker, in a kind of burnt orange — a remnant of the 1969 campaign when everyone thought Whitlam would win."

This was the context in which the 13-year-old Davis experienced Whitlam's 1972 election victory: "The telecast was on and when it became clear that Whitlam was going to win, my father, in a fit of enthusiasm, decided the best thing to do was to go 'beat the drum' for the Labor party, which consisted of belting the metal base of the [water] tank in a rhythmic fashion with his fist for a half hour or so. Things had got pretty out of hand by then. About 6.30 am the next morning, when everyone was still asleep, a hail of half-bricks came through the front 'picture-window', shattering every single one of its six large panes. The tank, luckily, was spared."

Davis remembers the 1975 dismissal of the Whitlam government as something that was also a mediated experience: "The dismissal was a schoolyard rumour that spread like wildfire at Ashwood High, and I remember walking home from school not believing that it could be true in a Western democracy, and so on. When I got home I found mum in the kitchen, ear glued to the radio. Everything from then on took place in an atmosphere of disbelief. I can remember watching Brian Naylor, I think it was, on the news that night, and then Whitlam on the front steps of parliament — "You may well say, 'God save the Queen', because nothing will save the Governor General!" — it was a signal moment. We went to the various demos in the city and so on, full of righteous passion (yes, ironic distance and Timor Gap has taken its toll). I still hate [Liberal leader Malcolm] Fraser. All that third world stuff just doesn't wash. He'll always be the stony-faced, Easter Island type guy they interviewed on the news that night to me."

Lindsay Tanner was also a teenager during the brief flowering of the Whitlam Labor government. Gough's celebrity brought him even more directly into Labor culture than

Davis' participation in the anti-dismissal demontrations. Tanner was a branch volunteer on Whitlam's 1974 re-election campaign. "He was always a big hero and I spent countless hours busting a gut to get him re-elected", remembers Tanner.[17] Where for Tanner, Gough Whitlam's celebrity was a catalyst for directly political desires, for Tofts and Davis, it is part of quite different constellations of memories, desires, interests.

Part of the challenge for Labor at the end of the 90s became that of finding ways of articulating this broader, less directly political memory of Labor's past to the party's future electoral ambitions. The media vector distributes images of political culture far and wide, lobbing them right in the intimate space of home and suburb. This distribution of images of the political via the media is also their dispersal. They end of woven together with all kinds of images, used as resources for reading all kinds of experience.

When Gough Whitlam appeared on stage at the 1998 ARIA music awards ceremony, he was to present an award to the rock band The Whitlams. He opened the envelope and mocked surprise: "and the award goes to — my family!" The (musical) Whitlams are old enough to remember the (political) Whitlams, and to associate them with a certain kind of progressive, optimistic, enlightened culture, and hence to name a band after them. It's a striking instance of the political contribution to celebrity being drawn upon in turn by culture. The trick for the Labor Party is try this in reverse, and draw political support from the culture. Although in the unlikely event that there is ever a band called The Hawkes, I doubt they would be as melodious.

On My Left, Lindsay Tanner

Like Mark Davis, Lindsay Tanner might count as part of Generation Gough. Like Davis, he grew up in rural Victoria, in the town of Orbost. Like Davis, Tanner came from a politically self-conscious family. His mother was secretary to a minister in the Fraser government and his father was a member of the National Party. Where Davis found punk music and culture upon coming down to Melbourne, Tanner found student politics. While Davis occupies an urbane position within the politics of culture, it seems to me Tanner espouses a more suburban version of the culture of politics.

Orbost, Tanner says, was a "basic sort of place." He remembers a time before the town had electricity, gas, sewerage — or television. It's a life Tanner says "city types don't understand. Melbourne in the 40s was Orbost in the 60s." Like Ben Chifley, Tanner turned rural isolation to his advantage by becoming a reader. Encountering writers like George Orwell at an impressionable age probably provided the information with which to think of a life beyond. Given how pervasive the media have become since the satellite opened a vector that brings almost all of the Australian continent within its reach, Tanner may well be one of the last politicians not raised in its embrace.

Even a strict boarding school could not isolate Tanner from the media aftershocks that emanated from 60s activism. His chance to become a participant rather than a spectator came at Melbourne University in the late 70s, where he edited the student paper, *Farrago*. After that, his career is within the labour movement: with a labour law firm, party staffer, union secretary. He wrote two books, one on his union experiences and one on environmental policy.[18] Then preselection for a safe inner city Melbourne seat, which he won in 1993. This rich and varied experience may lie behind Tanner's distinctive blend of views.

Tanner identifies the resentment of 'political correctness' as a backlash against the extension of new ideas flowing from the 60s social revolution into everyday life. At a time when the 80s economic revolution introduced even more destabilising ideas, popular resentment rose against new thinking on any front. Anti-political correctness was a reaction by those formed by past accretions of suburban outlook who resent the untimely intrusion of new modes of thought and language.

For the most part Tanner appears to favour an urbane reassessment of Australia's history and the ongoing proposal of new images of identity. If it is a choice between being an open and forward looking nation, or a closed and backward looking one, Tanner's favours the former. He also rightly stresses the tensions caused by Labor's partial support for some of the libertarian ethos of the 60s, with its concern for civil liberties, sexual and racial equality, environmental protection. He understands that these once urbane notions have already partly filtered through suburbia. He also perceives that many in the community feel they have paid too high a price for liberation. The down side is the "loss of community which seems to afflict contemporary Australia."[19]

Community is something of a 'motherhood' term in Australian political culture, conjuring up images of a small town life where everybody knows everybody and there's always someone to lend a helping hand. John Button gives a contrasting portrait of the communal ideal in his memoir *As It Happened.* He describes growing up in Ballarat in the 30s and 40s, where his father was the Presbyterian Minister. What's striking to me is the "tribal bigotry" Button describes: "My father was sometimes criticised by his parishioners for having morning tea with the nuns at St Mary's." The Buttons dealt only with Presbyterian shop keepers and professionals. "Anglicans had second preference." They shunned Catholics. "The only people whom nobody gossiped about were the Chinese."[20] The limitations of a communal life are rarely acknowledged in the yearning for community. It's not all as jolly as *Sea Change.*

It's largely a fantasy that there were once happy little communities. What has really changed is that, thanks to libertarian social change and proliferating media vectors, Australians now have an open discussion about the social problems that have always existed. Sexual harassment, homophobia, spousal abuse and drug addiction are not new phenomena. These things existed, acknowledged mostly in the margins, throughout the golden era of suburban Australia. What was characteristic of the suburban culture was not that it made the world safe and warm for everyone, but that it appeared to be blocking access to information about the down side of modern life. Tanner gives the impression that social dislocation is a new problem. While the forms of social dislocation that people suffer change over time, the really dramatic change that Tanner doesn't acknowledge is the increasing availablity of information about it.

Tanner also identifies a tension in the culture expressed as that between individualism and community. I think that if there has been a transformation in Australian culture, it is not from the collective to individualism, it is from forms of compulsory solidarity to voluntary ones. Individualism is an illusion. We always confront each other in social life in packs, bands, bunches — and now in cyberspace, networks. The difference is that there's now more flexibility about belonging. It's better to suffer a bit of anxiety of choice than to be forced to conform to compulsory forms of association, such as the churches or the old style trade unions were in the supposedly good old days.

To my mind, Tanner concedes too much to the conservative view, that libertarian change has somehow gone 'too far', and that individualism has corrupted community values. But there is no mistaking his compassion for the sense of anxiety and loss people feel. He also correctly identifies as a fundamental issue the desire to reconcile liberty and solidarity. Tanner is closest to that section of the Labor Party that is educated, white collar suburbia. With its admixture of libertarian and progressive values, it's a fading residue of the 60s. Its anxieties about security are caused by feeling too exposed to the forces of economic change in the 80s.

The dilemma is whether adjusting to economic change requires a turn to more culturally conservative values, or whether it is possible to create a sense of security, trust and confidence that incorporates the best of the libertarian spirit. What's best in Lindsay Tanner, as a thinking politician, is his awareness of these ambivalences. He represents an advanced point in the rethinking of the values of what was once the left of the Labor Party.

The Left and the Leftovers

It's hard tell what is the left any more. Many of its once vocal talking heads have abandoned any coherent defence of the old left's faith in the centralised economy. They have also retreated from the libertarian and liberationist social views that bubbled up with the new left of the 60s. The left are in danger of becoming leftovers — a residual and resistant force without a positive and progressive culture of change.

Sometimes the old left and the old new left seem not to notice they have become the new new right. They favour government intervention in the economy, but only to arrest change and protect the interests of workers in a few unions, at the expense of other workers. They favour government intervention in culture, but only in the form of an authoritarian restriction on the free flow of information, to further the interests of inner suburban cultural mandarins. The critique of popular culture has quietly become a contempt for the people who express their aspirations via its images and stories. The left, in short, has become zealously suburban in outlook.

The critical distance the left maintains toward popular culture comes at a heavy price. Both the 60s liberationist and the 80s suburban moralist had their critiques of tabloid media. The former thought it too conservative and moralising, the latter too risque and immoral. In both cases the difficulty lies in identifying popular media only by particular elements in it, and then characterising it by these — mutually exclusive — stereotypes. The critique of popular media ends up doing exactly what it accuses popular media of doing — reducing things to their simplest level.

This is a problem for the Labor Party. Labor cannot allow itself to be too dominated by the values of the educated inner band of suburbia, because part of the culture of inner suburbia is its disdain for the tastes and desires of those it considers beyond the pale. This snobbery has a conservative expression, but also a superficially leftist one as well, a suburban absorption of leftist critique. It is always detrimental to the fortunes of the Labor Party to so openly despise the kinds of media vector that a lot of Labor voters embrace as their own. It was through not respecting popular taste that Keating really came unstuck with certain kinds of voters, who saw his hob-nobbing with urbane arty types as the snobbery of a self-important inner suburban.

Fortunately, Tanner sees the problem. "I wouldn't like to see the influence of people like me becoming more dominant", he told McGregor, because then the "traditional Labor base could get squeezed even more." In addition to retaining the trade union links, I think this problem has to be addressed more laterally, by thinking about how Labor can come to terms with the popular culture and media tastes of its lower suburban base. The "cult of celebrity" annoys a serious Labor thinker like Tanner, but it is not impossible for Labor to speak in a popular voice, as it did in Chifley's day.

As *True Believers* reminds us, much of the media were overtly hostile to Chifley. In Hawke and Keating's day, the so-called 'quality' media took Labor seriously. But if anything, the animosity of the editorial writers for Frank Packer or Keith Murdoch probably did Chifley more good than the embrace by the business scribes of Kerry Packer and Rupert Murdoch did Keating. Outer suburbia is quite capable of reading between the lines.

Perhaps some day Labor figures will get a run in the more popular end of the media controlled by James Packer and Lachlan Murdoch. Tanner's own story, from frontier country town to Federal Parliament, would make a great celebrity tabloid yarn. Tanner has a deep concern for reforming the apparatus of the Labor Party and overcoming its leftover culture of "arrogance, exclusivity and intellectual rigidity in an era in which these characteristics are alien to most ordinary people."[21] Part of the arrogance that needs to be addressed is arrogance toward popular taste.

Steering the Third Way Leftwards

Some on the left of the Labor Party, such as Tanner, are starting to see the light on the hill a little differently. It's no longer enough to grow the economy, tax it, and transfer some income to whoever a government decides most needs it. That might put money in the hands of people in need, but it doesn't always help those people *participate* in their culture, the economy or in public life. "Capacity to participate" is what Tanner identifies as the thing government intervention could take as a better objective, a light on a higher hill. What Tanner exemplifies is a left-leading version of an emergent third way between market and state. To me Tanner still has too collectivist and communitarian a view of this capacity to participate, but it is perhaps inevitable that a thinker like Tanner, who wants to be inside government, sees it so more than someone who values the liberty of thinking from the culture at large.

Everyday life contains many organised expressions of the desire for community. These provide individuals with a capacity to participate — and a capacity to choose how to participate, I would add. It's from these small entitlements to belong, these little worlds of sympathy we feel for the fortunes of those around us, that make it possible for people to think beyond the borders of their quarter acre block and beyond their suburb. Participation is not just a good thing in itself, it may also be the only way a small country can manage the kinds of changes required by its participation in a wider world of information flows, technological change and economic flux.

The Australian economy is not a static entity, and change is not just the result of economic rationalist policies. In Tanner's view, economic rationalism was a response to changes, rather than their cause. Both rationalists and traditionalists within the Labor government had to confront the fact that most of the Australian settlement "...on which traditional ALP faith has been founded — protectionism, conciliation and arbitration, high living standards and trade union strength — are in the process of being drastically weakened or destroyed by international forces beyond our control." The challenge for the left at the end of the 90s was to come up with its own version of economic literacy, one that did not retreat to the magic pudding, but accepted changing economic realities and looked for more equitable solutions within a realistic framework.

For a start, this means joining the public consensus on what actually happened in the 80s and 90s. The constraint within which the Hawke government's strategy had to accommodate itself was the decline in the value of Australia's commodity exports. By 1983, when Labor took office, it no longer sufficed to dig up rocks, chop down trees and grass, and export the resulting wood, wheat, and iron ore. As commodity exports declined, the export of legal, accounting, education, engineering, medical, managerial and creative services increased, but not enough to close the gap.

By the late 90s, over 27% of Australian adults were relying on social security as their main source of income, a proportion that doubled since the days of the Whitlam government. Thanks to the idea of 'targeted benefits', people receive this money under a plethora of different benefit categories with different eligibility criteria. No wonder there is an unspeakable majority obsessed with 'fairness'. As Tanner and others started to point out in the wake of Keating's defeat, people require a very high degree of moral legitimacy from welfare they are forced to pay for but not entitled to use.

In the fables of the left, Hawke and Keating presided over a Thatcherite reduction in welfare, and the public sector shrank dramatically. Actually, what the government takes out of the economy through taxation did fall slightly in the 80s and 90s, but after it had risen steadily throughout the postwar years. The real cause of the perception that government spent less is that there were more people that it has to spend money on. More people needed health, welfare and education, and so expenditure was stretched more and more thinly.

Other changes outside of government control also had equity effects. The work force changed significantly since the Whitlam years, partly as a result of Whitlam's tariff cuts, but also under the impact of information technology, becoming more flexible and fragmented. Demand for low skilled labour dropped. Even workers who work with their hands had to know something about the technologies involved. Not just skill but knowledge became a major differentiator of income, and income inequalities markedly widened. Even many of those with jobs did not feel that the job gave them a sense of autonomy and security.

Some of the more threatening images of global economic change can be overstated. It's true that as vectors of trade and information thread distant parts of the world together, concepts like national interest and national competitiveness lose their meaning. But the state is not necessarily in terminal decline. A small, high wage economy is not automatically doomed. Car makers, for instance, continue to fabricate in Australia, despite tariff reductions, because they want to hang on to market share. There may be places where wages are lower, but there are few places where highly skilled labour can be bought on the cheap.

Global capital markets may transact colossal sums, but 94% of total savings are invested in the country of the saver's origin. These global capital markets actually enhance a government's power, as it too can borrow abroad. There is not quite the same imperative for Chifley's fatal policy of nationalising domestic savings when there are private foreign lenders. When Keating privatised the Commonwealth Bank, he sold off one of the last remnants of the postwar reconstruction plan, but in the process he failed to come up with a strategy to ensure that when the deregulated banks went off in hot pursuit of big business customers, there would be an adequate retail banking service industry for ordinary people.

One role that could actually be enhanced is the state's involvement in the research and development of new technologies. Private investment comes too little and too late to applied science and technology. There are still good arguments in favour of government intervention in the economy, but on a somewhat modest scale. A range of smaller measures may generate more jobs and income than another Snowy Mountains scheme. While markets may be more efficient users of information and allocators of resources than centralised bureaucracies, there are many circumstances where market conditions do not prevail. There are situations where some firms have monopoly power, or where the assistance of other governments tilts the playing field. There are also situations, more positively, where an argument can be made that the "clustering" of related industries could generate jobs and growth, and where producing such a result requires a government with the information and planning powers to bring private interests together.

But in the main, the realistic option for the left is to argue that policy should focus on improving the quality of the inputs rather than trying to direct the production of outputs or protect them from competition. Micro-economic reform has been too obsessed with lowering the costs of power and transport — changes that might benefit heavy industry and mining but do little for the growing service and information industries. Environmental standards can improve the quality of resource inputs; education and training can improve the quality of labour.

The Australian economy still creates a lot of jobs, only it creates different jobs that benefit different people. The kinds of low skilled jobs that men used to do in the industrial economy evaporated; the kinds of low skilled jobs women used to do have expanded, as services and cyberspace grow, and the economy moves from an industrial to a postindustrial basis. Hence the support Pauline Hanson's One Nation Ltd received from blue collar males, who make a large part of the conscious, resistant information proletariat.

Unemployment is also very unevenly distributed, creating whole suburbs of continuous high unemployment. To make matters worse, there are still rather macho ideas about what counts as a real job. What this calls for is a major change in the culture of work.

Nobody on the left doubts that the Hawke and Keating era programs were not always satisfactory. The idea of "mutual obligation" sounds good in principle, but if someone is obliged to undergo retraining in order to get benefits, government agencies ought to be under obligation to provide training that is actually useful. In practice there is no way an unemployed person is in any position to 'participate' in questioning the government's end of so unequal a mutuality. This became a strong source of popular resistance.

Competition policy could also benefit from an engaged scepticism from the left. Competition policy may generate productivity improvements that can benefit commodity industries that compete on price by lowering the cost of major inputs like power and transport. The picture may be more complex for other industries. The left has every right to be sceptical about arguments for the benefits of competition that contain little or no empirical evidence. A greater emphasis on the analysis of outcomes in proposals for deregulation, might show whether the reality is likely to match the theory. It is only by acknowledging a wider public scepticism about economic policy making that a consensus might be rebuilt around a policy for change. If there is a benefit that can be leveraged out of the existence of hard Hansonism, it is not a soft Hansonism of retreat from reform, but a more empirical approach to it.

Education is a difficult issue for the left, not least because that is where it derives so much of its support. Increasing public funding for education is a hard case to argue without accepting greater accountability and, over the inevitable objections of the teacher's unions, testing of schools. If people are to trust the teacher's assessments, they are entitled to assessments of the teachers. *Silent Majority III* made abundantly clear that an increasingly well educated public is also a public increasingly sceptical about the self-interest of professionals who want to run their services without public accountability.

The old left has been slow to grasp the potential of the urbane world of the culture industries, not just to cause trouble and promote strange ideas, but also to contribute to the economy. Australia exports significant amounts of popular music, television programs, educational materials and other intellectual property. The way to get Australia into cyberspace economically is not to spend millions trying to entice Intel to set up a semi-conductor factory, but to further develop the successful media content industries.

As partly privatised communications utility, Telstra is a weird beast. It ties up a lot of capital in something that is no longer fully under public control. The debate in the media tends to polarise toward the extremes of a wholly public or wholly privatised future for Telstra. The left usually supports public ownership of basic communication capacity, but it is an open question in a technologically fluid environment as to what that means. The difficulty is to keep some basic vectors under the umbrella of public policy, while allowing a telecommunications industry to develop, and to encourage other information based industries to take advantage of cheap communications and technically sophisticated vectors.

The left has a sentimental attachment to public ownership, and can be as resistant to inquiries into the real benefits of public control as the economic rationalists can be about the real benefits of competition. The left also draws its support disproportionately from the public sector, and hence there is a strong resistance to addressing the issue. What the left has left too much to the right is the question of setting criteria for deciding on the appropriateness of public ownership. Such criteria might include: the extent to which the product is used universally, the contestability of the market, and the externalities associated with production and consumption of the product. Under such criteria, gas, water, electricity and communications ought to be in public ownership. There is plenty of room for debate there, but the crucial factor is to work on some reasonable terms for such a debate.

Postindustrial Class Struggle

If there is a reason why the left often appears to be struggling to keep up with the pace of change, it may be that the forces traditionally identified as 'left' no longer represent the front-line in the class conflict that, in Marxist thinking, determines the forward movement of history. Much of the agenda of the left seems either to be about resisting change completely or accommodating to it in ways that preserve the interests of certain constituencies, particularly those skilled workers in manufacturing and in the white collar public sector that belong to left wing unions.

Barry Jones identified an information proletariat, but he did not claim to have thought through the postindustrial society in terms of class conflict. His prophecy was that "the question of control of, and access to, information should become one of the major political issues of the 1990s", but he did not pose this question in class terms. Information may work as differently in the market economy as capital does to rent, and might therefore generate quite different kinds of class interest. I want to conclude this chapter with some highly speculative remarks that try, in a very abstract way, to advance the conceptualisation of the conjuncture of the late 90s. This last section is addressed to a certain kind of culture of the left. Those not so inclined might find the next chapter, which deals with Labor's culture of the right, more congenial.

"Rent is that portion of the produce of the earth that is paid to the landlord for the use of the original and inde-structible powers of the soil. It is often, however, confounded with the interest and profit of capital…".[22] So wrote David Ricardo, one of the original 'economic rationalists', in what was one of the first, although certainly not the last attempt to define the difference between rent and profit, the returns respectively on land and capital.

Land is of fixed quantity. There is only so much of it. Any economic activity based on land behaves in much the same peculiar way. When demand rises, prices rise, but if there is no more land to meet the demand for what land produces, then the high price does not encourage new competitors — by definition there can be no new competitors, as the quan-tity of land is fixed. If there were new competitors, they would add to supply, supply would match the new high level of demand, and prices would trend down again. But there is no more land, no new competitors, so as demand rises, prices shoot up, and owners of land collect a rent derived from possession of this fixed asset. In principle, a mine, an office block and a prime piece of farm land behave in much the same way in the marketplace.

Most things are not of fixed quantity, and don't offer an opportunity to extract rent. If a factory makes widgets, or a company offers a service, and demand for those widgets or that service rises, competitors can come into the market attracted by the high prices. These new competitors add to supply and drive down the price. This is where the more strictly capitalist economy thrives, by investing in bringing to market products or services that can be sold for more than the investment, and hence return a profit. Unlike rents, profits are not protected by the fixed quantity of the inputs. Of course, many capitalists would like their business to accrue rents rather than profits, and governments are often dragged in to the creation of artificial rent-producing monopolies in anything from steel to television.

People who own land or capital hire people who have neither to work for them. Owners have an interest in keeping down the wages they pay, whereas workers have an interest in driving them up. This conflict of interest may not be a complete one, however. In the modern world, workers require security and stability of employment, and come to have a shared interest with their employer in the maintenance of those conditions. Higher wages might be good in the short run, but not if this shuts off profits, sends the company broke, and tosses the worker out of a job. Owners and workers may have different interests, but their interests are not simply opposed to each other, unless you accept the fable that by overthrowing the owners, the workers will inherit the earth.

There is one significant difference between working for someone who owns land and someone who owns capital. When demand for land or what land produces is high, it's possible for the wage earner to make demands for much higher wages without sending the owner of land broke. The owner of land is much more likely to just pass the increased cost on to the purchaser. After all, new competitors can't come in to bankrupt the rentier, and hence the job of the worker is more secure.

This is why mining and building workers were, until recently, more able to extract wage increases out of owners of land than other workers were out of owners of capital. Demanding higher wages was unlikely to send the company broke. Actually, under a high tariff system, the whole economy can work more like a rent economy than a capital economy. Protectionism creates quasi-rent conditions for lots of businesses, and lots of workers can demand wage rises that just get passed on to the purchaser.

There are already two kinds of economy in this classical conceptualisation of how it all works. But what if we add a third kind of economy — the information economy? Actually, before Adam Smith or David Richardo got around to theorising rent and capital, the new information economy was already becoming a reality. When English law recognises the rights of authors and engravers to 'own' the content of their works, the concept of property was in principle extended to information.

Before then, any printer could copy any book — ownership resided in the thing, the book itself, not the ordering of the information within it. With copyright a reality, a new kind of property owner arises — the owner of copyright. Not coincidentally, a new kind of celebrity, and a new kind of urbanity arises at the same time as the recognition of this new kind of property. Samuel Johnson was one of the first writers to openly make his living from his trade, and became famous for it. Johnson claimed that "there seems to be in authors a stronger right of property than that by occupancy; a metaphysical right, a right, as it were, of creation…".[23]

Johnson realised that this property right had to be balanced against the common interest in that the knowledge contained in a book be "universally diffused among mankind." Hence Johnson argued for an exclusive right that would be limited in duration. As Mark Rose of the University of California argues, "at one level, the literary-property question was a legal struggle about the nature of property and how the law might adapt itself to the changed circumstances of an economy based on trade. At another, it was a contest about how far the ideology of possessive individualism should be extended into the realm of cultural production."[24]

As it turned out, it could be extended very far indeed. As

with the ownership of land or capital, the arguments made for it could be based on the doctrines of natural law. Someone is entitled to own whatever is the object and product of their own labour. But the creation of information as a form of private and tradeable property is no more natural than the creation of land and capital as private property. A fully market-based economy rests on the convention of property, backed by the authority of the courts.

Information can be an object of a law of property, just like capital or land, but does not necessarily behave the same way. What is distinctive about information is firstly that my possession of it need not deprive you of it. I cannot possess land that you at the same time possess, but I can know something that you at the same time know. The possession of information does not require the dispossession of another.

Secondly, copying information is distinct from creating it. If I grow wheat or make a shoe, the copying of either of these things takes as much effort as making them, and is in fact an identical act to making them. If I write a book or compose a song, the copying of it requires much less effort. An effort tending, from the invention of moveable type to the invention of the floppy disc, to diminish to nothing. In short, information behaves very differently to a physical thing, and as a form of property it is quite the opposite of land. Land cannot be copied and is in fixed supply; information can be endlessly copied, and the copying of it is simple compared to making it in the first place.

The principles of the information economy have existed for two centuries, and were worked out alongside the legal fictions for other kinds of property according to which a commodity economy would be regulated. It is late in the 20th century that the information economy has become conspicuous in size and influence, in part because the evolution of the technical means of storing and distributing information have advanced very rapidly.

Most information workers, like most agricultural and industrial workers, have to sell their capacity to work, and do not, in the end, own what they make. The worker might have the capacity in their head or hands to produce something, but lack the means to realise it. Where other workers confront owners of land or capital, information workers confront owners of what I call vectors. A vector is the physical and technical means of moving information across space, or preserving it across time. As with agriculture or industry, the technical development of information reaches a point where economies of scale dictate the formation of large enterprises which own and control vast vectors for the distribution of information, just as other businesses control vast tracts of land or physical plant and equipment.

What is often conceived as globalisation may just be the growth of the information economy due to the technical advance of the vector, and the subordination of the economies of capital and land to it. The reason for this is not hard to fathom. Markets presuppose the transmission of information about demand, supply and the prices that mediate between them, from one place to another. The information economy grows, in part, on its capacity to expand the opportunities for owners of land and capital.

What is often perceived as a shift in the balance of power from labour to capital in the 90s may rather be a shift in the centre of gravity of economic activity, from the economies of capital and land, to that of information. The most conspicuous beneficiaries of such a shift are the owners of vectors, the Murdochs and Packers. Less noticed are those beneficiaries who are not owners but merely workers in this expanding economy, which includes both information-specific businesses, and also the information component of the business of capital and land, of making things and growing things.

What appears as an information proletariat is a pool of unemployed or marginally employed people who have not made the transition from an economy dominated by making things to an economy dominated by making information. Just as the transition from agriculture to manufacturing produced an under-employed population, this second transition also produces such a proletariat, and once again, in its desperation, it is tempted to embrace populist solutions, involving a strong state that will maintain an economy to its liking.

The left has always been an unstable and uneasy alliance, and has always included the representatives of industrial labour, the most organised part of the economy of capital and the making and things. It has also included members of the information-working class. The difficulty for the left is that the interests of these different kinds of worker are further apart than ever. The former are tempted to struggle for the retarding of the shift in the centre of gravity toward the information economy. The latter have no interest in such a retrogressive step, and have their own agenda of conflicts over the conditions under which they sell the information they produce to the owners of media vectors.

The information economy is at the same time an information culture. As Mark Rose argues, the extension of "possessive individualism" into culture via the legal fiction that information can be private property is an old principle. It just became more obvious, late in the 20th century, what this commodification of information has all along implied: culture and economy are inseparable. There was always a market for information upon which the culture of everyday life depended. What changed is the development of new vectors, such as radio, television and the internet, which could be accumulated and co-ordinated, as elements of a powerful kind of market economy.

As a consequence, politics, no less than the economy, became saturated by vectors. The vectoral becomes the space of political action no less than of economic gain. The creation of political majorities becomes a matter of articulating popular desires via media images. This process has been advancing for some time, overcoming the social and communal basis of political affiliation. Politics in the information age is about the formation of majorities that are synchronised around particular images.

Majorities may be articulated on the basis of a shared desire *for* something, or *against* it. Both the left and the right have a history of the articulation of desire against things. The right depended on the articulation of desire in the form of hatred of communism throughout the cold war — a tactic that contributed to the weakening of the right when the Berlin wall came down. In this they merely succeeded where the left failed, in its attempt to turn the difference between the interests of workers and owners into an opposition that would pit workers against ownership in general — the class war.

Both the left and the right must share some culpability for the rise of a populism that has no qualms about identifying the most vulnerable minorities as the object of a majoritarian hatred. Populism exploits the pleasure machine of desire, as it works in the vectoral world, and can achieve substantial gains. The irony is that populism achieves its gains using the cultural machinery of information precisely because of discontent with the effects of the power of information to undermine the economic position of what now becomes an information proletariat.

Politics as desire *for* something, rather than desire which attempts to opposed a majority to a minority, faces the added difficulty that the articulation of mass desire must occur in public. Desire compounds desire, but also fragments, dissipates, comes in conflict with itself. If there is a majoritarian politics to be created, it might not be the politics of consensus, which presupposes community of interest, not just between capital and labour, but also between the economies of cultivating land, manufacturing things and processing information. It might be a politics of connection rather than consensus, of articulating networks rather than a corporatism rooted in the old manufacturing economy.

The politics of consensus assume a mass media that works rather like mass manufacturing. It composes its majority on the basis of blocks of shared interest that can be articulated in a few broad strokes in a mass media vector. The politics of connection, on the other hand, might be more appropriate for a world in which diverse vectors proliferate, and the interests that have to be composed to form a majority are not based firmly in a mass manufacturing economy, but span two different kinds of economy, that of the manufacture of things and the production of information.

In short, a 'political economy' of the age of information has to take account of what is specific to the information economy. Like land, information deviates from some key assumptions about the commodity economy of things. The commodification of culture has always been a part of the development of the information economy, no matter how much of a recent phenomena this may appear. It is implied in the original formulation of the legal fiction of information as property. A certain kind of celebrity, as someone who

in a sense owns an image and story of which they are the producer, is a byproduct of this commodification. It too is not
new, and in someone like Samuel Johnson there is a proto-
type for contemporary celebrity.

Celebrity, in turn, is a concept that can hold together the
economic and political aspects of this 'political economy' of
information. The appearance of celebrity is not just an artefact of the commodification of culture, but also of the
immersion of politics within the relations of the vector.
These are not ephemeral additions to the commodity
economy, they are aspects of it that have been developing for
some time. The creation of a form of property for information has just been waiting for the technical development of
the vectors of information relations to release the potential
latent in it.

This is just a rough sketch, starting with Barry Jones'
insight into the existence of an information proletariat, and
speculating on what larger picture it may fit into. It is somewhat removed from rather pragmatic approach of, say,
Lindsay Tanner. But perhaps what Tanner's insights into the
changing options for the left of the Labor Party needs is
some larger framework within which to plot the changes,
rather than reacting on the basis of out-dated maps of how
the commodity economy functions. In any case, the left no
longer have a monopoly on conceptual thinking in the
Labor Party and the labour movement, and perhaps it never
did. As I want to show in the next, and last, chapter, the light
on the hill can also be regenerated in terms quite outside
those of the left.

c h a p t e r **10**

Third way, second go

Do not be deceived: this last lamp does not give more light — the dark has only become more absorbed in itself.

Paul Celan

Or maybe the truth is not what lies beneath the sand but the sand itself, always shifting, never certain, so that once we cut away that which we cannot be sure of we are left with nothing but space. And echoes.

James Bradley

On My Right, Mark Latham

Mark Latham is a "heavy, strong-looking bloke with a palpable sense of reserve", writes Craig McGregor.[1] He is a "full on intellectual", but "dry, laconic." His story is pure Sydney westie made good. He grew up in Green Valley from the time he was four, when the Department of Housing moved his family out there. Encouraged by his parents, he studied hard, did well at school, and got in to Sydney University where he majored in political economy.

He was Gough Whitlam's research assistant for a while, and worked for Bob Carr. Fighting his way through the Labor ranks, Latham turned rightward, lost an ugly preselection battle, then ran Liverpool council for what McGregor calls "three controversial years". According to Mike Steketee, he "introduced dry economic notions of productivity targets, corporatisation, contestability and contracting out", but he also opened two new libraries, a cultural facility and new sporting facilities."[2] Winning Gough Whitlam's old seat of Werriwa in a 1994 by-election, Latham landed in parliament with a reputation as aggressive, hard-headed, single-minded. As Laura Tingle says, Latham is "the inheritor of Gough Whitlam's lofty intellectual arrogance as well as his seat."[3]

After Labor's electoral defeat in 1996, these and other media commentators identified Latham as a rising celebrity, a fresh face to replace the overly familiar roster of Labor heavies, with whom both the media and the electorate were a bit bored. He held the shadow portfolio of education. After Labor's electoral defeat in 1998, Latham found himself on the back bench, without a shadow portfolio, and highly critical of the policy development process within the parliamentary Labor Party. As senior NSW Labor figure Michael Easson said at the time: "Labor needs to think through new policies to extend its support... that's where Mark Latham has a point about policy development. Labor appeared... to proffer a soft form of economic Hansonism. Labor appeared retrograde on many of the policy reforms it took in the 80s... Where Latham is wrong is in seeking to influence the party from the backbenches... he needs to engage his colleagues more."[4]

Whether McGregor and others were right in pegging him as a future Labor star is of less interest to me than his book. He started writing *Civilising Global Capital* with Peter Baldwin, former member for Sydney, who is from the left of the party.[5] I think it is the most intellectually serious writing I've ever read by a member of the Australian parliament. In it I find a thinker who is no friend to either the old Labor fable of the state driven command economy, or of Labor's intellectual and special interest group fellow travellers. Yet it's a book that I think charts a course with which those who believe in justice, liberty and the fair go can usefully argue. This last chapter is a commentary on it, and its potential as a source of thinking for the renewal of Labor culture, and as a framework for thinking about a third way for Labor, lost in cyberspace.

Civilising Global Capital examines the policies and structures by which Labor might respond to the challenges of the postindustrial era and expand what Latham calls "social capability". His idea of updating the Labor fable is not to revise 'a chicken in every pot' to 'chicken nuggets in every microwave', but to try and think again about what the light on the hill means and how to achieve it. If Labor's goal has always been "civilising capitalism", then this goal changes as capitalism changes. Labor has made the transition from agrarian Labor to industrial Labor, but is stalled at becoming cyberspace Labor.

"The postwar certainties of the nation and welfare states have gone forever", Latham declares. In such a time "there is a powerful tendency to appeal to the perceived triumphs and legends of the past to guide the thinking and identity of the present." But what is distinctive about Latham is his lack of nostalgia, his almost completely consistent modernism. Latham is searching for a third way other than following the paths of American style market freedom and the servile states of Europe. In the process, he draws on an eclectic mix of ideas, and moulds them together in a prose style as thick as congealed vegemite.

Yet almost in spite of himself, *Civilising Global Capital* is a personal book, an essay on Latham's own experience. Various Latham personas glisten beneath the matt surface of his prose: the westie, the mayor, the suburbanite, the footy player, and most endearingly, the man who got an education and is determined to use it for his own advancement by linking his advancement to that of others. It's hard not to see in his passion for education an essay on what it means to be Mark Latham.

The Four Conflicts

Latham kicks off with one of his schematic overviews. He identifies four kinds of conflict with which Labor has to cope. Firstly, there is the traditional antagonism between capital and labour, the conflict that shapes the perceptions of what Lindsay Tanner calls the "traditional" wing of the party. Secondly, there is the conflict between the information rich and information poor, which sharpened in the late 90s with the rise of a resistant "information proletariat", to use Barry Jones' term. Thirdly, there is the conflict between the global and the local, which impacts on the former colonial dependency very strongly now that the Australian settlement has unravelled. The fourth conflict is between individualism and community, which strikes me as a different kind of conflict to the others on Latham's list. The other three detail forces at work in the world, where this fourth conflict seems to me a clash of values. As I hope to show, it can be better expressed as a conflict arising out of new vectors of communication.

The preoccupation with the conflict between capital and labour with the ALP tends to distract attention from the second conflict on Latham's list, which might be just as important in terms of the effect it has on people's lives, and on their "social capacity." As it shifted from agrarian Labor to industrial Labor, party members recognised a shift in the kind of property, the possession of which conferred power over labour. That the land itself was in the hands of the few was what agrarian Labor organised against; that capital, in the form of factories and workshops was in the hands of the few, this was what industrial Labor organised against. The property in dispute shifted from nature to second nature, from soil and water to steel and steam.

The conflict between the information rich and poor, or between the urbane specialised elite and the information proletariat, is about a different kind of property. It's about intellectual property, the ownership of what becomes third nature. As Latham perceives, this conflict does not neatly correspond to the conflict between capital and labour. Urbane specialists are not necessarily owners of intellectual property. Lachlan Murdoch or James Packer are owners of intellectual property, for a substantial proportion of the assets of a business like News Corporation or the Packer family's PBL are intangible things like the value of the banner of *The Australian* newspaper, or the Packer empire's accumulated capacity to dominate the magazine business.

It's possible to have a trained capacity to create or assess information that is very valuable without actually owning much by way of intellectual property, not to mention the means of capitalising on one's intellectual property. The urbane talking heads I described in an earlier chapter, swilling cocktails in Kings Cross, mostly do pretty well out of their skills, but don't own much of the information they make. Beth Spencer's sorry tale of begging for the rights to a Lou Reed song is a case in point.

What distinguishes most of the information rich, Latham says, is the ability to engage in "abstract thinking". But some information rich don't think abstractly, but very concretely. They don't think in concepts, but in pictures, sounds, sensations, feelings. A successful creative director in advertising ought to count as part of the information rich, but it isn't possible to specify in an abstract way how her process of thinking works. Thinking abstractly is one of the most valuable skills, but it isn't the only one. The information rich includes everyone who can make or discover new patterns or divergences in any flow of information at all. This is the heart and soul of urbanity: the ability to invoke the virtual side of any flow of information; the ability to create new flows by discerning what is immanent in what exists.

The difference between the information rich and information poor, between the urbane burghers and the intellectual proletariat, intersects the next level of Latham's list of conflicts too. The urbane are more inclined to be "cosmopolitan, progressively tolerant and confident, generally embracing the rhetoric and horizons of the global village." Not universally so, of course. Few people are completely urbane, purely cosmopolitan, completely at home in Marshall McLuhan's global village. But by tendency, the information rich value the opportunity to engage with global flows of information because they see new kinds of virtuality in it, new possibilities for creating concepts, perceptions, sensations, stories, or whatever. By contrast, the information poor tend to fear unwanted information flows, to be more attached to what Latham calls the "practical certainties of life". In short, suburban rather than urban in outlook.

This is where the first three levels of conflict Latham identifies cascade into the fourth, although I think it's wrong to think of this conflict as the opposition between community and individualism. Rather, it is the difference rather between defining one's identity negatively or positively. There are two ways of responding to a new flow of information: incorporating it into oneself and modifying one's identity to take advantage of new potentials that information incites;

resisting that information by defining one's self as precisely this capacity to resist. The former looks like individualism because it tends to create communities of diverse people pursuing different lifestyles and life chances. The latter looks like community because the production of this negative sense of self, as being that which resists, tends to happen on a collective basis. People tend to appeal to what they take to be common values in this act of resistance. But both are "communal" in the sense that it takes a communication among individuals for either way of living in the path of the vector to occur.

Labor's Response

"One of the reliable laws of modern politics is that policy vacuums are filled by polling results", Latham observes with the sardonic certainty of one who knows first hand. I think it's a good thing that Labor uses such research tools, but they are better deployed testing rhetorics than making policies, still less creating the abstract framework within which to conceptualise policies.

Latham's starting point for orienting himself in his four-fold diagram of conflicts is to start with the conflict between labour and capital, and Labor's traditional role as defender of the interests of those who do not possess capital. Or as he expressed it more colourfully to Craig McGregor, "I think our starting point is to stick to the working class like shit to a blanket."[6] The difficulty is that this is hard to piece together with the other levels of conflict. It isn't necessarily in the interests of workers to oppose the information rich (who have their own conflicts with capital) or to oppose globalisation (which creates new sources of efficient wealth creation as it destroys the old slothful ones). Nor is it helpful to align Labor's working class base too closely with a negative and reactive subjectivity in relation to new flows of information, as that not only sets workers against others Labor needs to put together electorally, it cuts them off from new kinds of work and new expressions of solidarity.

"New forms of social connectedness and solidarity, however, are not possible unless people find new things to do and express in common." Whether Latham is comfortable with it or not, recreating solidarity requires openness to new information and the invention of new forms. That in turn will require cooperation with members of the information rich. And whether anyone likes it or not, it will have to be open to the global information vector to some degree, for it is through globalisation that new sources of wealth creation will produce the pudding to be shared out to Labor's traditional base. The paradox is that the only way for Labor to honour its traditional commitments is a leap into a modern, perhaps even postmodern future.

Latham goes looking for a new cultural expression of solidarity by looking around internationally himself, and he hits upon the "new radical centre", a concept worked on in Britain by Prime Minister Tony Blair's New Labour and in the United States by the Democratic Party, including people close to President Bill Clinton. Latham expresses the new radical centre in slightly alarming terms as "new expressions of personal and collective responsibility".

As one might expect from someone who sees things in terms of the desire to govern, Latham thinks in terms of responsibilities; for those of us outside of it comes an equally insistent need to talk about rights. Fortunately, were Latham's vision of the light on the hill to come to pass, I think there would be a vigorous constituency outside of government to safeguard rights. So while I'm always wary of "governmentality", Latham's is not in the end of too authoritarian a kind.[7] Latham sees the role of government as providing resources so that people can avert insecurity but also so they can develop skills and extend their liberty.

Latham charges that Labor "has not responded adeptly to the question of social diversity." It responded to each new self-definition of difference by setting up a new category of administration. Taking his image from a television adventure series, Latham concludes that the "simultaneous pursuit of an equality of opportunity, material conditions, social goods, gender, culture, sexuality, race and other rights is, in practical terms, a *Mission Impossible*."[8] In the Hawke and Keating years, it was a matter of adding new constituencies, on the assumption that frictions with the old ones could somehow be finessed. Politics could work like that before cyberspace saturated social space. Politicians could speak one way to their blue collar constituency, another way when out bush. In a world of slow and disconnected vectors, constituencies need not notice this.

Labor's problem was that attempting to add constituencies actually had a subtracting effect. According to political scientist Andrew Scott, there has been a "major transformation of Labor's social base over the postwar period."[9] The party's membership has become overwhelmingly middle class. This middle class party confronted an increasingly polarised class structure in the 80s and 90s, as winners and losers in the economic modernisation process started to appear. Those who were unable to respond to Labor's political culture in the 80s and 90s were those who were unable to respond to the economic culture of that period, which rewarded workers who could identify new opportunities, acquire new skills, adapt to new information.

Those who were left behind economically were those parts of the working class who had become deep-suburban in outlook. They were resistant to new information, resistant to a more urbane culture of pluralism and its political expression, as well as to an urbane economic culture of adaptation and reskilling. This increasingly disenfranchised information proletariat came to define itself not in terms of a positive self-transformation, but negatively against hated others. They defined themselves negatively against the boss, but just as likely negatively against poofters, slopes and hairy leg feminists. While this is no more 'authentic a part of working class culture than that part of it that did become more urbane — and more prosperous if no more secure — it was the part of working class culture that would become "Howard's battlers", potential Labor votes lost to the conservative Coalition.

I don't think Latham is correct in identifying Labor's failed attempts at an urbane recognition of difference, and the social policies built on it, as the cause of this defection, although the resentment such policies caused is a significant symptom of the crisis of a once stable relation between the culture of fortress suburbia and economy of fortress Australia. As Latham puts it, "in this popular culture, some of the new categories — perversely enough — have cultivated a feeling of exclusion." Proliferating categories of difference based on personal characteristics hasn't worked. But rather than stop listening to the call for a fair go that responds to cultural differences, I think Latham wants to hear it in a different way.

Rather than define categories of need on a humanist basis, in terms of personal characteristics of subjectivity, Latham wants a more abstract concept of what it is that Labor in government responds to as a need. Labor stands for the fair go, but fair about what? His answer is social capability. This he defines as access to material resources, the skills to use those resources, and the liberty to do so. Rather than add new categories of people in need, Latham looks for a more sophisticated way of addressing what it is that is needed. In short, he wants to put industrial Labor and postindustrial Labor on the same conceptual footing, and so avoid a rift between these two incarnations of the party.

The Disenchantment of the Magic Pudding

If Labor is to achieve power on the promise of a fair go measured in terms of equity, it needs to achieve three things. Firstly, a new concept of what equity is; secondly, an approach to economic management that produces an economic gain to be shared; and thirdly a tax and transfer system to mediate between them. I won't go into Latham's tax reform ideas — it's a topic on which I would rather stay in deep suburban ignorance. In any case, for all the migraines tax reform talk causes, the cause itself is a banal one — achieving an efficient way of transmitting part of the economic surplus to government for redistribution. The health of the economy to be taxed, and the destination of the surplus transferred, strike me as more interesting issues.

Latham subscribes to a version of Paul Kelly's picture of the Australian settlement. Australian capital, labour and farming interests built between them an "historic compromise" out of which manufacturing received tariff protection, labour received centralised wage fixing. The Labor Party's "gain sharing practice" worked within this framework. Economic rents in agriculture and mining were distributed through wage fixing adjustments. Whitlam extended labourism into a wider program concerned with the rights of all citizens. His government began the shift to postindustrial Labor when it created an electoral majority by offering a slice of the lucky country pudding to everyone, in the form not just of transfer payments but through a whole host of services. These were designed to add a civilised social life to the second nature built by industrial capitalism. But this largess came just at a time when the pudding of government revenues no longer magically grew in the form of export income from the raw natural produce of farming and mining.

Hawke and Keating promised both a more competitive economy and a fairer social distribution. They were caught between a falling surplus generated by economic rents and rising demands generated in part by their own offerings to the electorate. But there was no magic way to meet expanded demand from revenues that were not growing. Hence the lengths to which both Hawke and Keating went in the disenchantment of public expectations — a policy which reached its limit with Keating's famous "banana republic" remark.

Latham acknowledges that basically Hawke and Keating were right in explaining, over and over, that "a small open economy, with low savings, cannot grow faster than its trading partners without a high proportion of the growth spilling over onto the external account", as foreign capital and imported goods come funnelling in. Without growth, there is no way to meet rising and increasingly competing demands on government resources other than rationing. If the unpopularity of petrol rationing helped defeat Ben Chifley, the unpopularity of welfare rationing certainly didn't help Paul Keating.

Where Latham differs from Keating is that he wants to tackle the problems of the Australian economy at their source rather than rely on macro economic tools. He is sceptical about the ability of rational models of economic activity to function as the sole arbiter of judgement in economic policy. He is not an economic irrationalist, and nor does he want to return to outdated fables of the traditionalists in the party. He just wants to approach economic policy with reasoning rather than rationalism. He is rational about reason, which means he has some appreciation of its limits.

While Latham recognises that the global economy is here to stay, he also recognises that it could be better managed.

Even economic rationalists are coming around to this view in the wake of the collapse of Asian economies in the late 90s. Australia cannot wait on achieving reasonable agreement in international forums. It has to do the best it can. Economic rationalists conceive of doing the best you can in terms of competitive advantage. This leads to the policy of driving down the costs of inputs into production. Both the Labor Party and the Liberal coalition believe in driving down the costs of inputs like transport and communication.

The difference is that where Labor pursued waterfront reform through negotiation, the Liberals backed confrontation. Latham would further differentiate Labor by working further on improving the quality of labour as an input into production, rather than trying to drive down its cost. This is one of the reasons for his focus on education, although as we will see, Latham sees education as the crossroads for all of the goals of the postindustrial Labor party. It's the elevator to the light on the hill.

From the 60s to the 90s, the government sector came under increasing scrutiny and pressure: "... the media, with their daily agendas driven by action and conflict, are forever keen to lift public expectations for the contemporaneous things governments can achieve." The government sector gets held accountable for the shortcomings of the private sector. The poor management skills and shonky investment decisions of the business sector are rarely called to account. If business management pulled its socks up as much as government and labour, things would improve dramatically.

It's not easy being in government. Governments are caught between the formation of capital on a global scale and the formation of electoral majorities on a national scale. The global versus national level of conflict is very apparent to governments, who are the membrane separating the national from its other, the global. "The global integration of capital has given the state more work to do, yet fewer resources with which to discharge these responsibilities."

Latham is probably pushing it uphill in attempting to appeal for sympathy for the unenviable lot of government. As the *Silent Majority III* report stressed, in the 90s, the public refused to recognise many claims to legitimate authority, including the claims of governments. But there is a significant cultural issue at work here, in the way that in Australia, hopes and desires for a better life are expressed in terms of expectations on government. Traditionalists on both the left and the right of the labour movement and the Labor Party still seem to expect government to pull off a miracle, in spite of Australia's poor international trading position. "The Hawke and Keating governments, remarkably enough, were able to manufacture a European-style social contract and safety net based on United States-style tax rates." And still many want it to play jingle-bells too.

Postindustrial Economics

Tanner would probably agree with Latham that "events have had a much greater impact on policy than political theory." The real reason for the rationing of government services in the 80s and the 90s was declining economic rents caused by deteriorating terms of trade, coupled with rising demand for services partly caused by the same decline in trade. Latham is not out to defend the reputation of economic rationalism, however. He is an economic empiricist, not a rationalist. "There are no natural laws in economics, only dogmatists who try to invent them."

Senator John Button, who held the industry portfolio under the Hawke government, provides a fine example of the difference between economic rationalism and economic empiricism. In 1985, the Australian dollar floated erratically, and then it sank. With the trade deficit worsening, Treasury officials were certain that the "J-curve" would come to the rescue. Secretary of the Treasury Bernie Fraser explained to Button how the worsening trade deficit led to a devaluation of the dollar, but that this would make imports dearer and exports cheaper, which would boost exports and narrow the trade deficit. The economy, Fraser seemed to Button to be saying, would behave rationally, responding to these price signals, and the curves would arc gracefully across the graph. Fraser's thinking is based on the understanding of the relationship of knowledge to the world that is economic rationalism: the real world is just a messy, gritty version of a purely rational set of quantitative relations — or if it isn't, it ought to be.

Bernie Fraser is a compassionate man. He is not an economic rationalist out of any great love of business interests. As Craig McGregor reports, this "working class bush boy from Junee" believes in government intervention, social safety nets, and scorns businessmen who "got fat from doing bugger all". No wonder John Hewson, when he was leader of the Liberal Party, wanted him sacked. "I'm well aware that the markets don't work very well", Fraser acknowledges, "you just can't let the markets run rampant and let all the human debris that's flung off that operation just pile up, so you have a scrap heap of unemployed people. That's never been part of my philosophy."[10] In short, Fraser's economic thought is not just driven by ideology.

Bernie Fraser is an intelligent man. It would be churlish to pretend, as Bob Ellis does in his rather eccentric attack on economic rationalism, that the reasoning of someone like Fraser can be easily faulted.[11] Fraser's reasoning about the relationship between the trade deficit, the value of the dollar and changes in imports and exports is sound. Economic rationalism usually is. There are sound ways of deciding if an economic theory is rational or not. It's a simple matter of testing the logic, although that logic may be fiendishly complex and require highly qualified specialists to debug.

The problem with economic rationalism lies not with its internal rational coherence, but with its relation to the world it claims to describe and for which it claims to proscribe. As John Button recalls, when listening to Bernie Fraser explain how the J-curve would work: "Some of these people, I thought, have no idea about the composition of Australia's major imports, and no idea about the patchy capacity of Australian manufacturing." Treasury could plot the graphs and forecast no growth in imports, and then, when the figures come in, imports had grown by 9.1%. Even John Edwards, former Keating staffer, an economist by training and broadly sympathetic to economic reform, notes in his blow by blow account of Keating's economic management that Treasury's line of reasoning could produce "egregiously wrong forecasts."[12] Treasury kept expecting the J-curve to work, but the J-curve was not expecting Treasury's faith in it.

As Button observes, rational models of the economy "were no doubt great fun, but knowing something about technology, corporate structures, business reactions and what was happening in the rest of the world were necessary to make sound judgements as the basis for government policy."[13] What Paul Keating called "guile", I am calling economic empiricism, an approach that works from the available evidence to reasoning to policy, not from the rational theory to policy by heavily discounting information that doesn't fit the model.

Clearly there were problems with the implementation of economic reform in the 80s and 90s. The solution to those problems is not a retreat into economic irrationalism. The magic pudding isn't an option. What is interesting about Latham's writing is his commitment to pursuing economic inquiry as a basis for formulating policy, in full and frank awareness of the dismal fact that Australia's economic difficulties can't be wished away, but that there is always a degree of uncertainty involved in the application of reason to actual problems.

So far I've posed the economic problem in terms of declining terms of trade — the world just pays Australia less and less for its wheat, wool, iron ore, coal and bauxite, and charges more for video recorders, four wheel drives and personal computers. An additional problem is that as vectors lace the world together, it gets easier for economic activity to escape from national boundaries. Latham is definitely not in favour of the kind of "industry welfare" that tries to keep factories inside the nation's borders by bribing companies to stay. This might save a few jobs in the short term but in the long term it's an ineffective way of negotiating the global versus local conflict. As an alternative, Latham is adamant that government investment needs to concentrate on those factors that are relatively immobile, such as infrastructure, but also people. Of course many Australians pack up their subsidised education and migrate abroad — a "leakage" Latham doesn't mention, but there is some benefit in this also, in the creation of cosmopolitan networks of Australians.

While most of the argument about government ownership revolves around fights over privatisation, Latham is adamant that government should be investing in the inventiveness of Australian people through education, science and technology. The old postwar development mentality is at work in thinking of the government sector of the economy in rather butch terms as consisting of big instrumentalities.

Economic policy can become too obsessed with tacking and trimming this or that macro economic variable, as if you just got the numbers right and the economy would take off, just like that. This was the 80s version of the magic pudding theory, in which it was market discipline rather than state authority that made the magic. Government needs to pay more attention to creating an environment for technological change, for that is the engine of new economic growth, and hence of the ability to create a surplus that can be taxed and transferred to Labor's traditional constituency.

Technology is a funny thing. Almost by definition, new technology cannot be accurately priced. Creating a new technology, as opposed to refinements of an existing technology, involve *qualitative* change. It's the kind of stuff good engineers thrive on, but it is anathema to accounting procedure, and consequently hard to model quantitatively. Technology is about the virtuality of the material world, when knowledge is applied to it.

Like Tanner, Latham sees a role for government in funding the start-up costs of new technologies, and in maintaining technical skills within the country. New technology is a public good. One of the disincentives to invest in new technology is that the investor rarely gets all of the advantage of the new technique. It gets copied or imitated. If technology has this characteristic of a "public good", then government has a rightful role in its development. I would say further that this policy will have to be an empirical one. Governments have to experiment with policies that nurture technological innovation. Those policies will have to manage complex information. The experiments on the lab bench and in the computer that are at the heart of technical research are designed with a high degree of virtuality. They are about possibilities, not predictable outcomes. Government has to see part of its own functions as an experiment too.

One striking idea that Latham hints at is that economic sovereignty is best thought of in terms of the knowledge and skill the people of the nation hold between them. What this implies is thinking about sovereignty not just in terms of owning land, plant and capital, but also in terms of intellectual capacity. The greater the collective intelligence of the country, the greater the virtuality of possible ways to create something out of whatever resources it has, and whatever international trading environment within which it may find itself. If the lucky country coasted along on its mineral and agricultural resources, then what I would call the virtual country is about as far from that as possible. It would trust its perception, its imagination and its capacity to reason.

Workers of the World Disperse

"Sector planning" is a popular idea in some union and manufacturing circles. The idea is for government to plan ways of clustering related segments of an industry together. Latham is more sceptical than Tanner about this. It may just create more dependency between government and declining industries. Certainly, sector planning has usually been thought of in terms of the industrial economy. It would be interesting to think about what it might mean for the postindustrial economy. But it is characteristic of postindustrial business that industry is dispersed. Small business and franchising are growing areas of employment.

Franchising is the bridge between global capital and local conditions. It is a global business response to the problem of combining the virtues of localised management with economies of scale into a kind of "global localisation". There is clearly a role for government in ensuring a fair go between the unequal parties of the local franchise holder and the often global business behind the scheme. Franchises may sound like a strange preoccupation for a Labor politician, but Latham claims that "more Australians are employed by McDonalds than by the steel industry." This statement shocked me at first, but now I see it as an index of just how much this has become a postindustrial economy, and how far Labor has to go to adapt to it.

In the 80s and 90s, the Australian economy created a lot of new jobs, but not in the locations or of the type that would be electorally useful. Latham breaks work down into three kinds of jobs. Firstly, there are new jobs for urbane specialists with skills that are mostly tradeable in the globalising part of the economy. Secondly there are new jobs providing tangible and personal services, particularly in the parts of town where people holding down urbane jobs live. Count the restaurants, hair salons, contract gardeners and dog walkers that advertise in the local papers for those parts of any city where the urbane congregate. Lastly, there are routine factory jobs, and these are declining. The shoes or pop-up toasters are now imported from countries like China or Thailand. To the extent that industrial jobs have a future, they are of a different kind. "White lab coats are replacing blue overalls on the factory floor."

The problem for Labor is to strike some kind of equity deal between these three kinds of worker. The first and second kinds of worker rarely belong to unions. Urbane workers often have bargaining power on their own. Service workers are just too hard to organise, being dispersed in so many small businesses. While there was substantial economic growth toward the end of the Hawke Keating years, it was not well distributed. The lowest paid workers need to be guaranteed a share of any economic growth. Security of employability, rather than job security, could be enhanced by access to education and training.

The Poverty Code

One of the hallmarks of the intellectual proletariat's resistance is to 'training' schemes, as came out in the *Silent Majority III* report. What is distinctive about Latham's approach to employment is that he wants to move beyond the platitudes. In one startling remark, Latham says that: "Full employment has actually been achieved, but only in a particular type of labour market in certain parts of the country." In other words, there's no magic solutions to be found by looking at the aggregate numbers.

The poverty code is no mystery. One of the most effective ways to measure a person's chances of finding a job is by looking at their postcode. Employment and unemployment are strongly concentrated in space. Where there are skilled urbane knowledge workers, they create service jobs. Where there aren't, then they don't create service jobs, which these days mean there are no jobs. "Suburbs have become the most appropriate unit of spatial analysis", and it's not hard to identify the problem areas. What's going on out there in high unemployment suburbs is a viscous cycle. Low levels of education lead to low levels of employment which leads to low levels of income which leads to low levels of service industry. This in turn leads to breakdowns in civility than can turn this into an abject downward spiral, where what results is the hopeless world pictured in movies like *The Boys* and *Idiot Box.*

Latham wants to respond by developing infrastructure projects and vocational training tailored for specific areas. Infrastructure projects can put income in the hands of unskilled workers and jump start the cycle. Vocational training can broaden the skills within the locality. Community organisations could be subsidised to generate further employment. Latham wants the whole package run by "place management", where all of the different government programs and services can be brought together and the resources focused on an area in need. By treating the locality as the unit of need, Labor can break out of identifying need in terms of the personal characteristics of individuals.

Looked at together, Latham's approach to industry policy and employment policy are complimentary. The former tries to assist economic growth wherever it is already strong, and the latter is a way of sharing some of the gain with the least well off areas. In short, "Scarce public resources need to be directed primarily at overcoming the inadequacies of the profit system — its failure to invest adequately in the skills of the nation's people; its failure to deal with the entrenched problems of economic exclusion on a spatial scale."

Social Rationalism

On economic and industry policy, Latham's thinking is refreshingly empirical. He looks for ways to build concepts out of the information available, rather than making the information fit a predetermined theory. But I think he lapses into "social rationalism" when he moves on to consider the question of the social justice component of the fair go.

The philosopher John Rawls' famous theoretical experiment of the "veil of ignorance" is Latham's starting point.[14]

Imagine you are asked to design a just society in which you will have to live, but without knowing what place you will have in it. Fans of Rawls thinks that with this device of the veil of ignorance, it is possible to create a rational model of an ideal social justice. Latham begins his thinking about social justice with this rationalist approach.

A more consistent approach might be to work, as post-modern ethical theory has tried to do, from the bottom up, from everyday encounters of a *practice*, rather than a theory, of social justice. Having abandoned the idea of the ideal market composed of universal rational economic agents, it's hard to then turn around and argue in favour of the idea of the ideal society based on universal rational social agents. Social thinking, like economic thinking, has to start empirically, with the perception of the difference circumstances and events that make up the social and the economic world, and creating concepts of those differences, as Latham does with his spatial concept for employment policy.

Having this ideal rational model of social justice in his head leads Latham off on a tangent, looking for reasons why reality does not conform to the model. "The cohesiveness of our public morality has been weakened in tandem with the rise of electronic media", he writes. "Politics is presented as infotainment, while public issues are portrayed solely through the prism of conflict." This is dangerous nonsense. What I think is lurking in the back of the Lathamite unconscious is Plato's republic, where the perfect rapport between politician guardian and grateful citizen is achieved by chucking the diversity of communication out of paradise. In order to account for the persistent gap between the ideal model of social rationality and messy social reality, Latham blames the media.

This is exactly the same as an economic rationalist blaming the persistent gap between the ideal model of market rationality and messy business reality on the 'distorting' effects of government. In both cases, the noisy differences that clutter up the actual world are not incidentals that distort the implementation of a pure model. Communication, no less than the economy, is noisy, messy, and irreducible to a pure ideal. In relation to communication no less than in relation to economics, politics is less a matter of trying to impose a pure

model on messy reality, as of trying to make messy reality productive, useful, functional. It's not a choice between messy
reality and pure policy, it's a choice between good and bad
kinds of mess. The fair go is not an ideal, a theory, it's a practice. It's an empirical art of making differences work
together rather than against each other.

In the Platonic view of communication, there is a hierarchy
of forms, with some kind of pure, rational and informative
discourse at the summit, and entertainment at the bottom, "a
long way removed from truth."[15] As I have tried to show,
whether it is the virtual optimism expressed in Kylie Minogue,
or the critique of fortress suburbia in *Muriel's Wedding*, entertainment is no less important a part of democratic communication. Images and feelings matter as much as facts and
figures. The politics of communication works less well when
it opposes media noise with pure policy, than when it tries to
make a connection between them. This was what Bob Hawke
pulled off in four successive election victories.

Politics has always been "infotainment", all that is new is
the portmanteau word for it. As for the "cohesiveness of
public morality", if ever there was such a cohesiveness in
living memory it was during the war, and it was very much a
product of the mass media. If it has declined, it is because in
the absence of a military emergency like the war against
Japan, or the phantom emergency of the cold war, people
saw less and less reason to fall into line behind authoritarian
figures. In the absence of a renewal of this culture of emergency, Latham will have to adapt his thinking to a more
empirical practice, rather than expect to adapt the culture to
his ideal.

Labor's real problem with social justice is not the media
but that it has not used the media wisely. It added different
kinds of difference together: differences of race, ethnicity,
language, gender, sexual preference and so on, making each
a special category of social justice supplicant. This was part
of the same logic as the proliferating categories of benefits in
welfare services. But these administered categories of difference created any number of anomalies and exceptions.
Social justice was "reduced to a zero-sum contest between
winners and losers designated, not by the uncertainties of
life, but by personal characteristics."

While the intention was to offer to anyone with such characteristics some measure of equal justice with people who lacked them, it created the impression among people who lacked them that they were unjustly ignored. An "entitlement politics" arose in which white, straight, English speaking suburbia saw itself threatened, not from above, but from below, from marginalised people like new migrants or Aboriginals. The result was "downward envy". John Howard exploited downward envy at the 1996 election to separate suburbia from urbane workers.

I don't think Latham actually wants to take benefits away from people who are black or gay, lesbian or nesbian. If there is a genuine shortfall in the social capacity such a person experiences, then they have an entitlement. All the same, Latham is not coming from the same direction as those who added these categories of entitlement to Labor's commitments. Labor needs to create more sensitivity to difference in its handling of fair go, rather than less. Establishing a few bureaucratic categories of entitlement is too crude an approach to difference. It creates the impression of some small groups on the margin who, in the songwriter Paul Kelly's words, get "special treatment" and an unspeakable majority who don't.[16]

A culture of resentment, of downward envy, then grows out of this bureaucratic identification of potential subjects for the resentment treatment. By moving to a more abstract measure of what social justice programs must address — social capacity — the idea would be to try and manage difference in a more subtle way, on a case by case basis. Which is the only way the fair go ever works. No two claims for justice are ever the same. There may be 'family resemblances' among such claims: case A is like B but not like C, case C is like A but not like B.

The problem with the 60s social liberation movements that provided the impetus for expanding Labor's social justice agenda is that they were not really social libertarian movements. They did not take as their premise the differences between people, they took as their premise one founding difference apiece — gender, race, ethnicity, sexual preference, and made this one difference the foundation for an essence of sameness. All gay men were assumed to be alike in respect to their gayness, for instance. Liberation rhetoric tended to create two categories that are different, but which each recognises in the other the principle of its sameness. To be gay is to be, first and last, *not* straight. Unfortunately, while there is a positive pay off for the minority this recognition generates, it comes at the expense of allowing an imaginary majority to constitute itself against the minority.

As I argued in *The Virtual Republic,* I think postmodern thinking has grappled with this problem for some time.[17] Rather than abandon minorities to right wing backlash, and the collapse back into invisibility, the strategy has mostly been to insist that there is more, rather than less difference at work within culture than the liberation movements of the 60s were capable of imagining. This is one of the things Christos Tsiolkas' novel *Loaded* was all about, with its dense and noisy mix of ethnic, sexual and class differences.[18] This thinking seems to me to matter, now that the additive incorporation of 60s style subjective difference into an electoral majority seems unlikely to work.

Latham at least acknowledges one difficult issue for representative politics, generational equity. "It is manifestly unfair for one generation to overload the commons knowing that, in all likelihood, future generations will not have the same opportunity to satisfy their collective interests." The interesting problem with inter-generational equity is that different 'generations' may come to have quite different ideas about what is equitable between them.

Like Tanner, Latham thinks there needs to be a "visible and direct" connection between what people do and what the public consequences are. Welfare payments create a passive relation between the recipient and government, and stigmatise the receiver in the eyes of people who don't qualify for such a payment. But Latham is not keen to join the right wing chorus calling for cuts to welfare. Rather, it's a question of rebuilding public trust in the concept of welfare.

Latham is critical of the "guild system" of public sector management — hospitals run by doctors, schools by teachers, transport by engineers, cities by town planners. Guilds have influence with government in terms of getting funding but aren't really answerable to the people they serve — and the public resents it, as expressed in *Silent Majority III*. He favours more flexible delivery of services. He sees no reason why the government sector should always have a monopoly on providing services. The light on the hill, he insists, is the service, not that a large government bureaucracy deliver the service.

Democratising Education

"The most effective form of collective action in an open economy and society now lies in ensuring that each of a nation's citizens can respond adeptly to the contingencies of change." Increasing people's social capacity requires education. Where other government services provide a particular good, education provides the capacity for people to create the good for themselves. "Education has become the critical item of social capability in the post-industrial age. It serves not only as a catalyst for new forms of economic and technological progress, but is also the means by which each individual can develop the skills of adaptability."

Education as a public good — all citizens eventually benefit, not just from the eventual spread of better techniques, but through the enhancement of people's capacity to think and act. Lack of education reduces people's capacities to deal with new information, and as the rise of the information proletariat shows, there is a social cost that comes with the unequal distribution of access to education. By not investing in education, Australia makes itself vulnerable to global capital movements —although a skilled work force is only a necessary condition for attracting investment — it is not a sufficient one.

For Latham, education is the perhaps the most central part of the Australian government's contribution to the economy. In a postindustrial economy, where applying knowledge to information becomes a key generator of wealth, governments role changes, "shedding its ownership of fixed industrial assets and investing ever more in the assets and capabilities of the learning society."

Social mobility in a postindustrial world relies on knowledge skills, but the urbane manage to keep a tight grip of access to education for their own children. Labor must not "allow the unequal distribution of primary goods from the industrial age to perpetuate itself, as society moves towards the information age, through the uneven distribution of learning capability." Latham wants to ensure a more merito-cratic access. He feels strongly about education as a lifelong process, about the importance of the early years of educa-tion, about the quality of the home environment to scholarly attainment. In a rare outbreak of moral outrage, he claims that parents dependent on welfare have "no excuse" for not upgrading their own skills as home educators. Latham writes here like a true believer, someone who takes this issue per-sonally.

There is something a little old fashioned about this. "The good society has always been an enlightened society, pushing the understanding and experience of its citizens towards the social habits of tolerance and cooperation". It's not neces-sarily the case that education produces tolerance. The underlying assumption in this view, which was typical of modern rationalism, was that enlightenment develops abstract thinking, and that abstract thinking approaches uni-versal understanding, so the closer people approximate to universal understanding, the more harmony there will be. It turned out in practice that enlightenment worked, and con-tinues to work, quite differently.

Whatever its contribution to the sciences may be, the con-tribution of enlightenment to the humanities and culture has been rather to develop and extend the differences in people's capacities. Enlightenment develops the virtuality of thinking in relation to being. But it turns out that what is at the core of our being is not some common essence that can be represented in a universal rational calculus. Rather, it seems that what is at the core of our being is a capacity to dif-ferentiate from each other, rather than to converge. The application of the tools of enlightenment to our being has resulted in new ways of becoming different, not in a conver-gence towards an ideal. Celebrities, for instance, express this very possibility of becoming different — sometimes fanati-cally different.

So while the good society may be an enlightened society, it has to be a society that does more than tolerate differences. The concept of tolerance still contains within in the core idea of an ideal norm, from which what has to be tolerated diverges. Suburbia tolerates differences, but a more urbane culture actually encourages differences. Or rather, encourages the productive, creative, innovative side of difference. As we embrace learning, as we think for ourselves and incorporate new information into our thinking, we become other than as we were.

An enlightening education is one that enhances differences. This enhanced difference is one of the reasons people feel that 'individualism' is on the rise, and that there is more alienation and less community. Learning weakens obedience to cultural authorities, including church and party. It weakens compulsory community based on sameness and encourages free association based on difference. Enlightenment teaches us that we are condemned to be free. In place of compulsory community, more voluntary forms of association emerge that enhance differences rather than merely tolerating them. Latham quite rightly sees education as more than just an economic tool, but the cultural transformation that is the virtual side of education may promise different, and more profound, changes than Latham imagines.

Even the thorny subject of migration turns up in Latham's thinking under the education agenda. Where Tanner is broadly accepting of Labor's immigration and multiculturalism focus, Latham favours migration of skilled people, but is against unskilled migration. "There are virtually no jobs available for unskilled migrants", and this "inevitably builds resentment." The sentiment Paul Sheehan thinks is unsayable in the Labor Party because of "political correctness" is here in plain view. What Latham fails to mention, however, is that many migrants can't get the skills and training they already possess recognised in Australia. This particularly unjust and wasteful problem surely merits mention in Latham's new thinking for Australian Labor.

Civility and Public Trust

'Social capital' is a term I intensely dislike. It is part of the practice of seeing everything as analogous to the capitalist economy, even things that are completely unalike. Social capital simply means civility, an idea that has been with us since the enlightenment thinkers reread their Machiavelli, who in turn was steeped in classical Greek and Roman public thought.[19] As much as I admire Latham's modernity, sometimes it's preferable to go back to the roots of western thinking than to get trapped in its more recent fads.

Civility means the "self government of community life", and embraces the practical negotiation of — autonomy and mutual aid. The problem is whether civility can exist in the shadow a strong government, or whether government 'crowds out' civility, as liberal thinkers such as Gregory Mellevish seem to imagine.[20]

Latham is at least prepared to admit the problem. "A decent safety net of transfer payments and service universality does not appear to have sustained a strong base of compassion and mutuality." But this may be more in the way government, and Labor governments in particular, have implemented a certain kind of relationship between government and the people. The problem is Labor's "habit of addressing every new issue by further raising popular expectations about the role of the state public sector — ultimately devouring its own programs." It creates the expectation that government is responsible for everyone's demands, and creates a client patron relation between people and government, at the expense of a self-organising and autonomous civility.

Latham resists the moralising tone of the burbling talking heads, and those in favour of a communitarian approach of moral authoritarian preaching to people about values. He is at some remove from this secularised wowser culture. But he acknowledges that cultural conditions determine economic and social possibilities. There is a virtuality to culture. It makes other kinds of connections possible and sustainable. In particular, culture can generate trust, which for Latham is the key to civility.

There are two kinds of trust that enhance civility. There are hierarchies of trust, where people trust those who have authority. There are networks of trust, where people rely on others without being subordinate to them. Latham recognises that both kinds of trust are important to Labor. Without trust, a Labor program of transfer payments lacks legitimacy. People will suspect the fairness of the social justice calculations involved, will resent those who get payments, and assume they must be bludgers. Had there been a stronger environment of trust in the 90s, the information proletariat might not have reacted so strongly and indulged in Hansonite conspiracy theories — a sure sign of weakened trust.

Latham puts social trust, the basis of civility, alongside social capability, the measure of social justice, as his two key desires, his light on the hill. In both cases, they are pragmatic, workman-like conceptual tools, built to tackle particular kinds of difficulty. Social capability helps resolve the tension between liberty and equality. Social trust helps reconcile freedom and collective necessity. They are both deconstructable terms, but I won't deconstruct them. I think it more politically and culturally helpful to see what can be made of them. Thinking about these issues has to be both critical and clinical, as the philosopher Gilles Deleuze puts it.[21] By clinical, Deleuze means looking at concepts in terms of whether they affirm life, whether they realise the possibility of the fair go. Latham invents the possibility of a people who could come into existence. It's about a way of becoming Australian under somewhat cramped international circumstances.

When social trust is good, people link their liberty to mutual action, and civility comes to mean doing things with other people voluntarily in the expectation that one's own liberty is thereby enhanced. Civility requires trust in relation to hierarchies and networks, but Latham sees networked trust as more important. The limit to hierarchical trust is that it establishes dependency, a lack of autonomy, and I would add a negative sense of identity. Under hierarchical social trust, one comes to a sense of self through the experience of domination by another's arbitrary will — which is certainly how a lot of people feel about welfare bureaucracies.

Government cannot create civility, but can have some indirect effect, by thinking of welfare as assisting the development of social capacity, for example, which might break down the culture of dependency. Or by funding community based projects and employment outside the government sector, as seeding funds for the autonomous development of networks of trust. As David Hume stressed, trust has to extend beyond family and clan, friends and acquaintances if it is to extend as far as civility.[22] It has to extend beyond the culture of mateship, which was and often still is premised on the exclusion of others (women, Blacks, gays...) from mutual aid.

Now that cyberspace makes available whole new vectors for creating networks, connections independent of locality that may be freely chosen, and that can evolve, divide, regroup to negotiate differences, surely is time to experiment empirically with how to make use of such a technology, not just for creating wealth, but also for creating trust, civility, the fair go.

Misrecognition of the Other

While busily building, from the ground up, a concept of the fair go that stretches beyond the suburb, Latham is once again drawn to a rationalist conception of the basis of social trust, just as he was in trying to ground social justice. Like a good NSW Labor right politician, Latham has rounded up the intellectual numbers to defeat economic rationalism, only he has drawn them from two incompatible factions: economic empiricism and social rationalism. In this section, where I unpack some of the thinking involved here, gets a bit abstract. Those not so inclined to thinking abstract might like to skip ahead to the slightly more fun stuff about the media, a bit further on.

Latham finds his concept of social trust in the most unlikely place, borrowing the idea of "recognition" from Francis Fukuyama, the American liberal, who borrowed it from his more conservative teacher Allan Bloom, who borrowed it from Alexandre Kojève, who worked on formulating the economic policy of the European Community. Kojève also lectured on the German philosopher Hegel, from whom he took this now famous theme of recognition. I've recounted the genealogy for this concept because it is a strange ancestry for any concept. Latham doesn't look too deeply into it, but rather opts for what Allan Bloom calls the "charm of political solutions", and rightly so, I think.[23] But the thing about concepts is that they are a virtual world out of which new ways of thinking endlessly generate themselves. There is more to recognition than what Latham would make of it.

What Kojève was looking for in Hegel was a way to understand the world from the point of view of a thinking, self-conscious being. We live within historical time. In each era, history shapes the way we think about ourselves and the world, making us think in different and only partially rational ways. How then is it possible to become a fully rational, thinking being?

Briefly put, Hegel's approach is to argue that reason becomes fully present in the unfolding of history itself.[24] History looks forward to an end to all of the partial and false ways of thinking and being in the world. Then when history comes to an end, the partial rationality comes to an end. For Hegel, the beginning of the end was the universal declaration of the rights of man at the time of the French revolution. This was the original press release for the concept of the 'fair go', but the declaration was just the beginning of the end of history. When the end of history itself comes to an end, so too do the differences in the way people think, and people can finally come together in a fully real and rational relation to each other and to the world.

The most influential restatement of at least part of this daring synthesis of reason and history was made by Francis Fukuyama, who saw the beginning of the end of history a bit later, in the collapse of the Soviet Union and the emergence of the liberal democratic state as the only contender for the prize of the final form of rational governance of rational man. For Fukuyama, history is over, and *we won*. Latham's book seems to me to breathe some of the same atmosphere. History simply doesn't exist in Latham's book. His is a Platonic world, a statement of the ideal republic, where all that remains is the realisation of the rational ideal of social justice and social trust. Latham stands outside history, thinking through the completion of the Australian state, in full self-recognition of itself and its world.

No wonder Latham is so keen on education. He sees it as the means towards the enlightenment that will make the rationalisation of Australian government self-evident. Latham is very much an optimist about the power of reason, and he seems to see no impediment in the unfolding of history to the realisation of a rational, self conscious life. This is the sense in which his thought is modern.

There is no mention of the sources of postmodern doubt about this faith in the connection between reason and history. The Holocaust and Hiroshima caused many postwar thinkers to think again. European thought looked back at the catastrophe of war and turned into a pillar of salt. Postmodern thought doubts that there is any connection between the unfolding of history and the realisation of reason. Or worse, sees a perverse relation between them. Postmodern thought has turned instead to the fables people tell each other about the events that transform their experience of the world.[25] It is a modest, step by step, reconstruction effort, trying to rebuild an ethical way of thinking, and acting, out of the ruins.

Postmodern thought took to seeing something sinister in this perfect state where all of our partial and historical forms of reason converge into a single pure form. For postmodern currents of thought there's virtue in the differences in the way people think. And as for the unfolding of history, "universal history is the history of contingencies", as two of the most radical postwar European thinkers, Gilles Deleuze and Felix Guattari, put it.[26] They prefer an empirical philosophy of thriving on the differences history throws up rather than a rationalist one that wants to see history as having meaning, purpose — and an end.

In the more conservative American thought that stems from Kojève, the split between history and reason results, not in doubts about both history and reason, but a privileging of one against the other. Francis Fukuyama seems to prefer a politically satisfying fable, according to which history works out, if not rationally, at least on our side.[27] Allan Bloom made the opposite choice, preferring reason to history. He preferred the closing of the American mind to opening it up to the flux of change and new information that history hurls at it.[28] But the most radical solutions, in the sense of getting to the root of the problem, are the postmodern critics of Hegel and his inheritors, who abandoned both the great fables of historical progress and the universal goodness of reason, let alone the grand synthesis of the two, in order to start a more modest reappraisal of what reasoning can achieve in the world.

Tactically, Latham wants to oppose economic rationalism, which reduces the goal of history to the perfection of one kind of universal rationality, that of the market. One of the places he goes looking for a weapon in that conflict is social rationalism, which reduces the goal of history to the perfection of another kind of universal rationality, that of the state. What might be more consistent would be to combine his economic empiricist approach, which acknowledges local differences and the limits of universal models, with a social empiricism that does the same in regard to cultural difference. One source for such a line of thinking is precisely the postwar, postmodern turn, which put the intellectual blowtorch to the rationalist faith in the market, but also to faith in the state.

Our relation to the world and to each other is never completely rational, and perhaps can never be completely rational. This is a problem that has bugged western thought ever since the waning of the first flush of enthusiasm for the French revolution and the gift of enlightenment it thrust on Europe on the point of Napoleon's bayonets. Hegel, who was in Jena thinking about reason and history when Napoleon marched into town, probably found that the presence of randy soldiers looting and pillaging concentrates the mind. He certainly thought intently and intensely on the problem of how our desire for things in the world forges our awareness, not just of the world but also of our selves, our *self-consciousness*, and how this in turn orients our actions.

Kojève excavated from Hegel the concept of recognition, on which Latham builds his idea of social trust. But nothing could be further from Kojève's intention that what Latham makes of it. For Kojève, recognition is not the foundation of mutuality and trust, but rather of slavery and domination. For Kojève, it all starts with desire, with a craving for something, an experience of lacking something. When I get the thing I desire, and devour and consume it, I come to know this thing I desire, but I don't come to know myself. What reveals me to myself, is not the thing desired, but the act of desiring. What makes me aware of the act of desiring is the desire of others. It makes me aware of my desiring self, and that this desiring self is a self-awareness of *lacking* something. My capacity to change, my immersion in the change that is history, stems from this awareness of lacking something. This sense of lack makes me not only desire something, but desire *desire itself.* I *want* to change.

My desire for desire is, in practice, my desire that others desire my desire. "The human being is formed only in terms of a desire directed towards another desire, that is — finally — in terms of a desire for recognition."[29] Recognition means imposing my desire on another. I have to be prepared to "go all the way in the pursuit of its satisfaction... in order to be recognised by the other", so that my desire can "impose itself on the other as the supreme value", and so that my desire is "realised, and revealed to itself and to others." Which sounds rather like Paul Keating — the "political killer" — at work.

Actually, I don't think the macho dialectic of recognition is a very comprehensive theory of human action, but it does explain a lot about the Labor party. A fabled anecdote from Graham Richardson's *Whatever It Takes* illustrates it perfectly.[30] The NSW Premier Neville Wran went to the party machine boss John Ducker and told him that he "wouldn't wear" a certain motion that Ducker was behind at the upcoming state conference of the party. Ducker let Wran say his piece, and replied: "I'll tell you what you'll fucking wear! Not only will you wear it, you'll fucking *move* it!" In this battle between competing desires, Ducker forced Wran to recognise the supremacy of his desire, and to act according to his desire.

This is in the end rather unsatisfying, for the master ends up being recognised, but by someone who in that moment at least is an inferior. In the clash of desires, the winner achieves recognition only momentarily, and consequently only achieves self-awareness in the moment of action. Which is perhaps why most of the memoirs written by former members of the Hawke and Keating governments, no matter how funny the anecdotes, lack a strong sense of self-awareness and self-knowledge.

What Kojève was looking for was a philosophy of conflict, not of trust. Conflict is the motor of his unfolding of reason in history. For while the master dominates the slave, the slave is forced in his domination to dominate things. He masters things and offers them up to his master, in turn. But having mastered things, the slave recovers the means to his freedom, and the means to overthrow the master. It is of course all rather more subtle than that, but quite removed from what Latham would make of it.

But now that I've mentioned the macho world of the right wing faction of the NSW Labor party, it occurs to me that it might be a way of explaining Latham's own desire. Rather than battle the party masters at their own game, Latham slaves away diligently, working on new concepts. By mastering concepts, Latham might free himself from the masters of the party's clash of desires. While that clash is illuminating in its brief flashes of triumph, the moral of the stories told, over and over, in the books written about the previous Labor government, is that in the end winning recognition brings with it a transitory lucidity at best. One is recognised by competitors who, in that very moment of defeat, are no longer one's equal, and who thereby no longer challenges one's desire with another active desire.

Perhaps that's why Keating seemed so much sharper, so much more self-possessed, when he had others to battle within his own party. Perhaps Latham's desire, or part of it, is not factional conflict, but intellectual work, work that represses the immediate desire to consume information unthinkingly, or to combat the desires of others and achieve transitory self-awareness. Intellectual desire is for an ongoing transformation of the lack in one's self of a quite different kind. Or if this is not what Latham desires, perhaps it could be. At least in part, given that the negative example of what happens to a Labor politician with a desire for ideas that is not matched by a desire for recognition is Barry Jones, "respected, but not feared."

What Do People Want?

The concept of recognition Latham wants is of a more peaceful, mutual kind. His purpose in to set the concept of recognition to quite a practical task: "the concept of recognition directly challenges modes of liberal thought reliant on the ideals of self-preservation and boundless accumulation." Actually, that's not quite true. It just expands the consequences of a selfish, individualistic concept beyond preserving the self as a subject and accumulating material objects. Recognition conceives of the self as not just self-preserving and self-enriching but also *self-defining*. It is part of an inquiry into where the self comes from in the first place that economic rationalism simply takes as given. It is also a concept that sees the self as something self-transforming.

Desire is a lack that drives the self into action. The self encounters objects that it consumes, that satiate desire — to the point of boredom. Consumerism is ultimately neither enlightening or very satisfying. The self encounters subjects that it recognises as also having desires, and thus can reflect on its own desires, and ultimately its desiring nature. The outcome of this encounter might be a clash of desires, as in Kojève; it might be an accommodation to mutual trust, but in either case, a transformation. Recognition is therefore not a very useful concept in the end for Latham's social rationalism, for it does not specify an alternative or additional calculus that explains human action, for the whole point of the concept is to argue that human action changes what it is to be human.

The desire for recognition is in any case only one of the things I might desire. What's more, the theory of desire as a lack that the self experiences is only one theory of desire.[31] I think Latham is on the right track in proposing a concept of recognition as something that people might desire that can, in part, be offered politically. But its just the start. There is the whole world of what people want in the objective sense, what material things they want to acquire, to work with, to play with, to make their lives richer, fatter, stronger, more fun, more secure from the wind and rain, whatever. His economic thinking addresses such wants. But there is also a whole world of what people want in the subjective sense, and for which there is no rational calculus.

An empirical approach to thinking about desire has to start by looking at things people actually do desire, in everyday life. Just because Mark Latham desires that people desire recognition does not make it so. It is unlikely that the electorate will feel obliged to recognise such a desire and adopt it on the strength of the sheer force of Latham's exposition of its rationality. So the empirical approach has to look at the different things people desire and start to make concepts that, rather than acting as a universal theory of what people ought to desire, can act as a tool for constructing particular things people might desire.

Latham is rightly disparaging of making policy according

to what Labor's opinion polling and focus groups say, but it seems to me that such information would be useful for making concepts about what things people might desire. Not having access to such information, I will have to look elsewhere for evidence of what people desire. Where better than the world of celebrity? Celebrity poses a fundamental question to Labor culture, namely: what can political culture learn about what people want from what the pleasure machine of celebrity culture expresses?

It is hardly trust and mutual aid that people who used to go to concerts by the Birthday Party desired. That desire might be closer to what Georges Bataille thinks of as the religious experience.[32] If our sense of self-awareness arises out of the desire for a particular thing, and self-consciousness from the recognition that what is desired also recognises us, or appears to, then something gets left out. The self forms in relation to something particular, finite. What is missing is the experience of the whole, the immersion in life that recognition hides from us. But at a Birthday Party gig, all sense of self, all boundaries could dissolve into a chaos of movement and noise. This is too scary an experience for most people, and so Nick Cave's celebrity is partly that he stands in for us as someone who has been over that edge and back. By recognising our desire in him we recognise something beyond recognition — but at a safe distance.

What happens when teenage fans pour out their adoration for Kylie Minogue is something else again. The unattainable image of desire, Kylie, acts as the object outside of the self around which the fan's self can form. The self is always defined negatively, by what it doesn't have, by the absence, rather than the presence of Kylie. The psychoanalyst Jacques Lacan spent a lifetime spinning out the knotty relations of self to other that this kind of relation, not of recognition but of fantasy, creates.[33] The unreality, the unattainability of Kylie, is not an obstacle to desire, even though this might be held up as a kind of ridicule of such a stupid kind of desire. For Lacan, fantasy is precisely this impossible relation out of which all desire flows. Desires of a quite immediate and variable kind are always what short-circuit another kind of desire, the desire for a rational and unified 'public sphere'. But such a thing never existed.

Hanson's Celebrity

Ultimately it hardly matters which celebrity provides the image that appears to motivate desire, or what more objective observers think of it, for it is desire that creates the celebrity as object of desire, even thought it may appear that the celebrity, Kylie for instance, is being desired. This is another way of understanding the pleasure machine of celebrity. It is a machine made up of the labours of TV producers, video camera operators, make-up artists, publicists, gossip columnists, and the vectors along which they ply their various trades. Celebrity is also a machine made out of the desires that this machinery articulates together. Between the image of celebrity and the public lies the pleasure machine that connects one to the other. While the concept of desire usually conceives of it as something private and human, it also has public and technical dimensions.

I was watching an angry, seething crowd hurl abuse at Pauline Hanson on a *Four Corners* documentary, in 1998. The crowd were really mad, and Hanson, behind a straining line of cops, stood her ground and shouted back: "I'm not going to go away!". I'm reminded of the desire for Kylie, but also the desire for Nick Cave. An angry mob is one in which one can lose oneself, become part of something larger, pretty much like a Birthday Party gig. Some of the desire for Hanson as a celebrity was not that different from the desire for Kylie, even though it was a desire that might be turned towards accumulating power rather than money. Hanson is an object produced by a certain kind of fantasy, but in which it is not so much Hanson that is desired but the desire itself.

Journalists can be even less aware of how desire works than politicians, and *Four Corners* is obviously produced by journalists who have not thought much about desire, for this Hanson documentary was a brilliant video clip promoting Hanson's celebrity as an object of desire. The producers probably patted themselves on the back for finding a few inconsistencies on statements and policies by Hanson and her entourage, but the logic of Hanson's policies is no more the object of desire here than Kylie's ability to sing. This lesson of this story is not reason, it is desire. What *Four Corners* really showed was Hanson at her best, which is to say, being an object of desire. That *other people* desire her was what the show confirmed for any budding Hansonite. Her failings actually add to her allure, making her just that little bit more accessible, while the sweeping shots of her massive entourage, the glare of the lights, the adoring and even the hating crowds, make her unattainable, and that combination is the essence of celebrity.

What makes celebrity such a unique kind of desire is that someone who desires a celebrity is in the company of a great mass of others who also desire that celebrity. There may be many different reasons people have their particular desires, but what the media vector makes possible is a simultaneous awareness of a mass collective act of desiring. What will end this collective act of desiring is the collapse of this collective fantasy space.

While it was a commonplace of the late 90s to blame the media for creating Hanson, it is in the end only the media that could destroy her. Editors and producers lack any self control over their desires, so it is not likely that a enforced silence about Hanson, a refusal to put her image out over the vector, could succeed. The desire of editors and producers in the media was really no different to that of Hanson's minders, David Oldfield and David Ettridge, which was to realise their desires through the public's desire for Hanson. The difference is that the latter had some patience, and were able to defer and husband their own desires, whereas their media colleagues can't wait to shoot their wad. So the other strategy was more likely to succeed: that if the object of desire cannot be removed from the fantasy space so that it might collapse, it could be so overexposed that the fantasy space implodes.

While the fans may think they cannot get enough of Pauline Hanson, in reality what they cannot get enough of is their own desire. That desire appears to originate from its image only as long as the image is at the right distance within the fantasy space. Saturating the media vector with an image will in the short run ramp up desire, because what accumulates is not desire for the image but desire to belong to the collective fantasy of desire. But in the long run it dissipates, and for this reason: People who already desire the image of a celebrity become, in the space of the fantasy, part of what is desired. The image of Hanson, like the image of Kylie at her peak, is not just an image of an individual, it is an image also of the individual's celebrity. So while the celebrity's popularity continues to rise, or appears to rise, the fan can put himself or herself into the fantasy as part of what becomes desired as more and more people join the fantasy.

This is why perceptions of the rise of a celebrity are a cause, not a consequence of that rise, and perceptions of the decline in popularity are likewise a cause of decline. When saturation point is *perceived* as being reached, it is reached. The image has exhausted itself, and many of the fans will disperse and perhaps attach to other celebrities, or more interestingly, to other kinds of desire. The exponential rise of celebrities ramps up very quickly when media vectors are dense and rapidly circulate images to be desired, and of what others desire. But it also subsides very quickly, which is why there are all those old Kylie records in the second hand stores.

Hating the Media

Politicians rarely love the media. It makes them work much harder for their celebrity than singers, cricketers, game show hosts, even criminals. When out canvassing votes or working their way up through the party machine, politicians at least have some control over how they appear to others. Once they reach the point where the media vector makes their connection to the public, they find a whole host of reporters and producers cramping their style. Entertainers often have the opposite experience — having survived hecklers and dodgy promoters, it gets easier once they can afford a first rate pleasure machine of minders and handlers. Politicians have survived the evolution of cyberspace so far, but they are falling behind other kinds of celebrity as cyberspace becomes more extensive, and as people pass a more educated gimlet eye over what its vectors offer up to them.

Latham is not exempt from this unease about the media, and like many he would like to blame the media messenger for mucking up suburbia. "The neighbours most commonly invited into Australian homes are from the fictitious Ramsey Street". True, but one of the things people talk to each other about is shows like *Neighbours*. When Kylie 'married' Jason, it was the subject of many a natter over the back fence. Teenage girls watched it at home alone, but talking at the same time to a friend on the telephone who was also watching the show. Media vectors do not replace social relations, but they do provide social relations with access to images and stories beyond the local compass of experience. The media vector is the transmitter of images, around which desires of many kinds form.

Latham persists in misunderstanding how the media work and the real nature of the changes the media created, and continue to create. "Many people see something inherently worrying about a society which has lost so much of its personal interaction. A significant proportion of the things we now respond to as citizens are impersonal: concepts and images we shall never actually see, touch or experience at first hand." But this rests on a silly conservative bedtime story. Concepts and images have been impersonal for many centuries. John Hartley punctures this conservative fantasy quite nicely: "The medieval Catholic church was an effective mass medium", it communicated just as impersonally, "in audio-visual and performative form: songs, sights, stories, speech." Just like a TV variety show, "it employed the highest, leading edge technologies and massive capital investment to produce its hardware (cathedrals, carvings, manuscripts) and its software (liturgies, laws, rites, rituals). Its output was organised into genres, schedules and seasons, and it was dedicated to audience maximisation...".[34] The mass was mass media. The fantasy of a social world free from mass media of any kind, ancient or modern, is really a fantasy about being free from desire, by being free from the fantasy space mass media create for collective desire. While this is superficially attractive to people in politics, in reality, political parties have always been impersonal generators and users of vectors along which flow concepts and images.

The mass political party was something produced alongside modern mass media. It has to re-invent itself for the postmodern cultural world of cyberspace. The combination of media and communication vectors with widespread education has resulted in a decline in respect for hierarchical organisations. People no longer subordinate themselves to community leaders who once held a monopoly on the ability to interpret information, and so they no longer go to church or party meetings to be told how to interpret events. Nor do such organisations necessarily have better access to information than what people can glean by themselves from the media. The tendency of party machines to hoard information once gave them a monopoly over its interpretation that a rank and file might value, but now it just makes them obsolete.

The proliferation of media vectors and of the genres, celebrities and stories they propose has weakened the mobilisation ethos that was a lasting legacy of wartime mass communication practices. The decline in popularity of authoritarian organisations, from political parties to old fashioned surf clubs, took quite a long time — so effective were wartime media practices. Indeed the whole idea of a 'cold war' would have been unintelligible had a generation not experienced wartime media mobilisation, and indeed the cold war is unintelligible to many Generation X people whose media education did not occur in such an hysterical and paranoid culture. This is clearly a problem for the Labor Party, which has not entirely recovered from either its fantasy of postwar reconstruction or the wounds it inflicted on itself in the cold war.

Latham rightly observes that: "It is as if, as our communication networks have globalised... society has found other ways in which to compensate through new, less hierarchical forms of participation." Or rather, culture has found ways to weave people together, from the bottom up, drawing in part on the images and stories the media make available, but also on rising levels of education, which make the authoritarian ways of party or church, if not obsolete, then certainly optional. "In the global village, hierarchy is having less success in telling people what to do."

Just when Latham starts to get it, he slips back into a nostalgia that early on in his book he declared off limits. "When civil society was strong there was no such thing as a celebrity". This is not strictly true. While there are distinctive forms of modern and postmodern celebrity, their predecessors include the saints whose relics became objects of pilgrimage. Then there were the heroes whose legends sustained the hopes of enslaved people. William Wallace was a celebrity.

It's quite appropriate that the people of the Scottish town of Stirling would want to erect a statue to him in the visage of Mel Gibson, who retold the fable of William Wallace in his movie *Braveheart,* to commemorate the 700th anniversary of Wallace's short-lived victory over the English oppressors.

Civil society is only strong when there are a lot of celebrities. It is weak when celebrity is reduced to one. The weakness of authoritarian regimes is their elevation of a single celebrity, such as "the man-god Joseph Stalin, floating in fireworks over Moscow with his moustache ends dripping stars", as Dorothy Hewett memorably put it.[35] It was the founding weakness of Pauline Hanson's One Nation Party Ltd, in which rivalries and jealousies, paranoias and resentments, all pass through a fantasy space containing only one central image of desire.

Latham mentions in passing a more convincing source of the loss of civility than television and the media: "over-geared mortgages, hand-to-mouth living standards and a disengagement from formally organised institutions... a 'do not disturb' generation." Suburbia can work, it can be a valid and viable fantasy of the fair go, but when securing the bunker for a completely privatised family life at the expense of a barely serviceable mountain of debt becomes the sole aim, then civility is doomed. Not surprisingly, for many people who have committed themselves to such a life, and found that reality did not promise a continuation of stable conditions in which to sustain it, but change and uncertainty, a new desire arose. The desire for a leader who could defend fortress suburbia with a return to the strong state of fortress Australia.

The Future of the Future

"The fewer answers politicians have about the future the more inclined they are to talk about the past", and to associate themselves with talking heads who specialise in prophecy of the past. Latham is a reluctant nostalgic. "It is difficult to identify a golden age of community values... in Australia", he declares. The past weighs like a migraine on the minds of the Labor Party. Perhaps what is needed is not an historical fable about a legacy or a tradition, but a conceptual fable about Labor's options in the present. Put simply, there are three ways to go: The first way is help the people. The second way is help yourself. The third way is help the people to help themselves. While many people thought the Hawke and Keating years were about the second way, I think it was an incomplete go at the third. Latham's project is a second go at the third way, framed not in terms of nostalgia and principle, but in terms of a pragmatic desire to learn from experience.

Latham is critical of Labor's desire to help people rather than help people to help themselves. The unspoken side of altruism is the dependency it creates. Labor culture "needs to broaden its political goals beyond the state to citizen relationship." It needs, I think, to inquire more about everyday life. Three keys to everyday life are celebrities, culture and cyberspace: the images through which people formulate what they want, the resources and practices they have for acting on those wants, and the vectors along which the information connecting the former to the latter travels.

Politics is ultimately about virtuality, about the creation of a space within which people can become what they want. This requires some degree of security, otherwise people do not become anything except fearful that somebody else will take away what they desire. A secure people extend and expand their capacities, social or otherwise. There may be conflict — Latham seems to overestimate how *civil* civility actually is in practice. But with some security, conflict can be useful, affirmative, creative. Kojève was right in thinking that conflict confronts desire with desire, revealing something of the process of change, the hidden world of virtuality.

Without security, conflict turns negative, it becomes a struggle to preserve what is, rather than to create what can be. Or worse, it becomes a desire to punish or exclude whatever is different, to suppress virtuality, to refuse to change. "In a nation culturally weaned on the ethos of sameness, the virtues of diversity and openness need to be supplemented by new types of social assurance."

"I sometimes wonder if the Labor Party really exists, or if it's just a dream at the top of the hill", Ben Chifley asks, or rather Ed Devereaux the actor who plays Ben Chifley asks, in the TV series *True Believers*. Of course the Labor Party is just a dream, a fantasy that creates desires — but no less real for that. *True Believers* is a fable that invokes the fantasy of Labor, its actors acting the parts of the machine that produced its celebrity. But the Ben Chifley that Ed Deveraux plays was also an actor, invoking a fantasy. When Mark Latham says: "it makes best sense for the ALP to draw strength from the continuity of its political goals", what I hear him say is that it makes best sense for Labor to continue to desire, and to continue to desire its desire, rather than to make a fetish of this or that object of fantasy it has created for itself. Or as Lindsay Tanner says, "Our task is to write the New Testament, not destroy the Old." Amen to that.

chapter **11**

Epilogue and acknowledgements

> *The aim is not to rediscover the eternal or the universal, but to find the conditions under which something new is produced.*
>
> Gilles Deleuze

> *Appropriation is the hallmark of contemporary culture. The reinvention of old forms, the repositioning of said things.*
>
> John Kinsella

The Light from the Screen

A young man with peroxide hair bursts into frame. He puts a coin in the slot of a do-it-yourself business card machine, the kind you find in railway stations and airports. He prints himself up a card and holds it to the camera: John Safran: Media Tycoon.

Safran first lunged into view as a contestant on ABC TV's *Race Around the World*. In one of the ABC's few successful attempts to break out of its burbler world view, *Race* offered young wannabe film makers the chance to win a course at the prestigious AFTRS Film School in Sydney. In its first series, *Race* impressed with the grace of its host, Richard Fidler, and with the antics of contestant John Safran. Where most of the other young film makers set off to make worthy documentaries from various foreign parts, Safran chose to make television about himself — and about television. Particularly inspired was his last piece, in which he showed how to get in to Disneyworld without paying. He put up a plaque in the Disney museum in recognition of Walt Disney's flirtation with the Nazis in the late 30s.

That Safran's pilot for *John Safran: Media Tycoon* will probably not be picked up by the ABC is probably more telling about the suburbanising of the national broadcaster in the 90s than anything that has actually aired. Safran's show would have been a critique of the media, but it would not pretend to be any less cynical than the programs and program genres it attacked. "I'm quite ambivalent about the things I'm criticising", Safran once remarked.[1] The show's departure from the suburban assumption of a moral high ground from which to criticise the media was a radical break with the suburban conventions of media propriety.

Rather like Malcolm McLaren's antics in the early days of the Sex Pistols, Safran became famous for work that did not go to air. Tapes of *John Safran: Media Tycoon* circulated informally. In one segment, Safran proposes a new marketing idea for a brand of cheese — a pack that has the cheese slices popular with children aged 6–12, but with a cigarette included in the pack for those growing out of the cheese segment of the market. His point is that the conglomerate that markets cheese to 6–12 year olds, also markets cigarettes that attract a following among the 12–16 year old generation.

In another segment of the pilot, Safran appears in the kind of television kitchen familiar from countless cooking shows. Safran observes all of the conventions of the genre, popping ingredients into the pan and explaining his actions as he goes along. After the onions go over the flame, Safran comes to the meat. While maintaining the chatty, instructional voice of the cooking show host, the pictures suddenly cut to an abattoir, and Safran calmly narrates as we watch a cow being killed and butchered. "Next, cut your cow down the middle", Safran intones, as a meat worker wields a giant saw, and we watch as cow innards splatter on the floor. It's a brilliant satire on the conventions of suburban television, in which whole aspects of life are simply absent from the screen.

In attacking the genre of current affairs, Safran adopts its tone and techniques. He sets out to expose bludgers — workers who slack off on the job, "costing the economy millions". Only his target are not council workers, but the staff of the most popular TV current affairs show, *A Current Affair*. Using the 'hidden camera' technique, Safran films the staff of *A Current Affair* in their own office and canteen, and discovers them doing — bugger all. The Roman satirist Juvenal asked: Who guards the guards? In the 90s a more relevant question might be: Who exposes the exposers?

Safran's pilot proved too hot for the ABC to handle. Some parts of the pilot would clearly be in breach of the Broadcasting Act, but even with those excesses trimmed, Safran was beyond the limit of what the suburban space of the broadcast media could accept as information. The exposure, in the sanctity of the suburban living room, of images of a cow being butchered would be going 'too far'. Perhaps more to the point, Safran was prepared to attack corporate life as well as political life. "You can say what you like about politicians", Safran observes, "but if you present- ed a sketch about McDonalds, it would go straight to the legal department."

It's not surprising that Safran's home page proved popu- lar.[2] For a generation raised on television, Safran not only exposed its concessions to suburban restrictions on the free flow of information, he provided a salient instance of the emergent qualities of cyberspace celebrity. Cyberspace can potentially be the return of the urbane to information flows. At the end of the 20th century it can potentially be as chal- lenging and diverse as the mass popular print culture of end of the 19th century.

As Safran says: "Everything is chaos theory with so many facets. People are always trying to reflect the mood of Australia, but with 20 million people, it's impossible. It's like there's too many variables to nail." Broadcast media, trapped in suburban conventions, doesn't even try. The proliferation of vectors, from cable TV to the internet and beyond, promises to destabilise fortress suburbia, by exposing it to a much wider variety of information flows, and flows not tai- lored to suburbia's self-justifying assumptions about the world.

This is why attempts to censor and restrict postbroadcast vectors have to be resisted. The internet is not like television.

It does not present the world to suburbia as if the world existed as a series of tightly filtered images, composed for suburbia's benefit. Just as the flow of printed matter in a previous
era made it possible to know that the sun does not revolve
around the earth, so in our time the internet makes it possible to learn that the earth does not revolve around fortress
suburbia.

Soft Hansonism is in the end not much different to hard
Hansonism, in that it wants to stop the world so that suburbia
can get off. But if there is an opportunity for life in the postindustrial part of the world at the beginning of a new millenni-
um, it is not in continued reliance upon the economies of
agriculture and manufacturing. Nor is it in the growth of the
'service' sector. Many services, such as the fast food empires of
McDonalds and its competitors, are really just part of a manufacturing economy. A McDonalds is a factory that makes burg-
ers rather than shoes or car parts. It is wealth creation based
on information rather than the productivity of the soil or of
physical capital that provides the basis for a virtual revival of
fortunes, whether in the outer suburbs of Sydney or the
provincial cities of Britain and the United States.

The postindustrial economy comes with a postmodern culture. Suburbia has to adapt and incorporate new kinds of
urbanity. Surburbia has always been a filterer and absorber of
urbanity. It applies the common sense test of everyday life to
the sometimes impractical new perceptions, affections and
conceptions generated by the urbane. This process slowed
down significantly between the 60s and the 90s. As Australian
movies of the 90s such as *Strictly Ballroom* or *Muriel's Wedding*
attest, there is trouble in fortress suburbia. Information is not
passing through its membranes into everyday consciousness.
There is an awareness of this as a problem, particularly
among younger film makers and writers.

It remains to be seen whether broadcast media can adapt
to the demands of a postindustrial world, in which urbane
information generating practices more readily feed into suburban life. The postindustrial economy has established itself
in Australia as a branch plant for global information industries. Global information businesses specialising in accounting, legal services, banking and advertising all operate offices
in Sydney or Melbourne, or sometimes Brisbane. The estab-

lishment of the Fox studio complex in Sydney provides a high profile emblem for this more diffuse transformation of the Australian economy. But the success of these industries depends not just on factors like the intellectual property and taxation environment, or even on the provision of a well trained information work force. It depends also on a culture that can thrive on the flows of information from which such businesses make their living. It means the reform of assumptions about the suburban way of life.

The New Empiricism

In proposing the need for a new relationship between suburbia and information flows, I don't want to appear to be saying this is just a question of the *quantity* of information. Most people with any stake at all in the information economy, that is pretty much everyone except the information proletariat it excludes, finds there is always too much information about already. It's not a question of more information, its a question of the rules of thumb of a theory of knowledge for handling information.

If there is a characteristic of the suburban approach to forming knowledge out of information, it is, broadly speaking, an emphasis on rationalism. By this I mean a bias towards pre-formed categories into which new information is to be slotted, rather than a bias towards creating categories out of the new and unexpected patterns imminent in new information itself. Rationalism, understood in this broad sense, is a common feature of suburban thinking. It is what creates the suburban tendency to resist new information when it doesn't fit the assumed order of the world.

It is precisely this unthough order in which thinking is to take place that John Safran's cut to the abattoir challenges. Why should only the sequence of steps in preparing food that actually take place in the kitchen be included in a program that gives information about how to cook something? What if we examine all of the steps in the process of food preparation and find another order in them? This more open approach I want to call empiricism. By that I don't mean the view that facts are simple things and that knowledge is just a matter of gathering facts. On the contrary, I think of empiricism as a highly conceptual way of handling information — but one that looks for patterns in flows of information rather than fitting flows of information into fixed patterns.

Empiricism starts, as the philosopher Gilles Deleuze says, from "the concrete richness of the sensible", but it need not flatten that richness out into an abstract principle. Empiricism apprehends the world as flux, as difference, as information: "Empiricists are not theoreticians, they are experimenters: they never interpret, they have no principles."[3] It's not about measuring the world according to an abstract, other-worldly principle and finding what is lacking in it. Rather, it is a matter of apprehending the world in its variability, and looking for useful, productive, and creative ways to make a life out of the events of *this* world.

Deleuze elaborates: "In so-called rationalist philosophies, the abstract is given the task of explaining, and it is the abstract that is realised in the concrete. One starts with abstractions... and one looks for the process by which they are embodied in the world which they make conform to their requirements." The abstract calculus of economic rationalism might be an example here, but so too would be the abstract diagrams of desire that Mark Latham tries to turn into a basis for his theory of the social. What is distinctive about rationalism, as more than a theory of knowledge, as a practice also of action in the world, is this attempt to make the world conform to the abstraction.

"Empiricism starts with a completely different evaluation", Deleuze declares. It is a matter of "analysing the states of things, in such a way that non-pre-existent concepts can be extracted from them. States of things are neither unities nor totalities, but multiplicities."[4] Viewed in this way, empiricism, or pluralism as Deleuze also terms it, is quite distinct not only from economic rationalism, but also from a lot of alternatives to it, whether it is the social rationalism of some new kinds of social democracy — or for that matter, the moral rationalism of some kinds of cultural and media studies.

The suburban predilection for rationalism seems to run pretty deep, and across several different kinds of knowledge. So too does the practice of dividing the world up between different kinds of rationalism. Suburbia accommodates the need for knowledge through specialisation, even if the lines defining the boundaries between one speciality and another are arbitrary. Rationalism composes an internally unified space for thinking about a particular thing, the economy for example, by dividing it conceptually from anything that might make it appear more heterogeneous.

Rationalism is the dominant mode of managing information in the suburban world. The historical origins of this kind of intellectual division of labour are industrial and bureaucratic. They are the imprint of the industrial economy on the culture that sustained it. But there is also a minor mode within suburban culture that handles information quite differently. As Barry Jones discovered, political culture has harboured a quite peculiar kind of specialised way of working with information — one based on not specialising. The experiment in economic reform of the first Hawke cabinet was an interesting instance of political empiricism in practice. It was informed partly by economic rationalism, but only partly. It was informed by the moral rationalism of party dogma, but very partly. In the main, it was an empirical approach to managing the eventful character of politics caught in the flux of global economic and information flows.

Clearly, that reform process failed to identify, let alone solve, many problems, including many thrown up by the process of reform itself. There were also mistakes of judgement that appear with hindsight, like the faith in the J-curve or Paul Keating's "recession we had to have". But overall, it was the empiricism of experimentation of the 80s that produced the more dynamic and outward looking Australian economy of the 90s — an economy robust enough to survive the economic crisis that overtook many Asian economies. The Hawke legacy is a laboratory of empirical experiment that is, among other things, a 'third way' between dogmatic insistence on a politics of rationalism and a do-nothing politics of pragmatism.

Empiricism of this kind is not for the faint hearted. It offers no guarantees of the right choice. It offers no moral absolutes. It's just about making decisions, based on imperfect information, by producing concepts out of that information, concepts that acknowledge the way things can change. This is not really a foreign idea. It may be contrary to some of the intellectual underpinnings of leaned culture, but it is how most people negotiate everyday life.

Actually, even deep in suburbia there is a frank acknowledgment of the empiricism of everyday life. This expresses itself in celebrity. Celebrities are monstrous exceptions. Each celebrity is his, her — or it's — own peculiar and singular mix of ordinary and extraordinary attributes. What is celebrated in celebrity is making the best of things, putting peculiar circumstances to a productive end. There is no general principle to which celebrities can be reduced. They cannot be rationalised, although they can be reasoned about, on a case by case basis. Here I think David Marshall is almost but not quite right when he thinks of celebrity as rationalisation from below.

Suburbia is often host to a quite healthy scepticism about rationalisms that appear to come from without. Neither the economic rationalism of the free market or the social rationalism of political correctness was ever all that popular. The problem is more that suburbia doesn't encourage too much thinking about the rationalism implied in the culture of suburbia itself. The corollary is that in the 90s both political and cultural talking heads were often dismissive of the empiricism of the everyday, as expressed, for instance in the suburban taste for celebrity. In chastising suburbia for its trashy tastes, political and cultural talking heads often pined instead for an absurdly rationalist idea of the public sphere, one shorn of all its vitality and plurality. In short, suburbia's disdain for rationalism from without rarely became a critique of rationalism within; while the critique of the empiricism of everyday life conducted by talking heads actually attacked the one thing of most value in suburban culture.

There is a positive side to the lucky country, in its empiricism: in the capacity to respond to events, to make use of circumstances, to enjoy the moment, to cultivate options. Adding a more conceptual way of thinking, and way of life, to this instinctive empiricism seems to me an appropriate goal for talking heads, whether coming at it from an economic, political or cultural competence. It's a matter of finding ways to combine different kinds of reasoning, about economic, political and cultural matters, rather than of asserting the dominance of one kind of rationalism over the whole of life.

Culture and Pluralism

Culture plays its role alongside, indeed inextricably interwoven with, economics and politics. They form a multiplicity. The medium through which economic or political change or negotiation takes place is always partly cultural. The exclusion of the cultural from political or economic rationality is invariably the exclusion of difference, plurality, the messiness of everyday life.

The way back to an empirical concept of politics as a practice is through culture, through the tangible and actual moments of lived experience. Suburban rationality is too concerned with imposing its views of what *ought* to be the means and ends of culture to see what actually takes place in the interchange between cultural practices and popular media fables and images. By not starting from what *is*, it misses the virtuality of culture, the new ways of being that people compose for themselves out of it.

When Scott wants to break with dancing that is 'strictly ballroom', or when Muriel wants to reinvent herself out of ABBA songs, what takes place is at once both cultural and political. Both assert a desire to break with communities of coercion and to find communities of choice. There is also an economic dimension to their actions — who owns the steps that Scott incorporates into his routine? What contract does Muriel enter into in exchange for her wedding? As information becomes more and more commodified, the cultural uses of that information come under scrutiny from its owners and traders. The ownership and control of information creates new kinds of class conflict, alongside those that take place over the ownership and control of land and capital.

Culture is the medium for an empirical ethics. It is through the fables of the famous that people discover templates for assessing the rightness or wrongness of actions. Celebrity appears within mediated culture as the face of possibility. Celebrity can be aspirational, like Kylie or Elle. Or critical, like Peter Garrett, a one-man image of the engaged citizen. Or celebrity can be about a radical otherness, as in a Nick Cave song that gestures to the radical absence of order in the world. These are often more effective images than the more respectable talking heads of high culture, mainstream politics or organised religion have to offer. Rather than bewailing the lack of interest suburbia evinces towards traditional talking heads, perhaps it would be more useful to think about what sorts of things these organic celebrities express.

In any case, the forms celebrity takes are an index of the changing geometry of the vectors that connect culture together that scholars such as Scott McQuire and Darren Tofts explore. What I find in John Safran or Pauline Pantsdown is an interesting development: media celebrities who quite intentionally exploits the limits of broadcast culture. They become famous via the mass media, but even more famous by the absence of their work from the mass media, whether via legally imposed censorship or the timidity of broadcasters. The possibility expressed in these images is of a more plural cyberspace.

Meanwhile, Beth Spencer explores the composition of communication in such an emergent world, where all kinds of experience can be appropriated, cut and mixed in an empirical fashion. Catharine Lumby experiments with the composition of a knowledge and scholarship of the media that is at the same time immersed in its flows. In their different ways, all of these different people invent practices that work on the juncture between media and culture.

Elsewhere, in political life, a development to which all these others have to be related is the emergence of the political intellectual or intelligent politician as a kind of celebrity. These are phenomena blocked, in part by residual suburban ideas about the ideal rational public sphere, but blocked on a more practical level by the difficulties in using the emerging vectors of cyberspace to develop a politics of knowledge. The political future of leaders like Lindsay Tanner and Mark Latham may hinge on the development of a politics of information within the Labor Party, and between the Labor Party and some potential constituencies for it in the emerging information economy.

The expression 'the light on the hill' suggests two elements that have to come together. The light itself is the virtual side of politics, the will to minimise human suffering through collective action. The hill that provides the vantage point for communicating this concept is the tactical combination of economic, political and cultural circumstances. If there is a 'third way' for social democracy it is I think a practical but not pragmatic, reasoned but not rationalist, radical but not utopian practice of experimenting with the given elements and events of everyday life.

acknowledgement

Celebrities, Culture and Cyberspace is a book that was written in its own peculiar way, as a series of experiments with fitting events and ideas together, conducted in public, through a wide variety of print and electronic media. Therefore I would like to thank all of the editors and referees of the publications where the essays, columns and squibs out of which the ideas for this book grew first appeared, or if they didn't appear, who stumped up a generous kill fee: *Age, Angelaki, Australian, Australian Left Review, Australian Quarterly, Australian Style, Continuum, Eddie Magazine, Geekgirl, Meanjin, Media International Australia, Mute, Nettime, New Internationalist, New Statesman, Overland, Sun Herald, 21C, Weekend Australian, Wired UK, World Art.* An earlier version of 'Homage to Catatonia' appeared in *Australian Cultural Studies: A Reader,* edited by John Frow and Meaghan Morris.

I would like to thank the producers and researchers of all of the radio and television shows on which I have appeared, including ABC Radio National, the ABC Metro and Regional stations, *Lateline* on ABC TV and *Insight* on SBS TV. I would like to thank my fellow participants on listserver discussion lists such as *Nettime* and *Recode.* I would also like to thank the reviewers and interviewers — too numerous to list, who engaged with my previous book, *The Virtual Republic.* May I just say, following Stendhal, that every time I find serious, critical reviews, I re-read them carefully "and decide afresh which one of us is right."[5]

Thanks to the organisers and participants at various conferences where I also tried out some of these ideas, including: *Beyond the Culture Wars* at Artspace, the *Nexus* Conference at the Museum of Sydney, the Cultural Studies Association Annual Conference at the University of Melbourne, the Royal Australian Institute of Planners Biannual Conference, the Perth Institute of Contemporary Art, The Zadok Institute for Christianity and Society, the

Newcastle Young Writer's Festival, and the Sydney Writer's Festival. Thanks also to my comrades in the Heretics group.

Lastly, special thanks to Tony Moore, Fiona Giles, Milissa Deitz, Christen Clifford and Catharine Lumby for essential contributions of many and various kinds. *Celebrities, Culture and Cyberspace* is dedicated to 'BushWark TNG': Kate, Scott, and Tim. Boldly go.

e n d n o t e s

Chapter 1 30 years, 15 minutes

1   Jill Roe, 'The Australian Way', in Paul Smyth and Bettina Cass (eds), *Contesting the Australian Way: States, Markets and Civil Society*, Cambridge University Press, Melbourne, 1998, pp. 69–80

2   McKenzie Wark, 'Europe's Masked Ball: East Meets West at the Wall, *New Formations*, No, 12, Winter 1990, pp. 33–43, at p. 39

3   See, for example, Alex Hall, *Scandal, Sensation and Social Democracy: The SDP Press and Wilhelmine Germany, 1890–1914*, Cambridge, London, 1977

4   http://www.netnexus.org/

5   See Mark Gibson, 'Richard Hoggart's Grandmother's Ironing: Some Questions About 'Power' in *International Cultural Studies*, Journal of International Cultural Studies, Vol. 1, No. 1, April 1998, pp. 25–44

6   Craig McGregor, *People, Politics and Pop: Australians in the Sixties*, Ure Smith, Sydney, 1968

7   Craig McGregor, 'Drawing Blood', *Sydney Morning Herald*, 21st March, 1998, Spectrum, pp. 6–7s

8   Chandran Kukathas and William Maley, 'Mainstream Takes Refuge in Soft Hansonism', Opinion, *Australian*, 23rd September, 1998

9   Terry McCrann, *Weekend Australian*, 9th March, 1996

10   Gerard Henderson, *Sydney Morning Herald*, 6th October, 1998

11   Andy Warhol and Pat Hackett, *Popism: The Warhol '60s*, Harper & Row, New York, 1980, p. 130

12   Stephen Muecke, 'Bob Hawke's Country Practice: A Deconstruction', in *Intervention*, No. 22, 1988

13   Meaghan Morris, 'Politics Now', in *The Pirate's Fiancée*, Verso, London, 1988, p. 177. I've modified the periodisation a bit, but I think the point still stands.

14   Donald Horne, *The Lucky Country*, Penguin, Ringwood Vic., 1998, revised edition, p. 20

15 Donald Horne, *The Avenue of the Fair Go: A Group Tour of Australian Political Though*, Harper Collins, Sydney, 1997, p. 8

16 Two key works were reprinted in the 90s: Marshall McLuhan, *Understanding Media: The Extension of Man*, MIT Press, Cambridge Mass., 1994; Marshall McLuhan, *The Medium is the Message*, Hardwired, San Francisco, 1996

17 Mark Dery, *Escape Velocity: Cyberculture at the End of the Century*, Grove Press, New York, 1996, p. 8

18 Dale Spender, *Nattering on the Net: Women, Power and Cyberspace*, Spinifex Press, North Melbourne, 1995; Jon Casimir, *Postcards from the Net*, Allen & Unwin, Sydney, 1997; Daniel Petrie and David Harrington, *The Clever Country?: Australia's Digital Future*, Lansdowne Publishing, Sydney, 1996

19 John Nieuwenhuizen, *Asleep at the Wheel: Australia on the Superhighway*, ABC Books, Sydney, 1997, p. 180

20 K. T. Livingston, *The Wired Nation Continent*, Oxford University Press, Melbourne, 1996, p. 9

21 The classic source for this argument is Harold Innis, *The Bias of Communication*, University of Toronto, 1991

22 Richard McGregor, 'Unmasked: The Most Secretive Force in Politics', *Weekend Australian*, 17th October, 1998, p. 4

23 Graeme Osborne and Glen Lewis, *Communication Traditions in 20th Century Australia*, Oxford University Press, Melbourne, 1995, pp. 169–170

24 Scott McQuire, *Visions of Modernity*, Sage, London, 1998, p. 7, and below, p. 2 and p. 85

25 Darren Tofts, *Memory Trade: A Prehistory of Cyberculture*, Gordon + Breach Arts International, Sydney, 1998, p. 15

26 McKenzie Wark, *Virtual Geography: Living With Global Media Events*, Indiana University Press, Bloomington, 1994

27 An argument first proposed by James Carey, *Communication as Culture: Essays on Media and Society*, Unwin Hyman, Boston, 1989

28 Anthologised in Ashley Crawford and Ray Edgar (eds), *Transit Lounge*, Craftsman's House, Sydney, 1997

29 Robert Manne, 'Strong Women, Stronger Morality', *Australian*, 8th April 1996

30 Brian Toohey, 'Naked Truth on Redheads', *Sun-Herald*, 28th June, 1998

31 Robert Dessaix, *Speaking Their Minds: Intellectual and the Public Culture in Australia*, ABC Books, Sydney, 1998, p. 6

32 Peter Blazey, *Screw Loose: Uncalled-For Memoirs*, Picador, Sydney, 1997, p. 139

33 Michael Pusey, *Economic Rationalism in Canberra: A Nation-Building State Changes its Mind*, Cambridge University Press, New York, 1991

34 Paul Sheehan, *Among the Barbarians*, Random House, Sydney, 1998

35 Liz Johnson, 'The Hanson Cult', *Bulletin*, 16th June 1998, p. 27

36 McKenzie Wark, *The Virtual Republic: Australia's Culture Wars of the 90s*, Allen & Unwin, Sydney, 1998

37 Elspeth Probyn, quoted in Mary Zournazi, *Foreign Dialogues*, Pluto Press, Sydney, 1988, pp. 32–33

38 Two enduring works from the 60s liberationist perspective, originally published in the early 70s are: Anne Summers, *Damned Whores and God's Police*, revised edition, Penguin, Ringwood Vic., 1994; Dennis Altman, *Homosexual: Oppression and Liberation*, Serpent's Tail, 1996.

39 Donald Horne, *The Lucky Country*, 5th edition, Penguin, Ringwood Vic., 1998

40 See Phillip Adams (ed), *Retreat From Tolerance*, ABC Books, Sydney, 1997

41 Julianne Schultz, *Reviving the Fouth Estate*, Cambridge University Press, Melbourne, 1998

42 John Langer, *Tabloid Television: Popular Journalism and 'Other News'*, Routledge, London, 1988

43 Stuart Littlemore, *The Media and Me*, ABC Books, Sydney, 1996

44 Three classic works from a left wing perspective on media and hegemony: Humphrey McQueen, *Australia's Media Monopolies*, Widescope International, Camberwell Vic., 1997; Bob Connell, *Ruling Class, Ruling Culture*, Cambridge University Press, Melbourne, 1997; Bill Bonney and Helen Wilson, *Australia's Commerical Media*, Macmillan, Melbourne, 1983

45 Ien Ang, *Living Room Wars*, Routledge, London, 1997; Virginia Nightgale, *Studying Audiences: The Shock of the Real*, Routledge, London, 1996

46 Craig McGregor, *Soundtrack for the Eighties*, Hodder & Staughton, Sydney, 1983, pp. 7–11

Chapter 2 the murmur of the waves

1 The photographer was Jez Smith, illustrating Andrew Stafford, 'Wark's World', *Studio For Men*, No. 20, Autumn, 1998, pp. 100–102

2 Helen Razer, *Everything's Fine: A Beginner's Guide to Thwarting Primary Nihilism*, Random House, Sydney, 1998, p. 41

3 Robert Hughes, *Nothing If Not Critical: Selected Essays on Art and Artists*, Collins Harvill, London, p. 247

4 An idea I've borrowed from Catharine Lumby's forthcoming book, *Gotcha!: Life in a Tabloid World*, to be published by Allen & Unwin.

5   *Cleo*, August, 1998; *Ralph*, September, 1998

6   Marcus Casey, Evie Gelastopoulos and Morgan Ogg, 'Hutchence's Last Hours', *Daily Telegraph*, 24th November, 1997

7   Larry Writer, 'A Life in Excess', *Who Weekly*, 8th December, 1997, p. 32

8   Toby Creswell, 'A Life Lived INXS', *Juice*, No. 60, January 1998

9   Ed St John, *Burn: The Life and Times of Michael Hutchence and INXS*, Transworld, Sydney, 1998, p. 246

10 This may be Camille Paglia's only good idea, but it is, I think, a powerful one. See her *Sexual Personae*, Random House, New York, 1991

11 Bob Ellis, *Goodbye Jerusalem: Night Thoughts of a Labor Outsider*, Random House, Sydney, 1997, p. 472

12 Natalie Imbruglia, *Left of the Middle*, RCA, 1997

13 See Camilla Griggers, *Becoming Woman*, Minnesota University Press, Minneapolis, 1997, chapter 1

14 Caroline Overington, 'Beauty And Truth Both Missing', Agenda, *Sunday Age*, 20th September 1998, p. 16

15 Dave Graney and the Coral Snakes, *The Soft'n'Sexy Sound*, id/Mercury, 1995

16 quoted in Marian Wilkinson, *The Fixer: The Untold Story of Graham Richardson*, William Heineman Australia, Melbourne, 1996, p. 297

17 Jack Marx, 'That Video', *Australian Style*, No. 23, 1997

18 Wendy Tuohy, 'Why So Many Love it When Sam's In A Jam', *The Age Online*, 27th May, 1997

19 Chris Cobb, 'The Age of Celebrity', *Montreal Gazette*, 6th September, 1997

20 Samuel Johnson, *Selected Essays from the Rambler, Adventurer and Idler*, Yale University Press, New Haven, 1968, pp. 106–107

21 William Hazlitt, *Selected Writings*, Penguin, Harmondsworth, 1985, p. 162, p. 279

22 David Marshall, *Celebrity and Power: Fame in Contemporary Culture*, University of Minnesota Press, Minneapolis, 1997

23 See Joshua Meyrowitz, *No Sense of Place: The Impact of Electronic Media on Social Behaviour*, Oxford University Press, New York, 1985

24 Gustave Le Bon, *The Crowd: A Study of the Popular Mind*, T. F. Unwin, London, 1921

25 T. S. Eliot, *Selected Prose*, Faber & Faber, London, 1975; F. R. Leavis, *Mass Civilisation and Minority Culture*, Minority Press, Cambridge, 1930

26 Theodor Adorno. *The Culture Industry: Selected Essays on Mass Culture*, Routledge, London, 1990

27 Dwaine Marvick, *Harold Lasswell on Political Sociology*, University of Chicago Press, 1977

28 Paul Lazarsfeld, *The People's Choice: How the Voter Makes Up His Mind*, Columbia University Press, New York, 1965

29 See Martin Barker and Julian Petley, *Ill Effects: The Media/Violence Debate*, Routledge, London, 1997; David Buckingham, *Moving Images: Understanding Children's Emotional Responses to Television*, Manchester University Press, 1996;

30 David Morley and Kuan-Hsing Chen, *Stuart Hall: Critical Dialogues in Cultural Studies*, Routledge, London, 1996

31 Catharine Lumby, *Bad Girls: The Media, Sex and Feminism in the 90s*, Allen & Unwin, Sydney, 1997

32 See Elspeth Probyn, *Outside Belongings*, Routledge, New York, 1996, p. 135

33 See for example, Luke Slattery, 'Blurring the Boundaries', *Weekend Australian*, March 29, 1997; Kath Kenny, Feminists on the Front Line', *Sydney Morning Herald*, 22nd March 1997; John McDonald, 'Art of the States', *Sydney Morning Herald*, June 7th, 1997. For a more constructive reading, see Marilyn Lake, 'Good Women, Bad Girls', *Meanjin*, No. 2, 1997, pp. 338–345

34 John Hartley, *Popular Reality: Journalism, Modernity and Popular Culture*, Edward Arnold, London, 1996

35 Ien Ang, *Living Room Wars*, Routledge, London, 1996

36 McKenzie Wark, *Virtual Geography: Living With Global Media Events*, Indiana University Press, Bloomington, 1994

37 See Mulvey's classis essay 'Visual Pleasure and Narrative Cinema', in Laura Mulvey, *Visual and other Pleasures*, Indiana Unversity Press, Bloomington, 1989

38 On the virtual, see Brian Massumi, *A User's Guide to Capitalism and Schizophrenia*, MIT Press, Cambridge, 1992, pp.3–4ff

39 Lumby here follows the arguments of Moira Gatens, *Feminism and Philosophy: Perspectives on Difference and Equality*, Polity Press, Cambridge, 1993

40 Naomi Woolf, *The Beauty Myth*, Vintage, London, 1991

Chapter 3 the ass and the angel

1 Colin Cave, et al, *Ned Kelly: Man and Myth*, Cassell Australia, Melbourne, 1968, pp. 8–9

2 Robert Drewe, *Our Sunshine*, Picador, Sydney, 1991, p. 35

3 Paul Kelly, 'Bradman', on *Songs of the South: Paul Kelly's Greatest Hits*, Mushroom Records International, 1997

4 Not without some misgivings. See Michael McGirr, 'At Home in Memory', in Cassandra Pybus (ed), *Columbus' Blindness and Other Essays*, University of Queensland Press, St Lucia Qld, 1994

5 Dino Scatena, *Kylie: From Girl Next Door to International Icon*,

Penguin, Ringwood Vic., 1997, p. 12

6   Peter Wilmoth, *Glad All Over: The Countdown Years 1974–1987*, McPhee Gribble, Ringwood Vic., 1993

7   Kylie Minogue's, 'Locomotion' and 'Better the Devil You Know' are on *Greatest Hits*, Mushroom Video, 1992

8   See Stuart Cunningham and Toby Miller, *Contemporary Australian Television*, UNSW Press, Sydney, 1994, pp. 127–135

9   Craig McGregor, *Class In Australia*, Penguin, Ringwood Vic, 1997

10 Tom O'Regan, *Australian National Cinema*, Routledge, London, 1996, p. 50ff

11 Jean Baudrillard, *Seduction*, Macmillan Education, London, 1979

12 Kylie Minogue, 'Confide In Me', *Kylie Minogue*, Mushroom, 1994; see also *The Kylie Tapes 94–98*, Roadshow/Mushroom, 1998

13 Susan Sontag, 'Notes on Camp', in *Against Interpretation*, Anchor Books, New York, 1990, pp. 275–292

14 'Where the Wild Roses Grow', on Nick Cave, *Murder Ballads*, Mute/Mushroom, 1996

15 Greil Marcus, *Lipstick Traces: A Secret History of the 20th Century*, Harvard University Press, Cambridge Mass., 1989

16 Friedrich Nietzsche, *The Birth of Tragedy*, Penguin, London, 1993, p. 26; see also Friedrich Nietzsche, *Twilight of the Idols/The Anti-Christ*, Penguin, London, 1990, pp. 116–121

17 The Birthday Party, *Hits*, Shock Records, 1996

18 Nick Cave and the Bad Seeds, *The Firstborn is Dead*, Liberation Record, 1990

19 Dick Hebdige, *Subculture: The Meaning of Style*, Methuen, London, 1979

20 Bernard Cohen, *Snowdome*, Allen & Unwin, Sydney, 1998, p. 3

21 Antonin Artaud, 'The Theatre and Its Double', in *Collected Works*, Calder and Boyars, London, 1974, p. 65, p. 4

22 Nick Cave, *And the Ass Saw the Angel*, Penguin Books, London, 1990, p. 9

23 Arthur Rimbaud, 'Letter to George Izembard', *Collected Poems*, Penguin, London, 1986, p. 6

24 Nick Cave and the Bad Seeds, *Tender Prey*, Liberation Records, 1990

25 Arthur Schopenhauer, *Essays and Aphorisms*, Penguin, London, 1990, p. 43

26 Fredrich Nietzsche, *Beyond Good and Evil*, Penguin, London, 1990, p. 68

27 Nick Cave and the Bad Seeds, *The Good Son*, Liberation Record, 1990

28 *Johnny Suede*, directed by Tom DeCillo, 1991

Chapter 4 homage to catatonia

1 Constitutional Commission, *Individual and Democratic Rights*, Report of the Advisory Committee to the Constitutional Commission, Canberra, 1987, Preface

2 Lesley Sly, *The Power and the Passion: A Guide to the Australian Music Industry*, Warner/Chappell Music, Sydney, 1993, pp. 16–17

3 Peter Wilmoth, *Glad All Over: The Countdown Years 1974–1987*, McPhee Gribble, Melbourne, 1993

4 Hirst, quoted in Sly, op cit, p. 321; Garrett quoted in Wendy Milson & Helen Thomas, *Pay to Play*, Penguin Australia, 1986. See also Toby Creswell's chapter in Clinton Walker, (ed), *The Next Thing*, Kangaroo Press, Sydney, 1984

5 Peter Garrett, *Political Blues*, Hodder & Staughton, Sydney 1987, p. 76. Unacknowledged quotes from Garrett are from *Political Blues*.

6 Rob Hirst, quoted in Sly, op cit, p. 332

7 See McKenzie Wark, 'From Fordism to Sonyism: Perverse Readings of the New World Order', *New Formations*, No. 15, Winter 1991, pp. 43–54

8 Milsom & Thomas, p. 35

9 Milsom & Thomas, p. 7

10 Not all publicity is good publicity. See *The Centralian Advocate*, 16th July, 1986; *The Age*, 15th July, 1986; *Melbourne Sun*, 19th Feb 1987; *Melbourne Herald*, 16th July, 1986

11 Garrett wrote a number of 'Comment' columns for the *Melbourne Herald*, for example, 'Goose-stepping with the New Right', 11th Sept 1986 and 'Is Our Constitution in Crisis?', 9th October 1986. Also 'The Beat Goes On' in *Rolling Stone*, No. 409, Aug 1987. Some of these were collected in *Political Blues*, Hodder & Staughton, Sydney, 1987

12 Marcus Breen in *Arena*, No. 74, 1986

13 Michael Birch in *Meanjin* Vol. 43 No. 4, and in Marcus Breen, (ed), *Missing in Action*, Verbal Graphics, Melbourne, 1987. All quotes are from the latter, revised version.

14 Craig McGregor, 'On Mass Art', in *Soundtrack for the Eighties*, Hodder & Staughton, Sydney, 1983, p. 37; John Anderson, 'Art and Morality', in *Art & Reality: John Anderson on Literature and Aesthetics*, Hale & Iremonger, Sydney, 1982

15 Antonio Gramsci, *Prison Notebooks*, International Publishers, New York, pp. 3–24

16 David Rowe in *Australian Journal of Cultural Studies*, Vol. 3, No. 2, 1985

17 Toly Sawenko, 'ACF's Energetic Crusader', *Habitat Australia*, October 1989, p. 13

18 On 'The Rise and Fall (?) of the NDP' cf Marian Quigley, in *Current Affairs Bulletin*, Vol. 62, No. 11

19 'In the Valley', *Earth, Sun and Moon*, Columbia 1993

20 'The Power and the Passion', *10,9,8,7,6,5,4,3,2,1*, CBS, 1982

21 quoted in John Pilger, *A Secret Country*, Vintage, London, 1989, p. 219

22 Peter Garrett, 'Myths, Magic Potions and the Reality of Survival', *Habitat Australia*, April 1990, p. 10

23 Paul Kelly, *The End of Certainty*, Allen & Unwin, Sydney 1992, pp. 536–8

24 cf Megan Cronly's excellent analysis in *New Music Articles*, Melbourne, No. 3, 1984

25 *Constitutional Commission Bulletin*, No. 2, September 1986

26 Russell Ward, *The Australian Legend*, new illustrated edition, Oxford University Press, Melbourne, 1978

27 Craig Mathieson, 'Back In Red', *Rolling Stone Australia*, Issue 552, September 1998, pp. 52–55

28 Midnight Oil, 'Redneck Wonderland', on *Redneck Wonderland*, Columbia, 1998

Chapter 5 subdivision cultures

1   Paul Kelly, 'Little Kings', *Words and Music*, White/Mushroom, 1998

2   Paul Kelly, 'Careless' and 'Dumb Things', *Songs of the South: Paul Kelly's Greatest Hits*, Mushroom, 1997. The other song mentioned here, 'From Little Things Big Things Grow' is also on this compilation.

3   Paul Kelly, *The End of Certainty*, Allen & Unwin, Sydney, 1992. p. 2

4   Kelly, p. 674

5   Donald Horne, *The Lucky Country*, (5th edition), Penguin, Ringwood Vic., 1998, pp. 10–11

6   David Williamson, *Bulletin*, 2 April 1996; Beatrice Faust, *Australian Rationalist*, No. 38, 1995

7   Donald Horne, *The Public Culture: The Triumph of Industrialism*, Pluto Press, London, 1986

8   Sally White and Sue Cummings, *Silent Majority III: The Everyday Problems of the Average Australian*, Clemenger Advertising, Melbourne, 1997

9   Robert Manne, *The Culture of Forgetting*, Text Media, Melbourne, 1996

10 See for example Jock Collins and Antonio Castillo, *Cosmopolitan Sydney*, Pluto Press Australia, Sydney, 1998

11 Pamela Williams, *The Victory*, Allen & Unwin, Sydney, 1997

12 Elaine Thompson, *Fair Enough: Egalitarianism in Australia*, UNSW Press, Sydney, 1994

13 Paul Kelly, 'Special Treatment', *Hidden Things*, Mushroom, 1992

14 Geoffrey Dutton, *Snow On the Saltbush*, Penguin, Ringwood Vic., 1985, p. 16

15 See Ian Turner, *Room For Manoeuvre*, Drummond, Melbourne, 1982, pp. 216–228; Allan Ashbolt, *An Australian Experience*, Australasian Book Society, Sydney, 1974, pp. 29–43; Humphrey McQueen, *Social Sketches of Australia 1788–1975*, Penguin, Harmondsworth, 1978, pp. 208–211

16 Chris McAuliffe, *Art and Suburbia*, Craftsman's House, Roseville East, NSW, 1996, pp. 11–13. The following quote is from p. 58

17 Tim Rowse, *Australian Liberalism and National Character*, Kibble Books, Melbourne, 1978, p. 212

18 John Hartley, *Popular Reality: Journalism, Modernity, Popular Culture*, Edward Arnold, London, 1998, p. 54

19 Craig McGregor, *People, Politics and Pop*, Ure Smith, Sydney, 1968, p. 163

20 David Marshall, *Celebrity and Power: Fame in Contemporary Culture*, Minnesota University Press, Minneapolis, 1997, p. xii

21 Michael Pusey, *Economic Rationalism in Canberra*, Cambridge University Press, 1992; Eva Cox, *A Truly Civil Society*, ABC Books, Sydney, 1995; James Walter, *Tunnel Vision: The Failure of Political Imagination*, Allen & Unwin, Sydney, 1996; Moira Rayner, *Rooting Democracy: Growing the Society We Want*, Allen & Unwin, Sydney, 1997; Fred Argy, *Australia At The Crossroads: Radical Free Market or a Progressive Liberalism?*, Allen & Unwin, Sydney, 1988; Gregory Melleuish, *The Packaging of Australia: Politics and Culture Wars*, University of NSW Press, Sydney, 1998; Humphrey McQueen, *Temper Democratic: How Exceptional is Australia?*, Wakefield Press, Kent Town SA, 1998; Frank Brennan, *Legislating Liberty: A Bill of Rights For Australia?*, University of Queensland Press, St Lucia Qld, 1998; Bob Ellis, *First Abolish the Customer: 202 Arguments Against Economic Rationalism*, Penguin, Ringwood Vic., 1996

22 Kenneth Slessor, 'A Portrait of Sydney', in Dennis Haskell (ed) *Kenneth Slessor: Poetry, Essays, War Despatches, Journalism, Autobiographical Material and Letters*, University of Queensland Press, Brisbane, 1991, p. 72

23 Dulcie Deamer, *Queen of Bohemia*, University of Queensland Press, St Lucia Qld, 1998

24 Craig McGregor, *Class in Australia*, Penguin, Ringwood Vic., 1997, p. 126, p. 69, p. 158

25 *Strewth!*, No. 1, Spring 1998, p. 3

26 Sylvia Lawson, *The Archibald Paradox*, Allen Lane, Melbourne, 1983

27 John Docker, *The Nervous Nineties: Australian Cultural Life in the 1890s*, Oxford University Press, Melbourne, 1991, p. 233
28 Peter Kirkpatrick, *The Sea Coast of Bohemia: Literary Life in Sydney's Roaring Twenties*, University of Queensland Press, Brisbane, 1992, p. 3
29 Richard Neville, *Hippie Hippie Shake*, William Heinemann Australia, 1995, p. 10
30 Anne Summers, *Damned Whores and God's Police*, Penguin, Ringwood Vic, 1995, revised edition, p. 109
31 Justine Ettler, 'Happy Hours', *HQ Magazine*, January 1998
32 *Bohemian Rhapsody*, written and directed by Tony Moore, ABC, 1997
33 Mandy Sayer, *Dreamtime Alice: A Memoir*, Random House, Sydney, 1998, p. 4
34 John Clare, *Bodgie Dada and the Cult of Cool: Australian Jazz Since 1945*, UNSW Press, Sydney, 1995
35 Anne Coombs, *Sex and Anarchy: The Life and Death of the Sydney Push*, Viking Penguin, Ringwood Vic., 1996
36 See Gary Wotherspoon, *The City of the Plain: History of a Gay Subculture*, Hale & Iremonger, Sydney, 1991; Graham Carbery, *A History of the Sydney Gay and Lesbian Mardi Gras*, Australian Gay and Lesbian Archives, Parkville Vic., 1995
37 Andrew Conway, 'Not As Easy as ABC', *The Guide*, *Sydney Morning Herald*, 10th June, 1996, p. 2
38 Amruta Slee, 'Sympathy for the Devil', *HQ Magazine*, No. 60, September, 1988, pp. 36–43, at p. 40

Chapter 6 screening suburbia

1 Chris McAuliffe, *Art and Suburbia*, Craftsmen's House, Sydney, 1996, p. 91
2 See *Good News Week: Unseen and Obscene*, directed by Martin Coombs and David Rector, ABC Video, 1998
3 Amruta Slee, 'Sympathy for the Devil', *HQ Magazine*, No. 60, September, 1988, pp. 36–43, at p. 40
4 Allan Ashbolt, *An Australian Experience: Words from the Vietnam Years*, Australasian Book Society, Sydney, 1974, pp. 9–10
5 John Pasquarelli, *The Pauline Hanson Story*, New Holland Press, French's Forest NSW, 1998, pp. 70–72
6 *Wildside* screened on ABC TV in 1998
7 *Metal Skin*, directed by Geoffrey Wright, Village Roadshow, 1994
8 *Sea Change*, written by Deb Cox, produced for ABC TV by Artist Services
9 Samuel Johnson, *Selected Essays from the Rambler, Adventurer and Idler*, Yale University Press, New Haven, 1968, p. 184

10 For information on *Heartbreak High*, see
http://www.abc.net.au/heartbreak/episode/default.htm

11 *The Castle*, directed by Rob Sitch, Working Dog, 1995

12 Robin Boyd, *Australian Ugliness*, F. W. Cheshire, Melbourne, 1960, pp. 9ff

13 *Muriel's Wedding*, directed by P. J. Hogan, Village Roadshow, 1994

14 *Idiot Box*, directed by David Ceasar, Globe Films, 1996

15 Mark Latham, *Civilising Global Capital*, Allen & Unwin, 1998, pp. 113–115

16 John Hartley, *Popular Reality: Journalism, Modernity*, Popular Culture, Edward Arnold, London, 1996, p. 157

17 *The Boys*, directed by Rowen Woods, written by Stephen Sewell from a play by Gordon Graham, 1998

18 Diane Powell, *Out West: Perceptions of Sydney's Western Suburbs*, Allen & Unwin, Sydney, 1993, p. xviii

19 Graeme Turner, *Making It National: Nationalism and Australian Popular Culture*, Allen & Unwin, Sydney, 1994, p. 8, p. 129

20 *Parkland*, written and directed by Kathryn Millard, Australian Film Institute, 1996

21 *Dead Letter Office*, written by Deb Cox and directed by John Ruane, 1998

22 *The Interview*, directed by Craig Monahan, Pointblank Pictures, 1998

23 Chris McAuliffe, *Art and Suburbia*, Craftsman's House, Roseville East, NSW, 1996, p. 60, p. 71

24 *The Adventures of Priscilla, Queen of the Desert*, directed by Stephan Elliott, Village Roadshow, 1994

25 Max Harris, *Ockers: Essays on the Bad Old New Australia*, Maximus Books, Adelaide SA, 1974, p. viii, and p. 22

26 John Docker, *Postmodernism and Popular Culture: A Cultural History*, Cambridge University Press, Melbourne, 1994, p. 168ff

27 Paul Kelly, 'Sweet Guy', on *Songs from the South: Paul Kelly's Greatest Hits*, Mushroom, 1997

28 *Doing Time for Patsy Cline*, directed by Chris Kennedy, Dendy Video, 1997; *Kiss or Kill*, directed by Bill Bennett, New Vision, 1997; *True Love and Chaos*, directed by Stavros Andonis Efthymiou, 1997; *Heaven's Burning*, directed by Craig Lahiff, Becker Home Video, 1998

29 McKenzie Wark, *The Virtual Republic: Australia's Culture Wars of the 1990s*, Allen & Unwin, Sydney, 1997, pp. 239–271

30 Les A. Murray, *Selected Poems: The Vernacular Republic*, Angus & Robertson, Sydney, 1976

31 Graeme Turner, *Making It National: Nationalism and Australian Popular Culture*, Allen & Unwin, Sydney, 1994, p. 9

32 quoted in Gay Alcorn, 'Hanson Loses Control', *Age*, 12th September, 1998

33 *Sylvania Waters*, directed by Brian Hill and Kate Woods, BBC TV in association with ABC TV, 1992

34 John Hartley, *Popular Reality: Journalism, Modernity*, Popular Culture, Edward Arnold, London, 1996, p. 174

35 Graeme Turner, *Making It National: Nationalism and Australian Popular Culture*, Allen & Unwin, Sydney, 1994, p. 155. See also Graeme Turner, 'Suburbia Verité', *Australian Left Review*, October, 1992, pp. 37–39

36 Tom O'Regan, *Australian National Cinema*, Routledge, London, 1996, p. 256

37 quoted in Tom O'Regan, *Australian Television Culture*, Allen & Unwin, Sydney, 1993, p. 116

38 See also David Rowe, 'The Federal Republic of *Sylvania Waters'*, *Metro*, No. 98, 1994, pp. 14–23; Jon Stratton and Ien Ang, '*Sylvania Waters* and the Spectacular Exploding Family', *Screen*, Vol. 34, No. 1, pp. 1–21

39 Craig McGregor, *Class In Australia*, Penguin, Ringwood Vic., 1997, p. 144

40 Bob Gregory and Boyd Hunter, 'The Macro Economy and the Growth of Ghettos and Urban Poverty in Australia', *Australian National University Centre for Economic Policy Research Discussion Paper*, No. 325, April 1995

41 See Craig McGregor, *Class in Australia*, Penguin, Ringwood Vic., 1997, pp. 158ff; Mark Latham, *Civilising Global Capital: New Thinking For Australian Labor*, Allen & Unwin, Sydney, 1998; pp. 100ff

42 Paola Totaro, 'We've Given Up the Quarter-Acre Block', *Sydney Morning Herald*, 6th March, 1998, p. 2

43 Peter O'Shea, 'Telecast Threat', *Capital Q Weekly*, 8th November 1996

Chapter 7 true believers

1 Craig McGregor, *Class in Australia*, Penguin, Ringwood Vic., 1997, p. 86

2 Linda Jaivin, 'U Got the Look', *Confessions of an S&M Virgin*, Text Publishing, Melbourne, 1997, p. 104

3 Craig McGregor, *Time of Testing: The Bob Hawke Victory*, Penguin, Ringwood Vic., 1983, p. 13

4 *Labor in Power*, produced and directed by Sue Spencer, ABC Video, 1993

5 Norman Lindsay, *The Magic Pudding: The Adventures of Bunyip Bluegum*, Angus & Robertson, Sydney, 1996, first published in 1918

6 Thomas Keenan, *Fables of Responsiblity*, Stanford University Press, Stanford CA, 1997, p. 45

7   *Rats in the Ranks*, produced and directed by Bob Connolly and Robin Anderson, Film Australia and Arundel Films, 1996

8   Bob Ellis, *Goodbye Jerusalem: Night Thoughts of a Labor Outsider*, Random House, Sydney, 1997, p. 260, quoting Dennis Healy.

9   *The Dismissal: The Power Struggle that Split Our Nation*, executive producers Byron Kennedy and Dr George Miller, directors George Miller, Phillip Noyce, George Ogilvie, Carl Schultz and John Power, Kennedy-Miller, 1982; *Labor in Power*, devised, written and reported by Philip Chubb, executive producer, Paul Williams, ABC Video, 1993; *True Believers*, written by Bob Ellis and Stephen Ramsey, directed by Peter Fisk, executive producers, Sandra Levy and Matt Carroll, Roadshow, Coote and Carroll, 1988

10 On John Curtin, see Geoffrey Serle, *For Australia and Labor: Prime Minister John Curtin*, John Curtin Prime Ministerial Library, Perth, 1998; Lloyd Ross, *John Curtin: A Biography*, Macmillan, Melbourne, 1977; Kim Beazley (snr), *John Curtin: An Atypical Labor Leader*, ANU Press, Canberra, 1972

11 John Curtin, 'The Task Ahead', originally published in the Melbourne *Herald*, 27th December 1941, reprinted in David Black (ed), *In His Own Words: John Curtin's Speeches and Writings*, Paradigm Books, Curtin University WA, pp. 193–196

12 From a radio broadcast of 1943, in Black, p. 226

13 John Pasquarelli, *The Pauline Hanson Story*, New Holland Publishers, Sydney, 1998, pp. 54–55

14 On Ben Chifley, see Scott Bennett, *J. B. Chifley*, Oxford University Press, Melbourne, 1973; L. F. Crisp, *Ben Chifley: A Biography*, Longmans, London, 1961

15 A.W. Stargardt (ed) *Things Worth Fighting For: Speeches by Joseph Benedict Chifley*, Melbourne University Press, 1952, p. 9

16 John Anderson, *Studies in Empirical Philosophy*, Angus & Robertson, Sydney, 1962, p. 399

17 Bob Ellis, *Goodbye Jerusalem: Night Thoughts of a Labor Outsider*, Random House, Sydney, 1997, p. 173. He attributes it to Nugget Coombs.

18 On H.V. Evatt, see Ken Buckley, Barbara Dale and Wayne Reynolds, *Doc Evatt: Patriot, Internationalist, Fighter and Scholar*, Longman Cheshire, Melbourne, 1994; Peter Crockett, *Evatt: A Life*, Oxford University Press, Melbourne, 1993; Kylie Tennant, *Evatt: Politics and Justice*, Angus & Robertson, Sydney, 1972; Allan Dalziel, *Evatt the Enigma*, Lansdowne, Melbourne, 1967

19 Judith Brett, *Robert Menzies' Forgotten People*, Macmillan, Sydney, 1992, pp. 51ff

20 H.V. Evatt, *Post-War Reconstruction: A Case for Greater Commonwealth Powers*, Prepared for the Constitutional Convention at Canberra, November, 1942, Commonwealth Government Printer, Canberra, 1942, pp. 6–8

21 See Paul Kelly, *November 1975: The Inside Story of Australia's Greatest Political Crisis*, Allen & Unwin, Sydney, 1995

22 John Button, *As It Happened*, Text Publishers, Melbourne, 1998, p.160

23 See Peter Love, *Labour and the Money Power*, Melbourne University Press, Melbourne, 1984

24 Max Harris, *Ockers: Essays on the Bad Old New Australia*, Maximus Books, Adelaide SA, 1974, p. 18

25 Bob Hawke, *The Hawke Memoirs*, William Heineman Australia, Port Melbourne Vic., 1994; p. 549; Peter Walsh, *Confessions of a Failed Finance Minister*, Random House, Sydney, 1996, p. 125

26 Niccolò Machiavelli, The Discourses, Penguin Books, Harmondsworth, 1983, book 1.6, p. 123

27 Graham Richardson, *Whatever It Takes*, Bantam Books, Sydney, 1994; Marian Wilkinson, *The Fixer: The Untold Story of Graham Richardson*, William Heinemann, Port Melbourne Vic., 1996

28 quoted in Michael Gordon, *A Question of Leadership: Paul Keating, Political Fighter*, University of Queensland Press, St Lucia Qld, 1993, p. 10

29 Meaghan Morris, *Ecstasy and Economics: American Essays for John Forbes*, EmPress, Sydney, 1992, p. 20

30 André Glucksmann, *The Master Thinkers*, Harper & Row, New York, 1980

31 Bob Hawke, *The Hawke Memoirs*, William Heinemann Australia, Port Melbourne Vic., 1994, p. 251

32 Bob Ellis, *Goodbye Jerusalem*, p. 185

33 Dean Jaensch, *The Hawke-Keating Hijack*, Allen & Unwin, Sydney, 1989; Peter Beilharz, *Transforming Labor: Labour Tradition and the Labor Decade in Australia*, Cambridge University Press, Melbourne, 1994; Graham Maddox, *The Hawke Government and Labor Tradition*, Penguin, Ringwood Vic., 1989

34 Carol Johnson, *The Labor Legacy: Curtin, Chifley, Whitlam, Hawke*, Allen & Unwin, Sydney, 1989

Chapter 8 generational ganglands

1   Camilla Nelson, 'We're Young, Angry, Cynical — and We Vote', *Australian*, 14th February, 1996

2   Mark Latham, *Civilising Global Capital: New Thinking for Australian Labor*, Allen & Unwin, Sydney, 1988, p. 239

3   Hugh Mackay, *Generations: Baby Boomers, Their Parents and Their Children*, Macmillan, Sydney, 1997

4   Helen Townsend, *Baby Boomers: Growing Up In Australia in the 1940s, 50s and 60s*, Simon & Schuster, Brookvale NSW, 1988

5   Douglas Coupland, *Generation X: Tales for an Accelerated Culture*, Abacus, London, 1992

6   Beth Spencer, 'X-ed Again or: Whatever Happened to the Seventies?', *Australian Book Review*, December, 1995, also at: http://home.vicnet.net.au/~ozlit/crit0002.html

7   Catharine Lumby, 'The Squeeze Generation', *Sydney Morning Herald*, 28th December, 1996

8   George Lukács, *The Historical Novel*, Merlin, London, 1989, p. 23

9   *Literati*, by Heartbeat, a division of Kalaidescope, Sydney, 1998. Disclaimer: I am a member of the editorial advisory board for this research. The views expressed here are my own and not those of Heartbeat.

10   David Marshall, *Celebrity and Power*, Minnesota University Press, Minneapolis, 1997

11   Samantha Trenoweth, 'The Big Guy', *Juice*, No. 69, October, 1998

12   See Richard Neville. *Out of My Mind*, Penguin, Ringwood Vic., 1996

13   'New Pollution gets Down With Richard Neville', in Sean Healy et al (eds), *The New Pollution: National Zine Anthology*, Loud, Sydney, 1998, p. 2

14   Les A. Murray, *A Working Forest: Selected Prose*, Duffy & Snellgrove, Sydney, 1997

15   *Frontline*, written, produced and directed by Santo Cilauro, Tom Gleisner, Jane Kennedy and Rob Sitch

16   Mark Davis, *Gangland: Cultural Elites and the New Generationalism*, Allen & Unwin, Sydney, 1997

17   Richard Neville, *Hippie Hippie Shake*, William Heinemann Australia, 1995

18   A partially satisfying rethink of the 60s is Julie Stephens, *Anti-Disciplinary Protest: Sixties Radicalism and Postmodernism*, Cambridge University Press, 1988

19   Darren Goodsir et al, 'Death of a Caring Cop' and other stories, *Sun-Herald*, 1st March, 1998

20   Richard Hill, Tony McMahon and Judith Bessant, 'Don't Damn Young Law Abiding Majority', *Australian*, 4th September, 1996

21   Paul Sheehan, *Among the Barbarians*, Random House, Sydney, 1988

22   As Clinton Walker shows in *Stranded: The Secret History of Australian Independent Music 1977–1991*, Macmillan, Sydney, 1996

23   Michelle Griffin, 'Generate', *Overland*, No. 143, Winter 1996, p. 15

24   See Justine Ettler, *The River Ophelia*, Picador, Sydney, 1995; Andrew McGahan, *Praise*, Allen & Unwin, Sydney, 1992; Edward Berridge, *The Lives of the Saints*, University of Queensland Press, Brisbane, 1993.

25 Christos Tsiolkas, *Loaded*, Random House, Sydney, 1995

26 *Head On*, directed by Ana Kokkinos, released by Palace Films, 1998

27 Sasha Soldatow and Christos Tsiolkas, *Jump Cuts: An Autobiography*, Random House, Sydney, 1996; Beth Spencer, *How To Conceive of a Girl*, Random House, Sydney, 1996; Chris Gregory, *Twins*, Penguin, Ringwood Vic., 1997

28 Beth Spencer, 'X-ed Again or: Whatever Happened to the Seventies?', *Australian Book Review*, December, 1995, also at: http://home.vicnet.net.au/~ozlit/crit0002.html

29 Cate Rayson, *Glued to the Telly*, Elgua Media, Redhill SA, 1996, p. 88

30 See Peter Wilmoth, *Glad All Over: The Countdown Years 1974–1987*, McPhee Gribble, Melbourne, 1993

31 Sherryn George, 'The Warp Manifesto', in Kathy Bail (ed), *DIY Feminism*, Allen & Unwin, 1996, p. 36

32 at time of writing, the recording and a transcript of the lyrics were available at: http://www.geocities.com/CapitolHill/Lobby/5192/index.html

33 quoted in Richard Ackland, 'Decision for Hanson Has Disturbing Effect', *Sydney Morning Herald*, 2nd October, 1998

34 Howling Wolf, 'Back Door Man', on *Moanin' and Howlin'*, Chess/Charly, 1988

35 Pauline Pantsdown, 'I Don't Like It!', TWA Records, 1998

36 Caroline Overington, 'Pantsdown Pulls Socks Up For Senate Bid', *Age*, 18th September, 1998

37 Benedict Watts, 'Please Explain', *Juice*, November 1998, p. 30

38 Beth Spencer, 'I'd Like to Have Permission to be Post-Modern, But I'm Not Sure Who to Ask', *Jacket*, No. 1, 1997, http://www.jacket.zip.com.au/jacket01/spencer.html

Chapter 9 regenerating labor

1 Geoffrey Barker, 'Respected By All, Feared By None', *Australian Financial Review Magazine*, August 1998, pp. 12–17, at p. 14

2 Barry Jones, *Sleepers Wake!: Technology and the Future of Work*, second edition, Oxford University Press, Melbourne, 1995, pp. 175ff

3 John Pasquarelli, *The Pauline Hanson Story*, New Holland Publishers, Sydney, 1998, p. 112

4 Adams, Phillip, and Lee Burton, *Talkback: Emperors of Air*, Allen & Unwin, Sydney, 1997

5 John Button, *As It Happened*, Text Publishing, Melbourne, 1998, p. 367

6   Here I draw on Craig McGregor, 'After the Fall, Labor Seeks a New Messiah', *Sydney Morning Herald*, 12th October, 1996; Craig McGregor, The Anointed One', *Good Weekend Magazine*, 13th September, 1997; Mike Stekete, 'Labor's Young Turks', *Weekend Australian*, September 20th, 1997; Laura Tingle, 'Capital Ideas', *Sydney Morning Herald*, 4th April, 1998; Mark Latham, 'Tricky Examination Ahead for New Labor', *Australian*, 30th April, 1998

7   John Button, p. 280; p. 246

8   Mark Latham, *Civilising Global Capital: New Thinking for Australian Labor*, Allen & Unwin, Sydney, 1998; Lindsay Tanner, *Open Australia*, draft manuscript courtesy of Lindsay Tanner and Pluto Press, 1998

9   Craig McGregor, *The Australian People*, Hodder & Staughton, Sydney, 1980

10   David O'Reilly, *Cheryl Kernot: The Woman Most Likely*, Random House, Sydney, 1998; Peter FitzSimons, *Beazley: A Biography*, Harper Collins, Sydney, 1998

11   Tony Wright, 'Kim and John Slay the Ghost of Paul', *Age*, 9th October, 1998. I've altered the quote slightly to bring out the television program title quoted in it.

12   Lindsay Tanner, 'Labourism's Last Days', *Australian Left Review*, June 1991, pp. 10–14, at p. 10

13   Anne Summers, *Gamble for Power: How Bob Hawke Beat Malcolm Fraser, the 1983 Federal Election*, Thomas Nelson, Melbourne, 1983, pp. 106–107

14   John Button, *On The Loose*, Text Publishing, Melbourne, 1996, p. 134

15   For a useful sample, see John Frow and Meaghan Morris, *Australian Cultural Studies: A Reader*, Allen & Uwin, Sydney, 1995, in which my chapter 'Homage to Catatonia' previously appeared.

16   Quotes from Darren Tofts and Mark Davis from personal email communications.

17   Peter Best, 'A Likely Lad', *Australian Quarterly*, November 1997, pp. 22–27, at p. 25

18   Peter Russ and Lindsay Tanner, *The Politics of Pollution*, Visa Books, Melbourne, 1978

19   Lindsay Tanner, 'Relationships and Community, *Labor Essays 1998*, Pluto Press Australia, Sydney, 1998

20   John Button, *As It Happened*, Text Publishing, Melbourne, 1998, p. 12

21   Lindsay Tanner, 'Labourism's Last Days', *Australian Left Review*, June 1991, pp. 10–14, at p. 12. Other published essays of Tanner's consulted are: 'Time for an Indicator of Real Progress', *Financial Review*, 4th June, 1994; 'Building an Inclusive Society', in Gary Jungwirth (ed), *Labor Essays 1997: Renewing and*

Revitalising Labor, Pluto Press in association with the Australian Fabian Society, Sydney, 1997; 'Relationships and Community', in Gary Jungwirth (ed), *Labor Essays 1998: New Visions for Government*, Pluto Press in association with the Australian Fabian Society, Sydney, 1998; and a draft manuscript for *Open Australia* Pluto Press, forthcoming

22 David Ricardo, *On the Principles of Political Economy and Taxation*, Cambridge University Press, 1952, p. 67

23 James Boswell, *Life of Johnson*, Oxford University Press, 1964, vol. 2, p. 259

24 Mark Rose, *Authors and Owners: The Invention of Copyright*, Harvard University Press, Cambridge Mass., 1993, p. 92

Chapter 10 third way, second go

1   Craig McGregor, 'The Anointed One', *Good Weekend*, 13th September 1997, pp. 16–25

2   Mike Stekete, 'Labor's Young Turks', *Weekend Australian*, 20th September, 1997

3   Laura Tingle, 'Capital Ideas', *Sydney Morning Herald*, 4th April, 1998

4   Michael Easson, 'No Easy Way for Labor', *Sydney Morning Herald*, 26th October, 1998, p. 17

5   Mark Latham, *Civilising Global Capital: New Thinking for Australian Labor*, Allen & Unwin, Sydney, 1998

6   Craig McGregor, 'After the Fall, Labor Seeks a New Messiah', *Sydney Morning Herald*, 12th October, 1996

7   A term coined by followers of Michel Foucault. See G. Burchell et al (eds), *The Foucault Effect: Studies in Governmentality*, Harvester, London, 1991, pp. 87–104

8   *Civilising Global Capital*, p. xxxvii. I have put the last two words in title form to highlight this apparently unconscious borrowing from television culture.

9   Andrew Scott, *Fading Loyalties: The Australian Labor Party and the Working Class*, Pluto Press Australia, Sydney, 1991, p. 2

10 quoted in Craig McGregor, *Class in Australia*, Penguin, Ringwood Vic., 1997, pp. 49–50

11 Bob Ellis, *First Abolish the Customer: 202 Arguments Against Economic Rationalism*, Penguin, Ringwood Vic., 1998

12 John Edwards, *Keating: The Inside Story*, Penguin, Ringwood Vic., 1996, p. 367

13 John Button, *As It Happened*, Text Publishing, Mebourne, 1998, pp. 322–324

14 John Rawls, *A Theory of Justice*, Harvard University Press, Cambridge Mass., 1971

15 Plato, *The Republic*, Penguin, Harmondsworth, 1983, p. 426.
16 Paul Kelly, 'Special Treatment', *Hidden Things*, Mushroom, 1992
17 McKenzie Wark, *The Virtual Republic: Australia's Culture Wars of the 1990s*, Allen & Unwin, Sydney, 1997
18 Christos Tsiolkas, *Loaded*, Random House, Sydney, 1995
19 See J. G. A. Pocock, *The Machiavellian Moment*, Princeton University Press, New Jersey, 1975
20 Gregory Melleuish, *The Packaging of Australia: Politics and Culture Wars*, University of NSW Press, Sydney, 1998
21 Gilles Deleuze, *Essays Critical and Clinical*, Minnesota University Press, Minneapolis, 1997
22 David Hume, *A Treatise of Human Nature*, Penguin, London, 1985, pp. 529ff
23 Allan Bloom, 'Editor's Introduction' to Alexandre Kojève, *Introduction to the Reading of Hegel*, Cornell Univesity Press, Ithaca, 1986, p. viii
24 See Charles Taylor, *Hegel*, Cambridge University Press, New York, 1975
25 I'm thinking, for example, of Jean-François Lyotard, *Postmodern Fables*, University of Minnesota Press, Minneapolis, 1997
26 Gilles Deleuze and Felix Guattari, *Anti-Oedipus: Capitalism and Schizophrenia*, Athlone Press, London, 1983, p. 140
27 Francis Fukuyama, *The End of History and the Last Man*, H. Hamilton, London, 1992
28 Allan Bloom, *The Closing of the American Mind*, Simon & Schuster, New York, 1987
29 Alexandre Kojève, *Introduction to the Reading of Hegel*, Cornell Univesity Press, Ithaca, 1986, p. 7
30 Graham Richardson, *Whatever It Takes*, Bantam, Sydney, 1994, p. 55
31 For starters, see Patrick Fuery, *Theories of Desire*, Melbourne University Press, 1995
32 Georges Bataille, *Theory of Religion*, Zone Books, New York, 1989
33 On Lacan, see Slavoj Zizek, *Looking Awry: An Introduction to Jacques Lacan Through Popular Culture*, MIT Press, Cambridge Mass., 1991
34 John Hartley, *Tele-ology: Studies in Television*, Routledge, London, 1992, p. 49
35 Dorothy Hewett, *Wild Card: An Autobiography 1923–1958*, McPhee Gribble, Ringwood Viv., 1990, p. 233

epilogue and acknowledgement

1 John Safran, quoted in Catherine Caines, 'Game Boy', *Australian Style*, No. 29, 1998, pp. 63–65

2   http://www.geocities.com/Hollywood/Studio/8442/index.html
3   Gilles Deleuze and Claire Parnet, *Dialogues*, Columbia University Press, New York, 1987, pp. 54–55
4   Gilles Deleuze, 'Preface to the English Language Edition', *Dialogues*, p. vii
5   Stendhal, *Memoirs of an Egotist*, Chatto & Windus, London, 1975, p. 89

index